RETAIL ACCOUNTING AND FINANCIAL CONTROL

LOUIS C. MOSCARELLO, C.P.A.
FRANCIS C. GRAU, C.P.A.
ROY C. CHAPMAN, C.P.A.
PARTNERS OF COOPERS & LYBRAND

FOURTH EDITION

A RONALD PRESS PUBLICATION
JOHN WILEY & SONS, New York • Chichester • Brisbane • Toronto

Copyright © 1936, 1956, 1961, 1976 by John Wiley & Sons, Inc.

All Rights Reserved

Reproduction or translation of any part of this work beyond that permitted by Sections 107 or 108 of the 1976 United States Copyright Act without the permission of the copyright owner is unlawful. Requests for permission or further information should be addressed to the Permissions Department, John Wiley & Sons, Inc.

ISBN 0 471 06793-8

Library of Congress Catalog Card Number: 76-24550

PRINTED IN THE UNITED STATES OF AMERICA

10 9 8 7 6

Dedicated to the Memory of

Hermon F. Bell, C.P.A.

Partner, Friend, and Teacher

Preface

Published in earlier editions under the title *Retail Merchandise Accounting*, this book was originally issued in 1936 under the authorship of Hermon F. Bell, with subsequent revisions in 1956 and 1961. Written out of many years of professional experience, it is designed to supply detailed and useful insights into accounting and taxes and financial and operating controls as they specifically relate to the retail trade. As such, this book is directed to retail executives charged with responsibilities for finance, control, operations, and merchandising; to public accounting practitioners with retail clients; and to students of retailing.

The book provides the background and details of day-to-day operations, together with the related requirements and procedures for maintaining effective managerial control in today's retail environment. The federal income tax aspects of retailing are dealt with at length. Special attention is given to the LIFO method of inventory determination under the retail method and the use of alternative dollar-value methods. Tax planning and computations under installment sales accounting are also fully discussed. Every effort is made to reflect the significant changes that have taken place since publication of the last edition, notably the dramatic growth of multi-unit companies, increased mechanization and computerization of systems and procedures to process and analyze data, operational innovations, and revised accounting and financial reporting concepts.

Throughout, we have attempted to facilitate the understanding of complex problems with concrete examples and illustrations demonstrating sound accounting and management practices. Where feasible, alternative approaches and techniques have been included. It is hoped that these aids, together with the numerous operating forms, formulas, and tables, will enhance the book's usefulness as a working manual, as well as a policy and planning guide for retailers, regardless of size.

Louis C. Moscarello
Francis C. Grau
Roy C. Chapman

New York, New York
September, 1976

Acknowledgments

A book of this kind is, in reality, the product of the dedicated effort of many persons. We were fortunate to be able to draw upon the background and experience of many of our partners and professional staff knowledgeable in various aspects of retailing. We gratefully acknowledge the research performed and initial drafting of certain chapters by our partners, Marvin L. Baris, Leo J. Cannon, Harvey A. Creem, Clark Chandler, James L. Dodd, George R. Fitzsimmons, Thomas C. Flanagan, Charles F. Jacey, Jr., Jay S. Kamen, Walter F. Maischoss, Vincent M. O'Reilly, Frank J. Tanki, Bernard Tinkoff, Alan Vituli, and Warren G. Wintrub; and members of our professional staff, Michael J. Cohen, Donald Merry, and Charles A. Shipley.

Our special thanks are due to William Morris of our Firm's tax department who, together with Lawrence M. Friedman and James R. McCann, materially contributed to the tax chapters dealing with LIFO and the installment method of reporting.

We are also indebted to some of our former business associates, as well as representatives of client companies, Alan Batkin, Dean S. Campbell, Daniel Di Pietro, James Heeley, William D. Lang, Daniel J. Pedriani, Jr., Gerard Sampson, and George Sutton, for their comments, criticisms, and suggestions and for their review of certain chapters.

We wish to express our appreciation to the National Retail Merchants Association for its numerous valuable publications. The *Retail Accounting Manual* in particular (revised in 1976) has made a major contribution to the practical approaches and concepts relating to retail accounting and financial reporting.

As a final gesture of appreciation and thanks, we would like to single out with gratitude the gracious, patient, and almost endless assistance rendered by Dorothy Kasman, chief librarian of our Firm, and Miriam F. Werner of our Industry Research Group, who assisted with the basic research that was so essential in completing this work, and the efforts of Perley B. Hart who labored long hours in reviewing, revising, and correcting manuscript.

L.C.M.
F.C.G.
R.C.C.

Contents

1	Distinctive Features of Retailing	3
2	Types of Retail Businesses; Department Store Organization	7
3	Definition and Discussion of Important Terms	23
4	Methods of Merchandise Control	41
5	Budgeting and Financial Planning and Control	70
6	Inventory Dollar Control, Including the Retail Inventory Method	93
7	Accounting Problems of the Retail Method	133
8	Discounts in Inventories and Discounts Earned	158
9	Taking Physical Inventories	181
10	Determination of Purchases	209
11	Determination of Net Sales	231
12	Shortages and Shortage Control	261
13	Branch Store Operations	278
14	Non-Retail Operations (Workrooms)	298
15	Leased Departments	311
16	Statements Reporting Operating Results	322
17	Limitations in the Use of Percentages	348
18	Mathematics of Retail Merchandise Accounting	352
19	Development of LIFO for Retailers	378
20	Election, Carryovers, Revisions, and Termination of LIFO	386
21	Retail Price Indexes	404

CONTENTS

22	Computation of LIFO Inventories on the Retail Method	413
23	Dollar-Value LIFO	442
24	Installment Sales of Personal Property	457
25	Leasing of Real and Personal Property by Retailers	488
	Index	503

Figures

1	Functional organization chart for a department store	18
	(a) Merchandising	19
	(b) Operations	20
	(c) Finance and administration	21
2	Purchase orders placed report	48
3	Summary open purchase order listing	50
4	Open purchase orders	51
5	Open-to-buy report	52
6	Accounts payable due date summary	54
7	Price change summary report	55
8	Price change report	61
9	Slow-selling stock report	62
10	Seasonal stock report	64
11	Merchandise plan	77
12	Departmental stock ledger (abbreviated form)	105
13	Departmental stock ledger (detailed form)	106
14	Merchandise statement and stock ledger (combined)	109
15	Departmental stock ledger (based on percentages)	110
16	Purchase record summary	112
17	Price changes	116
18	Departmental rates of discounts	165
19	Sales division instructions for taking of physical inventories	192
20	Inventory sheet	198
21	Inventory tag	199
22	Inventory tally	199
23	Inventory certificate and cut-off sheet	201
24	Reconciliation of book and physical inventories, at retail	204
25	Inventory reconciliation sheet	205
26	Bill apron	212

FIGURES

27	Invoice register	214
28	Purchase record	215
29	Merchandise transfer sheet	222
30	Reconciliation of cycle controls with general ledger control	238
31	Branch store organization	283
32	Daily report of branch	285
33	Types of expenses in branch store operation	293
34	Individual store location operating statement	294
35	Individual store location sales report	296
36	Workroom operating statement	306
37	Comparative income statement	324
38	Merchandise departmental operating statement	328
39	Statement of operating expenses by expense summary	336
40	Statement of operating expenses by natural divisions	338
41	Comparative classification report	343
42	Comparison of sales and stock report	344
43	Computation of reserve for unearned discount at cost under retail method and on LIFO basis	428
44	Summary of merchandise inventory, retail departments, before and after unearned discounts	429
45	Buy-versus-lease analysis of an asset	494

RETAIL ACCOUNTING
AND FINANCIAL CONTROL

1

Distinctive Features of Retailing

In perhaps the last two decades, retailing as a trade has experienced rapid growth and undergone dynamic changes, in a confrontation with massive changes in society and in its own modes of operations. Population dispersions, often in conjunction with the explosion of suburban centers, have been widespread. Consumer mobility has increased. Consumer needs, responding to such factors as the changing age mix, increasing affluence, and improved education of consumers, have significantly affected buying patterns and have had dramatic effects on retailing. Furthermore, as government agencies have become increasingly concerned with retailing, the trade has experienced the advent of consumer legislation such as the fair labeling law, expanded credit availability, limitations on service charges, price controls, and the enactment of varied and often onerous taxes. In addition, the formation of consumer activist groups has made more troublesome the conditions under which retailers must operate.

Historically, the role of accounting in retailing has been to inform management as to what has been done, how it was done, and the present status of affairs. However, with all of the problems inherent in today's retail trade, accounting and the entire information compilation and analysis function are vital to a retailer's future survival.

During this same relative time frame, the accounting profession also has experienced more changes than ever before in its history. The advent of the Accounting Principles Board (APB) and the promulgation of its Opinions; the subsequent formation of the Financial Accounting Standards Board (FASB) and the issuance of pronouncements and interpretations by this successor to the APB; the increasingly dominant role of the Securities and Exchange Commission (SEC) in matters affecting financial reporting and disclosure requirements—all these have created a veritable storehouse of rules, promulgations, and principles to be followed. However, accounting is still an art and not a science. It cannot be guided solely by rules and definitions. Accountants in today's business environment must face its challenges and develop new methods of coping with the problems that are generated by the forces affecting that environment.

To understand retail accounting, including particularly retail merchandise accounting, one must have an appreciation of the current environment surrounding the retailer. The purpose of this introductory chapter is to give a brief listing of those problems and conditions that exercise a governing influence over the development of retail accounting procedures.

Distinctive Features of a Retail Business

Retailing differs radically from many other forms of business activity in the following principal respects:

1. The numerous lines of merchandise handled and the constant change of product lines in response to changing consumer needs.
2. The extensive assortments of items in many of the lines or departments of merchandise handled.
3. The great number of sales transactions involving a relatively low average dollar amount.
4. The service feature of the business, occasioned by its dealing with the ultimate consumer.
5. The absence of standardized products for which detailed planning is possible or past experience can serve as a guide.
6. The relatively short sale periods during which much of the merchandise is currently salable and can accordingly be more profitably sold.
7. The large number of employees who deal directly with customers (as compared with a manufacturer, who has a relatively compact and easily controlled sales organization).

Ch. 1   DISTINCTIVE FEATURES OR CONDITIONS OF RETAILING

8. The fact that the everyday contact of the public with the store is largely through employees other than those entrusted with management authority and initiative.
9. The fact that the store's goodwill is so vitally dependent upon the way in which rank-and-file employees reflect daily to customers the spirit and policy of the store (as distinguished from a manufacturing company, where the factory workers are under close daily supervision of superintendents and foremen and have practically no contact with the manufacturer's customers).
10. The difficulties in maintaining adequate control over the significant investment in merchandise because of:
    a. Its great variety, often with only one or a few items of a kind.
    b. The fact that merchandise is displayed openly and is easily accessible to the public and to employees.
    c. The transferral of merchandise into the custody or control of so many employees—salespersons, stock clerks, delivery men, and housekeeping personnel.
    d. The fact that the merchandise is appealing, is often small in size, and can be easily stolen by a dishonest customer or employee.
    e. The fact that clerks sell and deliver merchandise in exchange for cash, or on account.
11. The difficulties in maintaining adequate control over cash and charges to customers' accounts, since both types of transactions originate at all the sales counters throughout the store.
12. The problem of establishing sales prices that will achieve satisfactory gross margins when so many different products and departments are involved in the sale of merchandise; also, the problem of prices that are fixed in advance, often for considerable periods of time, for use in mail-order houses or departments.
13. The problem of merchandising in numerous locations, through chain stores or branch stores, and the related necessity to determine the extent of centralized control versus decentralized autonomy of operations.
14. The necessity to establish desired departmental margins sufficient to absorb direct and overhead expenses and provide a residue of profits.
15. The increasing percentage of part-time employees, principally occasioned by extended store hours.
16. The problems associated with adhering to governmental legislation in areas of pricing, consumer protection, and taxation.
17. The difficulties in maintaining adequate controls over costly and ever more sophisticated electronic data processing operations and equipment.

Resultant Procedures of Retailing

The distinctive problems and conditions of retailing described above have necessitated:

1. Some form of departmental, as well as functional, organization.
2. Some form of inventory control, particularly including the retail method, usually based upon departmental statistics.
3. Daily audit, basically comprising a daily compilation of sales and transactions (the sales statistics are correlated with daily cash receipts and charges to customers' accounts).
4. Development of extensive training programs for sales personnel, to accommodate part-time and seasonal help and turnover of employees; usually coupled with close supervisory control of sales clerks, to assure projection of the "store image" and as a key element in any shortage control program.
5. Use of more sophisticated equipment to capture and analyze information more rapidly.
6. Establishment of departmental standard or goal percentages for markon, both initial and maintained, and of standard or goal figures for departmental volume of business and for departmental expenses, both in ratios and dollar totals; in short, the division of a store into homogeneous departments and the conduct of operations on a departmental basis.

Merchandise Control

The distinctive problems and conditions that vitally affect retail accounting procedure largely center around merchandise control. Problems and conditions of merchandise control, and the related methods of resolving or adapting to such problems and circumstances, are the principal subject matter of this book. Since department store accounting is the most highly developed form of retail accounting and its methods and procedures can be adapted with appropriate changes to practically all the various types of retail operation, the main focus is upon department stores.

2

Types of Retail Businesses; Department Store Organization

Types of Businesses

The most prevalent types of retail businesses are general stores, single-line stores, specialty stores, department stores, chain stores, discount stores, mail-order houses, and other miscellaneous types. General descriptions of their approaches to merchandising and their accounting procedures are given in the following sections.

General Stores. These stores serve the smaller communities and carry as many different lines of merchandise as are currently in demand. They are usually under close personal supervision and are without departmentalization on any extended scale. Constant "hands-on" supervision and control by the owner or manager is the most predominant mode of organization, although simple accounting procedures along modern lines are proving of great value to these owner/managers.

Single-Line Stores. In these stores the merchandise carried is of one general line, for example, groceries, jewelry, men's clothing. Most single-line stores have the beginnings of departmental organization; for instance, a men's clothing store may offer selections of shirts, hats, and neckties. Close personal supervision of the proprietor is again the most common form of organization. Simple accounting procedures are used, but more attention is given to control of merchandise by class of goods and to standard ratios of markon and maintained gross margin. There is little necessity for departmentalization of expenses in these stores; however, simple expense classifications by natural divisions such as payroll, property rentals, and advertising are essential. Since expenses have to be met from gross profit on volume obtained, it is important that these expenses be controlled by comparison against previous periods and against budgets for the current period which are related to planned sales volume. Expenses should be adjusted currently, as may be appropriate, depending upon the current sales volume.

Specialty Stores. This term has come into common usage for single-line stores in the larger centers of trade where volume is sufficient to permit specialization in a particular kind of merchandise and its related classifications. For example, a ladies' dress shop would be called a specialty store when it is large enough to specialize in various price lines of dresses and ensembles, and to carry accessories, cosmetics, lingerie, and similar lines of merchandise geared to one type of consumer. In such a store, departmental organization is carried further than in the single-line store. Both merchandise and expenses are classified departmentally. Also, separate accounts, not normally found in a single-line store, must be set up for such transactions as layaways, alterations, commissions, and advertising allowances.

Department Stores. A selling unit which provides a broad line of merchandise to various classes of consumers is most commonly referred to as a department store. In addition to their variety of merchandise, department stores generally offer a full line of related services such as alteration and workrooms, custom shops, delivery, and various types of repair services. Beauty salons, soda fountains, cafeterias, and optical departments are often present. Credit facilities such as charge accounts and layaways are common.

Accounting for department stores represents the most complex and highly developed form of retail accounting. Department stores require departmental control of merchandising, with further refinements termed merchandise classifications within departments, and departmental classification of direct expenses. Procedures differ as to departmental allocations of indirect or general expenses: they can be prorated in one total on an approximate basis, or a complete allocation can be attempted, on various bases, of most or all of the expense elements involved. In recent years there has been a trend against departmental allocation of indirect expenses, in line with the so-called contribution profit concept. In applying this concept, standards or goals are set up departmentally for gross margin less direct expenses. These goals represent amounts that the department should earn or contribute toward indirect expenses and profits.

However, the direct expenses included as offsets to gross margin should comprise direct expenses over which a measure of control can be exercised. Defining which expenses are direct and controllable is a difficult question, and the answers will vary among different operations. Generally, the variations in the definition of direct expenses will parallel the differences in management philosophy. However, some form of measurement and control must be incorporated into the internal accounting systems. Normally this measurement is at some point between calculation of the gross profit and net operating figures, and reflects the contributions which respective departments should make toward indirect expenses and profits. These contributions supply a basis for the evaluation of actual results of operations on a departmental basis.

It is very common for department stores to have branch stores located in the surrounding suburban areas. Depending upon the markets which these branch stores serve, they may vary in size and consequently may not offer the full line of merchandise and services provided at the main store. Branch stores are generally controlled and to a certain extent serviced by the main store. In a recent variation on the use of branch stores, operations that have expanded beyond one geographical area have established a series of main stores, each of which controls and services a cluster of branches within its area. Measurement of the performance of a branch store is comparable to the measurement of the previously discussed merchandise or selling department. Accordingly, the same troublesome problems exist—defining controllable branch expenses, and reaching agreement on the desirability and equity of allocating general overhead expenses. One school of thought advocates the use of "four-wall" controllable expenses as a form of measurement. In this approach, only those expenses which are directly related to a specific location are used to measure performance. Alternatively, it is believed that operations should absorb all the costs within the organization, and all expenses should therefore be allocated to the operating units. Whatever definition is used for the measurement of store or buyer performance, it is important that this measurement be consistent from period to period and be understood by those being measured.

As can be expected, the department store accounting operation is often centralized, and the accounting systems and procedures required are more complex than those deemed necessary for the types of retail establishments described earlier. Department stores require many accounting checks and balances which must produce meaningful information in order to provide guidance and to control the various merchants, operations, and locations.

Chain Stores. Generally a chain store group represents a number of single-line stores, specialty stores, or department stores under one management. For any chain of stores the basic question that arises is the extent of centralized control that should be exercised by a headquarters group and the degree of autonomy, initiative, and responsibility that should be allowed local managements. Notwithstanding that in the true chain practically all authority is centralized, experience has shown the difficulty of operating a chain of stores with authority centralized in too much detail. In practice, there are several varieties of chain store organization, ranging from strictly centralized management to extensive local autonomy which is questioned only when profits are deemed unsatisfactory. An instance of the latter is where a number of department stores are under common management or ownership by a central holding company. In this situation headquarters personnel determine general policies and maintain central offices for merchandising counsel and comparison and interpretation of operating results, but headquarters insists upon and encourages a large degree of initiative and autonomy by individual stores.

In the strictest sense, a chain store may be contrasted with a department store by the fact that whereas a department store carries many lines of merchandise or operates many departments in a single location, a chain store operates one or a few departments in a great many locations. However, a department store that has geographically dispersed main stores and clusters of branches, as described above, is in essence a chain of department stores.

A measure of centralized control in true chain store groups is possible and desirable. Local managements are charged with custody and sale of merchandise, while expenses are generally standardized and closely controlled centrally. Often merchandise is billed to stores at retail amounts, to be accounted for at such prices. Price changes are often centrally authorized, and accounting for wastage and losses completes the cycle of inventory control for each store. Daily operating reports are provided to the central office, which is kept apprised of current conditions on a timely basis. Assets such as stock, cash, and certain types of receivables such as layaways are often verified by traveling auditors. Central control is maintained over stocks of merchandise in warehouses, both for incoming merchandise and for merchandise shipped to all stores.

Some chain stores are retailers for specific manufacturers which either own the chain or otherwise control its operating policies. The principles of retail merchandise control are not affected thereby, except in manner and detail of application. For example, if a chain is operated for distribution of shoes, control can be built around price lines.

Discount Stores. These stores generally offer a wide variety of merchandise, usually not concentrating on the higher price lines, and are somewhat similar to specialty and department stores. However, the full range of services normally offered by specialty and department stores is substantially curtailed or eliminated. Discount stores generally do not offer in-house credit facilities except on "big ticket" items. They encourage self-service and open selling, utilize mass check-out points, and complete most sales on a "cash-and-carry" basis with little or no repair or delivery offered. By limiting or eliminating these services and reducing the number of personnel required for the selling floors and for other services, economies are realized which can be reflected in pricing, since the gross margin realized is applied to a reduced level of operating expenses. Further, economies are anticipated by purchasing in bulk quantities and utilizing centralized warehousing and distribution. Discount stores work on smaller margins and place greater emphasis on volume and turnover. Discount stores are often part of a chain, and the comments regarding chain stores are equally applicable.

Buyers' and store managers' performance should be measured. The measurement techniques employed are similar to those encountered in department stores, and the difficulties in defining and allocating costs are equally troublesome. Any attempt to allocate costs is further complicated by the significant warehousing and distribution costs generally incurred on behalf of numerous departments and by costs of warehousing and distribution which can be directly related to the use of blanket advertising.

Mail-Order Houses. In some respects, mail-order organizations resemble department stores; in others, they resemble chain stores. Like department stores, mail-order houses carry a great variety of lines and types of merchandise. Generally speaking, however, mail-order houses attempt to standardize the merchandise in each line, and to carry more staples and fewer style or novelty items. Stocks of merchandise can be centrally controlled, as in the chain store warehouses.

Merchandise gross profit margins may be determined departmentally in the mail-order business. Expense classifications in mail-order houses differ somewhat from those of department or chain stores, with catalog expense, warehouse control, filling of orders, and transportation charges outward comprising important expense items.

A distinctive feature of the mail-order business is that prices are fixed in advance for more or less definite periods. Such prices are not subject to daily revision to meet competition, or to give effect to changed conditions, as they are with stores trading locally. If the market drops, the sale of merchandise will be affected adversely; if the market rises, an unanticipated customer demand may cause difficulties unless the mail-order house is protected by purchase agreements with its vendors. Supplemental price lists reflecting price changes may be used at times.

Mail-order houses have devised methods of forecasting seasonal demand based upon past experience and the experience of the present season to date. On the basis of careful planning and constant flexibility of plans, contractual arrangements are consummated with vendors. The correct balancing of seasonal purchasing with consumer seasonal demand is obviously exceedingly important and comprises elements of both art and science.

Special accounting problems relate to the handling of incoming cash and refunds for unfilled orders and to keeping track of orders until completed by delivery or refund.

Other Miscellaneous Types. In addition to the specific types of retailing mentioned, there are numerous special types, such as operation of leased departments, made-to-order workshops where customers' requirements are satisfied, service stores (e.g., beauty parlors, cleaning establishments, and restaurants), and catalog stores. Some organizations operate a chain of leased merchandising or service departments. In a real sense they are chain store groups, but they are subject to special conditions and problems arising from the leasing arrangements.

Some retailers manufacture a large portion of the merchandise they handle, and incur all the additional production and cost accounting problems common to manufacturers. Such manufacturing may be comparatively restricted to special custom work in the higher price ranges or it may include most of the merchandise sold.

Department Store Organization

In department stores, the most complex mercantile unit, a general standard of organization has been developed. To some degree the functional groupings utilized are natural for other types of retailing. In this chapter organization is discussed only as a reference or as an aid to a better understanding of the merchandise accounting problems and procedures outlined in succeeding chapters.

Most organizations have a chief executive who may bear any one of a number of titles but has the responsibility for making final decisions. In a department store operation, this chief executive may be the owner, or an officer unencumbered by any of the main functional or divisional duties and responsibilities. Under these circumstances, the chief executive is a coordinator of all functions. Alternatively, the chief executive officer may be one of the principal functional heads, such as the merchandise manager or general manager, and still have overall responsibility for the entire operation.

The final test of a good or a faulty organization is not the degree to which it approaches some theoretical or standard organization chart, but its effectiveness in actual everyday practice. Sometimes necessary changes in executive personnel may require the realignment of functional divisions or responsibilities as originally structured in the organization chart.

Outline of Standard Organization. The normal or standard practice has been to have a two-, three-, or fourfold divisional organization coordinated by the president or owner. A typical fourfold divisional organization is as follows:

1. *Merchandise manager.* This executive is responsible for active control and direction of merchandising, both buying and selling, which are different sides of the same activity.
2. *Operations manager* (sometimes called store manager or general superintendent). The operations manager is in charge of personnel (with certain notable exceptions, as, for example, buyers), upkeep of premises, and service to the public, including delivery, and is at least partially responsible for expense control, especially as it relates to the day-to-day operations of the facilities.
3. *Chief financial officer.* The duties of the chief financial officer may be consolidated in one executive or, alternatively, they may be split between a treasurer and controller, who have equal executive status. In larger organizations, it is common practice for the treasurer and controller to report directly to the chief financial officer. In any event, the controller (or controllership function) should be responsible for the store's accounting department, for accounting systems and procedures, and for accounting control over operations.
4. *Publicity and sales promotion.* This is an exceedingly important division whose efforts should be closely coordinated with the merchandising division.

In many details the four functions overlap, and there are twilight zones where it may be theoretically difficult to state where the authority of the individual functional divisions begins or ends. The spheres of influence of the chief functional executives often are affected by historical relationships and responsibilities in a store, as well as by personal factors. Frequently, the publicity and sales promotion function is combined with the merchandising function under a single executive. In moderate-sized stores, the store management and the control functions may similarly be combined under one principal head. In any event, whatever the size of a store or the form of its organization, a successful and viable operation requires coordinated, cooperative effort among the key executives.

In smaller or medium-sized stores a twofold divisional organization (for example, merchandise manager and operations manager) may be better and more efficient than the three- or fourfold functional alignment. In larger organizations, it may be desirable to establish personnel as a fifth major functional division. Personnel management—dealing with the selection, training, supervision, and development of employees; labor policies (including union contracts and employee benefit plans); and the study of wage and hour problems—is an office which is assuming ever increasing importance in the field of retailing since retailing obviously is a people-oriented business.

Functional and Departmental Organization. In a department store the departmental organization runs across the functional organization. For example, the buyers and assistant buyers are primarily responsible to the merchandise manager, whereas the departmental sales and service personnel are under the jurisdiction of the operations or store manager. Departmental operating results are compiled and analyzed in the control division, and thereafter made available to other executives, including buyers. Buyers are vitally concerned with departmental publicity and advertising allotments and must maintain continuous contacts with the director of publicity.

Details of Functional Organization. The following alignments should not be considered definitive since any functional division of duties and responsibilities should give due consideration to a store's specific problems and the experience and capabilities of its executive personnel. It is presented simply as a framework for the discussions of merchandise and expense control and related problems in the chapters which follow:

General Merchandise Manager:
    Divisional merchandise managers (stores which exercise strictest control over buyers are apt to have more divisional merchandise managers than those which grant buyers a large degree of responsibility and initiative)
    Merchandise office
    Fashion and home coordinators
    Buyers and assistant buyers

Unit stock controls (preferably in cooperation with the controller)
Buyers' office clerks (preferably in cooperation with the controller)
Bureau of standards, testing of materials
Comparison shopping department

Operations Manager:
Store manager
Selling and nonselling service superintendents
Factory manager, factory foreman, and factory personnel
Warehouse manager and warehouse personnel
Building superintendent, draftsmen, carpenters, painters, plumbers, electricians, and other housekeeping mechanics
Supply purchasing agent
Receiving manager, traffic manager, employees engaged in receiving, checking, and marking merchandise, and stockkeeping personnel
Cleaning (housekeeping) department
Telephone operators
Store detectives, uniformed guards, and watchmen
Delivery supervisor, delivery clericals, delivery drivers, helpers, loaders, sorters, route clerks, stubbers, and other delivery personnel
Mail and messenger service
Elevator starters, freight and passenger elevator operators
Wrapping and packing manager, supervisors and clericals, floor cashiers, cashier wrappers, package collectors and inspectors
Personal shoppers
Mail and telephone order personnel
Merchandise adjustment department
Service desks
Floor superintendents, floor managers, and service or sales managers
Salespersons

Chief Financial Officer:
Corporate controller
Retail controller
Tax and insurance specialists
Chief accountant and bookkeepers
Credit and collections department
Customer accounts department

Accounts payable department
Sales audit office
Cash offices (general cashier and personnel of all cash offices)
Timekeeping and payroll department
Budget and expense controller (it may be preferable to have this department, with its emphasis on budget and cost control and systems and methods research and modification, responsible directly to the chief executive)
Shortage controller
Bill adjustment department
Data processing department
Real estate department

Sales Promotion and Publicity Director:
Advertising budget and cost controller
Advertising, public relations, and display directors
Artists and photographers
Copywriters
Direct mail department
Advertising production personnel
Store interior decorators and window trimmers
Sign painters
Special events personnel

Personnel Manager:
Labor relations counselor, job evaluation personnel
Employment director, hiring personnel
Training department
Doctors, nurses, and dentists
Employee welfare department

In addition, an internal auditing staff will be responsible directly to the chief executive, or, alternatively, the chief financial officer.

Figure 1 and the related subfigures 1(a), 1(b), and 1(c) present a threefold divisional organization which, to a large extent, follows the above descriptions. Those situations where alternative jurisdictions may exist have been appropriately footnoted. Although these charts represent what might be deemed preferable lines of authority, they may have to be modified to take into account specific store circumstances and the strengths and weaknesses and experience of the key executives.

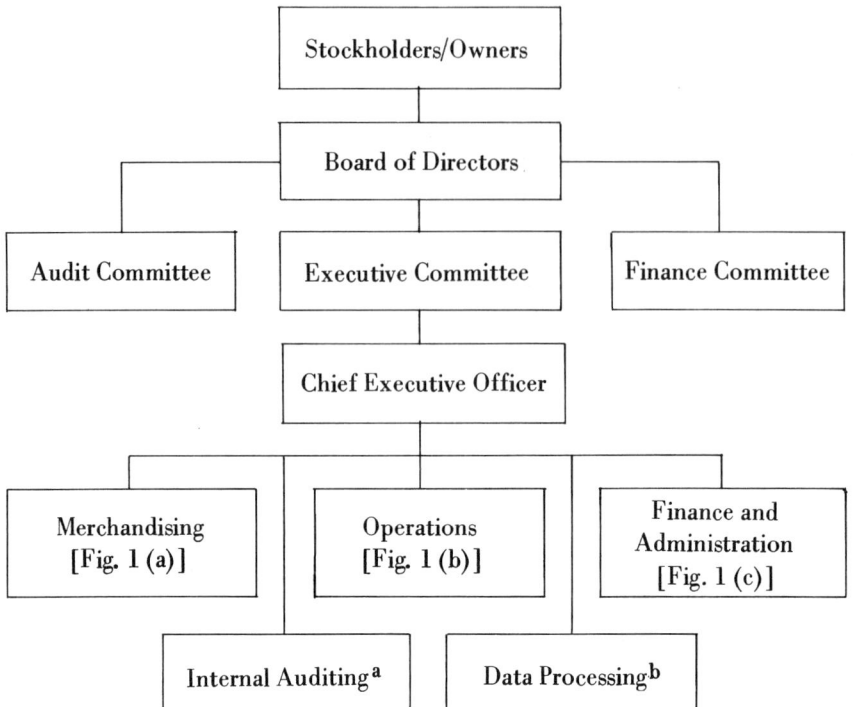

[a]The internal auditing function often reports to the Chief Financial Officer; however, it is preferable to have this function report directly to the Chief Executive Officer.

[b]Also called management information systems (MIS), electronic data processing (EDP), or similar titles. This department often reports directly to the Chief Financial Officer. However, since most if not all functions utilize its services, it should be independent of any one function.

FIG. 1. Functional organization chart for a department store.

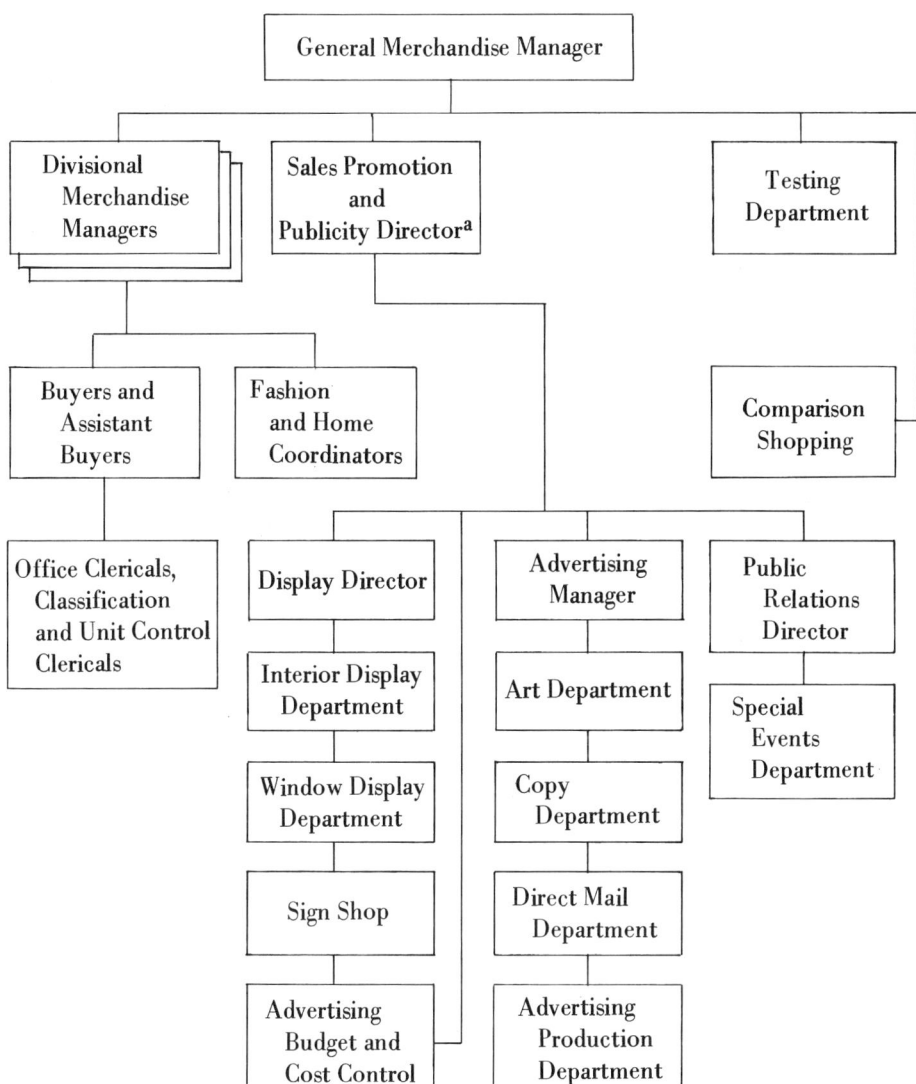

[a]This function in larger organizations reports independently to the Chief Executive Officer.

FIG. 1(a). Merchandising.

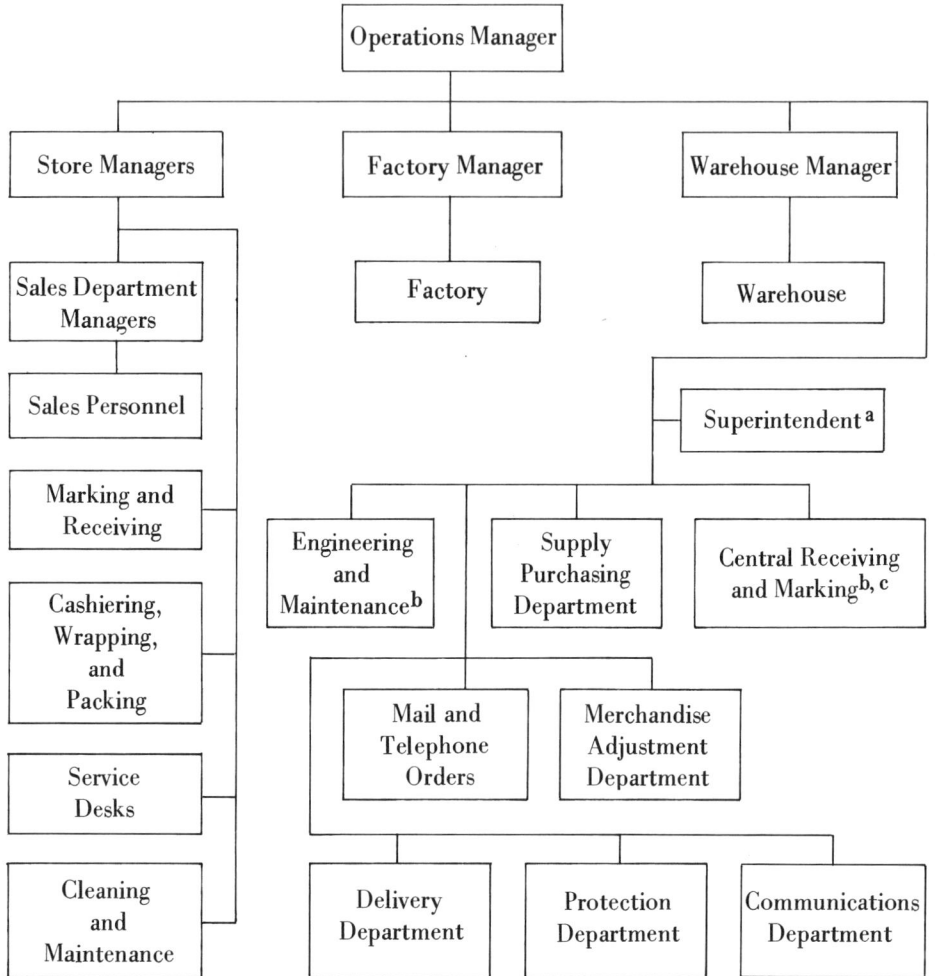

[a]This function can be separated into selling and nonselling services, depending upon the size of the operations and degree of centralization.
[b]These functions may be completely decentralized and therefore placed under the direct control of the store managers.
[c]In some operations, this function is under the control of warehouse managers.

FIG. 1(b). Operations.

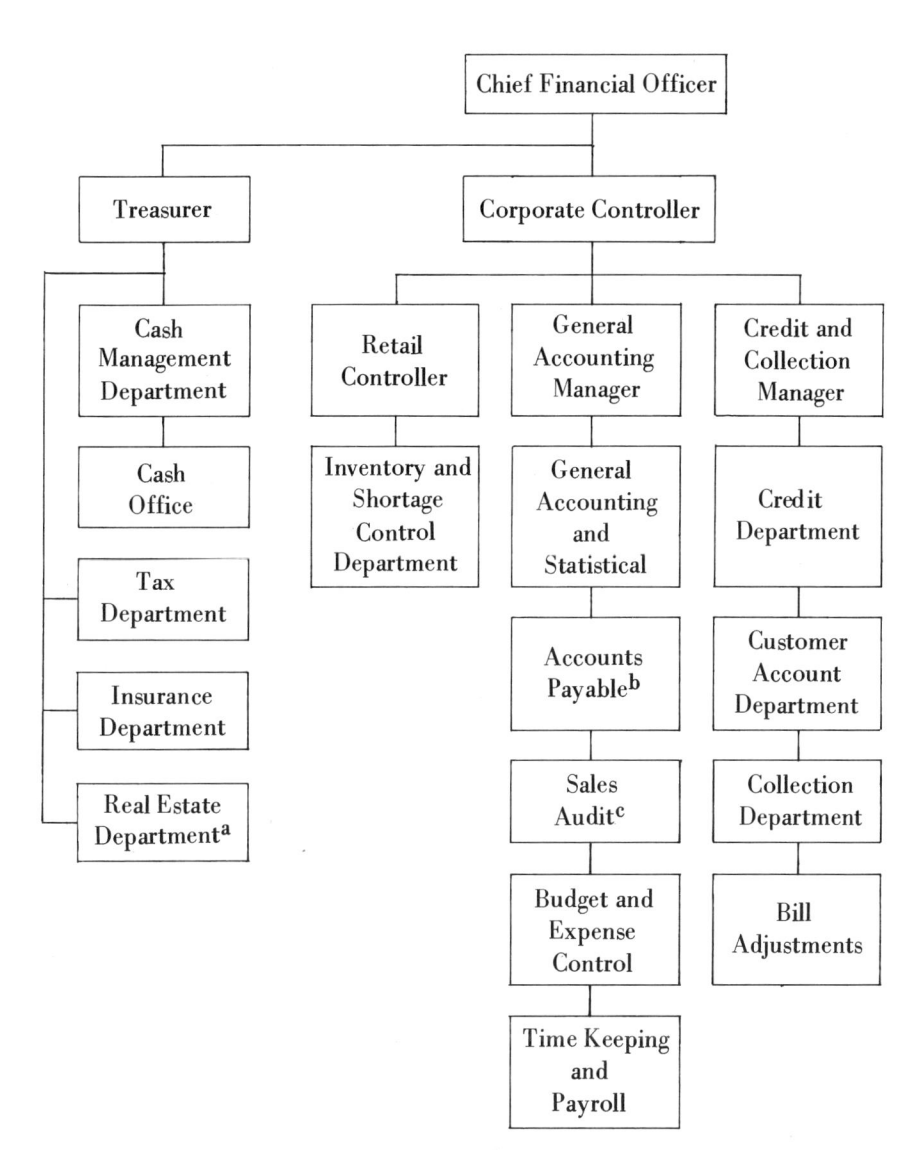

```
                          ┌─────────────────────┐
                          │ Chief Financial Officer │
                          └─────────────────────┘
                    ┌───────────────┴───────────────┐
            ┌───────────────┐              ┌─────────────────────┐
            │   Treasurer   │              │ Corporate Controller │
            └───────────────┘              └─────────────────────┘
```

```
Treasurer:                    Corporate Controller:
  - Cash Management Department    - Retail Controller
  - Cash Office                     - Inventory and Shortage Control Department
  - Tax Department                - General Accounting Manager
  - Insurance Department            - General Accounting and Statistical
  - Real Estate Department[a]       - Accounts Payable[b]
                                    - Sales Audit[c]
                                    - Budget and Expense Control
                                    - Time Keeping and Payroll
                                  - Credit and Collection Manager
                                    - Credit Department
                                    - Customer Account Department
                                    - Collection Department
                                    - Bill Adjustments
```

[a] This department is also commonly found under operations.
[b] Occasionally found under retail controller.
[c] Occasionally found under credit and collection manager.

FIG. 1(c). Finance and administration.

Retail Accounting Manual. While this book is primarily concerned with retail merchandise accounting rather than retail expense accounting, no outline of functional organization, however brief, should fail to mention the "Retail Accounting Manual—Revised" (1976) published by the Financial Executives Division of the National Retail Merchants Association (NRMA). The "Retail Accounting Manual—Revised" is an update of the "Retail Accounting Manual" published in 1962 by the then Controllers' Congress of the NRMA. This revised manual came into being as a direct result of the significant branch store expansion program implemented by many retailers which created a new series of problems related to accounting for expenses. The manual provides retailers with a great deal of flexibility in designing internal accounting systems regardless of the size of the retail operation. It stresses the need to assign responsibility for specific areas of activity and to have the accounting measure the performance of these activity centers. The manual provides ten expense summaries which can be further broken down into expense centers and subexpense centers, depending upon the size and complexity of an organization. Furthermore, "Retail Accounting Manual—Revised" sets forth the concept that each store should be treated as a selling location, without regard to whether a store is a branch, main store, or downtown store. (For further discussion of the underlying expense center concepts contained in "Retail Accounting Manual—Revised," see Chapter 16.)

The development and implementation of expense center accounting must take into account the organizational structure, as well as the capabilities and responsibilities of the various echelons of management. Expense accounting, and the directly related effective control over expenses, can be successful only if it follows clearly defined organizational lines of authority and responsibility and provides timely data with which to measure performance. In this connection, the use of expense centers provides a framework which, when combined with productivity and backlog data and effective supervision, can be used to control expenses.

3

Definition and Discussion of Important Terms

Introduction

As in any other specialized branch of accounting, retail accounting, especially retail merchandise accounting, uses terms or expressions that require definition and some discussion of their practical application. This chapter includes only the more important, commonly used terms relating to retail merchandise accounting. Terms relating specifically to the last-in, first-out (LIFO) method of inventory determination are not included here but will be found in later chapters dealing with LIFO and related procedures.

Retail Inventory Method

The retail inventory method is a method of book control of merchandise stocks at retail price amounts. Determination of inventory amounts at "cost" under the retail method is accomplished by applying the complement of cumulative markon percentages (cost multipliers; see page 25) of the selling departments to the departmental inventory amounts at retail prices. This method is discussed and illustrated in considerable detail in Chapter 6.

Markon

Markon is the amount added to cost to arrive at original marked retail (selling) price, plus any additional markups; stated differently, markon is the excess of original marked retail (selling) price, plus any markups, over cost.

Illustration. Purchases which cost $100 are marked originally to sell for $150. The $50 added to cost is the markon. If, however, the retail price of $150 is revised upward to $155, the markon is $55.

The term markon may refer to markon on specific purchases, or to total markon on purchases for a month (or four- or five-week period), season, year, or other period. It is, however, to be differentiated from cumulative markon.

Cumulative Markon

Cumulative markon is the difference between the aggregate of originally marked retail prices (plus markups) of the purchases of a period and the aggregate of the corresponding cost of such purchases *plus* the markon in the opening inventory; that is, cumulative markon represents the excess of retail of opening inventory plus retail (before markdowns) of purchases for a period, over cost of opening inventory plus cost of purchases for the period.

Illustration. Inventory at beginning of period is $100 at cost and $225 at retail. Subsequent purchases cost $200 and are first marked to retail at $350, then revised upward to $360. Markdowns amounting to $30 are taken, none of which specifically cancels any part of the markup of $10. Cumulative markon is markon of $125 in opening inventory plus markon of $160 on purchases, a total of $285.

Markon Percentage

Markon percentage is the percentage which markon bears to originally marked retail, plus markups.

Cumulative Markon Percentage

Cumulative markon percentage is the percentage which cumulative markon bears to the sum of retail of opening inventory and originally marked retail of purchases plus markups. This percentage is applied to an inventory at retail to determine the amount to be subtracted to reduce such inventory to cost. (For a fuller explanation, see Chapter 6.)

Alternative Terms

Sometimes other terms such as initial markup, initial markon, original markup, original markon, purchase markup, or purchase markon are used. Markon has been selected as the best term to use in this volume.

Complement of Markon Percentage

Markon percentage is the ratio of markon to the aggregate of original retail and markups. Cost is therefore expressed as a percentage of the corresponding retail by taking the complement of the markon percentage; that is, 100 less the percentage of markon. If 40 per cent is the markon percentage, then 60 per cent is the related complement.

Cost Percentage or Cost Multiplier

The complement of the markon percentage is sometimes referred to as the "cost percentage" or "cost multiplier." It is the percentage that is applied to retail of inventory to obtain cost.

Markups

Amounts added to the original marked retail prices to revise them upward are known as markups.

Illustration 1. If a marked retail price of $500 is subsequently revised upward to $515, the increase of $15 is a markup.

Since markups are adjustments of original retail prices, they are taken into consideration in determining markons and percentages of markon. Accordingly, markups during a period are added to the sum of inventory at the beginning of the period and purchases during the period (both at retail) when deriving the cumulative markon.

Illustration 2. The difference between revised retail of $515 (originally retail of $500) and $300 (the cost of opening inventory plus cost of purchases) represents cumulative gross markon in the amount of $215. The percentage of cumulative markon in this case is the ratio of $215 to $515, or 41.75 per cent.

Markup Cancellations

When an error occurs in adding markups to the original marked retail prices, a correction is necessary to reduce or eliminate the markup, thereby obtaining either a new or the original marked retail price. Such changes are known as markup cancellations. Although in a technical sense they may be viewed as markdowns, they are applied to reduce the amount of markups previously taken. However, the fact that a reduction in retail price follows an increase through a markup does not necessarily justify treating the reduction as a markup cancellation rather than a markdown. A markup cancellation is generally used to correct an unintentional error in re-marking. Markup cancellations may also be used where the original markup is of a special nature, and understood to be temporary at the time it was made and subject to reversal at a later date.

Generally speaking, price reductions are to be treated as markdowns and not as markup cancellations. To do otherwise, except in very rare and clear cases, is to open the door to abuse and permit the concealment of markdowns. This potential abuse is so troublesome that some controllers deem it desirable not to recognize markup cancellations at all.

Markup cancellations are to be taken only to correct markups on purchases of a current season. They should not be applied as corrections of cumulative markon in inventory as at the beginning of a season. Any corrections of such cumulative markon should be recorded as markdowns.

Markdowns

Amounts deducted from original marked retail prices (or from adjusted retail prices resulting from application of previous markdowns or markups) to arrive at reduced retail prices are termed markdowns.

Illustration. Assume purchases which cost $100 were marked to sell for $150. If this retail price is reduced to $140, the $10 reduction is the markdown. There may be further markdowns; for example, the retail price may be reduced to $130 and then to $120. The additional $10 reductions in each instance are markdowns.

As previously noted, markups are included when deriving cumulative markon. Markdowns, however, are not taken into consideration and do not affect cumulative markon.

Markdown Cancellations

After merchandise has been reduced in retail price by markdowns, it may be found desirable to restore the original selling price or increase the retail to some intermediate price. This most frequently occurs where merchandise has been marked down temporarily, as for a special sales event, and the original price is restored on any unsold merchandise. It also may be done to correct other previous markdowns. These price changes, although upward revisions, are treated as markdown cancellations, to be offset against markdowns previously taken.

Illustration. Goods originally marked to sell for $150 were marked down by $30 for a special sale. At the conclusion of the sale, the remaining merchandise was restored to its original selling price by processing a price change of $10. This $10 is not considered as a markup in the usual sense but as a partial offset to the markdown of $30. In this illustration the markdown would not be considered to be $30, but $30 less the markdown cancellation of $10, or $20.

Markdown cancellations are applicable only when they offset markdowns taken within a season. Restorations of retail prices on merchandise which was marked down prior to the beginning of the season are considered as markups, rather than as markdown cancellations.

Corrections of Retail

Originally marked retail of purchases is sometimes revised downward, either to correct unintentional errors in original pricing or to reflect the retail of rebates granted by vendors which are directly related to the amount of markdowns incurred by the retailer. Such corrections are recorded as reductions of purchases at retail rather than as markdowns.

Care should be exercised in classifying price changes as corrections of retail, to guard against the manipulation of markons through the treatment of markdowns as corrections of original retail.

Corrections of retail that arise where markdowns are offset by related rebates from vendors should be limited to the proportionate amount of the markdown covered by the rebate, based upon the departmental markon percentage. For example, if the markdown is $2,500 where the rebate is $1,000, in a department with a markon of 50 per cent, purchases at cost would be reduced $1,000 and purchases at retail would be reduced by $2,000. The difference of $500 ($2,500 less the rebate at retail of $2,000) would be recorded as a markdown.

Net Markon

This term relates to the excess of reduced retail price over cost, that is, the amount of markon, or cumulative markon less markdowns.

Net markon is not to be confused with gross margin (see page 34). There is some similarity between the two, but gross margin includes purchase discounts and is calculated after all retail reductions and after workroom and alteration costs. Net markon is a limited term useful for descriptive purposes. It does not enter into computations under the retail method, except as required when the LIFO method of inventory determination is used (see discussion of the lower of cost or market on page 37, and subsequent LIFO chapters).

Retail Price and Maintained Markon

Since markdowns, sales discounts, and shrinkages intervene between the original marking of merchandise and its ultimate sale, it is necessary to distinguish between the original (or revised) stock retail and sales retail. The retail placed upon stock is not the price expected to be realized on all merchandise sold. Some part of many purchases will probably be marked down before sale, and there also may be sales discounts and stock shrinkages. These factors are taken into consideration in fixing stock retail, so that sales retail (that is, after markdowns, sales discounts, and shrinkages) will produce the projected maintained or realized markon.

Stock retail is usually higher than sales retail just as cumulative markon is usually higher than maintained markon. Therefore, in deriving cost from stock retail it is necessary to reduce retail by cumulative, rather than by maintained, markon. In comparing markon on purchases and stock with maintained markon on sales, it should be recognized that they are not percentages of the same base, although both are expressed as percentages of retail. Also, maintained markon is usually less as a percentage of sales than gross margin, since the latter includes discounts earned, although after deduction of alteration and workroom costs.

Price Lines and Markon

Initial markons are usually established with the expectation that the resulting maintained markon will be sufficient to absorb alteration and workroom costs and operating expenses, as well as to allow some margin of merchandising profit in addition to discounts earned. However, the establishment of departmental markons is not solely a mathematical process; it must take into consideration all competitive and other pertinent factors such as, for example, the desirability of maintaining a complete line of certain products, or special sales events. With the goal ratio or markon in mind, the individual marking is adjusted to meet existing conditions. In effect, the same markon cannot be placed upon every purchase of every merchandise classification.

For a considerable number of merchandise classifications, price lines are established on the basis of a store's experience with the desires of its customers, as well as to buttress the image the store is attempting to project in its trading area. Merchandise is then "brought in" to such price lines, with resultant variations in markons of specific purchases above and below the desired average markon for the department or the merchandise classification.

Sales Discounts

Retail accounts receivable are not subject to trade discounts or cash discounts on remittances, as may be true with the accounts receivable of wholesalers or manufacturers. However, a special class of sales discounts is made available to employees of the retailer, and sometimes to decorators, dressmakers, selling agents, institutions, and clergymen. These discounts either are deducted from the sale price of the merchandise as the transaction is recorded, or are recognized at settlement dates (on payment of accounts). Just as with markdowns, sales discounts are not considered in determining markon or cumulative markon.

Shrinkages

This term refers to differences between actual stocks on hand and the corresponding amounts reflected in the stock records, where the latter amounts are greater than the actual stocks on hand. Such differences are also termed stock shortages. Excesses of actual stocks on hand over the amounts shown in the stock records are referred to as stock overages. Stock overages are rarely, if ever, representative of actual conditions. Apparent overages may result from inaccuracies in physical inventories or in the records. A shrinkage ordinarily represents an aggregate of stock record-keeping errors and actual physical losses of merchandise and samples through such factors as theft, breakage, and spoilage. Shrinkages have no effect on markon or cumulative markon, but are recorded in the accounts in the same manner as markdowns.

Total Retail Reductions

The sum of markdowns, sales discounts and allowances, and shrinkages constitutes total retail reductions. Percentages of total retail reductions and of each of the three constituent classifications are computed on net sales.

Net Sales

Net sales are gross sales less returns and allowances (except policy adjustments) and less discounts to employees and others. The sum of net sales and total retail reductions is the total amount at retail deducted from opening inventory plus purchases (net of returns and including departmental transfers and markups, all at retail) to obtain the closing inventory at retail. This is the inventory as per the books of account that periodically should be checked by a physical inventory.

Net sales do not include (a) alteration sales, (b) carrying charges on option, revolving credit, or installment accounts, (c) sales and excise taxes, (d) transportation charged to customers, (e) sales of supplies and waste, and (f) departmental or interstore transfers. The items mentioned are respectively treated as: (a) offset to alteration costs, (b) credits to expense or other income, (c) tax liabilities, (d) and (e) credits to expense or other income, and (f) credits or debits to purchases.

Purchases

In this chapter there have been included simple illustrations of markon on purchases and cumulative markon on inventory and purchases. The term purchases is now defined so that there will be a clear understanding of the basis of markons. The total of departmental purchases upon which markon of a period is based includes:

1. Billed cost of domestic purchases and landed cost of imported merchandise, both net of trade discounts, less returns and allowances (including quantity discounts) received from vendors. There may be included in billed cost of domestic purchases transportation charges, manufacturers' excise taxes, and charges for containers or prepacking. Landed cost of imported merchandise includes commissions, fees, freight, insurance, and duties, but excludes the cost or any allocation of buyers' traveling expenses and costs and expenses associated with the operation of the import office or function.
2. Charges for transportation of merchandise from manufacturer or wholesaler to store or warehouse.
3. Production cost of goods obtained by merchandise departments or manufacturing workrooms.
4. Consignment purchases, when such merchandise is not segregated in the accounts. Ordinarily, consignment goods are treated in the same manner as regular purchases except in those situations where there is a permanent arrangement to carry some of a vendor's merchandise in a store or warehouse for convenience in making deliveries.
5. The net amount of transfers between departments (whether retail or cost departments) and to workrooms or expense accounts. There is ordinarily a net credit amount of transfers resulting from charges to workrooms or expense.
6. Miscellaneous cash purchases for departments, including comparison shoppers' purchases, unless they are charged in part or in total to expense.
7. Vendor price concessions, where these concessions or allowances represent deductions from purchases. On the other hand, allowances received from vendors representing reimbursements of advertising disbursements should be offset against advertising expense.

Retail amounts are tabulated for these various elements of purchases insofar as applicable. Corrections of retail are deducted from retail totals of purchases. Markups, at retail only, are included in accumulations of purchases at retail.

Department Transfers

Retail operations are usually departmentalized. Records are maintained departmentally, and this necessitates reflecting transfers in the records whenever merchandise is moved from one department to another or is taken from departments for use in workrooms or expense divisions. Such transfers are known as department transfers or merchandise transfers. They are not recorded as sales but as adjustments of purchases.

Alteration and Workroom Costs (Net)

This term refers to the net cost of service departments (workrooms) maintained for altering or repairing merchandise sold or in stock and for making goods ready for delivery. Net cost comprises labor, materials, supplies, and other expenses (and the amounts paid for similar services purchased from outside sources), less charges made to customers. Frequently, while there may not be a workroom as such, departmental payroll and other expenses are incurred for repairs or alterations or in preparing for the delivery of merchandise to customers. These expenses are aggregated and are also termed workroom costs.

Alteration and workroom costs (net) are not included in cost of purchases in deriving markons, but they comprise part of total merchandise costs and are included in the determination of gross margin. Percentages of net alteration and workroom costs are computed on net sales.

Discounts Earned

In the foregoing definitions of markon and cumulative markon, reference has been made to cost figures. It should be understood that such cost figures are gross of cash discounts on purchases. In deriving markon and cumulative markon, cash discounts are not deducted from cost of purchases or from inventories, although they do enter into the determination of gross margin. It should be noted, however, that trade discounts, which have no bearing on invoice terms, do enter into markon computations.

There are two basic approaches to the accounting for cash discount income. One school of thought maintains that it is sound procedure in retailing to defer recognition of cash discount income until the related merchandise is sold, regardless of when discounts accrue or are received. Proponents of this method basically maintain that income is generated by the sale, not the purchase, of merchandise, and, accordingly, discount income should be deferred until the merchandise is sold. Discounts on purchases under this deferral method should be understood to represent the discounts applicable to the purchases of a period, without regard to when payment for such purchases is made. This would include all discounts applicable to purchases made during the period, whether such discounts were received upon payments made before or after the close of the period. Stated differently, the discounts are computed on an accrual basis rather than a cash basis. The accrual basis discounts are recognized as earned to the extent the related merchandise is sold. The remaining unearned balance is reflected as a deduction of inventories on the balance sheet.

Another school of thought considers cash discounts as a function of cash management, rather than merchandise income. Accordingly, cash discounts are reflected in income when received. In effect, it is maintained that decisions concerning the timing of invoice payments are not related to the sale of the merchandise purchased. Moreover, it is pointed out that the earlier payment of invoices to obtain discounts generally increases the burden of financing the inventory, which in turn either increases interest expense or decreases income from short-term investments. Such increased expense or decreased income is, of course, reflected in its entirety in the current period. Given these circumstances, it is believed that the recognition of cash discounts in income on a when-received basis results in a better matching of revenue and expense.

The authors believe that in most instances discounts earned should be recognized as merchandise is sold during the period.

Chapter 8 more fully describes and illustrates discount problems, including those arising in connection with so-called "loaded" discounts.

Percentages of Discounts

In operating statements percentages of discounts are generally computed on net sales. Basing such percentages on net sales probably results from ease of presentation since most other elements of income and expense are expressed as percentages of net sales. This percentage relationship also reflects the more prevalent practice of recognizing discounts as earned when the related merchandise is sold.

Gross Margin

The difference between net sales and total merchandise costs (net) constitutes gross margin. Total merchandise costs (net) are the sum of:

> Any decrease in inventories (before deduction of cash discounts) during the period;
> Purchases, including transportation inward; and
> Alteration and workroom costs, net;

less the sum of:

> Discounts earned on merchandise sold during the period; and
> Any increase in inventories (before deduction of cash discounts) during the period.

Percentage of Gross Margin

The percentage of gross margin is computed on net sales for the period. The percentage of cumulative markon can be reconciled with the percentage of gross margin by taking into account:

> The percentage of earned discounts on net sales.
> The percentage of retail reductions on net sales multiplied by the complement of the percentage of cumulative markon.
> The percentage of alteration and workroom costs (net) on net sales.

Illustration.

Cumulative markon percentage		41.5%
Add: Percentage of earned discounts		3.5
		45.0
Deduct:		
Percentage of retail reductions, 6.5%, times the complement of the percentage of cumulative markon, 58.5% (100 − 41.5)	3.8%	
Percentage of workroom and alteration costs (net)	1.2	5.0
Percentage of gross margin		40.0%

Classification of Departments

In a retail store the merchandise departments may be classified as retail departments, cost departments, leased departments, and workrooms. The retail departments sell merchandise at retail to the public and carry their inventories at retail on the statistical records. They include all items of a usual retail department, such as ready-to-wear, domestics, home furnishings, and appliances. The cost departments sell either merchandise or services at retail to the public but carry inventories, if any, only at cost. Examples are fur storage, beauty parlor, restaurants, barber shop, and workrooms that generally deal directly with customers. Leased departments may include retail or cost departments or workrooms, but such departments are operated by lessees rather than by store personnel. Lessees may be charged a fixed rental, or a rental based on sales, or a fixed rental with an override based on sales.

Markons and merchandise statistics at retail are obtained for retail departments, but these factors are not normally developed for cost departments. It is usually unnecessary for the store to keep any merchandise statistics for leased departments other than net sales.

Workrooms may be classified as manufacturing workrooms and subsidiary or service workrooms. Manufacturing workrooms produce merchandise for sale in retail departments. The relation of this type of workroom to the department is that of a vendor–supplier. The subsidiary or service workroom primarily assists in facilitating the sale of the merchandise carried in the selling departments or in servicing such merchandise after it is sold. Examples are the men's and women's garment alteration room and the furniture finishing room. Frequently, workrooms combine the functions of manufacturing and service. An example would be a millinery workroom which produces for stock and also alters merchandise sold.

A third class of workrooms, termed cost inventory workrooms, principally deal directly with customers. Although they are workrooms, they can be classified with cost departments. Examples are picture framing, stationery engraving, carpet laying, drapery and upholstery workrooms. Some of these workrooms may do work for other departments of the store, or they may be operated as adjuncts to selling departments.

For a more detailed discussion of workrooms, see Chapter 14.

Expressions as to Inventory Amounts

Explanations of the retail inventory method usually state that the merchandise records are kept at retail and also at cost, that is, "cost" as computed under the retail method. This resultant inventory valuation has been variously described as inventory at cost, inventory at the lower of cost or market, inventory as computed under the retail method, and inventory on the basis of the lower of cost or market as determined by the retail inventory method.

The tax authorities have focused on this problem, and the following is taken from Income Tax Mimeograph, Coll., No. 3077, dated March 23, 1923: "The 'retail method' is essentially a cost method of valuing inventories, but the rule is not inflexible. On a constant or rising market it is approximately a 'cost' method, but on a falling market it may result in a reduction to cost or market whichever is lower."

Section 1.471–8 of the Treasury Regulations says of inventories under the retail method: ". . . the total of the retail selling prices of the goods on hand at the end of the year in each department or of each class of goods is reduced to approximate cost. . . ."

In other words, it is impossible to describe with complete accuracy the basis of inventory valuation termed the retail method. For example, the application of the cumulative markon percentage, where there have been numerous markdowns, tends to reduce an inventory, insofar as marked-down goods are on hand, to somewhat below cost. But if no reductions whatever have been taken and other factors are normal, the inventory may be at or close to actual cost. There are all shades of variation, depending upon whether costs have been rising or falling, the range of purchase markon percentages, the total of markdowns taken, and the mix of items in the inventory (whether they represent merchandise bearing relatively high or low markons or marked-down merchandise, rather than merchandise carried at original retail prices, and in which proportions).

The inventory derived under the retail method is commonly described as cost although it is recognized that it is not cost. In fact, the inventory derived under the retail method is an amount clearly distinguished and different from cost. A term has been required to describe it. In the first edition of this book, inventories derived under the retail method by deduction of cumulative markons from inventories at retail were described as inventories on a mercantile basis, or, concisely, as inventories at mercantile. That term seems now to be widely accepted.

The following listing represents some of the numerous bases for computing and describing inventories of retailers:

> Inventories at original retail prices (before giving effect to any reductions)
> Inventories at retail (at marked retail prices)
> Inventories at cost (at actual cost)
> Inventories at mercantile
> Inventories at the lower of cost or market

Inventories at the Lower of Cost or Market

For retailers the term "market" has primary significance as probable selling price, rather than replacement cost. Retailers are trained to think in terms of consumers' market, which basically represents probable prices obtainable from prospective customers. Retail merchants will ordinarily replace little except what can be expected to yield a proper markon based upon probable selling price. A "proper markon" would, of course, include a provision for an anticipated normal gross margin. Accordingly, the retail inventory method generally results in a conservative inventory valuation since inventories will not only be stated at amounts which are not in excess of estimated net realizable but *at amounts which should provide a normal gross margin when the merchandise is sold during the ensuing period.* Except in limited staple lines, retailers do not really "replace" the exact merchandise carried in stock, but rather make replacement with other similar items of merchandise expected to yield a consistently comparable markon.

At this point it is important to distinguish between cumulative markon and net markon in connection with the valuation of inventories under the retail method. As noted earlier, under the retail method the cost (or mercantile) of inventories is computed by deducting cumulative markon percentages of retail from inventories at retail. Inventories at mercantile are never to be computed by deduction of net markon (i.e., cumulative markon, net of markdowns) percentages of retail from inventories at retail. The reason for this prohibition is that the effect of recognizing markdowns is to reduce the percentage of markon and automatically increase the cost multiplier which is applied to the inventory at retail. This is demonstrated by the following illustration of the difference in inventory valuation using net markon versus cumulative gross markon:

	Cost	Retail	Cost Multiplier
Cumulative Markon:			
Opening inventory plus purchases	$60,000	$100,000	60%
Deduct: Markdowns		10,000	
		$ 90,000	
Inventory valuation (60% × $90,000)	$54,000		
Net Markon:			
Opening inventory plus purchases	$60,000	$100,000	
Deduct: Markdowns		10,000	
	$60,000	$ 90,000	66⅔%
Inventory valuation (66⅔% × $90,000)	$60,000		

As indicated, use of the cumulative markon effectively reduces the inventory valuation (to $54,000) in recognition of the inherent loss of value. Moreover, using the cumulative markon, the ultimate sale of the merchandise will result in the realization of the normal departmental gross profit of 40% (i.e., $36,000 on $90,000).

However, as noted, the use of the net markon would preserve the initial cost of the inventories, and the ultimate sale of these inventories would result in the realization of a lower than normal gross margin of 33⅓%. It can be seen that inventories valued using a cumulative net markon would not yield a normal gross margin upon sale. In effect, this resultant valuation can be said to be in excess of the lower of cost or market, which would not be in accordance with generally accepted accounting principles.

The discussion above presupposes that proper markdowns have been taken in timely fashion. Given this assumption, inventory at mercantile, less unearned discounts, is for all practical purposes widely considered as inventory at market. However, if proper markdowns have not been taken, reasonable reserves for future markdowns and/or losses may be required to reduce the inventory to market. Assuming such reserves are material in amount, the alternative balance sheet presentations may be as follows:

Inventory at mercantile, net of unearned discounts	$2,000,000	
Less: Reserve for future markdowns	125,000	$1,875,000

or

Inventory at mercantile, net of unearned discounts, less reserve of $125,000 for future markdowns	$1,875,000

In summary, in describing inventories valued under the retail method, the preferable statement is simply at the lower of cost or market, with cost indicated as the retail method either in a footnote or parenthetically following the word cost. Interpreted broadly, this phrase should mean that the inventory is, with a reasonable degree of tolerance, valued at amounts which are expected to provide the ensuing period with a normal gross margin upon the sale of such inventory. However, it should not be overlooked that under certain circumstances and conditions the term market cannot be applied unless provision is first made for future markdowns or loss, based upon such pertinent factors as age and condition of stock.

Merchandise Turnover

Merchandise turnover represents the rate of merchandise movement. This rate is derived by dividing sales for the designated period by the average inventory, at retail, for that period.

Stock-to-Sales Ratio

The stock-to-sales ratio reflects the relation between current stock and current sales. This ratio may be stated in terms of either units or dollars. If ratios are determined based on dollar amounts, retail figures should be used for stocks (and for sales).

Stock-to-sales ratios are an important aid to management in ascertaining whether a sound relation of stock to sales is being maintained on a current basis.

Using retail figures, the stock-to-sales ratio is derived by dividing the stock at the beginning of a period by the actual (or projected) sales for the period. The period commonly used is a month or four- or five-week period. For example, if the departmental stock, at retail, on April 1 is $10,000, and sales for the month of April are $2,500, the stock-to-sales ratio is 4.

For practical use in monitoring and planning stock and sales, the buyer or department manager in this example may not wish to wait until the end of April to derive the stock-to-sales ratio. At the beginning of the month, or at any time during the month, it may be useful to develop this ratio utilizing estimated sales or actual sales to date and estimated sales for the balance of the month. Since the purpose of deriving the ratio is to be able to plan operations more knowledgeably on a day-to-day basis, an estimate can be made sometime during the month of April of the probable stock at the end of the month. Then, on the basis of planned sales for May, the estimated stock-to-sales ratio for May can be developed. If deemed unsatisfactory, it may be possible to revise departmental plans to achieve more desirable results.

The stock-to-sales ratio is a tool of day-to-day department management which may be derived from actual results or estimated partially or wholly upon projections. Monthly departmental tabulations of this ratio over past periods, together with comparisons with estimated and goal ratios, should be an informative, useful aid to merchandise control.

4

Methods of Merchandise Control

Importance of Control

The primary function of a retail store is the buying and selling of merchandise. Merchandise represents the most important asset of retail business and is its chief income-producing factor. The term "merchandise control" is used in different senses, signifying, for example, (1) custody of the physical property, (2) maintenance of book records to record transactions and indicate the amount of stock that should be on hand, or (3) guidance of merchandising operations with the aid of accounting records and reports. It is in this last sense that the term is most widely used in retailing and will be used in this chapter.

Merchandising by its very nature is a complex operation. The type of merchandise to be sold in a particular store is determined by the merchandising philosophy of the merchant. For instance, certain retailers desire to deal exclusively in quality and fashion, others may emphasize discount or bargain merchandise, and still others may concentrate on a middle-price-range line of merchandise. Once the merchandising philosophy has been formulated, the merchant must determine the extent of working capital available for investment in the desired lines of goods. In planning for the dollar investment in inventories, the merchant should consider the following related questions.

What type of merchandise is required at each location?
When is the particular merchandise required?
What quantity of merchandise is required?
How should the merchandise be priced?
When and to what extent should the initial price be adjusted?

Accounting Tools of Merchandise Control

Among the more important accounting tools utilized to assist management in answering the above questions are:

1. Merchandise plan or budget
2. Open-to-buy records
3. Unit stock records
4. Book inventory records
5. Departmental subdivision
6. Markdown procedure and analysis
7. Slow-selling merchandise reports
8. Merchandising statistics

Other control measures are concerned with protection of the physical merchandise by systems and procedures for the receipt, checking, and marking of merchandise; taking of physical inventories; and accounting for the successive movements of the merchandise. Some of these control problems are the topics of separate chapters of this book. This chapter briefly discusses their important implications.

Merchandise Plan or Budget. The preparation of a plan or budget for future operations comprises one of the basic initial financial controls bearing upon the overall control of merchandise. The customary procedure is to prepare a budget for each department, with the aggregate of the departmental budgets comprising the overall store merchandise plan. A measure of control over the size of departmental stocks is obtained by correlating purchase orders placed on a current basis to the budgeted totals of purchases. The budget can be revised, as may be warranted or appropriate, to reflect changes in anticipated conditions. A detailed discussion of the merchandise budget is presented in Chapter 5.

Open-To-Buy. The merchandise budget sets tentative limits for dollar purchases during a season. The control problem is to keep purchase commitments within the limits fixed in the budget as originally prepared or as revised, without adversely affecting sales volume. One means of coping with this control problem is the use of an open-to-buy system. Traditionally, open-to-buy records are maintained by department, although they may be further subdivided by merchandise classifications within departments.

To maintain an effective open-to-buy system it is essential that all orders for merchandise pass through a central office prior to final approval and placement with vendors. This central office maintains records for orders placed, orders filled and unfilled, and orders canceled, and uses these records to produce open-to-buy amounts, i.e., the amounts that can be expended in the future to acquire merchandise. Traditionally, the central office that prepares the open-to-buy reports and maintains the records of purchase order activity has been the budget office within the Controller's Department. However, some organizations use an Inventory Control office to perform this function, while others prefer to assign it to the Merchandise Management organization.

At the beginning of a season, open-to-buy is the planned purchases for the season, less any orders outstanding. Similarly, at the beginning of any period (a month, or four or five weeks), where the budget is currently revised, open-to-buy for the period is the revised planned purchases for that period, net of outstanding orders for delivery within the period. After a part of the month (or four- or five-week period) has elapsed, open-to-buy must be separately calculated. The procedure to be followed is dependent on whether stock on hand on the calculation date is known or must be approximated. Stock is usually known when the stock records are closed more than once during each period; it will have to be estimated when stock records are closed only at the end of each period. When the stock is known, the calculation is as follows:

Requirements at Retail:
  Planned stock, end of period $_____
  Planned sales, rest of period   _____
  Planned price reductions, net, rest of period   _____
    Total (A) $_____
Available Stock at Retail:
  Stock on hand at present   _____
  Outstanding orders for this period, at date   _____
    Total (B)
    Open-to-buy for period, at retail (A − B) $_____

When the stock at date of calculation is not known, the calculation may be made as follows:

Requirements at Retail:
  Planned stock, end of period $_____
  Net sales:
    Actual to date $_____
    Planned rest of period   _____   _____
  Price reductions, net:
    Actual to date   _____   _____
    Planned rest of period   _____
      Total (A) $_____

Deduct:
  Retail stock, first of period $_____
  Net orders placed for this period, at retail:
    Orders placed for this period $_____
    Less: Merchandise returns   _____   _____
      Total (B)   _____
  Open-to-buy for period, at retail (A − B) $_____

The open-to-buy at retail is converted to cost on the basis of departmental markon percentages. These same open-to-buy calculations may show an overbought condition rather than an open-to-buy. When this occurs, merchandise orders should be referred to the controller and the merchandise manager for their approval before being placed. This situation often highlights the need for close study of a department's operations and for revision of previously prepared budgets.

The figures used for planned sales and price reductions, net rest of period, should not represent the difference between the total planned for the period and the actual results to date. Rather, they should represent realistic expectations for the remainder of the period.

Some retailers have modified the above approach by excluding price reductions, net (principally comprising markdowns and shrinkage), from the total requirements at retail. The practical effect of this modification is a reduction in the open-to-buy since the buyer is penalized to the extent of such price reductions. This conservative approach can result in an understocked situation if not closely monitored, particularly during periods of heavy price reductions for sales or promotions.

It was mentioned earlier that open-to-buy is based upon the budget either as originally prepared or as revised to take cognizance of new conditions or actual performance. The disciplines and benefits inherent in open-to-buy systems can be substantially minimized if actual performance data on receipts of merchandise, sales, and markdowns are not reflected in the system on a reasonably accurate and timely basis. Integrating the open-to-buy system with the accounting system can in many instances improve the reliability and timeliness of the various open-to-buy reports, provide a better basis for forecasting cash requirements, and achieve economies in operating the system. To the extent that unit control systems are used, decisions as to future purchases as well as price changes should be predicted upon an analysis of the data generated by both the open-to-buy and unit control systems.

The Nature of Unit Stock Control. Where warranted by the nature of the merchandise, the inventory management information system should include data regarding the periodic status of units of merchandise by description, style, color, and size, in addition to price. The underlying concept is that departments are selling merchandise units, not dollars, and that all basic merchandise information, and the related planning, should be in terms of such units broadly identified by merchandise classifications. A control system that uses units of merchandise enables the merchandiser to maintain a better balance between stocks and sales, effectively supplementing the departmental dollar control over merchandise. Both types of control are essential in keeping stocks properly balanced and at appropriate levels.

Unit control is used in some form throughout the retail trade. The small independent merchant may utilize a visual observation of the units of merchandise on hand, to determine stock requirements. The sophisticated multi-store operation may utilize computers that report inventory levels as part of the automatic preparation of purchase orders. The manner in which the merchant determines the stock assortments desired must take into account the physical characteristics of the units of merchandise and the customer demand for the product. Stated differently, control of merchandise units and adequate information regarding the changing status of these units are obvious keys to successful retailing.

Since the retailer is selling merchandise units and not dollars, the retailer's merchandise information reporting system must supply significant data on units, to relieve the buyers of laborious details. More important, it should enable buyers to move away from intuition and toward informed decisions.

Too often, the dollar basis for open-to-buy planning is not correlated with underlying data in terms of units, price lines, or types of goods within merchandise classifications. Further inquiry will often disclose the unavailability of departmental information regarding the specific items or classifications that produce relative percentages of dollar sales, and the correlation of these data with supplying vendors. For years, manufacturers have established required inventory levels based on anticipated sales levels, recognizing that a disproportionately small percentage of merchandise items will account for a disproportionately large percentage of sales volume. In tests made by retailers in the past, 10 per cent of items in selected departments accounted for approximately 50 per cent of sales, while 50 per cent of items accounted for 90 per cent of sales. Also, it was determined that 10 per cent of vendors accounted for 50 per cent of sales, and 50 per cent of vendors accounted for 97 per cent of sales. The critical information revealed by looking at the units of merchandise can be used to eliminate resources who contribute little to sales and to remove slow-moving items from merchandise lines.

In addition, information on merchandise unit turnover may help solve the problem of stockouts, especially with high-volume items. Detailed information on units sold is obviously essential, but the retailer should also consider the adequacy of information on lost sales. Information regarding units that could have been sold, had the merchandise been available to satisfy customer demand, is obviously important, especially in light of tests made by retailers disclosing departmental stockouts as high as 35 per cent.

Like all control systems, unit stock control can only supply the data upon which judgments may be based. Naturally, the information made available, whether manual or computerized, should be accurate and pertinent, but its translation into practical action is, in the last analysis, dependent upon the judgment and decision of the merchant.

Advantages of Unit Stock Control. When properly utilized, many advantages can accrue from an effective unit stock control system. Well-balanced stocks and a proper assortment of merchandise stock are indispensable to a good merchandising operation. The unit stock control records should disclose whether a balanced assortment is on hand. The status of the stock—by classification, price, style, size, and color—in relation to customer demand (expressed as planned sales) should be readily available in such form that quick action may be taken by merchandisers and buyers.

The unit stock control records should disclose fast-moving and slow-moving items and their rates of movement. The desired merchandise can then be adequately stocked and re-orders can be placed promptly so that the absence of a particular style or color or size will not result in lost sales. Fast-selling items are easily spotted, and a base stock of profitable "never out" items becomes a foundation around which a department may be built. Moreover, a fast-selling item may indicate that a special promotion is in order.

Slow-moving merchandise is usually indicated by age codes which appear on the unit stock control records. This older merchandise which does not achieve customer acceptance must be constantly reviewed for special promotion, markdown, or changes in display. The early recognition of slow-moving items should minimize future losses from markdowns.

The examination of unit stock control records may indicate a fashion trend or a fad. Proper timing of purchases becomes critical, and correct anticipation of the beginning or the wane of a fashion will have a significant effect upon sales and profits. The operation of any open-to-buy should always be sufficiently flexible to allow for special purchases dictated by seasonal considerations or special opportunities. Anticipating or recognizing a fashion trend and making opportune use of available purchasing power will usually have a beneficial impact on volume and profits.

Another advantage of maintaining unit stock control is that minimum stock levels can be established for certain classifications of staple merchandise items. Reordering of these items can then become an almost automatic clerical function.

Unit control records should also serve to disclose important data on vendors, differentiating those that contribute to the retailer's overall viability from those that do not. Because a resource is accepted once—or considered too low in quality to be accepted—is not necessarily a judgment in perpetuity. Constant reassessment of consumer demand in relation to vendors' products is essential, and should be useful as a guide to future purchases.

Integration of the Accounting, Open-To-Buy, and Unit Control Systems. Extensive sums have been expended in connection with the development of computerized open-to-buy and unit control

PURCHASE ORDERS PLACED REPORT—SUMMARY

Dept. No.	Class. No.	Type of Merchandise	This Week				Year to Date					Total Retail on Orders Placed—More (Less) Than Budget
			Cost	Retail	Actual Average Markon (%)		Cost	Retail	Actual Average Markon (%)	Budgeted Average Markon (%)		
1	1	Regular Promotion Total Class.										
	2	Regular Promotion Total Class.										
	All Class.	Regular Promotion Total Dept.										
2	3	Regular Promotion Total Class.										
	4	Regular Promotion Total Class.										
	All Class.	Regular Promotion Total Dept.										
Line 1	All Depts.	Regular Promotion Total Line										
All Stores	All Lines	Regular Promotion Total										

Note: This report produced weekly by department, by classification. Purchase orders placed are net of orders canceled.

FIG. 2. Purchase orders placed report.

systems. However, if the information generated is not both timely and reliable, the impact on the merchandising operation is likely to be adverse. Once the credibility of computer-generated merchandise information is suspect, buyers and managers tend to develop their own informal, independent systems (often manual and costly to operate) for controlling stock levels and for buying purposes. These systems cannot cope with an expanding multi-unit retail operation. The results are costly merchandising mistakes caused by a lack of required reliable data or a reversion to inventory management by intuition. One method of improving the timeliness and reliability of open-to-buy and unit control systems is to integrate them with the accounting records, thereby subjecting these systems to the disciplines usually inherent in an efficient accounting function.

The specific design of an integrated system must, of course, be tailored to the merchandising and operational philosophies, and to the accounting system, of the particular merchant and is accordingly beyond the scope of this book. However, for purposes of this chapter, the authors have selected a computerized multi-store, multi-department environment and a system which would provide for:

> The placement of a purchase order to update concomitantly the purchase order file and the on-order portion of both the unit control and open-to-buy systems;
> The receipt of merchandise to concomitantly update the purchase order file, transfer the appropriate data from the on-order to the on-hand portion of the unit control and open-to-buy systems, and create an accounts payable file; and
> The concomitant entry in the open-to-buy and accounting records of markdowns and sales data, and the separate entry, on the unit control records, of the number of marked-down units.

Figures 2 through 7 illustrate the type of reports generated and merchandise control benefits that can accrue from such an integrated system. With the proper designs and safeguards, such an integrated system can incorporate a number of corollary advantages and controls. These could comprise the ability: to streamline the receiving and invoice processing functions; to guard against duplicate payment of invoices and loss of discounts; to highlight both early receipt and overdue merchandise; to facilitate effective cash management; and to provide the data base necessary for vendor profitability analysis.

Figure 2 is a summary of all purchase orders written during the current week and to date for the current year. All amounts are net of purchase orders that have been canceled, and the type of merchandise (regular versus promotional) is indicated for each entry. The annual budgeted markon percentage is shown next to the computed year-to-date actual markon percentage. The budgeted aggregate year-to-date retail is not shown on the report. However, the difference between such amount and the actual year-to-date retail is shown in the last column of the report, "Total Retail on Orders Placed—More (Less) Than Budget."

Analysis of a report of this type will enable buyers, merchandise managers, and managerial personnel to obtain a quick reading on the degree to which the pricing of merchandise conforms to the expectations of the merchandise plan, and to estimate the potential aggregate effect of deviations from the plan.

Figure 3 summarizes all outstanding purchase orders according to the month in which the merchandise is to arrive, and is a digest of the report shown in Figure 2. Figure 4 shows each open pur-

SUMMARY OPEN PURCHASE ORDER LISTING

Dept. No.	Class. No.	Month to Arrive	Regular Retail	Regular Markon (%)	Promotional Retail	Promotional Markon (%)	Total Retail	Total Markon (%)
1	1	Feb. Mar. Apr. May						
	2	Feb. Mar. Apr. May June						
2	3	Feb. Mar. Apr.						
	4	Feb. Mar. Apr. May						

Note: This report issued weekly by department, by classification. (A similar report can be produced for open purchase orders by department, by classification, by store.)

FIG. 3. Summary open purchase order listing.

OPEN PURCHASE ORDERS—DETAIL LISTING

Dept. No.	Class No.	Purchase Order No.	Vendor Name	Vendor Number	Cost	Retail	Markon Percent	Month to Arrive	Month to Pay			
									Feb.	Mar.	Apr.	May
1	1	R1-1										
		R1-3										
		R1-4										
		R1-6										
		P1-2										
		P1-4										
		P1-5										
	Total Class.	Regular										
		Promotion										
		Total Class.										
	2	R2-1										
		R2-3										
		R2-4										
		P2-2										
		P2-3										
	Total Class.	Regular										
		Promotion										
		Total Class.										
	All Class.	Regular										
		Promotion										
		Total Dept.										
Line 1	All Depts.	Regular										
		Promotion										
		Total Line										
All Stores	All Lines	Regular										
		Promotion										
		Total Chain										

Note: This report generated weekly by department, by classification, by purchase order number.

FIG. 4. Open purchase orders.

OPEN-TO-BUY REPORT

Dept. No._____ Class. No. _____   Month __October__

	This Year		Last Year	
	Actual	Plan	Actual	Plan
Beginning inventory, at retail	$190	$175	$168	$176
Add: Merchandise receipts at retail	42	46	41	40
Markups, MTD	2	1	2	2
Other (transfers, etc.)	1	1	1	1
	235	223	212	219
Less: Sales, MTD[1]	32	38	37	34
Markdowns, MTD[1]	6	4	4	4
Other (estimated shrink, transfers, etc.)	2	1	1	1
	40	43	42	39
Estimated actual stock at retail	195	180	170	180
Merchandise on order at retail[2]	71	68	73	74
Total commitment at retail	266	248	243	254
Planned sales and markdowns, balance of month	(10)	(10)	(8)	(8)
	$256	238	$235	246
Estimated EOM commitment		(256)		(235)
Open-to-buy (Overbought)		($18)		$ 11

	Month To Arrive			
	Oct.	Nov.	Dec.	Jan.
Estimated open-to-buy (Overbought), BOM		$(18)	$(18)	$ 8
Less: On order, at retail		(42)	(21)	(8)
		(60)	(39)	—
Planned sales and markdowns		42	47	19
Estimated open-to-buy (Overbought), EOM	$(18)	$(18)	$ 8	$19

MTD = month to date.
BOM = beginning of month.
EOM = end of month.

[1] Percentage of deviation, year or season to date, from plan; sales: +(−)(5%); markdowns: +(−) 1%.
[2] Amount by which initial markon on merchandise on order more (less) than planned amount: $4.

FIG. 5. Open-to-buy report.

chase order at cost and retail, the month when the merchandise is to arrive, and the month when the invoice is to be paid. At the bottom of the report, all amounts are totaled by merchandise line, and grand totals are shown for all lines on an all-stores basis. These grand totals can be useful in forecasting future cash requirements.

If the open-to-buy report illustrated in Figure 5 were integrated with the accounting system, the same source documents would initiate the recording of merchandise receipts and accounts payable in the accounting records; merchandise receipts would appear on the open-to-buy report; sales, markups, and markdowns would be shown in both the accounting and open-to-buy reports. Furthermore, the estimated shrinkage percentage used for accounting purposes would be used for the open-to-buy report.

The system would, as shown in Figure 5, reflect the amount by which the initial markon on merchandise on order differs from the budgeted markon. The amount of this difference on merchandise which has already been received should, of course, be reflected in sales or actual stock on hand. The open-to-buy report would also indicate the percentage deviation of sales and markdowns on a year-to-date or season-to-date basis, as appropriate. These data can be useful in realistically appraising planned sales and resultant estimated open-to-buy amounts for ensuing months on the basis of actual experience during the year or season to date. In addition, the system would generate a listing of those merchandise departments or classifications where markon, sales, or markdowns have deviated from predesignated percentages. This listing could, of course, serve to focus attention on areas where the merchandise plan should be re-examined.

As described earlier, an integrated system would, among other things, create an accounts payable file concomitant with the receipt of merchandise. Figure 6 is a report summarizing accounts payable by due date. Intended for use by the Treasurer and Accounts Payable Manager, the report reflects the gross amount of the invoice, vendor chargeback amounts, trade and cash discounts, and the net amount due by the due date. Credit memoranda would also be reflected on this report.

The price change report summary in Figure 7 would be produced for buyers and for the Merchandise Managers weekly by department and classification on an all-stores basis, and monthly by department and classification for the individual store.

ACCOUNTS PAYABLE DUE DATE SUMMARY

Vendor Name	Vendor Number	P.O. Number	Invoice Number	Invoice Date	Due Date	Gross Amount	Charge Backs	Adjustment Gross Amount	Trade Discount	Cash Discount	Net Amount

Note: This report generated weekly by vendor (also generated weekly by due date with subtotals by due date).

FIG. 6. Accounts payable due date summary.

PRICE CHANGE REPORT—SUMMARY

Dept. Class.	Net Sales	% of Class. Sales to Total Sales	Markdowns*									Net Price Changes		Total Markdowns as % to Class. Sales		Class. Sales as % to Total Sales	
			Buyer-Originated						Store-Originated		Total							
			Regular		Promotional												
			Amount	% Class. Sales	Amount	% Class. Sales	Amount	% Class. Sales	Amount	% Class. Sales	Amount	% to Class. Sales	Budgeted	Last Year	Budgeted	Last Year
1-1																
TW	1,000	2.9	150	15.0	50	5.0	10	1.0	210	21.0	170	17.0				3.6
MTD	3,000	3.8	400	13.3	300	10.0	60	2.0	760	25.3	460	15.3	13.0	22.0	4.2	4.1
YTD	10,000	4.1	1,000	10.0	300	3.0	180	1.8	1,480	12.8	1,180	11.8	12.5	13.6	4.6	4.4
1-2																
TW																
MTD																
YTD																
All Class.																
TW																
MTD																
YTD																
2-3																
TW																
MTD																
YTD																
2-4																
TW																
MTD																
YTD																
Company																
TW																
MTD																
YTD																

TW = this week
MTD = this month to date
YTD = this year to date
* = net of cancellations

Note: This report issued weekly by department, by classification, on an all-stores basis, and monthly by department, by classification, by store.

FIG. 7. Price change summary report.

Each amount on the report is shown for the current week, the current month, and the year to date. Store-originated markdowns are computed as the difference between total markdowns reported and buyer-originated markdowns. Net price changes are reported as the difference between total markdowns and total markups. Total markdowns as a percentage of sales for the current month and the year to date are compared to both the budget and the prior year's experience.

The monthly report makes possible an analysis of each class by store. Subtotals are printed for each department and class on an all-stores basis. At the bottom of the report, all amounts are summarized by merchandise line, and grand totals are shown for all lines.

Book Inventory Records. These records supply necessary information as to the amount of departmental stocks on hand, without incurring the labor and expense involved in the taking of physical inventory. The existence of such records makes it possible to determine the inventory as of a specific date with reasonable accuracy.

There are two general methods for computing book inventories: the "cost method" and the "retail method," with the latter used extensively in retailing. Both methods are discussed in great detail in Chapter 6.

Departmental Subdivision. In the preparation of a departmental merchandise budget, and also in the usual operation of book inventory methods, each selling department is considered as a separate entity. This is a necessary first step in controlling departmental stocks and in bringing about a proper relationship between stock and sales.

As a further step, it is often very useful to analyze the operations of selling departments by ascertaining the relationship between stocks and sales of the different classifications of merchandise sold in such departments. Such data and relationships are developed on a dollar basis, but departmental subdivision also provides the groundwork for control by units. In effect, this is a plan whereby units of various classifications of merchandise are controlled in relation to sales of those units. It is not advisable to attempt unit control in all departments of a store because the nature of the merchandise handled in a number of departments renders unit control complicated, of questionable value, and unduly expensive. Departmental subdivision by major merchandise categories (classifications) will often serve as a useful substitute for unit control in such departments. Even for those departments where unit control is used, a partial combination of dollar and unit control on some intermediate basis may well be advisable; for example, dollars would be used for the department as a whole, and details by units would be maintained for certain specific classifications of merchandise carried in the department.

Departmental subdivision often envisions the recordkeeping for, and analysis of, designated merchandise classifications on the same basis as the total department. Accordingly, all of the elements of departmental merchandising—sales, purchases, retail reductions, and stock on hand—are developed by individual merchandise classifications. The following illustrates a typical departmental subdivision report setting forth these elements of merchandise by classification and for the total department:

	Dept. Total	\multicolumn{6}{c}{Classification}
		01	02	03	04	05	06
Inventory, beginning	$ 8,000	$2,000	$1,500	$1,200	$ 800	$1,100	$1,400
Purchases	5,000	1,000	600	800	600	900	1,100
Total	13,000	3,000	2,100	2,000	1,400	2,000	2,500
Less: Inventory, closing	7,000	1,400	1,400	1,000	700	1,100	1,400
Stock available for sale	6,000	1,600	700	1,000	700	900	1,100
Sales	5,700	1,500	675	950	660	870	1,045
Price reductions	$ 300	$ 100	$ 25	$ 50	$ 40	$ 30	$ 55
Percentage of sales	100%	26.32%	11.84%	16.67%	11.58%	15.26%	18.33%
Percentage of average inventory	100%	22.67%	19.33%	14.67%	10.00%	14.66%	18.67%

The information required for this type of report may be obtained in either of two ways:

1. A classification record based upon an analysis of physical inventories (beginning and end of period), purchases, and price reductions.

2. A classification record of opening inventory, purchases, price reductions, and sales which may be kept in the same manner as the departmental records under the book inventory method, and which effectively supplements the departmental records.

Under the first method, analysis by classification consists of the following:

1. (a) Physical inventory at the beginning of the period
   (b) Purchases during the period
   (c) Price reductions during the period
   (d) Physical inventory at the close of the period

Sales by classifications for the period are obtained by adding purchases to the beginning inventory and subtracting therefrom the markdowns (and other retail reductions) and the closing inventory. This first method provides the necessary information only when physical inventories are taken and only in total for the period between the inventory dates. In this respect it is less informative than the second method, which provides the requisite information on a continuing basis.

In operating the second method, analysis by classification is made up of:

2. (a) Physical inventory at the beginning of the period
   (b) Purchases
   (c) Price reductions
   (d) Sales

Utilizing the basic recordkeeping principle underlying book inventory methods—stock at the beginning of the period, plus purchases, minus price reductions and sales—provides the stock on hand at the end of the period. On the basis of these figures, reports may be prepared to show operations for a month (or four or five weeks) or shorter period, and the total for the months or periods of the season to date. This second method, however, is used only for departments where it is feasible to obtain sales by merchandise classifications.

Departmental subdivision has many advantages. It supplies a detailed picture of the elements of merchandising operations; it provides a valuable record upon which to base plans for future operations; and it supplies an excellent insight into a department's operations by informing management as to the successful and unsuccessful lines of merchandise carried, effectively identifying those areas requiring management attention.

Markdown Procedure and Analysis. Markdowns are considered in the preparation of merchandise budgets. They have an important effect on departmental operating results in that they represent sales dollars lost for whatever reason. Often, one of the best means of increasing merchandising profit may be a decrease in the amount of unnecessary markdowns. For this reason, wide attention has been given to the subject by retailers, and studies have been made of the reasons for markdowns, all with a view to minimizing future markdowns. However, resistance to initial markdowns, out of an excessive concern for budgetary restraints, can prove quite costly since the markdowns ultimately required to dispose of the problem merchandise may represent a far greater loss in sales dollars. Retailers have developed a pertinent maxim to the effect that "the cheapest markdown is the first markdown." Needless to say, the question of when to take a markdown, and to what extent, requires considerable professional judgment on the part of merchandising management.

Markdowns are subject to control under the ordinary operation of the merchandise budget. Requests for markdowns should be processed through prescribed channels for approval prior to being effected. Records of markdowns taken and an analysis by causative factor should be maintained by a central office, preferably within the Controller's Division. These reports should be used to monitor the amount of markdowns taken against plan; to alert merchandising management regarding markdowns taken in excess of plan; and to inform management periodically as to the underlying reasons which necessitated the taking of markdowns.

Fundamentally, the main reasons for markdowns are errors in buying and mistakes in sales direction and operation after purchases have been made. Some errors of both kinds are inevitable. The endeavor is to keep them to a minimum.

Specifically, the following represent the principal classifications under which markdowns may be grouped or analyzed:

1. Slow-moving or inactive stocks
2. Special sales from stock

3. Price changes
4. Broken assortments, remnants, discontinued lines, and damaged merchandise
5. Style changes
6. Out-of-season goods
7. Remainders of promotional purchases

A form for requesting a markdown, obtaining the necessary approvals, and ultimately repricing the merchandise is illustrated in Figure 8. This request for price change form can be used to handle all types of price changes.

Slow-Selling Merchandise Reports. The problem of slow-selling merchandise is closely related to that of markdowns since markdowns are often taken in order to move slow-selling stock. Effective merchandising presupposes a knowledge of the condition of departmental stocks, including such salient facts as the amounts by classifications and by age groupings, the amount of damaged goods, and the propriety of the price lines.

Not all the required information of this nature is available either in dollar or unit stock records, or in the physical inventory records. Therefore, it is necessary to supplement other merchandise control methods with procedures designed particularly to facilitate the control of slow-selling goods. A practical approach to the resolution of this problem is to periodically inspect and record slow-selling merchandise. Customary procedure is to list the slow-selling merchandise in detail on columnar departmental forms which provide space for showing monthly, or for each four- or five-week period, the quantities and unit retail prices of these merchandise items throughout a season. A comparative presentation of slow-selling merchandise is illustrated in Figure 9.

The form shown can be used for an entire season when inspection of the slow-selling goods is done monthly or at the end of each four- or five-week period. At a physical inventory date, the slow-selling merchandise is listed on the form in the first column under quantity and price. The age of the merchandise to be listed as slow-selling depends upon the specific department. It may range from 60 days or less for some fashion departments, to six months or one year for some staple and home furnishings departments. The columns under quantity and under price are for recording the

METHODS OF MERCHANDISE CONTROL

PRICE CHANGE REPORT
No. 34901
LIST ONLY ONE KIND OF CHANGE

"X" KIND OF CHANGE		PRICE CHANGE NOTICE NUMBER FROM BUYER	STORE NO.	DIV.	DEPT. NO.
MARK DOWN	MARK DOWN CANCELLATION				
MARK UP	MARK UP CANCELLATION		DATE / /		

	DESCRIPTION					ORIGINAL PRICE	UNIT SELLING PRICE		CLASS	UNIT DIFFERENCE	TOTAL UNITS	ACTUAL UNITS	TOTAL DIFFERENCE
ITEM	VENDOR NO.	STYLE	COLOR	SIZE	SEASON		PRESENT	NEW					
1	2	3	4	5	6	7	8	9	10	11	12	13	14
1													
2													
3													
4													
5													
6													
7													
8													
9													
10													
11													
12													
13													
14													
15													
16													

HOW MDSE WAS REMARKED	DATE	PRICE CHANGE FORM	DATE	"X"	REASON	TOTAL	
TICKETS BY		WRITTEN BY			1 COMPETITIVE PRICE ADJUSTMENT	BRT. FWD.	
REMARKED BY		AUTH. BY			2 GREEN TICKET	TO DATE	
OTHER		SALES MGR.			3 OLD STOCK		
REMARK CHECKED BY		DIV. MGR.			4 SALVAGE-MARKED OUT-OF-STOCK		
RET'D TO STOCK BY		STORE MGR.			5 SHOPWORN		

Yellow & Pink copies — with mdse. until remarked.
Yellow copy — the day mdse. is remarked, to General Accounting.
Pink copy — when mdse. placed in stock, to Div. Sales Manager (or Store Mgr.), to Div. Buying Manager, to Buyer.
Blue copy — remains in book for Sales Manager.

6 SPEC. PROM. / /	
7	
8	

FIG. 8. Price change report.

SLOW-SELLING STOCK REPORT

Department _____ Inventory Date, January 31, 19—

Style Number	Article	Season Letter	Quantity At Inventory Date						Retail Price Per Unit At Inventory Date					
			Jan.31, 19—	Feb.29, 19—	Mar.31, 19—	Apr.30, 19—	May 31, 19—	June 30, 19—	July 31, 19—	Jan.31, 19—	Feb.29, 19—	Mar.31, 19—	Apr.30, 19—	May 31, 19—	June 30, 19—	July 31, 19—
106	End Table	P	10	9	9	7	6	6	5	$15.00	$15.00	$15.00	$14.00	$14.00	$14.00	$13.50
110	End Table	N	3	1	1	1	1	1	1	8.00	8.00	8.00	8.00	8.00	8.00	8.00
261	Hall Clock	O	6	6	6	3	3	—	—	60.00	60.00	60.00	45.00	45.00	—	—
274	Hall Clock	N	2	2	2	2	2	2	2	100.00	100.00	75.00	75.00	75.00	75.00	75.00
314	Tea Wagon	M	5	1	—	—	—	—	—	22.50	18.25	—	—	—	—	—
319	Tea Wagon	N	6	6	3	2	1	1	1	27.50	27.50	27.50	27.50	27.50	27.50	27.50
416	Pedestal	M	4	1	1	1	1	1	1	12.50	10.00	10.00	10.00	10.00	10.00	10.00
420	Pedestal	O	8	7	3	1	—	—	—	20.00	20.00	15.00	15.00	—	—	—

FIG. 9. Slow-selling stock report.

status as at each inspection date in the ensuing months (or periods) of the season. In Figure 9 month-end dates are used, but in practice the actual inspection dates are inserted.

At the time of inspection, a conclusion may be reached as to why the merchandise is slow-moving and a remedy for the condition may be adopted. For example, it may be desirable to display the goods differently, to advertise them, to apply markdowns, to offer premiums to salespeople for moving them, or to change selling or advertising methods.

Figure 9 shows, at each monthly inspection date, the quantity of merchandise and the corresponding marked retail price. This information provides the rate of movement of the goods as well as the effect of markdowns on such movement. Departments with a high rate of turnover may require more frequent follow-up. For example, departments which carry highly seasonal merchandise may require monitoring on a weekly or even semiweekly basis.

At times a more condensed form, aggregating quantities and dollars at retail, by merchandise classifications, may be satisfactorily utilized. Alternatively, the merchandise classifications may be aggregated solely in quantities or in dollars.

The information obtained by this procedure may be augmented by departmental seasonal statements showing the relationship between decreases of merchandise stocks, classified by seasons, and the corresponding amounts of markdowns taken. The amounts of stock decreases represent differences between inventories at the beginning and the close of the season and include both sales reductions and retail reductions (markdowns, shrinkages, and discounts). Markdowns are analyzed according to the season letters of the goods marked down. By such a procedure and by the use of a form for seasonal stock report (see Figure 10) (reflecting amounts at retail), summarized movements of stocks of the various seasons entering into departmental stocks, as well as ratios of markdowns to stock decreases, are given.

Merchandising Statistics. Great reliance is placed by operating executives upon carefully prepared and worthwhile statistics of current and past operations. Reports containing such statistics are an important aid to the control of merchandising operations. Essential reports are:

SEASONAL STOCK REPORT

Department_____   Date July 31, 19X3

	Season	Inventory on Hand Jan. 31, 19X3	Inventory on Hand July 31, 19X3	Stock Decreases During Season	Markdowns Taken	Percentage of Markdowns to Stock Decreases
R	Spring 19X3	$ 77,300*	$47,100	$30,200	$1,540	5.1%
P	Fall 19X2	40,400	7,900	32,500	2,260	6.9
O	Spring 19X2	9,300	2,000	7,300	1,870	25.6
N	Fall 19X1	1,200	500	700	200	28.6
M	Spring 19X1	800	250	550	180	32.7
	Prior	200	10	190	50	26.3
	Total	$129,200	$57,760	$71,440	$6,100	8.5%

*Represents purchases of Spring 19X3 season.

FIG. 10. Seasonal stock report.

Kind of Report	How Often Prepared
Comparative departmental sales report, showing day's sales, and cumulative sales in the period to date, for present year and last year, by departments	Daily
Departmental sales and stock report, showing sales, stocks, purchases, markons, markdowns, and open-to-buy	Weekly
Departmental operating report showing sales, stocks, purchases, markons, markdowns, gross margin, expenses, department profit [for month (or four- or five-week period) and cumulatively for season to date]	Monthly (or every four or five weeks)
Comparative inventory report, showing departmental inventories in total and by age classifications	As inventories are taken
Stock shortage report, showing stock shortages by departments	As inventories are taken
Slow-selling merchandise report	Monthly (or every four or five weeks)
Markdown report, showing analysis of markdowns by causative factor	Monthly (or every four or five weeks)
Comparative departmental classification report showing, for the merchandise classifications within departments, sales, stocks, purchases, and markdowns	Monthly (or every four or five weeks) or seasonally

In addition to the above, there are the reports which can be prepared from information contained in unit control systems, and interim reports on open-to-buy and outstanding orders.

These various reports provide a fund of information concerning the operations of the store. Comparisons may be made with statistics of other stores, published from time to time by agencies such as the National Retail Merchants Association, the Federal Reserve Board, and the Harvard Bureau of Business Research. Furthermore, stores often form groups for the purpose of interchanging financial information and merchandising statistics.

Chapter 16 contains a brief description of the form and content of departmental operating reports.

Receipt, Checking, and Marking of Merchandise. This important phase of merchandise control involves the safe entry and handling of goods in the store until the time they are placed in stock for sale to customers. It is important that correct accounting figures be set up for charges to departmental purchases and stocks and also that invoices be thoroughly checked before being passed to the Treasurer's office for payment. A separate discussion of these problems is contained in Chapter 10.

Taking of Physical Inventories. Only on the basis of carefully taken inventories can the effectiveness of the principal control measures be determined and the true merchandising results for a period be ascertained. Chapter 9 is devoted to a separate discussion of the problems involved in taking physical inventories.

Accounting for Movements of Merchandise. The nature and the operation of the accounting controls on merchandise movements are described in various chapters of this book. The principal controls are listed here to show the safeguards which may be considered necessary to protect the store's investment in merchandise:

1. Confirmed purchase order required for all purchases.
2. Comparison of invoices against existing purchase orders on file.
3. Invoices kept under control.
4. Invoices and/or corresponding receiving reports bearing signatures of checkers and markers.
5. Various book inventory controls, either in connection with the retail method or unit control records.
6. Existence of a sales check in order to move any merchandise sold to customers from the store.
7. Sales checks bearing cash register imprint, which is referred to as "certification," under floor audit (not under tally audit).
8. Numerical control of sales checks by sales audit department.

9. Existence of chargebacks in order to return any merchandise to vendors.
10. Existence of chargebacks or memo charges in order to send goods out on memo or for repair.
11. Numerical control of chargebacks or memo charges by the accounts payable office.
12. Special methods of moving customers' own goods from the store, such as section manager's signature on a sales check, or special forms.
13. Control over departmental transfers.

Illustrative Problems and Solutions

Some of the procedures outlined in this chapter may be made clearer by the following illustrative problems and solutions. Space limitations prevent inclusion of more than a few of the many illustrations that might be given.

Open-To-Buy, Stock Known

Problem. Compute the open-to-buy amount as of January 7 for the rest of the month, based on the following figures at retail. The amount of stock on hand at the calculation date is known.

Planned sales, rest of month	$ 4,000
Planned price reductions, net, rest of month	240
Planned stock, January 31	9,380
Stock on hand, January 7	7,700
Outstanding orders for month of January, at January 7	1,320

Solution. Requirements at retail:

Planned stock, end of month	$9,380	
Planned sales, rest of month	4,000	
Planned price reductions, net, rest of month	240	
Total (A)		13,620
Available stock at retail:		
Stock on hand at present	7,700	
Outstanding orders for this period, at January 7	1,320	
Total (B)		9,020
Open-to-buy for period, at retail (A − B)		$ 4,600

If it is assumed that the departmental markon is 37½ per cent in the foregoing example, then open-to-buy on a cost basis is 62½ per cent of $4,600, or $2,875.

Open-To-Buy, Stock Not Known

Problem. Compute the amount of open-to-buy as of February 21 for the rest of the month, based on the following figures at retail. The stock at the calculation date is not known.

Stock on hand, February 1	$16,000
Planned stock, February 28	15,000
Planned sales, rest of month	2,000
Actual sales to February 21	8,000
Merchandise returns	900
Planned price reductions, net, rest of month	225
Actual price reductions, net to date	300
Orders placed for this period	7,000

Solution. Requirements at retail:

Planned stock, end of month			$15,000
Net sales:			
Actual to date		$8,000	
Planned rest of month		2,000	10,000
Price reductions, net:			
Actual to date		300	
Planned rest of month		225	525
Total (A)			$25,525
Deduct:			
Retail stock, first of month		16,000	
Net orders placed for this period at retail:			
Orders placed for this period	7,000		
Less: Merchandise returns	900	6,100	
Total (B)			22,100
Open-to-buy for period, at retail (A − B)			$ 3,425

Departmental Subdivision

Problem. Prepare two statements, (a) and (b), illustrating the two general methods of departmental subdivision, for the six months ended January 31, 19X3. Show the total amounts of the elements of departmental merchandise operations and the different classifications which enter into the total, using the classification data given below at retail.

	Classification		
For Statement (a):	A	B	C
Inventory, August 1, 19X2	$9,600	$14,400	$8,000
Inventory, January 31, 19X3	8,400	12,600	7,000
Purchases, six months to January 31, 19X3	6,000	9,000	5,000
Price reductions, six months to January 31, 19X3	360	540	300

	Classification		
	A	B	C
For Statement (b):			
Inventory, August 1, 19X2	$9,600	$14,400	$8,000
Net sales, six months to January 31, 19X3	6,840	10,260	5,700
Purchases, six months to January 31, 19X3	6,000	9,000	5,000
Price reductions, six months to January 31, 19X3	360	540	300

Solutions. Statement (a) is prepared from seasonal classifications based upon analysis of physical inventories, purchases, and price reductions:

		Classification		
	Total	A	B	C
At retail:				
Inventory, August 1, 19X2	$32,000	$ 9,600	$14,400	$ 8,000
Purchases for six months	20,000	6,000	9,000	5,000
Total	52,000	15,600	23,400	13,000
Less: Inventory, January 31, 19X3	28,000	8,400	12,600	7,000
Stock available for sale	24,000	7,200	10,800	6,000
Less: Price reductions	1,200	360	540	300
Sales for six months	$22,800	$ 6,840	$10,260	$ 5,700

Statement (b) is prepared from a cumulative classification of monthly sales, markdowns and purchases, and classification of opening inventory:

		Classification		
	Total	A	B	C
At retail:				
Inventory, August 1, 19X2	$32,000	$ 9,600	$14,400	$ 8,000
Purchases for six months	20,000	6,000	9,000	5,000
Total	52,000	15,600	23,400	13,000
Less: Price reductions	1,200	360	540	300
Stock available for sale	50,800	15,240	22,860	12,700
Less: Sales for six months	22,800	6,840	10,260	5,700
Stock on hand, January 31, 19X3	$28,000	$ 8,400	$12,600	$ 7,000

Seasonal Stock Report

Problem. From the following departmental information, prepare a seasonal stock report, all figures being at retail.

METHODS OF MERCHANDISE CONTROL

	Merchandise Purchased				
	Spring 19X3	Fall 19X2	Spring 19X2	Fall 19X1	Prior
Inventory, January 31, 19X3	$80,000	$55,000	$20,000	$5,000	$7,000
Inventory, July 31, 19X3	40,000	22,000	4,000	900	1,200
Sales	37,750	30,500	13,200	3,300	4,325
Shrinkages	363	365	160	75	35
Markdowns	1,887	2,135	2,640	725	1,440

Solution.

Season	Inventory on Hand January 31, 19X3	Inventory on Hand July 31, 19X3	Stock Decreases During Season	Markdowns Taken	Percentage of Markdowns to Stock Decreases	Shrinkages	Percentage of Shrinkages to Stock Decreases
Spring 19X3	$ 80,000	$40,000	$40,000	$1,887	4.72%	$363	.91%
Fall 19X2	55,000	22,000	33,000	2,135	6.47	365	1.11
Spring 19X2	20,000	4,000	16,000	2,640	16.50	160	1.00
Fall 19X1	5,000	900	4,100	725	17.68	75	1.83
Prior	7,000	1,200	5,800	1,440	24.83	35	.60
	$167,000	$68,100	$98,900	$8,827	8.93%	$998	1.01%

Note: All figures are at retail.

5

Budgeting and Financial Planning and Control

Introduction

In addressing the broad subject of financial planning and control in retail organizations, it should be recognized that certain principles are valid here that are applicable in any organization dedicated to the philosophy of optimizing its profit opportunities over the short and long term. The application of any profit planning and control program to a particular company, however, must take into consideration the special characteristics of the trade or industry in which the company operates. Such critical factors as the competitive environment, the extent to which a trade or industry is labor-intensive as opposed to capital-intensive, the impact of statutory authority on operations, and the relative degree of stability or volatility inherent in the business are a few of the characteristics that will have an impact in defining the profit objective and the operational plans adopted to attain it. Of necessity, this will involve making the best use of a company's resources—personnel, capital, borrowing capacity, and plant and equipment.

Management Commitment

It is important to emphasize that the successful implementation of a financial planning program throughout any organization requires the absolute commitment of all levels of management. By definition, financial planning underscores the specific undertaking on the part of management to influence events in order to achieve what has previously been established as a desirable level of profit performance. Financial planning requires that management do more than passively project future events and future profits. Management is effectively charged with the responsibilities of making or reversing a trend in the key processes, of adopting strategies to attain projected objectives, and thereafter of tracking actual performance against plan.

There are practical problems confronting any top management in the discharge of its basic responsibility of increasing profitability at the same time it is increasing the growth rate. The more diverse the overall corporate activities, the more geographically dispersed the operating entities; the more extensive the decentralization of managerial activities and related delegations of executive authority and responsibility, the greater the difficulties in exercising effective control. Stated differently, the greater the diversity, dispersion, and delegations of authority, the greater the need for assurance to top management that proper control is being exercised over all operations and that all operating entities are contributing their proper share of earnings and growth.

Anticipated Major Benefits

Certain major benefits should accrue to any company from the implementation of a formal profit planning and control program. It should provide a clear picture of the anticipated financial results of all business actions in advance of their occurrence. Since certain corporate goals and objectives will previously have been established, management will be in a position to ascertain how these goals will be attained by the profit plan. Further, the compilation and subsequent attainment of the profit plan requires coordinated, cooperative effort of many disciplines within the company. This effort should be effective in achieving a greater measure of rapport and mutual understanding among the contributing staff. Finally, since the profit plan should provide an equitable basis for measuring performance and identifying deviations from plan by individual managers, it will be possible to take necessary action to correct any situation that may be deemed to be unfavorable.

Budgeting

In broad terms, one of the first steps in a typical profit planning process is the establishment of corporate goals in such specific financial terms as targeted profits, return on investment, rate of sales and profit growth, and any other financial objectives. These specific objectives must be established so that meaningful comparisons can subsequently be made between the actual and forecasted performance.

Once these goals are established, the major programs required to attain them must be clearly identified. The identification of these programs has a twofold purpose: Management effectively communicates to all operating divisions and entities their respective principal responsibilities in achieving the company's objectives; and management effectively decides the question of proper allocation of available resources.

Once the goals and major programs are determined, the detailed planning required to implement the profit plan must be done. It is at this point that the budget becomes an integral part of the profit planning process. With the budget providing guidance, the responsible officials of an enterprise have the capability to analyze more intelligently the interim financial and operating statements, the statements of financial position at the end of a period, and the results of operations for the period. Comparison of actual results with forecasted figures is often of much more practical use than comparison of current statistics with those of a prior period. Changes in the current economic climate and in local situations may make comparisons with the past invalid, if not misleading. Moreover, the past may have been affected by unusual events, abnormalities, managerial performance, or inefficient operations, all of which would constitute a poor "norm" for measuring the effectiveness of current performance.

Principal Divisions of the Budget

There are three principal divisions of a complete budget, all interrelated and interdependent. It is usually necessary to prepare all three divisions of the budget to determine the reasonableness of the projections of the individual divisions and to have a comprehensive picture of the desired results. The principal divisions of a complete budget are as follows:

1. Forecast of operations.
2. Forecast of cash receipts and disbursements.
3. Forecasted balance sheets.

The forecast of operations is usually prepared first, and it forms the basis for preparing the other divisions of the budget. A retailer's operating budget is usually subdivided into a merchandise budget and an expense budget. The merchandise budget establishes the goal for the gross margin that is expected to be realized from sales, inventories, purchases, markons, markdowns, discounts and allowances, shrinkages, and net alteration and workroom costs. The expense budget is essentially a plan for control of expenses in the light of the planned gross margin so that a satisfactory net profit will be realized from operations. The form of the expense budget is dependent upon the chart of accounts in use and the amount of detail required relative to the various classifications of expenses.

In addition to the merchandise and expense budgets a forecast of retail operations takes into consideration miscellaneous non-merchandising items of income and expense. Examples of such items are income from leased departments, interest income, interest expense, and miscellaneous income such as expense discounts, income from vending machines, and sales of waste.

Period of the Budget

A retailing budget is usually set up by six-month periods, known as "spring" (February through July) and "fall" (August through January) seasons. Each season is comparable with like seasons of past years, but the two seasons are not directly comparable with each other. The breakdown within each season is on a monthly or on a four- or five-week basis, with each four- or five-week period ending on a Saturday.

The merchandise purchases of the months (or 26-week period) of February to July, inclusive, are considered as spring season merchandise, while the purchases of the months (or 26-week period) of August to January, inclusive, are considered as fall season merchandise. Since merchandise purchases fall naturally within these distinct periods in the business year, and since inventories are normally classified as to age in the same manner, it is evident that the planning of such key merchandise factors as markons, sales, markdowns, shrinkage, and discounts, both in dollars and in percentages, should be on the same seasonal basis. (It should be noted, however, that some purchases made within a season are for the season immediately following.)

The Operating Budget

The preparation of a preliminary operating budget has been found to be very helpful. Executives and operating heads can use it as a reference base when they lay the groundwork for a detailed preparation of the operating budget. In effect, a preliminary operating budget aids in establishing the general policies, goals, and limitations to be followed in the preparation of departmental and divisional forecasts. A preliminary operating budget is prepared in total, rather than departmentally, and shows the major items of operations with appropriate detail and classification:

Sales
Cost of sales
Gross margin (except purchase discounts)
Purchase discounts
Operating expenses
Operating profit
Other income and expense
Income before provision for income taxes
Provision for income taxes
Net income

The most desirable format for the operating budget is generally the same format used for reporting past results of operations. Data for the constituent elements that enter into the determination of net income are given by months (or by four- or five-week periods), and the total for the season is shown. Details supporting the operating budget show the plans for each subdivision of the budget period (a month or a four- or five-week period) for:

1. Sales by departments.
2. Cost of sales by departments (including all key factors such as inventories, purchases, discounts, markons, markdowns, and shrinkages).
3. Gross margin by departments.

Ch. 5   BUDGETING AND FINANCIAL PLANNING AND CONTROL   75

4. Breakdown of expense classifications into component elements in as much detail as feasible, on a basis which clearly correlates responsibility for control over expenses for designated functions or areas with specific executives.
5. Breakdown of other items of income and expense not allocated to departments or not classified as operating revenue or expense.

The Merchandise Budget

The merchandise budget, a subdivision of the operating budget, reflects the details comprised in items 1, 2, and 3 of the foregoing summary. A merchandise budget, subdivided for each month (or four- or five-week period), is prepared for each department. The aggregates of the departmental forecasts by months (or four- or five-week periods), and in total for the season, are brought forward to the operating budget.

The merchandise budget should be prepared by the best qualified personnel—the merchandise managers and department buyers. They should, however, consult with the controller or controller's representative for guidance and assistance in estimating the results to be accomplished.

Starting with inventory at the beginning of a period, the merchandise budget plans or forecasts the following merchandising factors:

1. Sales during the period.
2. Purchases during the period.
3. Alteration and workroom costs.
4. Price changes to be effected.
5. Discounts to be allowed.
6. Probable shrinkages.
7. Inventory at close of period.
8. Rate of inventory turnover.
9. Percentage of purchase markon.
10. Gross margin to be earned (excepting purchase discounts).
11. Purchase discounts to be earned.

An important feature of a merchandise budget is the projected balancing of stocks in relation to sales and the assistance this provides in attaining an adequate gross margin on sales. An effective control over purchases should prevent an accumulation of stocks above the targeted budget figures. Utilizing desirable stock-to-sales ratios and turnover ratios and bearing in mind timely customer requirements should minimize losses that may arise from markdowns required to move excess merchandise stocks.

A merchandise budget is the primary step in merchandise control, since it controls purchases. An important corollary feature is that it controls the gross margin to be earned on the purchases. Other measures of merchandise control are chiefly concerned with existing stock: to safeguard the merchandise, to determine the amount which should be on hand, to ascertain whether that amount is actually on hand, to study the flow of stock in general and in detail as a merchandising aid, and to maintain a stock balanced as to units, classifications, and assortments. Although these further steps render the control plan more complete and effective, they are independent of the budgetary procedure which is the initial step in the control process.

The merchandise budget shows the elements of the statement of income, down to gross margin, as the management expects or desires them to be for each month (or four- or five-week period) during the season and in total at the close of the season. Effectively, it establishes a standard of desirable performance for each selling department. It is essential that, at regular intervals, actual performance be compared with the budget, either as originally set up or as revised in the light of new conditions or new judgments arising after the commencement of the season.

Illustration of Budgetary Procedure

Figure 11, a monthly plan covering six months for one department, illustrates the formal budget. In practice, there would be supporting work sheets showing details and calculations, explaining the statistics set forth in the plan, and indicating the bases used in their derivation. The budget office would collect data on performance under the plan, adjustments, open-to-buy, and other information which it uses from time to time to control purchases and markdowns and to revise the plan, as may be appropriate.

Some of the more important elements of the merchandise budget are discussed in the following paragraphs.

Planned Sales. This is the basic item of the budget and is the first one planned. Since all other items of the budget are based upon the anticipated sales volume, sales forecasts should be pre-

Ch. 5 BUDGETING AND FINANCIAL PLANNING AND CONTROL 77

MERCHANDISE PLAN
From February 1 to July 31, 19—

Department 37
Merchandise: Hosiery

For Season:
Per cent purchase markon .... Last Year 39.0 / Plan 40.0
Per cent markdowns .... Last Year 5.4 / Plan 4.9
Per cent shrinkages .... Last Year 1.4 / Plan 1.0
Turnover (season basis) .... Last Year 2.2 / Plan 2.75

	February	March	Season	April	Season	May	Season	June	Season	July	Totals Season Actual
Sales:											
Last year	$4,320	$5,586	$9,906	$6,175	$16,081	$5,628	$21,709	$5,005	$26,714	$4,122	$30,836
Plan	4,300	6,000	10,300	6,000	16,300	5,600	21,900	5,000	26,900	4,200	31,100
Revised plan											
Actual											
Markdowns:											
Last year	230	35	265	52	317	75	392	390	782	875	1,657
Plan	200	100	300	185	485	90	575	345	920	610	1,530
Revised plan											
Actual											
Shrinkages:											
Last year	43	56	99	62	161	56	217	50	267	165	432
Plan	43	60	103	60	163	56	219	50	269	42	311
Actual											
Sales discounts:											
Last year	65	50	115	60	175	55	230	60	290	50	340
Plan	50	50	100	65	165	60	225	55	280	50	330
Actual											
Retail stock (1st of month):											
Last year ...... (†end of month)	11,100	12,220		15,840		16,230		15,740		14,200	†12,440
Plan .... (†end of month)	9,320	12,380		12,210		12,200		11,800		11,100	† 9,800
Revised plan											
Actual											
Retail purchases:											
Last year	5,778	9,347	15,125	6,739	21,864	5,324	27,188	3,965	31,153	3,452	34,605
Plan	7,653	6,040	13,693	6,300	19,993	5,406	25,399	4,750	30,149	3,602	33,751
Revised plan											
Actual											
Cost purchases:											
Last year	3,622	5,472	9,094	4,166	13,260	3,327	16,587	2,411	18,998	2,042	21,040
Plan	4,592	3,624	8,216	3,780	11,996	3,243	15,239	2,850	18,089	2,161	20,250
Revised plan											
Actual											
Gross margin:*											
Last year	1,479	2,093	3,572	2,302	5,874	2,081	7,955	1,647	9,602	943	10,545
Plan	1,544	2,274	3,818	2,214	6,032	2,117	8,149	1,730	9,879	1,259	11,138
Actual											
Per cent of gross margin:*											
Last year	34.2	37.5	36.1	37.3	36.5	37.0	36.6	32.9	35.9	22.9	34.2
Planned	35.9	37.9	37.1	36.9	37.0	37.8	37.2	34.6	36.7	30.0	35.8
Actual											

Note: For simplicity in this example it was assumed that the markon in opening inventories was the same as in planned purchases for the season and did not change from month to month. In practice this is not likely to occur. Also it was assumed there were no additional costs, such as workroom costs.
*Gross margin and percentages of gross margin are before including purchase discounts to be earned.

FIG. 11. Merchandise plan.

pared in careful fashion. The figures developed should represent amounts which can be expected to be realistically attainable under normal conditions, rather than illusory expectations.

A number of factors are to be taken into consideration in planning sales. Historical sales data should be utilized, but such factors as current and projected business conditions, style trends, the competitive environment, the projected impact of inflation, and new promotional programs should be given full recognition. External data such as statistics supplied by trade associations and government agencies, and studies of trends may be very useful in this regard. Projections of transactions and average unit sales data can be especially important, particularly during periods of inflation.

Planned Markdowns. Markdowns are included in the budget as a realistic acknowledgment that there will be price reductions and to ensure that the planned purchases will be sufficient to maintain the planned stock figures. Markdowns result in the loss of gross margin and should, therefore, be carefully planned. Analyses of prior-period markdowns, linked to vendors and to causative factors, should be used as post-mortems, with a view to minimizing future recurrence of markdowns. It should be useful to know whether prior-period markdowns were caused by overly optimistic sales projections, the carryover of excess merchandise from season to season, remainders of promotional purchases, an excessively high initial markon, style changes, damaged merchandise, incomplete assortments, or faulty selling methods and displays.

Shrinkages. Shrinkages in merchandise stock (as a result of thefts, damage, and breakage) are, in some measure, always present in retail merchandising and should realistically be anticipated. The purpose of planning an amount for shrinkages is to spread the incidence of the loss, in recognition of the fact that it does not fall entirely in the period in which physical inventories are taken.

Sales Discounts. The adverse effect of sales discounts on the budget is similar to that of markdowns and shrinkages. An important difference is that discounts are the result of store policies adopted after mature consideration and presumably are good for the business. Some stores treat employees' discounts as an expense element for budgeting purposes, rather than as a factor to be considered in merchandising plans.

Retail Stock. The planned retail stock may be based upon a number of different factors. A procedure sometimes followed is to choose turnover and stock-to-sales ratios and develop the closing stock figures on the basis of these ratios. That procedure, however, ignores elements that enter into stock planning, which is a process requiring considerable merchandising skill. While it is desirable to attain a good turnover rate and stock-to-sales ratio, it must be remembered that these ratios are the result of stock planned on the basis of other factors. The condition of the opening stock, the amount of markdowns which may have to be taken to move that stock, and the allowances needed for shrinkage and discounts must be given careful consideration. It may be necessary to study the opening stock to ascertain whether there is an accumulation of slow-moving goods that must be moved in order to place the department on a proper operational basis. It is desirable to have stocks reasonably complete while maintaining sufficient purchasing power to react quickly to rapidly selling items or to what appear to be opportunities for very advantageous purchases.

When the budget is being prepared, the beginning stock can usually be approximated with a fair degree of accuracy. Once the opening stock is determined, the plans for sales and purchases, the desired turnover and stock-to-sales ratios for the season, and the closing stock for the season can be developed. The turnover rate and the stock-to-sales ratio should be reasonably attainable. As noted in Chapter 3, the stock-to-sales ratio is the ratio of stock on hand at the beginning of the month (or four- or five-week period) to the sales of the ensuing month or period. It differs from turnover in that turnover is based on average stock of the period when the sales are made.

In subsequently planning the closing stocks for each month (or four- or five-week period) of the budget season, consideration is given to the desired turnover and stock-to-sales ratio for each such period. Past experience will be useful in this regard. As a rule the peak in stock comes just prior to the high point in sales and the low point in stock is reached just prior to the low point in sales. From the low point, stocks gradually rise to the high point.

Planned Purchases. The planning of purchases involves a mathematical calculation using figures of planned sales, markdowns, shrinkages, discounts, and stock. A method of deriving planned purchases is as follows (use is made of the March figures included in Figure 11):

Planned sales	$ 6,000
Planned markdowns	100
Planned shrinkages	60
Planned sales discounts	50
Planned closing stock	12,210
Total requirements at retail	18,420
Less: Beginning stock	12,380
Total to be purchased, at retail	$ 6,040
Planned purchase markon percentage	40%
Planned purchases at cost (60%)	$ 3,624

Planned purchases at cost is equivalent to 60 per cent of the amount at retail, that is, 100 per cent (full retail) less 40 per cent (purchase markon).

To control purchases it is important to keep them constantly within the limits planned. For this purpose, schedules can be prepared showing the amounts of merchandise which departments may buy and still keep within the budget limitations. These schedules are called "open-to-buy," and have been described in detail in Chapter 4.

Percentage of Purchase Markon. Planned markon should be sufficient to cover markdowns, shrinkages, sales discounts, departmental expenses, and a fair portion of overhead expenses, and still yield a profit. Since selling prices may well be governed to a considerable extent by competitive conditions, it may not be possible in every instance to use a markon sufficient to cover all these elements. However, the markon currently used or planned should be compared with the required markon. A formula for determining required markon, which may be worked out either in percentages or dollars, is as follows:

$$\text{Purchase markon} = \frac{\text{Markdowns} + \text{Shrinkages} + \text{Sales discounts} + \text{Expenses} + \text{Profit}}{\text{Sales} + \text{Markdowns} + \text{Shrinkages} + \text{Sales discounts}}$$

If purchase markon is being developed with percentages, use 100 as the sales percentage and for the other items use percentages as related to sales. In using the above formula any net alteration and

Ch. 5 BUDGETING AND FINANCIAL PLANNING AND CONTROL

workroom costs should be treated as an additional item of departmental expense.

The following example illustrates how the purchase markon formula can be used in the budgeting process.

Problem. Based upon previous experience, it is necessary to have a purchase markon percentage of 40 in order to obtain the departmental profit desired. Using the figures given below, calculate the planned sales necessary in order to arrive at a desired departmental profit, and prove the answer.

Planned or estimated:	
Markdowns	$3,000
Sales discounts	400
Shrinkages	900
Expenses	9,000
Profit	2,000

Solution. Substitute in formula:

$$40\% = \frac{3{,}000 + 900 + 400 + 9{,}000 + 2{,}000}{\text{Planned sales} + 3{,}000 + 900 + 400}$$

$$40\% = \frac{15{,}300}{\text{Planned sales} + 4{,}300}$$

Let

$$x = \text{Planned sales}$$

$$40\% = \frac{15{,}300}{x + 4{,}300}$$

$$x + 4{,}300 = \frac{100}{40} \times 15{,}300 = 38{,}250$$

$$x = 38{,}250 - 4{,}300 = 33{,}950$$

$$\text{Planned sales} = \$33{,}950$$

Solution. Gross margin (before purchase discounts) is 40 per cent of sales of $33,950, or $13,580; less 60 per cent of reductions of $4,300, or $2,580; that is, $11,000. After deducting expenses of $9,000, a departmental profit of $2,000 remains.

Alteration and Workroom Costs. This element of cost of sales enters into the plans of many departments, especially ready-to-wear and fashion departments. Since it is a charge against gross margin, it must be considered in the budgeting process. Ratios of these costs to planned sales may be selected after a review of past experience. For the sake of simplicity the merchandise plan presented in Figure 11 does not include provision for alteration and workroom costs.

Gross Margin (Not Including Purchase Discounts). All the figures planned up to this point enter into the calculation of planned gross margin exclusive of purchase discounts. Computation of gross margin approximates the amount by which sales exceed cost of purchases minus the increase in inventory at mercantile, or alternatively, the amount by which sales exceed cost of purchases plus the decrease in inventory at mercantile. The entry of gross margin on the planning sheet permits comparisons between actual and planned results. There is also the advantage of showing directly on the planning sheet the adverse effect of markdowns, discounts, and shrinkages on gross margin.

Purchase discounts are a significant element of gross margin. However, in the interests of simplicity, departmental merchandise accounting and planning customarily consider gross margin before purchase discounts, developing such discounts as a separate item.

The computation of gross margin before discounts is illustrated by the following example:

	Cost or Mercantile	Retail		Markon Percentage	Mercantile Percentage
Stock, beginning of period	$ 5,592	$ 9,320		40.00%	
Purchases	20,419	33,751		39.50	
	$26,011	$43,071		39.61%	
Cost of sales:					
Net sales		$31,100			
Markdowns		1,530			
Shrinkages		311			
Sales discounts		330			
	$20,092	$33,271			60.39%
Alteration and workroom costs	310				
	$20,402				
Net sales, as above		$31,100			
Cost of sales, as above		20,402			
Gross margin (before purchase discounts)		$10,698			

$$\text{Percentage of gross margin} = \frac{\$10,698}{31,100}, \text{ or} \qquad 34.40\%$$

The difference of 5.21 per cent between the cumulative markon percentage (39.61 per cent) and the gross margin percentage (34.40 per cent) was caused by the markdowns, shrinkages, sales discounts and alteration and workroom costs.

In the foregoing illustration cost of sales was obtained by multiplying the total retail deductions ($33,271) by the cost percentage of 60.39 (complement of the cumulative markon percentage), and then adding alteration costs of $310 to the result. This is a short-cut method of developing cost of sales which may be proved as follows:

Stock, beginning of period and purchases of period at cost	$26,011
Stock, close of period (retail stock of $9,800 multiplied by mercantile percentage of 60.39)	5,918
	$20,093
Alteration and workroom costs	310
Cost of sales	$20,403

(Difference of $1 caused by rounding of percentages.)

The difference of 5.21 per cent between the percentages of cumulative markon and gross margin also may be proved as follows:

Sum of markdowns, shrinkages, and sales discounts = $2,171 Percentage on net sales of $31,100	6.98%
Reduced to cost by multiplication by mercantile percentage of 60.39	4.21%
Percentage of alteration and workroom costs, $310, on net sales of $31,100	1.00
	5.21%

Chapter 6 contains a discussion and further illustration of the effect upon gross margin of the merchandising elements—markdowns, shrinkages, sales discounts, and alteration and workroom costs. The topic has been included here to illustrate the need inherent in merchandise accounting to take all of these factors into consideration when planning operating results.

Purchase Discounts. In most instances this item of gross income constitutes a major part of the income from retailing. However, as has been stated, departmental budgeting and accounting has been simplified by treating purchase discounts separately as an item to be added after gross margin, exclusive of such discounts, has been determined. Purchase discounts are to be planned in relation to planned purchases, on a departmental basis tested by experience of the past. (See Chapter 8 for a further discussion of the accounting problems relating to purchase discounts.)

Budgeting the Merchandise Classifications

Effectively, merchandise classifications represent a finer breakdown of departmental inventories. Composite departmental figures may be misleading. In planning merchandise purchases and sales, with the objective of keeping them in line with planned stocks and keeping stocks well balanced, composite departmental figures are not as useful as figures analyzed by merchandise classifications. In many instances the results from budgeting by classifications, rather than simply by departments, will prove well worth the time and effort involved.

The procedures utilized in budgeting by classifications closely parallel those outlined earlier for departmental budgeting. Where a complete merchandise budget by classifications is not prepared, the work sheets underlying the departmental budgets should contain analyses by major merchandise classifications of the key merchandising elements—stocks, planned sales, and planned purchases.

Revision of Budgets

The departmental budgets are likely to require revision from time to time to take cognizance of new economic factors that may arise, particularly those that will have an impact on sales, especially where actual sales may be significantly higher or lower than plan. If sales decline from the budgeted figures, serious consideration should be given to the curtailment of planned purchases if it is desired to keep stocks within the budgeted amounts. If sales are greater than plan, the purchase allotment should be increased in the interests of maximizing sales and preventing the reduction of stocks below amounts deemed normal and desirable. However, in making adjustments of planned purchases, care should be exercised that purchasing power is not arbitrarily restricted to the point where it adversely affects operating results. Even when there is no open-to-buy under the budget, merchandise in current demand should be purchased. Under such circumstances, the plan for the department should be reviewed carefully, and present stock and the operations to date should be analyzed to ascertain the nature of the underlying troublesome factors.

Budgeting by Units

Thus far this chapter has focused on budgeting in terms of dollar amounts. Ideally, however, a dollar budget should be integrated with the corresponding budgeted units, since a budget is greatly improved and made more realistic by including forecasts of units of merchandise to be handled. As noted earlier, a budget carefully planned and adhered to, but with sufficient flexibility to take care of unexpected conditions, is an invaluable aid in successful retail management. Nevertheless, it is possible to adhere to budget requirements and achieve the pre-established dollar profit goal and still suffer an undesirable imbalance of individual items of merchandise stock on hand. Budgetary control by units helps to maintain a more acceptable balance.

The essential purpose of budgeting is control, whether it be control over the amounts and quantities of merchandise stocks or over the elements that enter into net profit. A question to be resolved is whether such control can best be exercised in terms of dollars or units, or both. The nature and value of the merchandise, or of the methods of operation, have a bearing upon the answer to the question. Merchandise of high unit value, such as automobiles, furs, pianos, precious jewelry, costly clothing, furniture, and appliances, lends itself readily to planning by units. Regardless of the unit values involved, single-line stores and chain stores with few lines and a limited range of prices, or quantity handling of a few standardized products, are well adapted to unit planning procedures. However, given the nature, variety, and low unit value of merchandise handled in certain departments (e.g., ribbons, laces, notions, toiletries), it is impractical in these situations to consider either maintaining unit records or budgeting by units.

In summary, under all circumstances a dollar merchandise budget, preferably developed on a departmental basis, is essential for financial purposes. To refine the budget and heighten its control features, the departmental totals should be analyzed by merchandise classifications, and preferably integrated with budgeted units. (See Chapter 4 for a more detailed discussion of unit control of merchandise.)

The Expense Budget

The ultimate goal in an operating budget is net income (after all income taxes). As a consequence of completing the merchandise budget, the retailer is provided with the prospective gross margin. The difference between planned gross margin and desired net income would be the allowance for selling, and general and administrative expenses of operation, plus or minus nonoperating items of expense or income, and less federal and state income taxes.

Focusing on the aggregate store operating expenses, we find items that can be viewed, to a greater or lesser degree, as being either fixed or variable in nature. The more common fixed expenses are property rentals, real estate taxes, insurance, and depreciation, whereas the principal variable or more controllable expenses are payroll, advertising, supplies, and services purchased. The variable expenses are susceptible of greater management and control, and consequently are given particular attention in budget preparation. In any event, a storewide expense budget should be developed in consultation with the key executives and supervisors who are responsible for incurring designated expenses in conjunction with the discharge of their respective duties and functions. It is essential that these executives and supervisors thereafter be held directly responsible for adherence to their respective expense budgets, which they helped to prepare.

Once an aggregate expense budget is prepared, it is helpful to correlate total expenses with gross margin and with the desired net income goal. This correlation may necessitate some adjustment of the expense budget if the store is to operate at a profit; it may even require some adjustment of the markon percentage or a reduction in the desired net income.

Expense classifications vary with the comparative size of the business, its form of organization, and the amount of information desired by executives. The Financial Executives Division of the National Retail Merchants Association (NRMA) recognized the need for flexibility in preparing its revised Retail Accounting Manual. For purposes of accumulating expenses, this manual provides the following ten expense summaries:

Property and equipment
Company management
Accounting and management information

Ch. 5 BUDGETING AND FINANCIAL PLANNING AND CONTROL

    Credit and accounts receivable
    Sales promotion
    Services and operations
    Personnel
    Merchandise receiving, storage and distribution
    Selling and supporting services
    Merchandising

These ten major work centers or areas of responsibility are generally applicable to most store operations regardless of size or type of operation. For larger stores, or for those desiring a further breakdown of expenses, the "Retail Accounting Manual—Revised" provides 44 expense centers within the ten expense summaries. As an example, within the Sales Promotion expense summary, the manual provides four expense centers:

Sales Promotion:
    Sales promotion management
    Advertising
    Shows, special events, and exhibits
    Display

Similar expense-center breakdowns are provided for each expense summary.

For those desiring an even greater refinement, the manual provides for the use of 22 sub-expense centers within six of the 44 expense centers. As an illustration of this concept, using the above example, Sales Promotion could be broken down into the following detail:

Sales Promotion:
    Sales promotion management
    Advertising
      Newspaper
      Radio
      TV
      Direct mail
      Other
    Shows, special events, and exhibits
      Public relations
      Merchandise shows
      Special events and exhibits
    Display
      Display production
      Sign shop

Not all stores will want to use 66 expense centers; the size of their operation will not dictate such a refinement. Furthermore, some of the areas of expense suggested may not be present within a specific operation. Latitude is provided within the manual to use only those expense centers or sub-centers which are appropriate.

After a decision has been made with respect to the desired number of expense centers, the manual provides natural divisions of expense which categorize the specific charge or expenditure as to type or function. These natural classifications of expenses are as follows:

Payroll
Allocated fringe benefits
Media costs
Taxes
Supplies
Services purchased
Unclassified
Traveling
Communication
Pensions
Insurance
Depreciation
Professional services
Bad debts
Equipment rentals
Outside maintenance contracts
Real property rentals
Outside revenues and other credits

In effect, the previously mentioned storewide expense budget is developed from building blocks comprising the individual expense-center budgets, broken down by natural expense classifications. The use of expense centers in this manner fixes the responsibility for expense control upon designated executives and supervisors within the organization. Moreover, this budget preparation exercise by these executives and supervisors helps foster an association with, and responsibility for, specific costs incurred by the expense center. In effect, each such person becomes an interested party in the problem of expense control. This becomes particularly effective when industry-wide comparisons are made available and searching inquiry is made into the reasons for unsatisfactory store performance. Obviously, in terms of the planning process, expenses should be budgeted in the same manner that expenses will be accumulated in the records during the year.

Payroll

In budgeting payroll, it is necessary to distinguish between, and separately consider, selling and nonselling personnel, and related salaries. There are obvious differences in the respective number of personnel requirements. Moreover, the peak activity requirements, including the duration of such peak requirements, can differ significantly between selling and nonselling functions. Accordingly, in preparing payroll estimates for each function or area of responsibility, consideration will have to be given to the number of personnel and dollar requirements in specific time frames. Practically speaking, if it is to be most effective, the budgeting for payroll should be done on a weekly basis.

Given the peaks and valleys of retail activity, an important principle to bear in mind in budgeting payroll is that the store cannot afford to maintain permanently a staff which is geared to peak activity. Part-time or contingent personnel must supplement the full-time staff in the interests of providing a satisfactory level of customer service. Also, the payroll budget must be developed in terms of hours, analyzed by full-time and contingent personnel. Literally, since there are fluctuations in daily retail selling and nonselling activity, these data should be developed for each day of the week, on a weekly basis. Moreover, since overtime dollars generally bear a 50 per cent cost premium, a further definition in terms of regular hours and overtime hours is essential.

Inasmuch as payroll expense for the selling function will fluctuate throughout the year, depending on the season and scheduled promotional activities, estimates should be based largely on the forecast of sales. The overall control should be to keep payroll within a given percentage of sales volume. Percentages have been the traditional standards of reference. In more recent years, however, a great deal of attention has been directed toward costs by focusing on the number of sales handled per hour and per day by sales personnel. These data have been effectively utilized to develop hourly personnel staffing requirements by selling departments or selling area, with such data ideally adaptable to the payroll budgeting process.

With respect to nonselling payroll, each expense center should be carefully studied to establish the necessity and justification for the individual employee positions. This study should be related to the workload of each department, the anticipated productivity in terms of a common unit, and the effective pay rate. Increasing attention is being focused upon the direct costs of performing a specific function. These costs are then related to the common denominator represented by the work performed in a department.

As a final point, the payroll budgeting process should take cognizance of all related fringe benefit costs, which represent a significant percentage of direct payroll dollars. This consideration becomes particularly important when programming full-time versus part-time employees since the respective fringe benefit costs can vary widely.

Advertising

As an important controllable expense closely related to the sales forecast, advertising requires special attention and planning. However, like payroll, it can, in considerable measure, be effectively controlled through careful departmental allocation. Just as payrolls are planned so that store operations may be satisfactorily conducted, so must advertising be planned with a view to the requirements of individual departments, as well as of general store policy.

The total amount planned to be spent for advertising should be subdivided among categories such as newspaper, direct mail, radio, television, and shows and exhibits.

Other Expenses

The detailed budgeting process will necessitate focusing attention on the various categories of other expenses incurred by key executives and supervisory personnel in all divisions. Working in concert with the controller and purchasing department (non-merchandising), and utilizing prior-season statistics and sales forecasts, and projections of work activity, these personnel can develop reasonably valid and realistic budgets of all other expense categories. As previously emphasized, before expense budgets (including payroll) are submitted to top management for approval, the key executives and supervisors must accept them as workable and realistic budgets for their own functions. This attitude will maximize the potential for ultimate adherence to the budgets.

Cash Receipts and Disbursements Budget

This budget can be prepared only after completion of the operating budget, since key figures brought forward from the operating budget are basic to the subsequent development of estimated cash receipts and disbursements. However, whereas the operating budget is developed utilizing the accrual basis of accounting, the purpose of this cash budget is to estimate revenue as it will be received and expenses as they will be disbursed.

Receipts from cash sales, collections on charge accounts, including service charges, and miscellaneous revenues are estimated monthly (or on a four- or five-week basis). Cash expenditures for merchandise purchases and for payroll, advertising, and other expenses, as well as outlays for fixed assets and liquidation of debt, are also estimated on a monthly basis. The excess, or deficiency, of budgeted receipts as compared with budgeted disbursements is determined monthly and applied to the balance of cash on hand.

This budget is utilized to determine the necessity (if any) and the timing for borrowing to carry on the business. The budget will also help to determine whether excess funds are likely to be available for temporary investment, for reduction of fixed indebtedness, for dividends, or for other purposes.

Forecasted Balance Sheets

The actual balance sheet at the beginning of the period is the starting point in the construction of an estimated balance sheet. On the basis of the operating budget and the forecast of cash receipts and disbursements, a forecasted balance sheet can be prepared for the close of each month (or four- or five-week period) of the season. It is important that the forecasted balance sheets derived in this fashion be reviewed and revised periodically on the basis of intervening results materially different from those budgeted.

Summation

In the final analysis, the budgeting process establishes, in definitive fashion, an accountability and responsibility for designated functions or areas of activity within an organization. Thus, it facilitates a more equitable measurement of performance. Moreover, in establishing goals and objectives at various levels of management, it provides the equivalent of a road map to guide management in maximizing growth and profitability. It highlights troublesome trends or unsatisfactory performance on a timely basis and permits the taking of corrective action.

6

Inventory Dollar Control, Including the Retail Inventory Method

Introduction

Chapter 4 emphasized the necessity for adequate control over merchandise, and outlined a number of the principal methods by which merchandise is controlled in the larger retail organizations. For smaller retailers the same principles apply, even if it is not feasible to carry out the control measures in detail. However, cost restraints in the smaller organization often require reliance, to some degree, upon personal supervision without complete accounting control.

In any retail business, whether simple or complex, the proper determination of stock on hand at the close of a fiscal period is essential for the current evaluation of the results of operations, as well as for control over merchandise stock. Practically speaking, the control of stock and determination of the results of operations are to a considerable degree inseparable and are present whether the business is large or small.

METHODS OF INVENTORY CONTROL

There are three principal or distinctive methods of controlling merchandise:

1. Physical inventories, whether taken frequently or at established periodic intervals.
2. Book inventory controls maintained on a cost basis.
3. Book inventory controls maintained on a retail basis.

The method of control by physical inventories represents the opposite extreme from methods whereby control is exercised by means of book records or stock ledgers maintained on the basis of cost or retail. The physical inventory approach minimizes use of an accounting record of transactions as they occur, and relies principally upon summaries, such as totals of sales or purchases. Operations are checked through periodic inventories. Under the book control methods, every transaction is accounted for and the book records reflect the inventories that should be on hand as at specific dates. Physical inventories are taken at intervals, and the results of the inventories are compared with the corresponding book control figures. Differences may reflect actual loss of merchandise, errors in recordkeeping, errors in counting and computing physical inventories, or combinations of any of these factors.

Control by Physical Inventories

In a very small business or a very specialized retail business, the most satisfactory and effective procedure with respect to merchandise stock is to take inventory with great frequency—monthly, weekly, or even daily. For a very small operation carried on by one or a few individuals, this procedure affords a most satisfactory method for determining profits and monitoring the movement of merchandise stock.

This method is not only feasible but desirable for retail merchandise operations where the inventory at any given time is comparatively small or can be readily counted and summarized. Operations where this method is most effectively utilized can range from a simple retail business such as a newsstand to large and busy enterprises such as restaurants or workrooms of metropolitan stores. An individual operator of a newsstand can best determine inventory by counting the stock at the end of the day or at other frequent intervals. The stock on hand, when correlated with purchases and sales, affords information as to whether there has been a gain or a loss, and reveals any unaccounted-for merchandise shortage. For a restaurant, the stock on hand at the close of any day should be comparatively small, especially if merchandise purchased for use on the following day is kept intact and segregated.

The physical inventory method yields necessary information and may indicate a need for greater control and even for special research as to the reasons for losses. It is probably the most practical method for many small retail stores. As with all physical inventories, the pricing of inventories must give appropriate consideration to any diminution in the values of merchandise if profits are to be properly determined.

Cost Method with Book Controls

This method is preferable for certain types of operations which carry only a few lines of merchandise, with a limited number of price lines. Automobile dealers and piano stores or departments should be well suited to this type of inventory accounting and control. It is the method traditionally followed in furniture stores, although there has been some trend toward use of the retail method. (Department stores using the retail method have long been accustomed to applying the retail method to their furniture department as well.) There are also departments or sections of departments where specific articles are registered, for example, jewelry, sterling silverware, and the more expensive furs. This registration is essentially for identification and as a measure of protection against loss, but it can readily be coupled with the cost method of inventory control.

Specialty stores with only a few principal merchandise lines (for example, shoe stores or chains) can advantageously utilize a procedure that is an adaptation of this method, especially when they restrict themselves to a limited number of price lines.

The Book Record. The book control of the cost method is a cumulative record, using only cost figures, in which purchases (including transportation) are added to inventory as at the beginning of a period to determine total merchandise available for sale. The cost of sales (including transportation), and the cost of markdowns (inventory depreciation) are deducted from this total. If experience shows that shrinkages normally occur in the inventories, estimated shrinkage amounts, at cost, may also be deducted. The resultant amount is book inventory at the lower of cost or market, which can be checked by means of a physical inventory.

Physical inventories should, of course, be priced and summarized on the same basis as the book inventories; that is, they should reflect transportation charges and the applicable markdowns or depreciation charged into the book record. As a consequence of taking the physical inventories and reviewing the individual items or classifications of merchandise, a decision may be made to further write down the inventory. Such additional depreciation should be reflected in the book record either as a direct write-down or via the use of an inventory reserve. If an inventory reserve is utilized, the book record will reflect the inventory amount before reserve. Discounts in inventories are best handled through unearned discount accounts, rather than through the book control records. It is usually desirable to have the book controls subdivided into departmental or merchandise classifications.

Cost of Sales. Under the cost method of book control, the cost of each and every sale must be determined. Under this procedure, sales and costs of sales may be tabulated, either in parallel columns by items or in separate lists, comparing selling price and cost for each transaction. One procedure for obtaining cost of sales is to have each article carry a two-section price tag, one portion of which is torn off at the time of sale and retained for use in the sales tabulation. This portion of the price tag shows the cost in code or by reference to a number or stock card in an office file. Another method is to enter on the sales check a code or other reference that will enable the sales audit office to compute the cost. Since this is a somewhat laborious, and probably expensive, compilation procedure, it is easy to understand why this method, combined with unit or other stock records, is considered an excellent method of merchandise control only when there are few transactions and large-dollar units of merchandise.

Changing Index "Costs." Where the cost method is in use, it is possible to record markdowns and change the prices in the cost index file. Index "cost" prices should be reviewed for possible downward revision at the close of each fiscal period, at a minimum.

Whether review is done continuously throughout interim periods as markdowns are taken depends upon the particular system used. The procedure followed in this respect has a bearing upon the determination of cost of sales for current monthly or interim purposes.

Unless index costs are changed to adjust for marked-down inventory values at the close of a fiscal period, the cost of sales for that period would be understated. Moreover, the cost of sales in the ensuing fiscal period applicable to the sale of the marked-down items would be overstated to the extent of the previously unrecognized markdowns. This imperfection in the records would automatically be corrected when a new physical inventory, properly priced, was taken. However, this automatic correction would be reflected in the records of the period during which the inventory was taken, rather than the period when the diminution in value of the merchandise actually occurred.

As a possible alternative, all markdown provisions may be made utilizing inventory reserves, with the stock records maintained throughout at original costs. Employment of this procedure will require reversals of opening reserves and establishment of new reserves each time financial statements are prepared. In this connection, there are practical difficulties in constantly estimating differences between original costs and current inventory values.

If index costs are changed only at the close of fiscal periods, sales of items from inventory at the beginning of the period will ordinarily be costed for current monthly or interim purposes on the basis of the inventory valuations, ignoring any subsequent markdowns. Markdowns, as taken, should be included in cost of sales, as merchandise depreciation, for the month or other interim period. The merchandise depreciation to be included in cost of sales should then comprise the markdowns taken during the period on items sold *plus* the total markdown reserve required against the closing inventory of merchandise on hand.

Where markdowns are tabulated and also reflected immediately as "cost" price changes on the index cards, any markdowns taken are to be included as a separate element in the cost of sales. This is desirable because costs as tabulated for sales, by items, do not include the differences between opening or original costs and written-down costs. Consequently, all markdowns of the period—those on items sold, as well as those applicable to merchandise still in stock—have to be taken into account.

Costing by Price Lines. The cost records may be subdivided into the price lines of each merchandise classification, with statistics as to the number of units handled in each price line. Given these data, average costs per unit within price lines are readily available. Cost of sales for a period may then be obtained expeditiously by multiplying the number of units sold by the average cost per unit. This obviously avoids the onerous chore of separately costing each individual sale. Under this plan markdowns arise through transfer of units to a lower price line. Upon such transfer the cost of markdowns is readily computed since it represents the difference between cost values of units in the respective price lines multiplied by the number of units. Units of shrinkage are also costed by application of the average rates. The taking and pricing of physical inventories is similarly facilitated since inventory counts are made by price lines and costed out using the respective average unit costs.

Objections to the Cost Method. The cost method with book controls operates satisfactorily where the units are large and important, or where the classifications are few and price lines are definite and limited in number. In such instances it is not burdensome to tabulate the cost of each sale, enter cost codes on tickets or cards, change the codes for depreciation semiannually or at other intervals, allocate transportation, and cost the items in physical inventories. Also, as has been stated, in operations where statistics can be kept by units and price lines, the amount of work is reduced through aggregate computations at average costs.

The cost method becomes burdensome and unsatisfactory in stores and departments with lower dollar-value items and numerous classifications and price lines. In such instances individual costing of sales and allocating of transportation charges, combined with the necessity to keep cost records updated with regard to depreciation (i.e., diminution in value), becomes prohibitively expensive and risks the added hazard of getting out of control. Regardless of whether book controls are maintained, the work of costing each item of a large and diversified inventory is quite burdensome. Similarly, with such inventories it is troublesome to compute depreciation by items and difficult to select satisfactory bases for reduced inventory valuations.

Under certain circumstances and conditions, if the cost method of inventory control is to be used, it may be advisable to continue to carry all items at original cost in the cost record. At the fiscal closing time all items would be listed at cost and retail. The inventory at cost would then be reduced by an amount or reserve based upon inadequate profit margins between present retails and original costs. However, the original costs of inventories, by items, will continue unchanged. The aggregate reduction or reserve for the fiscal closing will be changed periodically depending upon the spread between retail and original costs, or more particularly upon those inventory items where the differentials between retail and cost fall below predetermined percentages.

Cost Method on Approximate Basis. There are a variety of ways in which a cost system may be applied; sometimes an informal and approximate routine is followed. For example, approximate percentages of gross profits for departments and classifications of merchandise may be determined from past experience and used to cost current sales. The results are to be accepted only as approximations, with the exact determination of profits (as with any cost method) dependent upon the results of physical inventories. It should be recognized that for interim reporting purposes the gross margin determined on this approximation basis is somewhat arbitrary in that it does not consider relevant factors such as the incidence of markdowns or changes in the number of merchandise items sold at varying markon percentages.

Another variation is to determine purchase or inventory markons occasionally during a season and to derive approximate cost of sales and cost of markdown provisions based upon such percentages.

Retail Method

The cost method fails to meet the needs of modern retailing because it is costly to operate under the circumstances and conditions found in most department stores and many other retail stores. Obviously, daily inventory taking is impracticable in most stores or departments. It is equally obvious that costing out each sale and reducing markdowns to cost entails an excessive expense in most operations.

The retail method has been developed to its present status gradually and is now widely used to meet the combined needs for adequate information, proper control, and feasibility as to cost of operation. Essentially, the retail method compiles merchandise facts and figures and seeks to control inventories on the basis of retail prices. It is easier to compile values of physical inventories at marked selling prices than at cost. To do the latter requires either the use of cost figures in code on price tickets or a search in files for cost figures. Also, there is always the likelihood that a cost code may be decipherable by persons who are not entitled to have this information.

Advantages of the Retail Method. The retail method has the following advantages:

1. It permits periodic determination of inventories and profits without resorting to physical inventories.
2. It renders feasible the taking of departmental inventories at various dates, other than the general fiscal closing, with appropriate adjustment of the related departmental book record.
3. Physical inventories can be taken more expeditiously since they represent compilations of marked retail prices which are readily available to counting personnel.
4. Depreciation of inventory values, evidenced by a reduction in selling prices, is obtained as an automatic by-product of the method as soon as retail prices are reduced.
5. It discloses the effect of markdowns on profits.
6. It discloses the amount of stock shortages.
7. It facilitates the knowledgeable preparation of merchandise budgets.
8. It provides a basis for insurance coverage and settlements.
9. It tends to disclose, through apparently erroneous results, deficiencies in operational and internal control systems and procedures or in their implementation.

The Retail Method as an Averaging Method. Against these merits there must be recognized one definite objection: the retail method is basically an averaging technique. As such it is subject to distortion by the inclusion of extremes in the mix which makes up the average, with the consequent possible inaccuracy in the derivation of inventory values. Under the retail method, the mercantile (i.e., "cost") of merchandise on hand at any time is arrived at by deducting from retail the cumulative markon, generally representing the combined result of the markon of the opening inventory and the markon of purchases for the period to date. The cumulative markon is thus an average relation between the total cost of all merchandise (generally including opening inventory at mercantile) handled between inventory dates and the total retail of the same merchandise. Given the employment of this averaging principle, the merchandise cost of sales determined for a department under the retail method is not exact cost. Operation of the retail method and its underlying theory are discussed later in this chapter.

The retail method, like any other inventory method, must be checked and tested periodically by comparison with physical inventories, and book figures should be adjusted to the physical count unless there is reason to doubt the accuracy of the latter. Like any other method of inventory control, its successful use is dependent upon the care with which all pertinent factors are recognized and reflected in the accounts. No method of control will give satisfactory results if accounting detail is compiled carelessly, inaccurately, or with the omission of material factors. Furthermore, as noted earlier, it is fundamentally a method of averages. Accordingly, its successful employment depends upon its application to departments or sections of departments where average results, especially the use of an average cumulative markon percentage, do not distort the general picture. Any group of transactions where the extremes are so great as frequently to make average figures untrustworthy is not suited to the retail method. However, by subdivision or other expedient a reasonably homogeneous inventory grouping can be achieved, thereby making feasible the use of the retail method.

Choice of Method

Over the years the retail method has been widely adopted. For department stores and for many other forms of retail operation, this method probably combines, more satisfactorily than any other, information and control at the lowest cost. It is, however, a serious mistake to disregard or ignore the advantages of the other methods for use under certain circumstances. In almost any retail store there will be departments where the cost control method serves the requirements of the business more adequately than the retail method, and other departments where the taking of frequent physical inventories without use of a control record may be preferable.

It is the part of wisdom to use the method that most adequately meets the specific needs of a department or section, regardless of whether a different method is used elsewhere in the store. While the retail method can well be adopted by many retailers who do not yet use it, it is equally true that the other methods, or combinations of them with certain supplementary features, can and do give the best results for some types of business.

OPERATION OF THE RETAIL METHOD

Operation of the retail method requires merchandise statistics at retail as well as at cost, and a separate compilation for each department or appropriate merchandise classification rather than aggregate totals. With respect to inventories, "cost" figures are those worked out under the retail method; for this so-called "cost" the term "mercantile" is used in this book.

The merchandise statistics for each department or classification commence with opening inventory at mercantile and at retail. Purchases are added at cost (plus transportation) and at marked retail. There are also added markups at retail. Totals of these items represent merchandise handled during the period at cost or mercantile, and at retail. Utilizing these totals the cumulative markon is obtained, which is the difference between retail and cost or mercantile of merchandise handled. The percentage of cumulative markon is derived by dividing the cumulative markon by the retail total of merchandise handled. For purposes of valuing the year-end inventory, most retailers include the markon inherent in the opening inventory in computing the cumulative markon. However, this is not a universal practice. Recognizing that they are increasingly subject to periods of changes in the mix of merchandise and changing markon percentages, some retailers have either exclusively used the markon on the current year's purchases or more heavily weighted this markon percentage in the year-end inventory valuation process. Such an approach, of course, is predicated on the assumption that the closing inventory predominantly comprises merchandise purchased during the current year. In the opinion of the authors, the method selected to compute the cumulative markon percentage should be that which most appropriately reflects the facts and circumstances, and normally should be applied on a consistent basis.

To obtain closing inventory at retail, the total of retail deductions is subtracted from the total of merchandise handled at retail. Total retail deductions comprise the sum of net sales, markdowns, allowances, sales discounts, and shrinkage (estimated or actual). Closing inventory at retail is reduced to mercantile by deducting the cumulative markon derived from the application of the percentage of cumulative markon to retail. Mercantile of closing inventory may also be obtained through multiplying retail by the complement of the percentage of cumulative markon; that is, one hundred minus the cumulative markon percentage. Such complement is also known as "cost percentage" or "cost multiplier," or "mercantile percentage."

Illustration.

	Cost or Mercantile	Retail	Cumulative Markon Percentage
Opening inventory	$5,683	$ 8,795	
Purchases and transportation, net	3,482	5,372	
Markups (less cancellations)		145	
Total merchandise handled	$9,165	$14,312	35.96%
Net sales		$ 3,369	
Markdowns (less cancellations)		280	
Sales discounts		15	
Shrinkage (estimated or actual)		68	
Total retail deductions		$ 3,732	
Closing inventory	$6,775	$10,580	35.96%

The closing inventory at mercantile, $6,775, represents 64.04 per cent (complement of the cumulative markon percentage) of $10,580, the closing inventory at retail.

The Stock Ledger

The principal record used in the retail method is a stock ledger which includes figures for each department or departmental subdivision. Single-line and specialty stores, and some other operations, may maintain stock ledgers with figures for merchandise classifications (or price lines, styles, etc.) rather than for departments. For example, a men's clothing store may maintain stock ledgers by different types of merchandise and the price lines of each type, rather than by departments. Similar procedures may be followed by a chain of shoe stores, the primary classifications being price lines within types of merchandise, which are supplemented by analyses by stores.

For branch stores a stock ledger may be maintained for the departments of each branch, separate from the ledger kept for the departments of the main store. On the other hand, where the branches contain simple subdivisions or adjuncts of the main store (as contrasted with a completely distinct and separate operation), it is often the practice to have only one combined stock ledger for recording all merchandise transactions (except sales) of the common departments without regard to store location. However, sales statistics are generally reflected in the stock ledger on a store-by-store basis. See Chapter 13 on branch store operations.

Retail operations commonly are divided into two seasons, and the cumulative merchandise statistics are kept on a seasonal rather than an annual or other periodic basis. For example, department stores on a January 31 fiscal year basis would record merchandise statistics for the spring season, from February 1 to July 31, and then start the records anew for the fall season, August 1 to January 31. However, this is not universal practice. In the interests of simplicity and reduced recordkeeping requirements, the records are sometimes kept on an annual basis and statistics are accumulated without regard to seasonal breakdowns.

The stock ledgers may be either abbreviated or detailed. With an abbreviated ledger a supplementary record is kept to accumulate purchase totals; where the ledger is detailed, the various purchase elements are entered directly. Figure 12 illustrates an abbreviated form of departmental stock ledger.

As illustrated in Figure 13, a detailed form of stock ledger consists of three principal parts: an upper section for accumulating cost or mercantile of merchandise handled; a middle section for accumulating the corresponding retail, as appropriate, of merchandise handled; and a lower section for determining closing inventory at retail and mercantile, and gross margin before discounts.

The forms illustrated in Figures 12 and 13 provide for separate seasonal accumulations of statistics and markons. Where records are maintained on an annual basis, the accumulations would be designated as "year to date" and they would be continued for twelve successive months (or four thirteen-week accounting periods where the 52–53-week convention is used).

The two forms of stock ledger illustrated in Figures 12 and 13 provide for recording, on one page for each department, all the transactions of the season or the year. In contrast is another

Ch. 6   INVENTORY DOLLAR CONTROL   105

DEPARTMENTAL STOCK LEDGER

Department _____

Period	Merchandise Handled			Retail Deductions				Closing Inventory		Alteration and Workroom Costs, Net (11)	Gross Margin Before Discounts Sum (4) + (10) − (1) and (11) (12)
	Cost or Mercantile (1)	Retail (2)	Mercantile Per Cent (1)÷(2) (3)	Net Sales (4)	Mark-downs (5)	Sales Discounts (6)	Shrinkage Provisions and Adjustments (7)	Total Sum (4) to (7) (8)	Retail (2)−(8) (9)	Mercantile (9)×(3) (10)		
Inventory, Feb. 1												
Month of February												
Season to date												
Month of March												
Season to date												
Month of April												
Season to date												
Month of May												
Season to date												
Month of June												
Season to date												
Month of July												
Season to date												

FIG. 12. Departmental stock ledger (abbreviated form).

DEPARTMENTAL

Season _____   Opening Inventory   { Mercantile _____
                                      Retail _____
                                      Markon % _____

Merchandise Charges at Cost or Mercantile	(1) Domestic Invoices	(2) Foreign Invoices (Landed Cost)	(3) Workroom Made Merchandise	(4) Freight, Express & Cartage, Inward	(5) Sundries	(6) Department Transfers (Debits)
February						
Season to date						
March						
Season to date						
April						
Season to date						
May						
Season to date						
June						
Season to date						
July						
Season to date						

Merchandise Charges at Retail	(12) Domestic Invoices	(13) Foreign Invoices	(14) Workroom Made Merchandise	(15) Markups	(16) Sundries	(17) Department Transfers (Debits)
February						
Season to date						
March						
Season to date						
April						
Season to date						
May						
Season to date						
June						
Season to date						
July						
Season to date						

Closing Inventory and Gross Margin	(24) Net Sales	(25) Mark- downs	(26) Sales Discounts	(27) Shrinkage Provision (%)	(28) Adjust- ment of Shrinkage Provision	(29) Total Retail Deductions (Sum 24–28)
February						
Season to date						
March						
Season to date						
April						
Season to date						
May						
Season to date						
June						
Season to date						
July						
Season to date						

A. Shrinkage reserve (27 plus 28) _____
B. Difference between book and physical inventories _____
C. Actual inventory shrinkage (A plus or minus B) _____

FIG. 13. Departmental stock

STOCK LEDGER

Department _____

(7) Department Transfers (Credits)	(8) Invoices in Transit (Debits)	(9) Invoices in Transit (Credits)	(10) Total Merchandise Received (Sum 1–9)	(11) Opening Inventory Plus Merchandise Received	Purchase Markon % (21−10)÷21

(18) Department Transfers (Credits)	(19) Invoices in Transit (Debits)	(20) Invoices in Transit (Credits)	(21) Total Merchandise Received (Sum 12–20)	(22) Opening Inventory Plus Merchandise Received	(23) Cost Percentage (11 ÷ 22)

(30) Closing Inventory Retail (22 − 29)	(31) Closing Inventory Mercantile (30 × 23)	(32) Alteration and Workroom Costs, Net	(33) Department Labor Costs	(34) Gross Margin Before Discounts	(35) % Gross Margin Before Discounts

D. Physical inventory at retail (30 minus or plus B) _____
E. Physical inventory at mercantile _____

ledger (detailed form).

method which uses a separate sheet for each department monthly and shows figures for the month and cumulative for the season or year. This latter method has the advantage of including in a separate small book the key merchandise data of each month (or four- or five-week period) and of the period to date for the entire store. Copies of the sheets can be supplied to buyers and executives as a monthly (or four- or five-week period) report of merchandising results, thereby avoiding the duplicate work of transcribing figures from the stock ledger to the monthly report of operations. One writing of the figures serves the purposes of recordkeeping and reporting. This type of form, as illustrated in Figure 14, reflects the accumulations of statistics on an annual rather than a seasonal basis, with the data for the departments of the main store and the branches all combined in a single stock ledger sheet and operating report. The theory underlying the pooled or common department concept is the universal applicability of a common departmental markon, with all retail deductions (markdowns, allowances, discounts, and shrinkage) shared in proportion to sales. Consequently, the same gross margin on the sales is "earned" by the department regardless of store location.

An abbreviated form of stock ledger is to be preferred when the records are kept on a weekly basis and where the departmental figures are subdivided by such factors as merchandise classifications, price lines, or branch store locations. A detailed form becomes unwieldy for other than monthly (or four- or five-week) aggregate accumulations. When the stock records are kept on a monthly (or four- or five-week) basis, the choice of form depends upon whether the preference is for as much detail as possible in the stock record, or for as condensed a record as feasible, with supplementary details recorded elsewhere.

Figure 15 illustrates a form of stock ledger which facilitates preparation of data on a weekly basis or for different subdivisions of departments and branch stores. This is done by eliminating the computation and entry of mercantile amounts of inventories and by deriving gross margin results using short-cut computations in terms of certain percentages.

The percentages to be entered in Figure 15 are the cumulative markon, and the markdown, sales discount, shrinkage provision, alteration and workroom cost, and gross margin (before discounts) percentages on net sales. The percentages of gross margin are

INVENTORY DOLLAR CONTROL

MERCHANDISE STATEMENT

Month of		Line			Year to Date	
Amount	%			%	Amount	
		1	COST: Inventory — First of Period			
		2	Domestic Purchases (Net)			
		3	Freight and Cartage — In			
		4	Foreign Purchases (Net)			
		5	Transfers (Net)			
		6				
		7	CUMULATIVE COST (% = 7 ÷ 14 for Year)			
		8	RETAIL: Inventory — First of Period			
		9	Domestic Purchases (Net)			
		10	Foreign Purchases (Net)			
		11	Markups			
		12	Transfers (Net)			
		13				
		14	CUMULATIVE RETAIL (Markon % = 7 ÷ 14 Fr. 100%)			
		15	NET SALES: Main Store			
		16	Branch A			
		17	Branch B			
		18	Branch C			
		19	Branch D			
		20	Branch E			
		21				
		22				
		23	Total Net Sales			
		24	Markdowns (% = 24 ÷ 23)			
		25	Allowances to Customers (% = 25 ÷ 23)			
		26	Discounts to Employees (% = 26 ÷ 23)			
		27	Shrinkage (% = 27 ÷ 23)			
		28	Total Retail Stock Ded. (23 to 27 Incl.)			
		29	INVENTORY: Retail — End of Period (14 − 28) (Ratio = 29 ÷ 23)			
		30	INVENTORY Cost — End of Period (29 × % 7 Yr. to date)			
		31	Workroom and Other Costs (% = 31 ÷ 23)			
		32	GROSS MARGIN BEFORE DISCOUNTS (23 + 30 − 7 − 31) (% = 32 ÷ 23)			
		33	Cash Discounts (___% of 28 for month) (% = 33 ÷ 23)			
		34	GROSS MARGIN (32 + 33)			

_____ Dept. No.   Dept. No. _____
_____ 19__ Period   Period _____ 19__

[For explanation of line 33, see page 168.]

FIG. 14. Merchandise statement and stock ledger (combined).

DEPARTMENTAL STOCK LEDGER

Department _____ Dept. No. _____

Period	Merchandise Handled		Net Sales	Retail Deductions				Closing Inventory at Retail	Alteration and Workroom Costs	Percentages					
	Cost or Mercantile	Retail		Mark-downs	Sales Discounts	Shrinkage Provisions	Totals			Mark-on %	Mark-down %	Sales Discount %	Shrinkage Provision %	Alteration Costs %	Gross Margin Before Discounts %
Inventory Feb. 1															
Month of February															
Season to Date															
Month of March															
Season to Date															
Month of April															
Season to Date															
Month of May															
Season to Date															
Month of June															
Season to Date															
Month of July															
Season to Date															

FIG. 15. Departmental stock ledger (based on percentages).

determined from the other percentages on the form, in accordance with a standard formula of the retail method:

> The percentage of gross margin (before discounts) equals the cumulative markon percentage, minus the sum of markdown, allowances, sales discount, and shrinkage percentages reduced to cost (that is, multiplied by the complement of the cumulative markon percentage), and minus the alteration and workroom cost percentage.

Some computations are hereafter presented which illustrate how this form of stock ledger facilitates the determination of departmental results with a considerable reduction in the quantity of work.

Merchandise Handled

This item includes opening inventory and all purchase elements that enter into the determination of cumulative markon. Purchases included in merchandise handled consist of the following items:

1. Billed cost of domestic purchases, less returns, rebates, and allowances.
2. Landed cost of imported merchandise; that is, billed cost plus duty, freight, insurance, commissions, etc., less returns and allowances.
3. Inward transportation charges (at cost only).
4. Cost of merchandise produced in store workrooms.
5. Department transfers in, less transfers out.
6. Sundries; that is, cash purchases, comparison purchases, adjustments, etc.
7. Markups, less cancellations and other corrections of retail (at retail only).
8. Invoices in transit.

In some instances, all elements of purchases (except invoices in transit) are accumulated departmentally in the equivalent of a purchase journal, in the order in which they arise. Totals from this purchase journal plus invoices in transit may then readily be carried directly to the stock ledger. However, this procedure may not be as satisfactory as separate accumulations of the constituent components of purchases, either in a record supplementary to an abbreviated form of stock ledger or directly in a detailed form of stock ledger. The separate accumulation of purchase elements permits

PURCHASE RECORD SUMMARY

Department _____ Season _____

	Period (Month or Week)		Period		Period	
	Cost	Retail	Cost	Retail	Cost	Retail
1 Domestic invoices (net)	$2,466	$3,722				
2 Foreign invoices (net) at landed cost	850	1,500				
3 Transportation, inward	76	—				
4 Workroom-made merchandise	72	120				
5 Transfers—in	60	100				
6 Sundries (cash and journal)	18	12				
7 Markups, etc.	—	145				
8 Invoices in transit, close of period (if any)	102	157				
	$3,644	$5,756				
9 Invoices in transit, beginning of period (if any)	$ 85	$ 135				
10 Transfers—out	30	50				
	$ 115	$ 185				
11 Total purchases	$3,529	$5,571				

FIG. 16. Purchase record summary.

a review of the individual factors that enter into the computations of markons. A form of accumulation of purchase is shown in Figure 16.

Invoices in Transit

In the determination of purchases for the stock ledger, a question arises as to whether the amounts for domestic and foreign invoices should include all invoices for merchandise received or only invoices which have cleared through the receiving and marking rooms and have been recorded on the equivalent of a purchase journal. In practice, certain invoices are always "in transit"; that is, the invoices have not been recorded on the purchase journal although the merchandise has been received. It is desirable to include as purchases all invoices for merchandise received, without regard to whether the goods have been checked and marked and placed in stock. This practice provides a more meaningful purchases statistic, as well as more precise open-to-buy statistics.

A number of retailers reflect as purchases solely the cost and related retail of invoices representing merchandise received, checked, and marked. Invoices in transit are ignored. As a practical matter, generally speaking, at month-end (or at the end of any four- or five-week period), invoices in transit representing merchandise received but not checked or marked will not be a significant factor. The larger amount of invoices in transit normally will represent invoices received from vendors bearing a date prior to the month-end (or end of the four- or five-week period) for which the corresponding merchandise has not yet been received.

The reason for omitting invoices in transit is the practical problem of having to separately tabulate such invoices at cost and at retail. Where such tabulations are made, the cumulative retail is generally estimated, departmentally, on the basis of the markon of the invoices recorded in the equivalent of the purchase journal. Under these circumstances, at the close of each accounting period the amount of invoices in transit is reflected in the stock ledger as a purchase debit. This amount is reversed in the ensuing period, and a new amount is set up at the close of that period.

Another method is to post to the stock ledger totals which include all invoices received, as reflected in the invoice register. Under this plan the invoice register serves as the purchase journal, the totals of the register being carried to the "purchases" account in the general ledger, with an offsetting credit to an account entitled "invoices in transit." As invoices clear through to the accounts payable office, debit entries are made to the account "invoices in transit," and credit entries to "accounts payable." Thus, at the close of any accounting period, the general ledger account "invoices in transit" reflects the aggregate liability for invoices in transit. The amount in this account is supported by open items on the invoice register. The invoice register will not reflect retail on invoices which are in transit. Consequently, this retail may be estimated on the basis of the markon of invoices which have cleared. Corrections of estimates will be required as actual retail is subsequently determined.

Forms and procedures for recording purchases are included in Chapter 10, which also discusses the problems connected with merchandise produced in store workrooms and transfers among departments and branch stores.

Mercantile Percentage

As noted earlier, the cumulative markon of a department is the difference between retail and cost or mercantile of the total merchandise handled. The percentage of cumulative markon results from dividing the amount of markon by the total retail of merchandise handled. This percentage is the factor used in determining the mercantile of closing inventories.

As it is mathematically simpler to use the complement of the markon percentage in computing inventory at mercantile, it is the complement percentage (otherwise known as the "mercantile percentage" or "cost multiplier") which may be reflected in the stock ledger. Subtraction of the complement percentage from 100 will, of course, provide the percentage of markon. The mercantile percentage is readily determined by dividing the total cost or mercantile of merchandise handled by the corresponding retail amount.

It is often useful to compare the departmental markon of individual accounting periods with the cumulative markon for a season or year, or with the corresponding accounting period of the prior year(s). As illustrated by Figure 13, a column can be provided in the stock ledger which shows such purchase markon percentages derived from the totals of retail and cost of merchandise received in the individual accounting periods.

Net Sales

Net sales represent sales net of all returns and allowances and net of sales discounts. Returns are deducted from gross sales because the merchandise has been restored to stock. When allowances are granted, no merchandise is returned to stock. To the extent that allowances are offset against sales they must be added to markdowns so that there is a complete accountability for merchandise at retail. Some allowances are classified as policy adjustments and are charged to expense rather than applied in reduction of sales.

Markdowns

Markdowns are entered as credits to stock on the stock ledger, in recognition of the reduction of the retail value originally charged to stock. Sales of marked-down merchandise are credited to stock only at the reduced prices.

Markdowns are frequently classified by causative factor, with a view to providing some insight into the effectiveness of buying and merchandising policies. The following classification of such factors is commonly used:

1. Promotional purchase remainders.
2. Slow-moving or inactive stocks.
3. Special sales from stock.
4. Price adjustments.
5. Broken assortments, remnants, discontinued lines, and damaged merchandise.
6. Allowances to customers.

Often the same form is used to control and record all types of price changes, including markdowns. A periodic analysis of such price change forms will supply the necessary information regarding the amounts of markups and markup cancellations, markdowns and markdown cancellations, and corrections of retail. Figure 17 illustrates a general form for handling price changes.

116 RETAIL ACCOUNTING AND FINANCIAL CONTROL Ch. 6

PRICE CHANGES

Department _____

Date _____ No. _____

Kind of change (check one)

Markup _____
Markup cancellation _____

Markdown _____
Markdown cancellation _____
Corrections of Retail _____

Season Letter	Quantity	Article	Classi-fication	Reason Code No.	Present Retail per Unit	Proposed Retail per Unit	Price Change per Unit	Amount of Price Change

Total _____

Authorized By _____   Buyer's Signature _____   Marker _____   Calculations checked by _____

FIG. 17. Price changes.

Sales Discounts

Sales discounts to customers and employees are deducted from the full sales prices at the time of sale or are deducted from charge accounts at the time of payment. Sales discounts deducted from sales are an appropriate recognition of the fact that the original retail price of stock will not be recovered from sales to customers or employees. Charge account discounts are not deducted from sales prices at the time of sale, and stock accounts are credited with full sales prices. However, a percentage of the sales price is rebated at the time of payment of the charge account. The amount of these charge account discounts is allocated departmentally and deducted from departmental sales, with a corresponding addition to sales discounts. Alternatively, employee discounts may be charged off to expenses, recognizing that such discounts represent a form of compensation or employee benefit cost.

Shrinkages

The provision for shrinkage as entered in the stock ledger is accumulated throughout a season as an estimate of probable shrinkage based upon past experience. Book inventories have, therefore, already been reduced by an estimated amount of shrinkage before they are compared with physical inventories. Where a difference exists between a physical inventory and a book inventory already reduced by an estimated shrinkage, the difference is equivalent to a correction of the estimated shrinkage; that is, it indicates that the estimate of shrinkage was either too great or too small. Therefore, an adjustment of the estimated shrinkage is in order, so that the stock ledger will reflect the actual shrinkage as at the date of the physical inventory.

If the indicated adjustment is large enough to reduce shrinkage below a minimum deemed "normal" for the specific department, or, on the other hand, to increase it to an abnormally large figure, a study should be made to ascertain the causative factor. It is not usual to make material adjustments of the shrinkage provision, especially those which are below normal, until the records have been reviewed for possible errors or until a second physical inventory has been taken.

Closing Inventory

Closing inventory at retail derives from the subtraction of total retail deductions from total retail of merchandise handled. It is subject to check by a physical inventory. Physical inventories are taken with more or less frequency but usually at least twice a year. As noted earlier, the inventory amount as shown by the stock ledger is adjusted to the amount of the physical inventory through the shrinkage provision.

Mercantile of closing retail inventory, whether the unadjusted book balance or the amount of physical inventory, results from the multiplication of the retail amount by the mercantile percentage.

Alteration and Workroom Costs, Net

These costs are not entered as purchases but as a separate element of merchandise costs to be used in the determination of gross margin.

Under this caption in the stock ledger are included the amounts charged to the departments by workrooms for alterations and repairs to goods in stock or goods sold, where there is no increase in retail price of the goods, net of payment by customers for the work performed. At least in theory, such customer charges should comprise the actual cost of the work performed, although estimates are often used. In addition to these charges, the selling departments are charged with their distributive shares of workroom net losses. Workroom net losses are determined by deducting from the total of operating costs the aggregate of amounts transferred to departments for stock work or free work and the amounts charged to customers for alterations. Such losses are periodically distributed to the departments closely associated with the respective workrooms.

The preferred practice is to consider workroom and alteration costs, net of charges to customers and to selling departments, as a separate element of merchandise costs to be used in the determination of gross margin (but not to be taken into account in the derivation of cumulative markon). This method is followed in the forms and illustrations in this book.

Not all of the alterations and similar costs arise through transfers from workroom accounts. Frequently, there are no established workrooms for handling such work. Under these circumstances, all alterations or work required to make merchandise on some orders ready for delivery is performed in the selling departments. These departments either employ separate workers for this purpose or have the work sent outside. In either case direct charges arise against departments for payroll, supplies, vendors' invoices, etc., which effectively comprise alteration and workroom costs, rather than purchases or operating expenses. For the abbreviated form of stock ledger illustrated in Figure 12 it is assumed that this kind of direct department charge will be combined with transfers from workrooms for entry in the column headed "Alteration and Workroom Costs, Net." For the detailed form of stock ledger illustrated in Figure 13, a separate column headed "Department Labor Costs" has been inserted for the specific entry of these direct departmental charges; whether or not such separation is made is not significant.

Gross Margin Before Discounts

Gross margin before discounts is derived by adding net sales and closing inventory at mercantile, and deducting therefrom the sum of total merchandise handled at cost and alteration and workroom costs. Stated differently, gross margin before discounts equals the excess of net sales over total merchandise costs (gross), the latter item representing the sum of opening inventory at mercantile, cost of merchandise received, and alteration and workroom costs (including department labor costs), less closing inventory at mercantile.

The stock ledger forms illustrated in this book do not include columns for entry of cost of sales (total merchandise costs, gross). Such columns could be included in the forms but were deemed unnecessary in the interests of simplicity and because the really important statistic is gross margin.

The illustrative stock ledger forms other than Figure 14 stop at the derivation of gross margin before discounts. Total gross margin of departments includes discounts earned, but ordinarily there is no need to enter discounts earned in the stock ledger or to show total gross margin. These data are entered in Figure 14 because that form is utilized for both the stock ledger and the selling department report. Gross margin before discounts is the important ratio in judging the result of departmental operations because it indicates how far the realized (or "maintained") markon percentage has fallen short of the cumulative markon percentage. Discussion of the procedure for obtaining the amounts of discount earned can be found in Chapter 8.

The stock ledger form illustrated in Figure 15 provides a method of determining the percentage of gross margin (before discounts) through the use of certain percentages. It is a short-cut method which avoids computation of inventory amounts at mercantile and total merchandise costs (gross), and eliminates several mathematical steps. The various percentages used in this form generally are computed as desirable statistical information, and thus do not involve additional work. The procedure for utilizing this form in deriving the percentage of gross margin (before discounts) may be illustrated by assuming that the following data have been obtained from a stock ledger:

	Amounts	Percentages on Net Sales
Opening inventory at mercantile	$ 20,880 *	
Purchases at cost	51,794 *	
Retail of merchandise handled	126,518 *	
Net sales	92,743	
Markdowns	5,653	6.10%
Sales discounts	1,079	1.16
Shrinkage provisions	368	.40
Closing inventory at retail	26,675	
Alteration and workroom costs	612	.66

* From these totals the cumulative markon percentage of 42.56% is derived.

From the foregoing percentages the percentage of gross margin (before discounts) is determined, as follows:

Percentage of cumulative markon		42.56%
Retail reduction percentages to be reduced to cost:		
Markdowns	6.10%	
Sales discounts	1.16	
Shrinkage provisions	.40	
Total	7.66%	
Percentage of retail reductions reduced to cost, 7.66 × 57.44 (which is 100 − 42.56)		4.40
		38.16
Percentage of alteration and workroom costs		.66
Percentage of gross margin (before discounts)		37.50%

Preparing a Gross Margin Statement

As proof of the correctness of the percentage of gross margin derived under the above formula, a method of preparing a departmental statement of gross margin from data in the stock ledger form (Figure 15) is illustrated below. As will be noted from the data used in the preceding example, the elements of a complete gross margin statement that are lacking are closing inventory at mercantile and the amounts of gross margin and earned discounts. Closing inventory and gross margin are derived while setting up the statement, but the discount amount must be obtained from discount records.

Illustration.

	Amounts		Percentages on Net Sales	
Net sales	$92,743	$92,743	100.00%	100.00%
Markdowns	5,653		6.10	
Sales discounts	1,079		1.16	
Shrinkages	368		.40	
Retail sales and reductions	$99,843		107.66%	
Merchandise costs:				
Inventory, beginning of period	$20,880			
Purchases	51,794			
Gross cost of merchandise handled	72,674			
Inventory, close of period	15,322			
Gross cost of merchandise sold	57,352		61.84%	
Alteration and workroom costs	612		.66	
Total gross merchandise costs		57,964		62.50
Gross margin before discounts		34,779		37.50
Discounts earned		3,849		4.15
Gross margin		$38,628		41.65%

Net sales, opening inventory at mercantile, purchases at cost, and alteration and workroom costs are available and can be entered directly on the statement. Since the percentage of gross margin before discounts is available, the corresponding amount is readily computed and entered. Net sales less gross margin before discounts gives total gross merchandise costs which may now be entered. The missing item, closing inventory at mercantile, is then derived by a subtraction process, that is, by deducting total gross merchandise costs from the sum of gross cost of merchandise handled and alteration and workroom costs. The correctness of the result may be checked by multiplying the closing inventory at retail, $26,675, by the cost percentage 57.44 (complement of the markon percentage of 42.56).

The final figure necessary to complete the statement is the amount of discounts earned. For this purpose it is assumed that the discount records show that this department has earned 4.15 per cent of net sales, or $3,849.

This illustration of a gross margin statement differs in one respect from that commonly used in published statistics. In published statistics discounts earned are deducted from the gross cost of merchandise sold in order to express the net cost of merchandise sold, and workroom and alteration costs are then added to obtain total merchandise costs (net). Thus, only one gross margin figure is shown—the one including discounts. The form illustrated here is more useful for operating purposes and is the one more commonly used for internal statements. Since it shows percentage of gross margin before discounts, comparison can be made between such gross margin and percentage of cumulative markon (which is based upon purchases and inventories gross of discounts) and attention can be directed to the extent by which gross margin has been reduced by retail reductions and alteration and workroom costs.

Controls Over the Stock Ledger

As was stated earlier in this chapter, the cost method is more practicable than the retail method for certain departments. It is not unusual to find both methods in use at the same time, with the cost method used for only a comparatively small number of departments where a store has adopted general use of the retail method.

The stock ledger forms used for the retail method may also be used for recording, in the appropriate columns only, the merchandise figures of the cost departments (that is, departments controlled by the cost method). Where figures under both methods are included in a single stock record, the latter is controlled by accounts in the general ledger representing totals for all departments. Sometimes the figures of retail departments (that is, departments controlled by the retail method) are controlled in the general ledger separately from cost department figures, with two distinct stock records being maintained.

In the stock ledger or ledgers there should be control (summary) sheets for entry of totals that are in agreement with amounts reflected in the general ledger. If there is a single stock ledger it will contain a control sheet for retail departments, one for cost departments, and a third for totals of all departments. The totals sheet should be in agreement with the general ledger. The control sheets in the stock ledgers represent totals of the respective dollar columns of the individual department sheets. However, the total inventory *at mercantile* for the retail departments is the sum of the computed amounts entered on the departmental sheets. It cannot be computed in total from figures on the control sheet itself.

Usually, the general ledger contains control accounts for net sales and cost of purchases, the latter including all the elements of purchases. There will generally be a separate account for costs and revenues of workroom operations, with revenues including charges to departments as well as to customers. A separate control account will be required for the charges made to departments as alteration and workroom costs. Such charges include transfers of costs from the workrooms account and costs charged directly to departments for such items as labor payroll, supplies, and cleaning and dyeing. In some instances net operating costs of workrooms are entirely distributed to the departments served; alternatively, the workroom operations show net losses (or gains).

Two different procedures are followed with respect to the inventory account in the general ledger. Under one method the amount is not changed during a season or even during a fiscal year, whereas under the other the amount is changed each month (or at the end of each four- or five-week period) to bring it into agreement with the stock ledger. Under the first plan the general ledger is not in agreement, as to inventories or net profits, with the interim monthly balance sheets and income accounts. Under the other approach the books are always in agreement with financial statements. For this reason the latter method seems preferable. It is not necessary to close out sales, purchases, expenses, discounts, etc., to a monthly profit and loss account if an account is opened to reflect the change in inventory during the period. This makes it possible to obtain all the required elements of the income account directly from the general ledger, except closing inventory, which equals the opening inventory as adjusted by the account which reflects interim changes.

The practice of transferring sales and purchases accounts monthly is not recommended because it complicates the feature of control by the general ledger over the stock ledger.

Stock Ledger Elements Not Subject to Control

There are two important component elements of the stock ledger not subject to control as part of the balanced system of accounts. These are the retail of purchases and price changes, notably markdowns. The retail of purchases as recorded in the stock ledger should represent the sum of the originally marked retail prices of merchandise placed in stock. Ordinarily, there is no mathematical proof of the accuracy of the retail of purchases, as there is with the cost of purchases. There may be errors in extensions or in tabulations, but they cannot be discovered by cross checking against a control account. This possible source of error in the operation of the retail method is important and merits particular attention for checking and rechecking. Markdown calculations and tabulations represent another source of possible errors under the retail method. They cannot be controlled to the same degree as sales. In this respect also, it is important that sufficient attention be directed to obtaining accuracy in the figures. There should be an accountability for the numerical sequence of all price change reports, and calculations and summarizations should be rechecked. In addition, each price change sheet should be examined for authorized signatures which evidence that the changes in price have actually been made on the merchandise.

When adequate care is exercised in recordings under the retail method, the shrinkages disclosed by its operation should properly represent the results of thefts, price tampering, and damage or losses.

SOME FORMULAS OF THE RETAIL METHOD

Under the retail method there is an interrelation among cumulative markon, retail reductions, alteration and workroom costs, and gross margin before discounts. The interrelation may be expressed by formulas applicable both to dollar amounts and to percentages.

Ch. 6   INVENTORY DOLLAR CONTROL   125

The percentages are expressed in terms of the common denominator, retail. Cumulative markon percentage is based upon the retail of merchandise handled during a period, but percentages of retail reductions, alteration and workroom costs, and gross margin are based upon the retail of merchandise sold during the period.

Illustrations of certain of these formulas follow. Dollar amounts and percentages are the same as those used in the illustration of a gross margin statement (page 121):

	Amounts	Percentages on Net Sales	Percentages on Merchandise Handled
Net sales	$92,743	100.00%	
Markdowns	5,653	6.10	
Sales discounts	1,079	1.16	
Shrinkage provisions	368	.40	
Total retail reductions	7,100	7.66	
Gross cost of merchandise sold	57,352	61.84	
Alteration and workroom costs	612	.66	
Gross margin before discounts	34,779	37.50	
Cumulative markon			42.56%
Mercantile percentage			57.44%

Gross Cost of Merchandise Sold

Gross cost of merchandise sold equals the sum of net sales and total retail reductions, reduced to cost by application of the mercantile percentage. The same formula is used to derive percentage of gross cost of merchandise sold. For example:

	Dollars At Retail	Dollars Retail × 57.44%	Percentages At Retail	Percentages Retail × 57.44%
Net sales	$92,743	$53,274	100.00%	57.44%
Total retail reductions	7,100	4,078	7.66	4.40
Gross cost of merchandise sold	$99,843	$57,352	107.66%	61.84%

Total Gross Merchandise Cost

Total gross merchandise cost is obtained by adding alteration and workroom costs to gross cost of merchandise sold. The percentage of total gross merchandise cost is obtained in the same manner. For the present example, $612 and .66 per cent, respectively, are to be added. Total gross merchandise cost is, therefore, $57,964, and the percentage thereof on net sales is 62.50. The results obtained represent cost of sales before deduction of discounts earned. Discounts are not considered in the present discussion because it is desired to illustrate derivation of gross margin before discounts. The relation of gross margin to cumulative markon is more clearly demonstrated when discounts are excluded because, as previously noted, cumulative markon is based upon figures that are gross of discounts.

Gross Margin

Formulas for gross margin and percentage of gross margin (both before discounts) may be stated as follows:

> Gross margin equals net sales times the percentage of cumulative markon, minus retail reductions at mercantile, and minus alteration and workroom costs.

> Percentage of gross margin equals the cumulative markon percentage minus the mercantile percentage of retail reductions and minus the percentage of alteration and workroom costs.

Illustration of these formulas, based upon figures already used, is as follows:

	Dollars		Percentages	
	At Retail	At Retail × 42.56% or at Mercantile	At Retail	At Retail × 42.56% or at Mercantile
Net sales	$92,743	$39,469	100.00%	42.56%
Retail reductions	7,100		7.66	
At mercantile		4,078		4.40
		35,391		38.16
Alteration and workroom costs		612		.66
Gross margin (before discounts)		$34,779		37.50%

The foregoing example illustrates how gross margin is reduced from the margin that would have been earned on the basis of cumulative markon, through the adverse effect on gross margin of markdowns, sales discounts, shrinkages, and alteration and workroom costs.

Cumulative Markon Percentage

Further illustration of the foregoing statements and examples can be found in the formula for deriving cumulative markon percentage:

$$\text{Cumulative markon percentage} = \frac{\text{Gross margin (before discounts)} + \text{Total retail reductions} + \text{Alteration and workroom costs}}{\text{Net sales} + \text{Total retail reductions}}$$

The formula may be worked out in both dollars and percentages, as follows (figures are the same as in previous examples):

	Dollars	Percentages
Gross margin (before discounts)	$34,779	37.50%
Retail reductions	7,100	7.66
Alteration and workroom costs	612	.66
Totals	$42,491	45.82%
Divide the foregoing totals by total of:		
Net sales and retail reductions	$99,843	107.66%
Result = Cumulative markon percentage	42.56%	42.56%

Cost of Sales

Cost of sales is based upon the following factors:

Inventory, beginning of period —
Purchases —
　Total = Gross cost of merchandise handled —
Deduct: Inventory, close of period —
　Difference = Gross cost of merchandise sold —
Alteration and workroom costs —
　Sum = Total gross merchandise costs —
Deduct: Discounts earned —
　Difference = Total net merchandise costs —

The factors stated are those which appear in a formal statement of cost of sales. However, other factors of cost—sales discounts, markdowns, and shrinkages—are not separately presented in a formal statement of cost of sales and gross margin.

Sales discounts are reflected in net sales, because the net sales are less than they would have been if a portion of the sales prices had not been rebated in the form of discounts to customers.

Markdowns are reflected partly in net sales and partly in inventories; that is, in sales for markdowns taken on items which have been sold, and in inventories for markdowns taken on items which are unsold at the close of a period. Markdowns not actually taken at the inventory date, but anticipated and provided for by means of inventory reserves for future markdowns, have the same effect on gross margin as have markdowns actually taken. Markdowns constitute a loss of part of the anticipated gross margin reflected in the marking of goods when they were first placed on sale. The loss of such anticipated gross margin effectively will be reflected in sales to the extent the merchandise is sold. Markdowns taken or provided for on merchandise in inventory represent losses expected to be realized in an ensuing accounting period. Both the realized loss and the anticipated loss are reflected in the operating results of the accounting period just ended. In effect, good accounting practice requires the recording of known or properly anticipated losses by computing inventories on the basis of realizable amounts, rather than carrying inventory amounts forward into a new period in excess of such amounts. Gross margins, therefore, although related to sales of a period, are affected by losses on merchandise which will not be sold until subsequent periods.

Shrinkages represent losses caused by disappearance, destruction, donation, or other disposition (e.g., samples) of merchandise which might otherwise have been sold to produce gross margin. The effect of shrinkages on gross margin is reflected through inventories since there is less merchandise to be carried forward to the new accounting period. Shrinkages increase the cost of sales although they have no direct relationship to sales.

Sales discounts, markdowns, and shrinkages are recorded in retail amounts, and percentages of these amounts are expressed in relationship to net sales. Net sales constitute a common denominator for expressing relationships, and the effect of the various elements of costs and losses upon gross margin can be determined from ratios based upon this common denominator. The amount of loss from sales discounts, markdowns, and shrinkages is not the retail at which they are recorded, but is the difference between retail and the cumulative markon contained in such retail. In other words, the amount lost is the amount required to purchase enough merchandise for sale, on the basis of the cumulative markon, to realize the retail total of sales discounts, markdowns, and shrinkages. For this reason, cost of the elements mentioned is determined by applying to their retail sum the mercantile percentage (100 minus percentage of cumulative markon).

Disposition of Markon

The gross income of a mercantile business arises principally from markons. As stated in preceding discussions, some part of markon provided is lost by reason of reductions and alteration and workroom costs. The remainder of markon is used to meet operating expenses, and it is hoped that some residue remains as profit. It is, therefore, obviously important that sufficient markon be provided when retailing invoices and that markon be safeguarded so that as little as possible be lost in reductions or alteration and workroom costs. It is also informative to have a record of the portion of remaining markon used to meet operating expenses and the balance that is realized as operating profit before discounts. By adding discounts earned, total operating profit is derived.

The forms on pages 130–32, both captioned "Report of Markon and Its Disposition," illustrate the previously cited accounting and financial reporting principles.

In effect, these forms show how departmental statements for a designated period may be prepared to show markon originally provided, the portion carried forward to a future period in the closing inventory, and the disposition of the amount available, with the uses made of markons realized. By indicating the percentages of markon used for various purposes, as related to total markon provided, a clear picture of the disposition of markon is supplied. This serves to emphasize the importance of conserving for expenses and profit as large a portion of markon as possible, rather than losing it in reductions and unknown costs.

Different types of forms can be utilized to present these data for separate departments, for groups of departments, or for retail departments in total. The first form provides more detail than the

REPORT OF MARKON AND ITS DISPOSITION
(Reconciliation Between Markon Provided and Total Operating Income)

	Markon	Markon Percentages	Amounts of Items — Cost or Mercantile	Amounts of Items — Retail
Provided:				
Markon in inventory, beginning of period	$175,000	35.00%	$ 325,000	$ 500,000
Markon in current purchases	562,500	37.50	937,500	1,500,000
Markups less cancellations	10,000			10,000
Total provided	$747,500	37.19%	1,262,500	2,010,000
Available for future:				
Markon in inventory, close of period	223,140	37.19%	376,860	600,000
			$ 885,640	$1,410,000
		Percentage of Used to Total Markon		
Total used	$524,360	70.15%		

		Percentages of Total Markon Used	Percentages on Sales
Total markon used	$524,360	100.00%	40.34%
Lost:			
Markdowns, less cancellations	$ 70,000	13.35%	5.39%
Sales discounts	15,000	2.86	1.15
Shortages	25,000	4.77	1.92
Total reductions	110,000	20.98	8.46
Alteration and workroom costs	5,000	.95	.39
	115,000	21.93	8.85
Earned:			
Gross margin before discounts	409,360	78.07	31.49
Discounts earned	40,000		3.08
Gross margin after discounts	449,360		34.57
Expended: Operating expenses	400,000	76.28	30.77
Realized:			
Operating income:			
From markon	9,360	1.79%	.72
From discounts earned	40,000		3.08
	$ 49,360		3.80%

Note: Deductions at retail amount to $1,410,000, of which retail reductions are $110,000, leaving $1,300,000 for sales.

REPORT OF MARKON AND ITS DISPOSITION
(Reconciliation Between Markon Provided and Total Operating Income)

	Markon		Markon Percentages
Provided:			
Markon in inventory, beginning of period	$175,000		35.00%
Markon in current purchases	562,500		37.50
Markups, less cancellations	10,000		
Total provided		$747,500	37.19
Available for future:			
Markon in inventory, close of period		223,140	37.19%

			Percentage of Used to Total Markon
Total used		$524,360	70.15%

			Percentages of Used to Total Markon
Total markon used		$524,360	100.00%
Lost:			
Markdowns, less cancellations	$ 70,000		13.35%
Sales discounts	15,000		2.86
Shortages	25,000		4.77
Total reductions	110,000		20.98
Alteration and workroom costs	5,000		.95
		115,000	21.93
Earned: Gross margin before discounts		409,360	78.07
Expended: Operating expenses		400,000	76.28
Realized: Operating income before discounts earned		9,360	1.79%
Discounts earned		40,000	
Operating income		$ 49,360	

second, in order to make clearer the manner in which the figures are compiled. While the second form omits some figures, it does supply the pertinent data. Reports may be made monthly (or for a four- or five-week period), for other intermediate periods, or for seasons or fiscal years.

7

Accounting Problems of the Retail Method

Introduction

The retail method, comparatively simple in theory, rests upon two fundamental assumptions: (1) as a method of averaging it will be applied where conditions are relatively homogeneous and averages are representative of current conditions, and (2) since retail prices are basic in the application of the method, marked retail prices shall reflect the seller's market. Actually, these conditions are present in variable degrees and, in fact, at times may not be present. Moreover, many special circumstances and conditions can be encountered in the practical application of the retail method. In this chapter a number of these special situations are considered, situations which provide useful insights into the practical applications of the retail method. The following subjects, as related to the retail method of inventory control, are discussed:

    Cancellations of markdowns and markups
    Effect of averaging high-markon and low-markon goods
    Inaccuracies reduced by departmentalization
    Separate markons for imported and domestic goods
    Effect of applying cumulative markons to marked-down goods in stock
    Effect of abnormal relationships on results of retail method

Markon percentage averages on time basis, and trends of markon percentages
Seasonal calculation of markon percentages
Monthly calculation of markon percentages
Seasonal vs. monthly calculation of markon percentages
Choice of cumulation period
Special sales events
Variable prices
Allowances from vendors
Departmental merchandise transfers
Merchandise turnover

Cancellations of Markdowns and Markups

In applying the retail inventory method it is basic that markups are taken into account in determining departmental cumulative markons but that markdowns are not. However, an exception to this general rule occurs in those relatively unusual circumstances when a markup represents the cancellation of a previous markdown. Since such markups cancel or offset markdowns (some of which may have been made temporarily for special sales), they should be applied against the markdowns. Under such circumstances, in the accounts, markdowns should be stated net of the subsequent markups that cancel markdowns or portions of such markdowns.

In the ordinary course of business, a reduction in selling price is deemed to be a markdown, without regard to the factors that may have occasioned the price reduction. The unusual circumstances that provide the exception are generally limited to the correction of an error in the initial markup or an understanding, at the very outset, that the markup applied to the merchandise is temporary and will be reversed with respect to unsold merchandise on hand. In these unusual circumstances it is proper to consider the markdown as a cancellation of the markup. With this exception, amounts added to cost to derive the selling price, whether in one or two or more of a series of markons and markups, are considered to enter into the retail price which is compared with cost in determining cumulative markon.

The foregoing distinctions cannot be too emphatically stressed. Before a markup is applied to reduce a markdown, it should be known that the markup actually cancels a markdown or portion of a markdown taken within the same season, and that the markdown was taken as a temporary measure or was made incorrectly. It is equally important to guard against the incorrect application of markdowns to reduce markups (and, therefore, cumulative markon). If price changes are treated incorrectly in material amounts, the result is a serious misstatement of inventory valuation, and consequently of gross margin.

The following illustration compares the results obtained in recording price changes correctly and incorrectly, and clearly illustrates the importance of recording them correctly.

Illustration.

	Cost or Mercantile	Retail
Assumptions:		
Opening inventory	$50,000	$85,000
Purchases	60,000	90,000
Markdowns		25,000
Markups		5,000
Markdown cancellations		7,000

Case A: Assume that the markups and markdown cancellations are correctly recorded so that the procedure for computing the closing inventory would be as follows:

	Cost or Mercantile	Retail	Cumulative Markon Percentage
Opening inventory	$ 50,000	$ 85,000	
Purchases	60,000	90,000	
	$110,000	175,000	
Markups		5,000	
		180,000	38.889%
Markdowns, less markdown cancellations of $7,000		18,000	
		162,000	
Sales		100,000	
Closing inventory	$ 37,889°	$ 62,000	

° $62,000 × 61.111% = $37,889.

Case B: Assume that the markups of $5,000 were incorrectly offset against the markdowns of $25,000, so that the procedure for computing the closing inventory was as follows:

	Cost or Mercantile	Retail	Cumulative Markon Percentage
Opening inventory	$ 50,000	$ 85,000	
Purchases	60,000	90,000	
	$110,000	175,000	37.143%
Markdowns		13,000	
		162,000	
Sales		100,000	
Closing inventory	$ 38,971*	$ 62,000	

* $62,000 × 62.857% = $38,971.

As is apparent, the erroneous treatment of markups in Case B resulted in an overstatement of closing inventory of $1,082 ($38,971 − $37,889), with a corresponding erroneous overstatement of gross margin as proved by the following computations:

	Case A	Case B
Sales	$100,000	$100,000
Cumulative markon percentage	38.889%	37.143%
Gross margin before depressing impact of markdowns	$ 38,889(a)	$ 37,143(a)
Markdowns	$ 18,000	$ 13,000
Cost multiplier	61.111%	62.857%
Impact of markdowns	($ 11,000)(b)	($ 8,172)(b)
Gross margin (a) − (b)	$ 27,889	$ 28,971

The gross margin in Case B ($28,971) exceeds the gross margin in Case A ($27,889) in the amount of the aforementioned inventory overstatement of $1,082. As illustrated, the practical effect of misclassifying markups as markdown cancellations is to erroneously increase gross margin.

Where merchandise is marked down for a day or two during a temporary promotional sale, and the unsold portion is restored to original selling price, there is no question that the markup on the unsold portion should be offset against the markdown on the whole quantity. Similarly, although a relatively rare occurrence, there may be a temporary markup for a day or two cancelled by a markdown. In this rare case it is proper to offset markdown against markup. However, when in the ordinary course of business merchandise that has been marked up is subsequently marked down (or, more rarely, when merchandise that has been marked down is subsequently marked up), the price changes should not be offset against each other.

Effect of Averaging High-Markon and Low-Markon Goods

It is possible that some goods entering into the cost or mercantile and the retail totals of merchandise handled during a period may bear a relatively high markon and some other goods a relatively low markon. As an example, the average percentage of markon on all merchandise handled in a department during a season may be 35. In arriving at this figure there may be merchandise, carried over in the beginning inventory or included in subsequent purchases, which carried various percentages of markon, say, 30, 35, and 40 per cent. The average mercantile percentage of merchandise handled by the department is 65 (100 − 35), and this percentage is applied to the retail inventory in order to arrive at mercantile. However, in order to derive an accurate inventory valuation, the relative proportions of goods bearing 30, 35, and 40 per cent markon in the inventory at the end of the period should be the same as in the total of merchandise handled during the period. Stated differently, in terms of markon percentages, the closing inventory should be representative of total merchandise handled during the period. When the closing inventory is not representative of total merchandise handled during the period, two results are possible under the retail method (except as may be modified by marked-down goods in stock):

1. An inventory stated at less than cost when closing inventory includes more high-cost (i.e., low-markon) goods than the average found in total merchandise handled.
2. An inventory stated at higher than cost when closing inventory includes more low-cost (i.e., high-markon) goods than the average found in total merchandise handled.

In situations involving departments handling high-markon and low-markon lines, it may be best to subdivide the department or at least classify merchandise statistics as set forth in the following paragraphs.

Inaccuracies Reduced by Departmentalization

The prospective problems posed by a large range in markon percentages and the possibly unrepresentative nature of the closing inventory are questions that must be considered on a case-by-case basis. When a store is adequately departmentalized, the likelihood of serious error is lessened. If it is impracticable to break up a department which consistently carries merchandise bearing widely differing markon percentages, stock records may be set up showing sales, purchases, and stocks for different sections within the department. Such records facilitate satisfactory operation of the retail method and aid in planning the elements of departmental operation. As a practical matter, certain retailers who maintain the stock ledger by merchandise classifications, rather than by the conventional selling departments, are effectively implementing a similar type of recordkeeping. The amount of information thereby provided is deemed essential for more effective merchandise control.

Illustration. The following example illustrates the manner in which operating results are distorted in a department with high and low markon percentage merchandise, when the rate of sale of the two classes differs. Low-markon merchandise usually moves faster than high-markon merchandise. For the sake of simplicity we assume two separate departments, A and B, and then show how the sum of the resultant inventories is affected by combining these two dissimilar departments in one department, C. The figures of Department C equal the aggregate of figures of Departments A and B, except that, as noted, C's closing inventory at mercantile differs significantly from the combined inventories at mercantile of A and B, *notwithstanding* that C's inventory at retail is equal to the combined inventories at retail of A and B.

Department A (low markon, rapid turnover):

	Cost or Mercantile	Retail	Cumulative Markon Percentage
Opening inventory	$ 40,000	$ 50,000	
Purchases	100,000	130,000	
	$140,000	180,000	22.22%
Markdowns		10,000	
		170,000	
Sales		140,000	
Closing inventory	$ 23,334	$ 30,000	

Department B (high markon, slow turnover):

	Cost or Mercantile	Retail	Cumulative Markon Percentage
Opening inventory	$ 75,000	$150,000	
Purchases	60,000	140,000	
	$135,000	290,000	53.45%
Markdowns		20,000	
		270,000	
Sales		130,000	
Closing inventory	$ 65,170	$140,000	

	Mercantile	Retail
Inventory, Department A	$ 23,334	$ 30,000
Inventory, Department B	65,170	140,000
Inventory, both departments	$ 88,504	$170,000

The result would not have been the same if these two dissimilar departments had been combined into one department, C, as follows:

Department C (Departments A and B combined):

	Cost or Mercantile	Retail	Cumulative Markon Percentage
Opening inventory	$115,000	$200,000	
Purchases	160,000	270,000	
	$275,000	470,000	41.49%
Markdowns		30,000	
		440,000	
Sales		270,000	
Closing inventory	$ 99,467	$170,000	

This inventory of $99,467 for Department C compares with $88,504, the aggregate for Departments A and B separately computed. Since the retail inventory method is an average method, it is clear from this sample that it should be utilized only when the use of averages does not provide distortive results.

Separate Markons for Imported and Domestic Goods

As a measure of departmental subdivision for the purpose of refining the averages, markons are sometimes separately accumulated for the imported and for the domestic merchandise handled in a single department. Imported merchandise ordinarily carries different markons than domestic merchandise. Such separate accumulation of markons is worthwhile principally for departments which handle a relatively large amount of imported goods. Departmental inventories are tabulated to obtain a total of the imported merchandise on hand as distinct from the total of domestic merchandise on hand. Mercantile of each subdivision of the inventory is computed separately by application of the respective markons.

Effect of Applying Cumulative Markons to Marked-Down Goods in Stock

Applying cumulative markon percentages to inventories which have been marked down from original retail prices results in an inventory at mercantile which is less than original cost. The purpose of the retail method is not to derive the original cost of merchandise on hand. Rather, it is intended to derive an inventory valuation stated at the lower of cost or market. In any determination of operating results, it is essential that inventories be determined on this basis in order to avoid overstatement of profits and of assets, always bearing in mind that in the retail trade the term "market" should represent selling market less a normal markon, rather than replacement cost.

Effect of Abnormal Relationships on Results of Retail Method

Discussions in preceding paragraphs have brought out the fact that the degree of accuracy to be obtained from the retail method in deriving inventories at mercantile depends largely upon: (1) the homogeneity of each departmental inventory with respect to the markon percentages of constituent elements; and (2) the extent to which markdowns have been properly recognized.

It should always be borne in mind that the retail inventory method, because it is based upon averages, occasionally produces unusual and unexpected figures because transactions during the period may be abnormal in relation to each other. A better understanding of the principles of the retail method and of its mathematical computations may be gained by study of some results caused by such abnormal relations of transactions. The three examples which follow are designed to illustrate the effect of selected abnormalities on results. In actual practice there may be compensating and offsetting distortions of results; however, distortions

Ch. 7   ACCOUNTING PROBLEMS OF THE RETAIL METHOD   141

may also be accentuated by cumulative effects. Consequently, one sound procedure where abnormal conditions exist to a marked degree is to consider departmental subdivision as a means of correction. As the following examples clearly evidence, there is a need for continual care in interpreting and analyzing operating results for possible distortions.

Illustration 1. Small opening inventory, large purchases with very low markon, considerable markdowns, but only nominal sales.

	Cost or Mercantile	Retail	Markon Percentage
Opening inventory	$ 10,000	$ 20,000	
Purchases	200,000	250,000	
	$210,000	270,000	22.22%
Markdowns		30,000	
		240,000	
Sales		10,000	
Closing inventory at retail		$230,000	

Inventory on a cumulative markon basis = $178,894

Comments. Obviously, large closing inventory and few sales indicate the probability of large future markdowns. The cumulative markon basis does little more than provide for markdowns already taken.

Illustration 2. Opening inventory entirely sold, but with heavy markdowns; none of the current purchases moved.

	Cost or Mercantile	Retail	Markon Percentage
Opening inventory	$ 60,000	$100,000	
Purchases	30,000	50,000	
	$ 90,000	150,000	40.00%
Markdowns, all applicable to opening inventory, none to current purchases		60,000	
		90,000	
Sales, clean-out of opening inventory of $100,000 after markdowns of $60,000 (none of current purchases sold)		40,000	
Closing inventory at retail		$ 50,000 *	

Inventory on a cumulative markon basis = $30,000

* It is noteworthy that this inventory represents current purchases, without any markdowns, and that actual cost of these purchases was $30,000.

Comments. In this extreme illustration, the inventory is overstated, notwithstanding that the retail method results in inventory of $30,000 which is at actual cost. Given the absence of markdowns on current purchases and the absence of related sales, there has been an obvious deferral of markdowns which will have to be taken subsequent to the fiscal closing. Effectively, the $30,000 is stated in excess of market. This illustrates how the retail method may provide misleading results when there is a failure to take markdowns on a timely basis.

Illustration 3. Opening inventory entirely sold, without markdowns in this period; one-half of current purchases moved with heavy markdowns; no markdowns taken on remaining stock.

	Cost or Mercantile	Retail	Markon Percentage
Opening inventory	$30,000	$ 50,000	
Purchases	60,000	100,000	
	$90,000	150,000	40.00%
Markdowns, all applicable to one-half of current purchases which were sold at a sacrifice because of a bad buy; no markdowns taken on other half of current purchases which remain, or on opening inventory, which is after markdowns in previous periods, but which was sold in entirety and without markdowns in this period		30,000	
		120,000	
Sales, clean-up of opening inventory without markdowns during period and sale of one-half of current purchases at heavy sacrifice		70,000	
Closing inventory at retail		$ 50,000	

Inventory on a cumulative markon basis = $30,000

Comments. It is noteworthy that inventory on hand represents one-half of current purchases which have not been marked down at all. This half of current purchases cost $30,000, so that its present valuation is at cost, which probably is in excess of a conservative market value.

Markon Percentage Averages on Time Basis, and Trends of Markon Percentages

In the preceding paragraphs discussion centered on the degree of accuracy of the retail method at any given point in time, considering the impact of varying rates of markon. The basic question raised was whether, at any given point in time, the averaging of high-margin and low-margin items concurrently handled in a department resulted in an inventory valuation that was reasonable and sufficiently accurate. A somewhat related question is the extent to which averages on a time basis are accurate.

Clearly, it is not beyond the range of possibility that markon percentages may fluctuate considerably from month to month or progressively throughout a season, either upward or downward. The problem is the extent to which the cumulative markon percentages may be affected by such fluctuations and may be unrepresentative of the inventory on hand. To illustrate, assume a situation in which markon percentages have been progressively increasing and recent purchases have moved rapidly so that there is a large portion of stock on hand dating from the commencement of the season. Under these circumstances, the larger margin reflected in the cumulative markon, because of the percentages of margin on the later months' purchases, may result in the older stock being carried at somewhat less than it would have been carried if the markon percentage had remained constant. This, of course, will result in a more conservative valuation of inventory. However, if opening stock has not moved in a period of increasing price spread, or rising retail prices, it should be carried at somewhat less than cost.

Assume, however, the same progressively increasing markon percentages but with practically all of the stock on hand comprising recently acquired purchases. Under these circumstances, there will be a tendency toward valuing the inventory above actual cost since the cumulative markon percentage will be somewhat lower than the markon applicable to the more recent purchases.

On the other hand, if the markon percentages have been decreasing, part of the older merchandise on hand (that portion which has not been marked down) will be carried at values in excess of cost, and part (that portion which has been marked down) probably in excess of the lower of cost or market. A preponderance of more recent merchandise on hand will probably result in an inventory valued at somewhat less than cost, by reason of the effect of higher markon percentages that enter into the cumulative figures through the opening inventory and purchases in the earlier months of the season.

Seasonal Calculation of Markon Percentages

The seasonal method for calculation of markon percentages provides for the accumulation of departmental markon for an entire season; that is, for six calendar months (or 26 calendar weeks) ending in July or January. For intermediate, season-to-date periods, cumulative markon percentages are used. For example, at the end of February, the cumulative markon is based upon the inventory at February 1, mercantile and retail, plus purchases for the month, cost and retail. At the end of March the markon is based upon the inventory of February 1 and the aggregate purchases of February and March, and so on during the season. By the end of July, the cumulative markon covers not only the opening inventory of February 1, mercantile and retail, but also the cumulative purchases for the six months, February to July, inclusive. The markon reflected in the inventory of February 1 is, in turn, a cumulative markon for the preceding six months to that date, including opening inventory and purchases for the six months.

The seasonal basis appears to be rather generally used among retailers. For that reason it is illustrated in the stock ledger forms presented in Chapter 6.

Monthly Calculation of Markon Percentages

Under the monthly calculation procedure, the opening inventory at February 1 and the purchases for February form the basis for the determination of a new book inventory at March 1. Similarly, that inventory, together with March purchases, forms the basis for a new inventory at April 1, and such procedure is continued for each month thereafter. This differs from the method illustrated by the departmental stock ledgers presented in Chapter 6, where intermediate inventories do not affect the season results. As noted earlier, only the inventory at the beginning of each season plus seasonal purchases to date are employed in the monthly calculation of markon percentages.

Seasonal vs. Monthly Calculation of Markon Percentages

In the keeping of retail stock ledgers the question arises whether monthly (or four- or five-week) closings should be made in preference to seasonal closings. In the operation of the retail method, final inventory at mercantile as at the end of a fiscal period may be materially different when determined on the basis of monthly closings as compared to a valuation computed on a seasonal basis.

Whether the seasonal basis results in lower or higher inventory than the monthly basis depends entirely upon the various factors involved. It cannot be generalized that one method always results in a higher inventory than the other; rather, the result will depend upon the nature, extent, and trend of the variable factors. This is illustrated in the examples on pages 146 and 147, where the same retail figures are used but markon percentages are made to vary, in one case progressively upward and in the other case progressively downward.

The second example reverses the order of the monthly markon percentages of the first example, but the same opening inventory at retail and the same monthly purchases at retail are used in both illustrations.

Choice of Cumulation Period

The rapidity of turnover should be taken into consideration when deciding whether to use monthly or seasonal periods for cumulation. If goods are cleared largely from stock within short periods, the monthly basis may be best because the more recent months' markons generally are applicable to the closing inventory. The use of the seasonal basis generally tends to stabilize the markon percentage, giving effect to markon in opening inventory and to the purchases of the season as a whole.

With diverse conditions as to the movement of stocks, there would seem to be no good reason why different periods should not be used for different departments, for example, using the seasonal basis generally, but using a monthly or quarterly basis for merchandise departments where clearance of stock is rapid.

Strictly interpreted, the Treasury Regulations (see Section 1.471-8) appear to call for cumulation throughout an entire year, rather than seasonally or monthly. However, in practice, the Internal Revenue Service has not objected to either method, or a combination of methods, consistently followed. In any event, the results of the retail method on any basis should be tested and reviewed to ascertain that the inventory derived is warranted by, and is reasonable in light of, the fact pattern.

EXAMPLE WHERE MARKON PERCENTAGES INCREASE PROGRESSIVELY

Seasonal Basis

	Cost or Mercantile	Retail	Markon Percentages
Opening inventory	$14,000	$20,000	30%
Purchases:			
February	5,520	8,000	31
March	6,120	9,000	32
April	5,360	8,000	33
May	3,960	6,000	34
June	3,250	5,000	35
July	1,950	3,000	35
	$40,160	59,000	31.9%
Sales and markdowns		40,000	
Closing inventory	$12,940	$19,000	31.9%

Monthly Basis

	Opening Inventories	Purchases	Totals	Markon Percentages
Cost or mercantile:				
February	$14,000	$5,520	$19,520	30.3%
March	16,030	6,120	22,150	30.8
April	17,300	5,360	22,660	31.3
May	16,490	3,960	20,450	31.8
June	13,640	3,250	16,890	32.4
July	12,840	1,950	14,790	32.8

	Opening Inventories	Purchases	Totals	Sales, Etc.	Closing Inventories Retail	Closing Inventories Mercantile
Retail:						
February	$20,000	$8,000	$28,000	$5,000	$23,000	$16,030
March	23,000	9,000	32,000	7,000	25,000	17,300
April	25,000	8,000	33,000	9,000	24,000	16,490
May	24,000	6,000	30,000	10,000	20,000	13,640
June	20,000	5,000	25,000	6,000	19,000	12,840
July	19,000	3,000	22,000	3,000	19,000	12,770

Closing inventory:
On seasonal basis $12,940
On monthly basis 12,770

EXAMPLE WHERE MARKON PERCENTAGES DECREASE PROGRESSIVELY

Seasonal Basis

	Cost or Mercantile	Retail	Markon Percentages
Opening inventory	$13,000	$20,000	35 %
Purchases:			
February	5,200	8,000	35
March	5,940	9,000	34
April	5,360	8,000	33
May	4,080	6,000	32
June	3,450	5,000	31
July	2,100	3,000	30
Totals	$39,130	59,000	33.7%
Sales and markdowns		40,000	
Closing inventory	$12,600	$19,000	33.7%

Monthly Basis

	Opening Inventories	Purchases	Totals	Markon Percentages
Cost or mercantile:				
February	$13,000	$5,200	$18,200	35 %
March	14,950	5,940	20,890	34.7
April	16,330	5,360	21,690	34.3
May	15,770	4,080	19,850	33.8
June	13,240	3,450	16,690	33.2
July	12,700	2,100	14,800	32.7

	Opening Inventories	Purchases	Totals	Sales, Etc.	Closing Inventories Retail	Closing Inventories Mercantile
Retail:						
February	$20,000	$8,000	$28,000	$ 5,000	$23,000	$14,950
March	23,000	9,000	32,000	7,000	25,000	16,330
April	25,000	8,000	33,000	9,000	24,000	15,770
May	24,000	6,000	30,000	10,000	20,000	13,240
June	20,000	5,000	25,000	6,000	19,000	12,700
July	19,000	3,000	22,000	3,000	19,000	12,790

Closing inventory:
On seasonal basis $12,600
On monthly basis   12,790

Special Sales Events

A store or its various departments will, at times, have special sales events. On occasion, special purchases are made for the sales events and there is no important variation in markon from the department's usual performance. Frequently, special sales events may represent considerable concessions on the part of the store; that is, the difference in price as compared with usual offerings may represent a considerable reduction from the store's customary markon. Such special sales events naturally tend to disrupt or disorganize any system of merchandise accounting which depends for accuracy upon a reasonable consistency of averages and of movements of merchandise.

If special sales form a material part of a department's operations, it may be advisable to subdivide the stock ledger accounts into "regular" and "special" classifications, maintaining separate markons, and thereby deriving more accurate inventory valuations. If there are no such subdivisions, accuracy in the records can be maintained by retailing the special merchandise utilizing the department's ordinary markon percentage and then entering a markdown for the difference between such derived retail and the offering price. These are, of course, "fictitious" markons and markdowns but the objective is desirable, and if the practice is not abused it should prove acceptable. In this regard, it should be recognized that any special merchandise remaining in inventory at the close of a season would be understated on the basis of the ordinary markon. Accordingly, if a material amount of such special merchandise remains in inventory, the imperfection may be corrected in one of two fashions: a markdown cancellation may be entered to raise the remaining portion to standard retail before applying the markon percentage; or two different markons may respectively be used in deriving the mercantile of the departmental inventory.

As a matter of statistical information, markdowns which are planned at time of purchase or before the offering of goods to the public should be tabulated separately from those markdowns that result from obsolete, damaged, or slow-selling stock, or that obviously reflect errors in purchasing or poor selling.

If special sales are relatively incidental in a department, it will probably be unnecessary to apply any correction factor for the differences in markons. In many such cases the low-markon merchandise will probably have only a negligible effect upon the departmental average.

Variable Prices

In the same category as special sales events problems are the questions which arise with respect to variable prices occasioned by variation in quantities sold. It is a general practice to make up certain articles into sets (for example, dinner service sets for stock patterns) for which the price may be somewhat different from the sum of prices of the component parts if sold separately. A different example of variable price occurs when prices less than marked retail are quoted to contract, wholesale, or institutional customers. Such special prices should be differentiated from regular discount terms allowed to individual customers or employees.

With regard to variable prices due to quantities sold or the combinations of articles into sets, there is, in theory, no difference from the special sales events just discussed. From a practical standpoint, except in special instances of importance, it is usually not feasible to tabulate and report these price changes as markdowns. As a matter of fact, this would be contrary to the theory and procedure that markdowns should be authorized before they are made effective, whereas these quantity changes in price are a matter of regular procedure. For the most part it may be satisfactory to consider that such price reductions are taken into account in the recording of departmental shrinkage provisions. The accounting records (retail of invoices) could reflect average retail prices of the items, rather than the highest or the lowest prices.

Reductions attributable to contract, wholesale, or institutional sales are variously treated according to the frequency with which such transactions occur and the general policy of the store. If such transactions are frequent, the store will sometimes operate a separate contract or wholesale department into which merchandise transfers are made from the various selling departments. It then becomes purely a problem for the contract department, which is one of those departments for which the retail method probably is not as satisfactory as the cost method or some modification of the cost method. If contract or wholesale transactions are rare, probably the best procedure is to put through special markdowns tabulated separately from markdowns in the usual course of business, a procedure which parallels the suggestion with respect to special sales events. An alternative procedure is to handle differences in price as special sales discounts.

Allowances from Vendors

Allowances from vendors are of several kinds. There are, for example, the so-called advertising allowances. Some of these allowances are clearly to be credited to advertising expense and should not in any way affect the merchandise stock accounts. Other advertising allowances may represent reductions of the purchase price of merchandise, and are properly applicable as credits to purchases. The definitive merchandise allowances or rebates of price may be received for different reasons. They may be granted by vendors as a form of price protection in a falling market, or they may represent quantity discounts based upon volume of merchandise purchases. Such allowances may be received during a season on current purchases or received at or after the close of a season or a year.

Merchandise allowances or price rebates, whether quantity discounts or not, may affect retail prices, or they may have no effect thereon. When retail prices are reduced as a consequence of an allowance, the retail of purchases should be credited with the amount of reduction, provided it is not in excess of the retail equivalent of the allowance received (determined on the basis of the cumulative or specific purchase markon percentage, whichever may be deemed appropriate under the circumstances). In other words, these reductions are not markdowns but are adjustments of the retail of purchases, provided, however, that, when the amount of retail reduction is in excess of the retail equivalent of the allowance, the excess is treated as a markdown. When no retail reduction follows a vendor's price allowance, the allowance is credited against purchases at cost with no adjustment of purchases at retail. This has the obvious effect of increasing the markon percentage.

When a considerable period of time intervenes between the specific dates merchandise was purchased and the receipt of material amounts of vendor credits, a special problem arises. This would ordinarily be the case with regard to seasonal or annual quantity or other allowances. A seasonal allowance distorts the purchase markon of the month in which it is entered, but for the season as a whole the markon may be only slightly affected, provided the markon is determined on the seasonal basis. An allowance on purchases of an entire year not only distorts the purchase markon of the month in which the allowance is entered but also affects the seasonal markon average. In this connection, it is necessary to consider whether the effect upon markon is great enough to warrant special procedure in handling an allowance of this type. It is desirable that markons not be unduly distorted, but allowances from vendors are proper departmental purchase adjustments and should enter into gross margin.

Two courses appear to be open where the distorting effect of purchase allowances is sufficient to call for special treatment. That part of the allowance not applicable to the current season may be treated as a special item of departmental gross margin, similar to discounts earned, and kept out of tabulations of purchases. In fact, the entire allowance may be so treated, including that part applicable to the current season; but this tends to keep the markon slightly lower than it otherwise would be, with a consequent tendency toward a corresponding inflation of inventory. Practically, however, the effect upon inventory may be so slight as not to require adjustment. Theoretically, it would be appropriate to estimate, at the close of each season, any allowances not yet received but accrued and applicable, and to appropriately adjust that season's purchases. The difference between the estimates already applied and the totals received will then fall into the purchases accumulations of the season of receipt.

Departmental Merchandise Transfers

Departmental merchandise transfers may be routine and may be required when one department requisitions merchandise from another department to fill an order. Such transfers are usually in relatively small amounts and, generally speaking, do not result in retail price changes. Merchandise is transferred out of the transferring department at marked retail and derived mercantile and is transferred into the receiving department at the same figures. It is possible that some departments so transferring merchandise may add a service charge or small percentage of profit, which effectively will be added to the mercantile of transfer. While this latter procedure will affect departmental cumulative markons, the effect may be so slight that it can probably be ignored, provided the method is used with care and extremes are avoided. Also, transfers at marked retail and derived mercantile may bear higher or lower markon percentages than are normal for the departments receiving the transfers. However, no special accounting procedure is ordinarily called for by such convenience transfers.

Accounting problems do arise under the retail method, however, when material amounts of transfers are made between departments having widely differing cumulative markon percentages, or when there is a significant disparity between the marked selling price in the transferring department and the anticipated selling price in the receiving department. Under these circumstances, the preferable approach is to use cost as the basis for the transfer.

Illustration. An upstairs department offers to transfer merchandise to a downstairs or basement department which is willing to take the merchandise. However, since the buyers of the respective departments are directly concerned with the results of their departments, it is necessary to agree on a mutually satisfactory transfer price. The following figures are assumed:

Upstairs Department:	
Retail of merchandise	$85,000
Markon percentage	42.857%
Downstairs Department:	
Expected retail of merchandise	$48,232
Markon percentage	37.800%
Cost of transferred merchandise as agreed upon by both buyers	$30,000

As far as the downstairs department is concerned, the records are correctly stated if the transfer is entered at cost of $30,000 and retail of $48,232. The effect of the transfer upon stock figures of the downstairs department may be illustrated as follows, assuming figures for merchandise handled, sales, and reductions are as shown:

	Cost or Mercantile	Retail	Markon Percentages
Merchandise handled	$320,000	$514,469	37.80%
Transfer-in	30,000	48,232	37.80
	$350,000	$562,701	37.80
Sales		$300,000	
Reductions		25,000	
		$325,000	
Closing inventory	$147,850	$237,701	37.80%

With respect to the upstairs department, the transfer-out at mercantile should be equal to the agreed-upon price of $30,000 and at the retail equivalent of this mercantile computed on the basis of the cumulative markon percentage before transfer. A markdown should then be taken for the difference between the marked retail of $85,000 and the computed retail of the transfer, as follows:

	Cost or Mercantile	Retail	Markon Percentages
Merchandise handled	$560,000	$980,000	42.857%
Transfer-out	30,000	52,500	42.857
	$530,000	$927,500	42.857
Markdown on transfer ($85,000 less $52,500)		$ 32,500	
Sales		600,000	
Reductions previously taken		40,000	
		$672,500	
Closing inventory	$145,715	$255,000	42.857%

In summary, under this method transfers are made as follows:

Retail of transfer-in = retail to be placed on goods in that department

Mercantile of transfer-in = retail of transfer-in, times the departmental mercantile percentage

Mercantile of transfer-out = mercantile of transfer-in

Retail of transfer-out = mercantile of transfer-out, divided by the departmental mercantile percentage

Markdown on transfer-out = excess of retail before transfer over retail of transfer-out

The method has certain advantages. The agreed-upon cost holds for both transferring and receiving departments, effectively keeping intact the "purchases" general ledger account. Further, the method maintains the accuracy of the markons in both departments and obviates any penalty to either department because of differences in customary markon percentages. It is true that the transfers-out at retail will not equal the transfers-in at retail. However, this "balancing" of retail as between the two departments is not essential "since the operation of the retail book inventory is a closed system within each department." [1]

Under an alternative method, the two buyers would agree on the

[1] "Retail Accounting Manual—Revised" (1976).

revised retail price of $48,232 for the merchandise transferred, and a new cost would be determined by utilizing the markon percentage of the transferring (upstairs) department. The upstairs department would then take a markdown measured by the difference between the original retail ($85,000) and the agreed-upon retail ($48,232), or $36,768. The receiving (downstairs) department would record the transfer-in at the same computed cost and agreed-upon retail utilized by the upstairs department. The effect on the upstairs department would be as follows:

	Cost or Mercantile	Retail	Markon Percentages
Merchandise handled	$560,000	$980,000	42.857%
Transfer-out	27,560	48,232	42.857
	$532,440	$931,768	42.857
Markdown on transfer ($85,000 less $48,232)		$ 36,768	
Sales		600,000	
Reductions		40,000	
		$676,768	
Closing inventory	$145,715	$255,000	42.857%

The effect on the downstairs department would be as follows:

	Cost or Mercantile	Retail	Markon Percentages
Merchandise handled	$320,000	$514,469	37.800%
Transfer-in	27,560	48,232	42.857
	$347,560	$562,701	38.234
Sales		$300,000	
Reductions		25,000	
		$325,000	
Closing inventory	$146,818	$237,701	38.234%

Merchandise Turnover

It is general retail practice to obtain turnover by dividing sales by average inventory at retail. Sometimes turnover is computed by dividing cost of sales by average inventory at mercantile. The first method is the one recommended. It gives a result different from that obtained under the second method, although it is often assumed that the two methods are interchangeable and produce identical results.

The following illustration shows the difference in result obtained in computing stock turns depending upon whether (1) sales are divided by inventory at retail or (2) cost of sales is divided by inventory at mercantile. Turnover is often obtained by utilizing an average inventory based upon thirteen month-end inventories. However, for purposes of this illustration, the average inventory has been derived by solely averaging the opening and closing inventories of a fiscal period.

	Cost or Mercantile	Retail	Cumulative Markon Percentage
Opening inventory	$100,000	$200,000	
Purchases	300,000	575,000	
	$400,000	775,000	48.3871%
Reductions		100,000	
		675,000	
Sales		425,000	
Closing inventory	$129,032	$250,000	

Summary of Merchandising Account

Sales		$425,000
Cost of sales:		
Opening inventory	$100,000	
Purchases	300,000	
	400,000	
Less: Closing inventory	129,032	270,968
Gross margin		$154,032
Average inventory at retail		$225,000
Average inventory at mercantile		$114,516

Turnover is computed as follows:

Sales divided by average inventory at retail (425,000/225,000) equals 1.88889.

Cost of sales divided by average inventory at mercantile (270,968/114,516) equals 2.36620.

The illustration chosen has large retail reductions. This factor accentuates the difference in result under the two methods. The basic reason cost of sales divided by average inventory at mercantile gives a higher rate of turnover is that the higher the reductions the higher will be the cost of sales figure (the dividend), with the average inventory (that is, the divisor) being decreased at the same time. On the other hand, under the preferred method, sales divided by average inventory at retail, the dividend (sales) is not affected by all reductions but only by those relating to merchandise sold. Sales are in fact decreased by the amount of markdowns and discounts, whereas reductions increase the cost of sales. The divisors of the two ratios (average retail inventory and average mercantile inventory) are affected by reductions in approximately the same proportions (in exactly the same proportions if the markon percentage in opening inventory and the cumulative markon percentage are the same).

Mention has been made of the fact that turnover is best obtained on the basis of averaging month-end inventories. This method is not always used. As in the preceding illustrations, opening and closing inventories for the year are sometimes averaged. However, this latter practice has only its simplicity to recommend it. Inventory as at February 1 and the succeeding January 31 are at low points of the year. Averaging those two inventories usually will not give a figure that is typical of the annual average. A procedure sometimes followed is to divide the sum of the inventories of February 1 and the beginning of each succeeding month of the fiscal year by twelve or to include also the inventory at the close of the year and divide by thirteen. An even better method is to average the inventories at the beginning and end of each month of the fiscal year, and divide the sum of these averages by twelve. All the inventories referred to are at retail.

The various methods of averaging ordinarily give different results, as indicated by the illustration on page 157. While the fourth method is to be preferred, this degree of refinement may not be required. Consistency of method is essential for comparing results.

The illustration is not to be interpreted as showing standard or normal relations between results under the four methods. However, as a general rule the average inventory derived under Method 1 is likely to be the lowest since inventories at the begin-

ACCOUNTING PROBLEMS OF THE RETAIL METHOD

ning and end of a fiscal year are likely to be below normal. The fourth method results in an average of monthly averages, and in the absence of special conditions seems most representative.

Illustration.

Dates 19X5	Inventory at Retail		Average Inventory for Month, at Retail
February 1	$ 200,000	February	$ 212,500
March 1	225,000	March	237,500
April 1	250,000	April	262,500
May 1	275,000	May	287,500
June 1	300,000	June	287,500
July 1	275,000	July	262,500
August 1	250,000	August	237,500
September 1	225,000	September	237,500
October 1	250,000	October	275,000
November 1	300,000	November	292,500
December 1	285,000	December	272,500
19X6			
January 1	260,000		
	3,095,000		
		January	255,000
January 31	250,000		
	$3,345,000		$3,120,000

Average inventory at retail:

Method 1. Average as at beginning and end of year,
$200,000 plus $250,000, divided by 2 .... $225,000

Method 2. Sum of inventories as at beginning of each month of fiscal year, divided by twelve

$$\left(\frac{3,095,000}{12}\right)$$ 257,917

Method 3. Sum of inventories as at beginning of each month of fiscal year and as at end of year, divided by thirteen

$$\left(\frac{3,345,000}{13}\right)$$ 257,308

Method 4. Sum of average inventories for each month of year, divided by twelve

$$\left(\frac{3,120,000}{12}\right)$$ 260,000

8

Discounts in Inventories and Discounts Earned

Introduction

Cash discounts comprise an important element of gross margin in retail merchandising. A distinction should be made between cash discounts, which are part of the invoice terms and are contingent upon payment of the invoice in accordance with such terms, and trade discounts, which effectively represent an adjustment of the sales price whether deducted directly on the face of the invoice, or whether already deducted in determining invoice amounts. All purchase statistics are net of trade discounts, and accordingly trade discounts do not pose accounting problems.

Cash discounts generally are greater than ordinarily would be allowed solely for the use of funds. Practically speaking, they represent a mixture of pure cash discounts and the outgrowth of trade practices and customs. Cash discount terms may run as low as one per cent or less for payment within ten or fifteen days, or as high as 8 or 10 per cent for payment within an approximate 46–47-day maximum period.

Problems as Affected by Accounting Methods

The accounting for discount income and for the related valuation of inventory is directly dependent upon the recordkeeping for purchases. In effect, purchases can be recorded net of cash discount or gross of cash discount, and the related discount income and inventory valuation treatments will coincide with whichever of these two recordkeeping practices is followed.

An occasional conventional retailer, and most discount retailers, will deduct all cash discounts from invoice totals, effectively recording purchases net of discounts. The practical effect of this practice is the derivation of higher markon percentages (in the retail ledger) as opposed to entering invoices at gross amounts. This, of course, results because the discounts effectively reduce the cost of merchandise purchased. However, gross margin percentages should not be affected. When purchases are recorded net of cash discounts, no account is set up for discounts earned; there is only an expense account for discounts lost. Discounts lost will comprise discounts which were deducted from invoices processed in the normal course of business but which, because payment was delayed or for other reasons, were not claimed or allowed at settlement.

Conventional retailers customarily record gross purchases based on gross invoice amounts, without deduction of discounts. This practice poses certain questions with respect to the subsequent valuation of inventories (whether or not the retail method is used) and to the determination of earned discount income.

The theoretical argument is sometimes made that discounts need not be deducted from inventories and that there is no objection to carrying merchandise at gross invoice cost. Proponents of this theory assert that discount earnings are not dependent upon the sale of merchandise but represent financial income arising from prompt payment of invoices. Accordingly, such discounts should be taken into income on a cash basis, as deducted at settlements, and not on an accrual basis. This theory may be appropriate under circumstances involving discount rates which are so low as to represent only reasonable interest for prompt payment. However, average discount rates of a mercantile business with varied lines of merchandise frequently are much higher than those that can reasonably be considered as interest, and vendor discount rates have never borne any particular relationship to the fluctuating costs in the use of funds. Moreover, vendors who offer retailers cash discounts effectively adjust for such discounts in the establishment of the selling prices of merchandise items.

Where discount rates are relatively nominal, or where discount deductions are not almost always taken, the discount earnings may be looked upon as "other income," a form of nonmerchandising income attributable to financial management. However, discount income normally is a significant factor entering into the determination of gross margin. Accordingly, there is near complete acceptance of the theory that purchase discounts should not be treated as other income, but as a component of cost of goods sold. Since gross margin can only result from sales, any discount on unsold merchandise should not be included in gross margin. As hereinafter discussed, this desired result is achieved by eliminating unearned discounts from merchandise inventories when such inventories are reduced to "cost." This, of course, presupposes that invoices are included in purchases on a gross-of-discount basis. However, a comparable adjustment in the valuation of merchandise inventories is automatically made when purchases are recorded net of purchase discounts.

In the interests of clarity with regard to the accounting for discounts, it is necessary to differentiate among the following:

Discounts accrued (on all purchases);
Discounts received (on a cash basis as vendor settlements are made); and
Discounts earned (on merchandise sold).

The following explanations of accounts pertaining to discounts outline the problems involved.

Discounts on Purchases

This account would include discounts applicable to all purchases made during the accounting period. It is usually equal to the discounts applicable to invoices paid during the period, *plus* the discounts to be received upon payment of accounts payable outstanding at the close of the period, *minus* the discounts received on accounts payable at the beginning of the period. In effect, it represents purchase discounts on an accrual basis directly related to purchases. A common recordkeeping procedure in this regard would be to enter purchases gross of discounts and accounts payable net of discounts, as follows:

Purchases (gross)	$45,000	
Discounts on purchases		$ 2,200
Accounts payable (net)		42,800

Discounts lost (for lapse of payment on due date or other reasons) will reduce the amount of discounts on purchases. However, if lost discounts are charged to an expense account, the credit to discounts on purchases effectively will represent discounts on all purchases on the accrual basis, whether realized or not.

Discounts Received

This account would include the discounts received on the cash basis, that is, discounts deducted from invoices when payments are made to vendors within the period. The amounts of the discounts on accounts payable at both ends of the period and also the discounts lost during the period represent the difference from "discounts on purchases" of the period.

When discounts are accumulated and reflected in the records on a cash basis, it is necessary at the close of each accounting period to adjust the figures for discounts deductible from open accounts payable. Adjustment may be made directly against accounts payable or via a "discount receivable" account which is offset against accounts payable. The offset to either of these two balance sheet accounts (i.e., accounts payable or discounts receivable) is the income account used to recognize discounts received. As a practical matter, only a net adjustment is normally made at the end of each accounting period for the net increase (or decrease) necessary to reflect the amount of discounts inherent in accounts payable at the end of the period.

Discounts Lost

When invoices and accounts payable are entered net, any discounts which are not allowable or deducted at settlements can be charged to an expense account which may be termed "discounts lost." Similarly, when invoices are entered on the gross basis and discounts are recorded on the accrual basis, any discounts not actually received can be charged to a comparable expense account. The taking of cash discounts is generally considered to be a financial rather than a merchandising decision. Thus, discounts missed or not taken are generally considered to be an expense rather than a reduction of gross margin.

Discounts Deductible (or Receivable)

This account would include the discounts related to accounts payable outstanding at the close of a period, which are deductible from such accounts upon settlement. On the accrual basis theoretically it would be proper to state the accounts payable net of discounts.

Purchases for a period include merchandise paid for and merchandise for which the corresponding liability is included in accounts payable at the end of the period. As explained above, the total of discounts on purchases includes discounts received, less such discounts as were deductible from outstanding accounts payable at the opening of the period (these discounts were recognized in income in the preceding period), plus discounts which will not be received until accounts payable outstanding at the close of the period are paid. It is necessary, therefore, to determine the amounts of discounts deductible from accounts payable outstanding at both ends of the period. As noted earlier, the offset to this net increase (decrease) in discounts applicable to accounts payable at the end of the period as compared to discounts applicable to accounts payable at the beginning of the period is an increase (decrease) in discount income.

Discounts in closing inventories should be deducted from income because they are not deemed to be earned until the merchandise is sold. Coincident with this accounting treatment, discounts in accounts payable outstanding should be added to income, either because such discounts are included in the discounts in inventories which have been deducted from income, or because such discounts have actually been earned for merchandise sold but payment has not yet been made. In effect, the payable discount calculation is a necessary complement of the inventory discount calculation.

The amount of discounts deductible from accounts payable is generally determined by applying to the total of outstanding accounts payable the overall average rate of discount on purchases. Where accounts payable are kept departmentally, calculations should theoretically be made on a departmental basis. It should be noted, however, that the average rate applied to accounts payable will probably differ from the rate applied to inventory. For the accounts payable computation, the average rate is based upon the invoice cost of purchases subject to discount—usually only domestic purchases. For the inventory computation, the average rate is based upon the total purchases, including such additional factors as transportation charges (i.e., freight-in), workroom-made merchandise, and imported merchandise.

Discounts Earned

This account would include the discounts on merchandise sold during the period. The amount would be equal to the discounts on purchases of the period, *plus* discounts applicable to opening inventory (not previously taken into income because the merchandise was not sold), *minus* discounts applicable to closing inventory (not taken into income because the merchandise is still on hand).

Discounts Unearned

Discounts are unearned when the merchandise on hand is unsold. Effectively, this account represents the adjustment applicable to closing inventory necessary to state such inventory on a net-of-discount basis.

Stated differently, this adjustment is necessary to state inventories at cost since, regardless of the method of inventory valuation, the actual cost of merchandise is invoice price *less* discount. When cost of sales is *charged* with the invoice price of purchases, it also is *credited* with the discounts allowed on such purchases. Therefore, inventories should not be priced at more than the net cost of purchases. Accordingly, at the end of each accounting period it is necessary to determine the amounts of "unearned discounts" remaining in inventories and to deduct such amounts from the inventories. Adjustments (debits or credits) of the unearned discount account from period to period are reflected in discounts earned.

Purchases Entered Net of Discounts

When purchases are entered net of discounts, accounts payable are automatically stated on a net basis and there is no separate accountability for discounts. Under this procedure the inventory valuation per books would be stated net of discounts. If the cost method is used, a physical inventory should be priced at net (of discount) costs; if only gross invoice costs are available, the discounts should be computed and deducted from inventory to arrive at the appropriate cost valuation. If the retail method is used with purchases entered in the retail ledger net of discounts, the departmental cost multiplier (complement of markon percentage) derived from the retail ledger will automatically result in a departmental inventory valuation appropriately stated net of discounts.

In summary, when purchases and accounts payable are entered net of discounts, there are no discount problems and discount adjustments are not ordinarily required. If information is desired with respect to discount totals, statistical tabulations can be made as to discounts on purchases, discounts deducted at settlements, or discounts earned.

Purchases Entered Gross of Discounts

The recording of purchases net of discounts has the virtue of simplicity and ease of accounting. However, there is a general conviction among retailers that more profitable merchandising results when buyers are forced to achieve a targeted markon percentage computed on a higher cost figure, notwithstanding that discounts earned are often credited to the individual selling departments. As an illustration of this practical goal to better merchandising performance, the achievement of a 40 per cent initial markon demanded of a buyer in a particular department is expected to yield higher sales dollars and presumably higher gross margin dollars if the 60 per cent "cost" factor used to establish selling prices is *gross* invoice cost rather than *net* invoice cost. So widespread is this belief in more profitable merchandising that a number of retailers have adopted the practice of "loading" additional amounts on purchase costs by means of the added discount device. The practical effect of grossing up invoice costs by the additional discount "load" factor is to place even greater pressures on the achievement of higher selling prices.

Departmental Discount Rates

From a theoretical standpoint, it is preferable to determine the average rate of discount for each selling department. If discounts are accumulated departmentally on the accrual basis from a record such as the purchase journal or invoice register, departmental totals of discounts are readily available and average rates can be computed with relative ease.

If discounts are analyzed and accumulated departmentally only as invoices are paid—that is, from the cash disbursements record—an additional calculation of discounts on unpaid invoices is required in order to obtain total discounts for a period applicable to purchases for that period. Figure 18 illustrates a tabulation that can be used to derive departmental rates of discount.

Department	Discounts Received During Month or Season	Add: Discounts Deductible on Accounts Payable, End of Month or Season	Deduct: Discounts Deductible on Accounts Payable, Beginning of Month or Season	Total	Total Cost of Purchases for Month or Season	Average Rate of Discount
1						
2						
3						
4						
5						
.						
.						
.						
Totals						

FIG. 18. Departmental rates of discounts.

An exact calculation of departmental rates of discounts is feasible only when accounts payable are analyzed departmentally. However, in many instances it may be possible to make a reasonably accurate calculation by dividing the total discount that is received during a month or season by the total purchases for the same period, without adjustments for discounts in opening and closing accounts payable.

As an alternative to precise rate computations for individual departments, some retailers compute and utilize a single store-wide average rate. Where departmental discount rates and the mix of merchandise are reasonably consistent from year to year and where the store-wide average is not statistically biased by extremes (e.g., special purchases, special discounts, or other factors), the use of a store-wide rate should provide an acceptable alternative. The following tabulation illustrates one approach in the determination of a single store-wide discount rate:

Total cost of purchases during period (gross of discounts)	$ 9,900,000
Accounts payable, beginning of period	450,000
Total	10,350,000
Deduct: Accounts payable, end of period	350,000
Total amount on which discounts were received	$10,000,000
Amount of discounts actually received	$ 550,000
Average rate of discount	5.5%

Computation of Unearned Discount

As noted earlier, the rates of unearned discount applied to departmental inventories to reduce such inventories to cost should be based on the relationship of discounts earned to departmental purchases of the specific period. The departmental purchases figures used to derive the departmental discount rates should be representative of the inventory on hand at the end of the period. The bulk of purchase discounts relates to domestic purchases. However, the departmental purchases statistic may include transportation costs, purchases adjustments such as special allowances and rebates, workroom-made merchandise and imported merchandise—all of which normally have nominal discounts, if any. Under these circumstances, therefore, the average rate of discount applied to the inventory should be derived taking into account all of the constituent elements of purchases which also comprise all of the constituent elements of inventory costs, whether or not such costs are determined under the retail method. Accordingly, the average discount rate applied to the inventory will almost always be less than the average discount rate earned on domestic purchases.

When imported merchandise is a considerable factor in merchandising and the inventory is classified as between domestic and imported merchandise, there should be separate computations of unearned discount on both types of merchandise in stock.

Theoretically, the inventory base to which the average rates are applied generally includes some amount of merchandise purchased in prior periods which conceivably may bear a different discount rate than the current year's rate. However, any such discount rate differential that may be applicable to the amount of prior-year inventory is usually too immaterial to be considered and is customarily ignored.

It must be acknowledged that, in general, discount calculations are not precise, primarily because they are based upon averages. Determination and application of discount rates for individual departments, rather than on an all-store basis, reduces the margin of error. Moreover, the overall discount rate on purchases used in the basic discount computation may not always be representative of the discount rate inherent in the accounts payable amounts (at both ends of the year) and in the year-end inventory. Notwithstanding, the approach and methodology set forth above provide reasonably reliable results which can be said to be satisfactory for most practical purposes.

Interim Figures for Discounts Earned

In reporting departmental gross margins it is important to bear in mind that there is a distinction among the discounts received on merchandise invoices paid (as taken from the cash records), discounts on all merchandise purchases (without regard to whether such invoices have been paid), and discounts on the merchandise sold. Obviously departmental results will differ depending upon whether discounts are allocated on the basis of discounts received or discounts on purchases, rather than on the more appropriate basis of merchandise sold.

For a season or year as a whole, the differential in gross margin that would result from the use of either discount allocation technique may not be significant, assuming there is no significant difference between inventories at the beginning of the season (or year) and at the end of the season (or year). However, throughout a season the amount of error in departmental and all-store gross margin will fluctuate as inventories rise and fall. Gross margin will be overstated in periods when retail purchases exceed sales and other retail deductions, and it will be understated when sales and other retail deductions exceed retail purchases.

Theoretically, this error could be remedied by computing monthly (or for each four- or five-week period) the amount of discounts earned on merchandise sold, but this would entail a considerable number of computations. For interim reporting purposes, a practical short-cut method would be to apply to current-period departmental sales the departmental earned discount percentages on sales of the preceding season or year. Departmental ratios of discounts earned to net sales normally would fluctuate within relatively narrow limits from year to year, and in all probability no significant error in the all-store gross margin would result from approximating discount earned on the basis of past experience.

Discount Computations Based Upon Retail Figures

An alternative method of allocating discounts earned departmentally for interim reporting purposes is to use the relationship of discounts earned to purchases at retail. Under this method, the departmental average rates of discounts on purchases (accrual basis) are computed in terms of the retail amounts of the purchases. That is, the discount amounts are divided by purchases at retail, rather than purchases at cost, to obtain the average discount rates. Such rates can be computed each month on the basis of cumulative purchases for the season or year to date with comparatively little effort.

These departmental discount rates can then be applied to the total of the individual department's retail stock deductions (i.e., the sum of net sales, markdowns, allowances, discounts, and shrinkage) to obtain the amount of discounts earned for the period. The underlying logic of this procedure is that the total of retail stock deductions represents the volume of goods moved from inventory during the period, at retail prices, and the discounts are earned as such movement occurs. At year end, the unearned discount applicable to the closing inventory should be computed in the conventional manner, with appropriate adjustments made, preferably on a departmental basis.

Discounts in the Income Statement

Different income statement presentations are possible with respect to discounts: they can be either netted against opening and closing inventories or shown broad. When discounts are deducted from opening and closing inventories, the purchases figure should be shown net of discounts, with no separate figure for discounts included in the income statement. Alternatively, the inventory figures used are inventories before deduction of discounts, and the figure used for purchases will also be gross of discounts. Under these circumstances, the amount to be used for discount income will then be the discounts earned on merchandise sold. An illustration of this latter procedure follows:

Ch. 8   DISCOUNTS IN INVENTORIES; DISCOUNTS EARNED

Cost of goods sold:
Opening inventory (gross of discounts)		$ 50,000
Purchases, including transportation (gross of discounts)		120,000
		170,000
Less: Closing inventory (gross of discounts)		60,000
		110,000
Discounts earned:		
Discounts on purchases	$6,000	
Discounts in opening inventory	2,500*	
	8,500	
Less: Discounts in closing inventory	3,000*	5,500
Total cost of goods sold		$104,500

* Assumed rate of discount applicable to both opening and closing inventory = 5 per cent.

This illustration sets forth the amount of discounts on purchases on the accrual basis ($6,000). As explained earlier in this chapter, in a situation where discounts are accumulated as received (from the cash book on invoices paid), discounts on opening and closing accounts payable must be taken into account in order to determine the discounts earned on purchases (i.e., on the accrual basis). As an example, the discounts earned ($5,500) could have resulted from a situation wherein discounts received had amounted to $5,750 and there were opening accounts payable of $20,000 and closing accounts payable of $25,000 with a discount rate of 5 per cent applicable to the opening and closing accounts payable:

Discounts earned:		
Discounts received (on invoices paid)		$5,750
Discounts on closing accounts payable (5% of $25,000)		1,250
Discounts in opening inventory (5% of $50,000)		2,500
		9,500
Deduct:		
Discounts on opening accounts payable (5% of $20,000)	$1,000	
Discounts in closing inventory (5% of $60,000)	3,000	4,000
Discounts earned		$5,500

Illustrations of Discount Computations

The following examples illustrate discount computations and the related valuation of inventories under the retail method.

Example 1

Opening inventory, February 1: at cost or mercantile (including unearned discounts of $5,000), $100,000; at retail, $175,000.

	Cost	Less Discounts of	Retail
Purchases:			
February	$ 60,000	4 %	$100,000
March	70,000	3	105,000
April	80,000	5	120,000
May	65,000	3½	102,000
June	78,000	4¼	110,000
July	58,000	3¾	98,000
	$411,000		$635,000
Additional data for six-month period:			
Freight, express, and cartage inward	$ 10,000		(no retail)
Workroom and alteration costs including departmental labor payrolls	2,500		(no retail)
Net sales			$500,000
Markdowns and other retail reductions			30,000

On the basis of the foregoing facts, inventory as at July 31 is determined under two cases:

Case 1, where purchases and accounts payable are entered net;
Case 2, where purchases and accounts payable are recorded gross.

Case 1

		Cost or Mercantile	Retail	Markon Percentage [*]
Opening inventory		$ 95,000	$175,000	
Purchases:				
February	$57,600		100,000	
March	67,900		105,000	
April	76,000		120,000	
May	62,725		102,000	
June	74,685		110,000	
July	55,825	394,735	98,000	
Freight, express, and cartage inward		10,000		
		$499,735	$810,000	38.3043%
Net sales			$500,000	
Markdowns and other retail reductions			30,000	
			$530,000	
Inventory, as per books		$172,748 [†]	$280,000	

[*] Workroom and alteration costs, including departmental labor, do not enter into the markon computation.

[†] 61.6957% of $280,000 (61.6957% is the complement of the markon percentage of 38.3043).

Ch. 8   DISCOUNTS IN INVENTORIES; DISCOUNTS EARNED   171

Case 2

	Cost or Mercantile	Retail	Markon Percentage
Opening inventory	$100,000	$175,000	
Purchases	411,000	635,000	
Freight, express, and cartage inward	10,000		
	$521,000	$810,000	35.6790%
Net sales		$500,000	
Markdowns and other retail reductions		30,000	
		$530,000	
Inventory, as per books	$180,099 *	$280,000	
Inventory at mercantile, as above		$180,099	
Deduct: Unearned discounts			
$\dfrac{521,000 - 499,735}{521,000}$ or 4.0816%		7,351	
Inventory at mercantile, less unearned discounts		$172,748	

* 64.3210% of $280,000 (64.3210% is the complement of the markon percentage of 35.6790).

It is obvious that the resultant balance sheet inventory valuation ($172,748) will be the same whether purchases are received gross or net of discounts.

Gross Margin Statements

	Case 1 Amounts	Case 1 Percentages on Net Sales	Case 2 Amounts	Case 2 Percentages on Net Sales
Net sales	$500,000	100.00%	$500,000	100.00%
Merchandise costs:				
Inventory, beginning of period	$ 95,000		$100,000	
Merchandise purchased	394,735		411,000	
Freight, express, and cartage inward	10,000		10,000	
	499,735		521,000	
Inventory, close of period	172,748		180,099	
	326,987		340,901	
Discounts earned on merchandise	—		13,914 *	
Net cost of merchandise sold	326,987		326,987	
Workroom and alteration costs, including departmental labor payrolls, net	2,500		2,500	
Total merchandise costs	$329,487	65.90	$329,487	65.90
Gross margin	$170,513	34.10%	$170,513	34.10%

* 4.0816% of $340,901.

It should be noted that in the above illustration the percentage of discounts unearned (in inventories) was computed on the basis of including opening inventory and freight, express, and cartage inward. If discounts were computed strictly on purchases for the six months (excluding opening inventory and freight costs) the ratio would be $16,265/$411,000 or 3.9574 per cent instead of 4.0816 per cent. Using this percentage the inventory valuation would be $172,972, determined as follows:

Inventory at mercantile	$180,099
Deduct: Unearned discounts (3.9574%)	7,127
	$172,972

Although theoretically incorrect, the resulting inventory valuation of $172,972 is not materially different from the aforementioned valuation of $172,748.

Example 2

Opening inventory, February 1: at cost or mercantile, $960,000; at retail, $1,750,000.

Purchases for year to January 31: at cost $6,000,000; at retail, $10,000,000. Freight, express, and cartage inward of $100,000 is included in purchases at cost.

Net sales for year, $9,400,000; markdowns and other retail reductions, $400,000.

Workroom and alteration costs, including departmental labor payrolls: at cost, $75,000; at retail, $30,000.

The above figures are taken from departmental records where all entries are net of discounts which are assumed to run uniformly at 4 per cent of invoice costs.

Accounts payable may be assumed to be $100,000 greater at the end than at the beginning of the period.

Case 1—Net Basis

	Cost or Mercantile	Retail	Markon Percentage
Opening inventory	$ 960,000	$ 1,750,000	
Purchases, including freight, express, and cartage inward	6,000,000	10,000,000	
	$6,960,000	$11,750,000	40.7660%
Net sales		$ 9,400,000	
Markdowns and other retail reductions		400,000	
		$ 9,800,000	
Inventory, as per books	$1,155,063 °	$ 1,950,000	

° 59.2340% of $1,950,000.

Case 2—Gross Basis

	Cost or Mercantile	Retail	Markon Percentage
Opening inventory	$1,000,000	$ 1,750,000	
Purchases	6,145,833 *	10,000,000	
Freight, express, and cartage inward	100,000		
	$7,245,833	$11,750,000	38.333⅓%
Net sales		$ 9,400,000	
Reductions		400,000	
		$ 9,800,000	
Inventory, as per books	$1,202,500 †	1,950,000	
Inventory at mercantile, as above		1,202,500	
Deduct: Unearned discounts (4%)		48,100	
		$ 1,154,400	

* $5,900,000 ÷ .96 = $6,145,833.
† 61.666⅔% of $1,950,000.

[See comparison of statements on page 174.]

The difference of $663 in inventory valuations and gross margins highlights the impact of theoretical imperfections on the discount computations. In Case 2 of Example 2, the total of discounts earned is derived *without* considering the effect of freight on the discount rate. Moreover, no effect was given specifically to an increase in accounts payable, since it was assumed that the 4 per cent on purchases was derived after taking into account all pertinent factors.

It should be further understood that, while inventories may be shown gross on the gross margin statement, all inventories should be reflected net of discounts on the balance sheet.

Loaded or Added Discounts

For stores that make use of "loaded" or "added discounts," as discussed earlier, an additional factor is introduced in the accounting for discounts and in the valuation of inventories. When the practice of loading is utilized, it is common to establish fixed discount rates on all the purchases of the individual selling departments. Thus, discounts of, say, 5, 6, or 8 per cent may be established depending on the department involved. Each purchase

Gross Margin Statements

	Case 1 Amounts	Case 1 Percentages on Net Sales	Case 2 Amounts	Case 2 Percentages on Net Sales
Net sales	$9,400,000	100.00%	$9,400,000	100.00%
Merchandise costs:				
Inventory, beginning of period	$ 960,000		$1,000,000	
Merchandise purchased	5,900,000		6,145,833	
Freight, express, and cartage inward	100,000		100,000	
	6,960,000		7,245,833	
Inventory, close of period	1,155,063		1,202,500	
	5,804,937		6,043,333	
Discounts earned on merchandise	—		237,733 [*]	
Net cost of merchandise sold	5,804,937		5,805,600	
Workroom and alteration costs, including departmental labor payrolls, net	45,000		45,000	
Total merchandise costs	$5,849,937	62.23	$5,850,600	62.24
Gross margin	$3,550,063	37.77%	$3,549,400	37.76%

[*] Discounts in opening inventory (4% of $1,000,000) $ 40,000
Discounts on purchases ($6,145,833 − $5,900,000)   245,833
    285,833
Less: Discounts in closing inventory (4% of $1,202,500)   48,100
    $ 237,733

invoice of the department is then expected to carry at least the fixed rate of discount. Any invoice with an actual rate of discount less than the fixed rate is "loaded" with an amount sufficient to bring the discount up to the established figure.

To illustrate, assume an invoice of $100 carries a 4 per cent discount, where the pre-established fixed departmental rate is 6 per cent. In this case there would be added to the gross invoice cost an amount which, together with the $4 of discount allowed by the

Ch. 8   DISCOUNTS IN INVENTORIES; DISCOUNTS EARNED   175

vendor, will give a combined figure for invoice and added discount equivalent to 6 per cent of the loaded cost. To obtain exactly the amount to be added to cost, a formula may be used:

> The amount to be loaded on cost equals gross cost *times* a percentage rate obtained by dividing the fixed department discount rate *minus* the invoice discount rate, by 1 minus the fixed department discount rate.

Utilizing the amounts in the illustration:

$$a = \text{percentage of cost to be loaded on cost}$$
$$a = \frac{.06 - .04}{1 - .06}$$
$$a = \frac{.02}{.94}$$
$$a = .0212766 \text{ or } 2.12766\%$$

Invoice cost	$100.00000
Amount loaded	2.12766
Total	$102.12766
Invoice discount	$ 4.00000
Added discount	2.12766
Total	$ 6.12766
Percentage of combined discount to loaded cost ($6.12766 ÷ $102.12766)	6.0%

(In actual practice, stores employing the loading practice utilize tables which show the percentage to be added to cost for various vendor discounts allowed.)

A store may use a rule-of-thumb method which gives an approximate result but greatly facilitates the calculation process. For example, in the above illustration it may be said that since the departmental rate is 6 per cent and the invoice rate is 4 per cent, an additional 2 per cent must be added to cost. The result is:

Invoice cost	$100.00
Amount loaded	2.00
Total	$102.00
Invoice discount	$ 4.00
Added discount	2.00
Total	$ 6.00
Percentage of combined discount to loaded cost ($6.00 ÷ $102.00)	5.882%

Elimination of Added Discounts from Inventories

Regardless of the method used, the practical effect of the added discount procedure is to increase purchases artificially by an amount which is offset by a credit to the added discount income account. Under the retail inventory method the loaded purchases figures are reflected in the records and influence the derivation of the departmental markon (and cost multiplier) percentages. Consequently, in the valuation of inventories under the retail method, it is necessary to eliminate the added discounts, as well as the conventional cash discounts, in order to properly state inventories at cost and to more accurately reflect discounts earned.

To eliminate added discounts from inventories it is necessary to determine the average rate of loading for each department. This rate of added discount is ascertained by dividing total added discounts for each department, accumulated during a month or season, by the total loaded purchases for each department. These departmental rates, when applied to departmental inventories, provide the amounts of added discounts included in such inventories. While it is theoretically better practice to calculate and utilize the loaded discount rates departmentally, a single all-store calculation is sometimes made on the basis of a store-wide average added discount rate.

The following example, whether applied on an all-store basis or departmentally, illustrates the determination of the added discount included in inventory:

Merchandise purchases for period, gross (i.e., including cash and added discounts)	$10,000,000
Added discounts, for period	$ 370,000
Percentage of added discounts to purchases	3.70%
Total merchandise inventory at end of period	$ 2,100,000
Added discounts in inventory (3.70% of $2,100,000)	$ 77,700

When both cash and added discounts are involved, as would be customary, the method of calculating cash discounts in inventories must be modified. Rates of cash discounts can be determined only after elimination of the amount of added discount-loading from the loaded purchases figures. Correspondingly, when applying cash discount rates to the inventories, the amount of added discount in the inventories must first be eliminated.

Calculation of discounts in inventory, where both cash and added discounts are involved, is shown in the following example:

	Cash Discounts	Added Discounts
Total purchases for period, gross of all discounts	$20,000	$20,000
Added discounts for period	480	480
	19,520	
Decrease in accounts payable	920	
Amount on which cash discounts were received	$18,600	
Cash discounts received	$ 818	
Rate of discount	4.4%	2.4%
Merchandise inventory at end of period	$ 5,000	$ 5,000
Deduct: Added discounts in inventory (2.4% of $5,000)	120	120
	$ 4,880	
Cash discounts in inventory (4.4% of $4,880)	$ 215	

The method of calculation illustrated in Figure 18 (page 165) should be substituted for that illustrated above where it is apparent that amounts of accounts payable and rates of discount thereon will have an effect upon the correctness of the result obtained.

Although theoretical distinction is made between cash discounts and added discounts, in practice they have the same effect upon merchandising operations. The amount paid for merchandise purchased is actually the face amount of the invoice minus discount. When purchases are charged with the face amount of invoices, they are loaded to the extent of the cash discounts. Any further loading of purchases by means of added discounts merely increases the load on purchases and increases the credit to discount income. It is, of course, necessary to remove this artificial load when stating inventories at cost.

Other Loading of Purchase Costs

Costs of imported merchandise are regularly charged with commissions paid to foreign buying agents. Some retailers also charge foreign purchases with a proportionate share of the expenses of foreign buying offices and with expenses of foreign travel. Ostensibly, such loading is designed to record purchases at an aggregate cost comparable to that which would have been incurred if the goods were purchased from importers in this country and to recover from higher selling prices the "extra" costs associated with the acquisition of imported merchandise. While these may be sound economic objectives, from an accounting standpoint there is a serious question as to whether these expenditures comprise merchandising costs or expenses of doing business that should be charged off as incurred.

In this regard, the authors concur with the long-established and predominant accounting practice which excludes foreign buying and foreign travel costs in the derivation of inventories where such items have been loaded in purchases basically to encourage improved markons. For this purpose, a valuation reserve is frequently set up against inventory of imported goods equal to the average percentage of loading included in such purchases.

Anticipations

Anticipations can be defined as additional discounts granted by certain vendors for payment made in advance of the discount date. Thus, if a vendor's invoice is dated March 26, 19—, terms 8 per cent E.O.M. (end of month), the retailer would be permitted the 8 per cent discount, provided payment was made by May 10, 19—. All invoices bearing E.O.M. datings conventionally allow the stipulated discount if the payment is made by the 10th of the month following. However, the month is deemed to run from the 25th of one month to the 24th of the following month. Accordingly, all invoices dated between the 25th and 31st (or 30th) day of one calendar month will be entitled to a discount if paid by the 10th day of the second following month.

Therefore, if the retailer made payment prior to May 10, 19—, a number of vendors would allow an additional discount (i.e., "anticipation"), based on the number of days between the payment date and May 10, at some rate which had previously been "bargained" between retailer and vendor.

Anticipations generally are included with cash discounts as an element of gross margin. Theoretically, much could be said in

Ch. 8   DISCOUNTS IN INVENTORIES; DISCOUNTS EARNED   179

favor of the practice followed by some retailers of treating anticipations as an element of other income, basically comprising a form of interest earned. However, in reality this is a form of cash discount that is bargained out between vendor and retailer and it effectively represents an element of purchase cost which is difficult to distinguish from cash discount. Under these circumstances, anticipations should be included as an element of gross margin on the income statement. On the ledger, however, it is preferable to segregate anticipations in a separate account. This will enable management to know the income thereby derived and to evaluate this practice by comparison with the current cost of money or with the alternative income that could have been generated by investing the relevant funds in merchandising or other activities.

Conversion of Discount Ratios from Sales to Purchases

In a gross margin statement, discounts earned appear in relation to sales. Utilizing the gross margin statement on page 174, the following ratios are derived, all representing percentages on sales:

	Amounts	Percentages on Sales
Net sales	$9,400,000	100.00
Opening inventory, plus purchases, and freight, express, and cartage inward, less closing inventory	$6,043,333	64.291
Discounts earned on merchandise	237,733	2.529
	5,805,600	61.762
Workroom and alteration costs, including department labor payrolls, net	45,000	.479
Total merchandise costs	$5,850,600	62.241
Gross margin	$3,549,400	37.759

As indicated, discounts earned are 2.529 per cent on sales. For statement purposes, all such ratios are based on sales and consequently are comparable from period to period. However, one naturally thinks of discounts as related to purchases. The approximate ratio of discounts to purchases may be derived by first substituting for sales the original retail; that is, adding retail stock reductions (basically markdowns and shortages) to sales. In this illustration the retail stock reductions were $400,000. Accordingly, the original retail would be $9,800,000, or 104.255 per cent of sales. The ratio of discounts to purchases is derived by dividing 2.529 (discount percentage on sales), by 104.255, and then dividing by the complement of the markon percentage (i.e., by the cost multiplier, which in this case is 61⅔ per cent).

Expressed in formula, the ratio of discounts earned to purchases in this illustration is 3.934 per cent, computed as follows:

$$\frac{(2.529)}{(104.255)} \div .61\tfrac{2}{3}\text{ or}$$
$$.0242578 \div .61\tfrac{2}{3} = 3.934 \text{ per cent.}$$

In the illustration, discounts were $237,733, and purchases, including increase or decrease in inventory, and freight, express, and cartage inward, were $6,043,333, or a ratio of 3.934 per cent.

9

Taking Physical Inventories

Introduction

Various phases of the problem of merchandise control have already been discussed from the viewpoint of accountability for inventory on any given date in terms of dollars and, in some instances, of units. Other phases of the control problem involve physical controls over merchandise stocks. In effect, all of the procedures involved with the receipt, storage, display, sale, and delivery of merchandise represent an integrated system of accounting and physical control over merchandise.

The test of how properly this system operates and how effectively inventory units are safeguarded is a physical inventory—a determination of the quantity and valuation of stock actually on hand as of a given point in time.

Necessity for Physical Inventories

Methods of maintaining book inventories in dollar amounts and units have reached a high degree of standardization and acceptability. Nevertheless, no retail business should be satisfied with book figures that are not checked by means of physical inventories taken either annually or semiannually; for some departments and lines of merchandise they should be taken more frequently. Physical inventories are a check not only on the accuracy of the book controls over dollar amounts and units, but on the efficiency of the systems of accounting and physical controls of stocks. Physical inventories may disclose evidence of erroneous or negligent record-keeping, as well as actual losses of merchandise by theft, damage, and other causes. In addition, physical inventories provide a basis and opportunity for detailed analyses of conditions and factors not normally obtainable from a review of the book records. Among these are:

1. The age of stock in accordance with seasonal and other selected age groupings.
2. The different classifications of merchandise included in departmental stocks.
3. The different price lines and their relative importance.
4. The number of units, and respective dollar totals, of different stock groupings.
5. The amounts of stock represented by imported and domestic goods, consigned goods, and materials and supplies.
6. The distribution of stock into forward stock, reserve stock, and warehouse stock.

Physical inventories are also the most satisfactory basis for merchandise insurance coverage.

Responsibility for Inventory Taking

The primary responsibility for the physical inventory rests with the controller. Frequently an inventory office is established under a supervisor who takes full responsibility for planning and executing the work of taking physical inventories. The duties and responsibilities of such an inventory office are principally as follows:

1. Arrangement of schedule of periodic inventories.
2. Preparation for inventory taking.
3. Supervision of inventory taking.
4. Tabulation, analysis, summarization, and reconciliation of inventories.
5. Investigation of inventory differences.
6. Review and critique of systems related to the movement and handling of merchandise and submission of suggestions for improvement.

Planning for Physical Inventories

The work of taking physical inventories should be planned with care. Sufficiently in advance of the designated inventory dates, general instructions should be issued to merchandise managers, buyers, and assistants, and to the service department managers concerned with inventories. Included in the latter are heads of receiving and marking, accounts payable, sales audit, accounts receivable, inspection, and adjustments. General instructions should cover the more important phases of inventory taking. Specific instructions relating to problems of various departments should be covered by conferences and consultations between the inventory office and department heads, and in meetings attended by department heads, salespeople, and others who do the actual listing and checking. It is important that the responsibility for the various phases of inventory taking be clearly established and set forth definitively in the instructions. (Detailed treatment of instructions appears later in the chapter.)

Problems of Inventory Taking

Many items must be covered in a plan for taking a complete and accurate inventory. The more important problems are discussed in the following sections.

Physical Layout of Departments. Department managers should be asked to submit sketches of the physical layout of their departments showing location of the various sections and cases, drawers, and other fixtures used for storage and display of merchandise. On the basis of the sketches the amount of forms and supplies for taking the inventory may be estimated. In addition, the physical layout can be used to estimate the number of personnel required to take the physical inventory and the number that must be assigned to specific areas. A determination can also be made as to the feasibility of precounting merchandise in reserve stock or other areas. The progress of the physical inventory can also be monitored through the use of the physical layout or floor plan.

Allocation of Forms and Supplies. The allocation of necessary forms and supplies for taking the physical inventory depends upon the physical layout, the method of taking, listing, and summarizing the inventory, and the type and nature of the merchandise to be inventoried.

The physical layout may indicate merchandise located on a variety of fixture types (racks, gondolas, cases, pegboards, etc.), each of which may have different requirements as to quantity or even the type of inventory forms required.

The methods used for taking, listing, and summarizing the inventory may include inventory sheets; tags and tallies, to be summarized manually; magnetically encoded or optical font tickets; mark-sense documents or optically readable tallies or count sheets for summarization by some type of data processing equipment. Price tickets bearing unit control data in the form of pinhole perforations are readily adapted to the taking of physical inventories. Where a multipart stub is available on each merchandise item, the detaching of the stubs from the merchandise in a controlled area would constitute the inventory-taking process. The basic problems would be verifying that a stub had been detached from each merchandise or stock item and control over the price tickets after they have been detached.

After they are detached, the price tickets can be converted into regular punched cards and subsequently summarized and tabulated. It is in summarizing and tabulating departmental inventory statistics, such as by classifications, price lines, manufacturers, etc., that the greatest advantages may accrue. This type of physical inventory can be an important supplement to the unit control of stocks.

For some types of merchandise, information as to style, size, color, or season may be desired for special listing and summarization. Further, the nature and type of merchandise in stock may require special forms or instructions for layaways, merchandise sold but not delivered, merchandise out for repair, or merchandise to be recorded at unit cost versus unit retail.

All inventory sheets, tags, or cards, whether used or not, should be accounted for by the inventory office.

Methods of Counting and Listing, and Subsequent Checking Procedures. The methods of counting and listing the merchandise must be carefully planned. Listing may be made directly on the inventory-taking forms, usually by having one person count and call the items and another enter them on the forms. There are a number of variations of the direct listing procedure, depending upon the extent to which it seems desirable to double-check the results. For example, after the first listing the caller and lister may change places and make a complete recount against the first listing; a second team of caller and lister may independently make a separate listing for comparison with the first; one person may do both the counting and entering and a second person cover the same ground, the two listings being compared; an independent checker may follow the inventory team and check its listings against the stock. Checking may be restricted to "spot" checks or tests but some measure of checking should be done, governed by the kind and value of the specific merchandise.

For large-unit merchandise such as furniture, preliminary counts may be made and entered on tags attached to the merchandise. Upon rechecking, the tags, or parts of them, are removed and assembled either for listing on sheets or for summarization without individual listing. The tag method is also well adapted to yard goods and house furnishings.

Assignment of Personnel. Assignment of personnel for inventory taking should be planned well in advance of the actual inventory date. Since store or department managers are usually responsible for the accuracy of the physical counts in their store or departments, they should have sufficient time to select and instruct the employees who are to work on the inventory. If there is an adequate number of trained clerks available for the inventory taking, the work is more likely to be completed with accuracy and dispatch.

Arrangement of Stock. The counting and listing of merchandise is facilitated by good arrangement of stock as to merchandise department classification, season letter, and selling price.

Examination for Proper Ticketing. A preliminary review of the stock is desirable to verify that all merchandise items are properly ticketed and that all price changes have been made.

Identification and Arrangement of Merchandise. To facilitate the inventory taking and correct summarization of the physical inventory, the following types of merchandise should be identified in advance and segregated or otherwise taken on separate listings:

    Merchandise on loan or consignment.
    Damaged, defective, soiled, or obsolete goods.
    Merchandise out for repair or refurbishment.
    Layaway merchandise.
    Merchandise sold but not delivered.

In addition, it is highly desirable that all goods received be processed and placed in inventoriable stock areas, preferably forward or reserve stock. Further, goods returned by customers should be returned to forward or reserve stock areas, and credits for such returns should be submitted to the accounts receivable department.

Establishment of Cutoff Procedures. Prior to the physical inventory taking, every effort should be made to clear through to the accounts payable office all invoices (or receiving reports for merchandise received without invoices) covering merchandise which has been opened and checked and placed in forward or reserve stock. Invoices covering merchandise not received or not placed in inventoriable stock should be stamped "Not Taken in Inventory." All unprocessed price change or merchandise transfer documents should be forwarded to the inventory control or statistical department for processing.

In effect, it is essential that, prior to the physical inventory taking, every effort be made to collect and submit all paper work bearing upon the inventory—invoices, receiving reports, merchandise transfers and credits, price changes, and sales checks—to the appropriate accounting or statistical department. This will also involve the establishment of special procedures regarding the handling and movement of merchandise prior to and after inventory taking, focusing on such aspects as goods sold, transferred, returned to vendors, marked and re-marked. The store can then focus on the important problem of fixing the point of "cutoff" between transactions prior to and after inventory taking. At some particular point the records of sales and purchases are closed for the period, and it is important that inventory listings exclude goods for which sales, or purchase returns, have been recorded and include goods for which purchases, or sales returns, have been recorded. For the stock ledger, also, it is necessary to use the same cutoff point for the recording of price changes and transfers so that book and physical inventories will be on the same basis.

Instructions

Instructions with respect to a physical inventory are prepared for use by store and/or department managers, the executive checkers of the counting and listing, and the personnel assigned to counting and listing. It is also necessary to notify all accounting, control, and operations supervisors that specific inventories are to be taken and, therefore, that the appropriate cutoffs should be established for departments being inventoried.

Instructions to buyers and assistants and/or department managers are really in the nature of reminders or suggestions helpful in making essential preparations for the inventory. They are reminded to keep the receiving and marking rooms clear of merchandise (to the fullest extent feasible), to make returns and markdowns in timely fashion, and to see that invoices, chargebacks, sales and credit checks, transfers, price changes, etc., applicable up to the time of inventory, have been sent to the appropriate accounting offices. A résumé of procedures for the distribution of inventory sheets, tags, or cards, and for listing and checking is usually included in these instructions, together with reminders of places where merchandise may be located and the requirements for separate listings of certain items of stock. There may also be suggestions regarding the arrangement of stock for the physical inventory, as well as guidance in reviewing, collecting, and arranging completed inventory sheets, tags, or cards and forwarding them to the inventory office.

Instructions to executive checkers cover their duties and procedures under the general inventory practices that have been adopted and the extent and manner of checking that is to be done. If separate listings of the same stock are made by independent inventory teams, the checkers' duties principally will comprise supervision and comparison of the duplicate listings. If original listings are completely rechecked by the inventory teams, or by another person, the executive checkers' duties will be largely supervisory. Where only test-checks are made, it is usual to assign such work to the executive checkers.

The following are illustrations of inventory instructions to store and/or department managers, executive checkers (in a situation where only test-checking is done), and to inventory-taking personnel. The specific inventory instructions to be adopted must follow the inventory procedure of the store or department.

INSTRUCTIONS TO STORE AND DEPARTMENT MANAGERS

1. *Introduction.* The actual taking of the inventory will be conducted in your store (or department) on the assigned dates. In order to assure the accurate recording of the inventory, it is im-

perative that adequate and trained personnel be scheduled, that control be maintained over all inventory documents issued, and that there be individual management supervision throughout the entire inventory taking. The following outline of the procedures concerning the recording of the inventory must be reviewed very carefully prior to inventory date to assure an accurate inventory.

2. *Inventory Personnel.* Inventory personnel will consist of experienced employees and contingents. On inventory morning the following must be adhered to:
   a. All inventory personnel must report to work promptly.
   b. All inventory personnel must be instructed on the proper method of taking the inventory.
   c. Inventory teams must be established consisting of one experienced employee and one temporary (contingent) employee. These teams will consist of a caller and a writer, respectively.
   d. Inventory teams will be assigned inventory sheets and the specific areas which they must inventory. Area supervisors should start off each team to be sure they are directed and started in the proper areas.

3. *Control/Inventory Forms.* Control over all inventory documents must be maintained to assure proper submission to the Home Office. In order to maintain this document control, the following must be adhered to:
   a. Numerically sequenced and controlled inventory sheets will be assigned to inventory teams. Inventory assignment sheets must be set up for each department. The following information must be recorded on the inventory assignment sheets:
   Starting sheet number
   Department name and number
   Signed out to: [Caller] and [Recorder]
   b. All other inventory forms must be completed by their related department managers and returned to the inventory control desk. All unused forms which have been distributed must also be returned to the inventory control desk.

   SPECIAL NOTE: Due to the importance of document control, it is required that a qualified employee be assigned the function of supervising the operation of the control desk. This will entail the assigning of all inventory sheets and the control of all other inventory forms.

4. *Inventorying Merchandise.* It will be the responsibility of each inventory team to be sure to inventory all merchandise which is located within their assigned area or section. In the inventorying of merchandise the following must be adhered to:

- a. Merchandise must be inventoried at the correct selling price, as shown on the ticket.
- b. When merchandise is not ticketed, items are to be pulled off the shelf, gondola, or rack and placed in a cart for the department manager to price and inventory.
- c. When merchandise is damaged, it is to be inventoried at the ticketed price, removed from the shelf, and placed in a cart labeled "Damaged Goods." The department manager will inspect this merchandise to determine whether a markdown is to be taken and a new selling price assigned. A separate listing of all such damaged goods must be prepared.
- d. Use one inventory sheet for each shelf, bin, or rack set forth in the floor plan.

5. *Inventory Supervision.* It is the direct responsibility of store management personally to supervise the taking of the physical inventory. It is extremely important that there be a check on all inventory teams, within one hour of beginning the inventory, to be sure they are following proper instructions and recording the inventories as prescribed. This will enable corrective action to be taken before too large an area has been incorrectly inventoried.

   Continued supervision must be conducted by management throughout the inventory day. Only through close supervision of all inventorying areas will store managers be able to assure themselves that an accurate inventory has been taken and thereby properly reflect the store's inventory position.

6. *Collecting Inventory Sheets.* When an area of the store has been completely inventoried (as outlined on the floor plan) and checked, inventory sheets can be collected, returned to the control desk, and placed in numerical order. All sheets must be accounted for.

Instructions to Executive Checkers

1. Make a detailed check of a fair sample of the work of each inventory team to assure yourself that the work is being done carefully and accurately.
2. The checker will look at the merchandise and carefully check the price ticket and compare it with the following entries on the inventory sheet: department number and price. The merchandise must be carefully counted so as to determine the quantity; the checking should be done both from the merchandise to the inventory sheet and from the inventory sheet to the merchandise. Exercise special care on the more expensive and larger quantities

of merchandise. You can detect errors quickly by scanning the columns. Watch for omissions.
3. If you feel that the inventory is not being taken correctly, contact your control supervisor.
4. No erasures should be made on the inventory sheet. If an error is found, call the control supervisor who will in turn consult the buyer, if it seems necessary to do so. If the error is verified, then draw a pencil line through the error and write in the right price, etc., above the entry in a clear, legible manner and initial it.
5. Call on a representative in the department who is familiar with the stock for any information regarding items on the inventory sheets which you do not readily locate. In all cases you must verify the quantity and price. As each sheet is checked, the checker will sign his or her name in the space provided on the inventory sheet.
6. When the inventory has been completed and you are satisfied that the merchandise has been listed correctly, the sheets will be collected in the order in which they were issued and examined to see that all the necessary information is entered thereon. After accounting for all the sheets that were issued to the department, the sheets will be bound together in books by classifications. Thereafter, the completed inventory, together with all unused material, will be delivered to the Inventory Office.

Special instructions covering the more technical phases of procedure are issued to personnel assigned to accounting and listing. General procedures are usually outlined to the inventory personnel in meetings with department heads and these are followed up by supervision. An illustration of technical instructions to counters and listers follows:

Instructions to Inventory Personnel

1. Report to work promptly on Inventory Day.
2. Write legibly; use numerals (1, 2, 3, 4, 5, etc.), not strokes.
3. You will be assigned to a two-man "team." Each team will be responsible for the *accurate counting* and recording of all merchandise in a specific area.
4. Record department name and number on each inventory sheet.
5. The caller will count and call the quantity and selling price shown on the ticket. The other person will repeat and record the information.
6. *Price Tickets.* Before inventory, be on the lookout for merchandise which is not properly priced. Where price tickets are missing, have them replaced by the buyer or assistant. All merchandise must bear a season letter.

7. *Listing Quantities.* It is strictly against the regulations to copy prices and quantities from stock books or scraps of paper. All listing must be done directly from the merchandise to the inventory sheets.
Never list more than one merchandise classification on a sheet.
Never list merchandise from two different shelves, bins, or drawers on the same sheet.
Never use dittos.
Season letters must be printed, not written.
Sheets must be signed in the space provided by the person who counts, and the lister.
8. *Multiple-Price Items and Packaged Merchandise.* All merchandise will be recorded on the inventory sheets at the *unit* retail price. This applies to all departments carrying packaged or multiple price items.

Examples:
a. Packaged merchandise which sells for a package price (package of three for $1.98) will be recorded as one unit at $1.98. If a package is broken (or if single item), record the actual number of pieces at the *unit* retail price (in this example, one at $.66).
b. Multiple-price items (other than packaged) will be recorded at the unit retail price.

Examples:
a. Items selling for three for $10.00 will be recorded as "so many" units at $3.33 (unit price).
b. Two for $1.50 will be recorded as "so many" units at $.75.
c. Two for $1.79 will be recorded as "so many" units at $.90.
9. *Unit Counts in Excess of 100.* In the recording of any unit counts which exceed 100 units, the recorder must circle the units in the quantity column of the inventory sheet. This will assure the proper extension of these large quantities by the Home Office.
10. Use one inventory sheet for each *shelf, bin,* or *rack.*
11. *Do not erase.* If you make an error, *void* the error by drawing a line through the entry.
12. When your "team" has completed taking its assigned Department Inventory, return *all* inventory sheets to the person assigned to the Control Desk. Make certain that he or she correctly records the last number used by your team on the assignment sheet.

A specimen of detailed instructions for the taking of physical inventory by Sales Division personnel appears in Figure 19 (pages 192–96).

INSTRUCTIONS FOR TAKING INVENTORY

Responsibility	Action
Floor Plans	1. Using Floor Plan worksheet, draw a block layout of fixtures in Stockrooms and Selling areas.
	1a. See last page of this notice for examples of plan and fixtures.
	2. On the Floor Plan, number Fixtures consecutively starting at the Main Entrance of each area. Always start numbering in Stockroom(s).
	2a. When an understock section of a Fixture is to be taken early and sealed, assign a separate Fixture Number to it.
	2b. Mark a block "Display" and list where "Out of Dept." mdse is located.
	2c. Mark a block "Office" if mdse is in an Office.
	2d. If a Fixture is added before Inventory, it can be added to the plan and the next Fixture number assigned. If a Fixture must be moved, it retains its original assigned number.
	3. Using special peel labels, number each Fixture, attaching the label to the upper left corner or at the point on Fixture where counting should start.
Fixture List	4. List all numbers assigned to Fixtures on Fixture List Sheet(s).
	4a. With Floor Plan and list, review Fixtures, decide on number of sheets per Fixture, and post on Fixture List.
	4b. Post the number of shelves, bins, drawers, or sections in each Fixture—an Inventory Sheet must be in each one.
	4c. Check any Fixture which will be difficult or take unusual time to count.
	4d. Check any Fixture which could be counted early and sealed.
	4e. Check Fixture which will require Deduction Sheet(s).
	5. Add the number of Inventory Sheets you will need.
	6. Post the number of Inventory Sheets needed on Fixture List.
	7. Make requisition for any extra personnel.
Team Planning	8. Review your Fixture Plan and decide, based on the number of teams, the actual Fixtures each team will count and in what order.
	8a. Enter the name of an employee in the Dept. assigned as one member of a team or just identify as Team 1, 2, etc. and decide on individuals later.

FIG. 19. Sales division instructions for taking of physical inventories.

Ch. 9   TAKING PHYSICAL INVENTORIES   193

Responsibility	Action
	9. Plan on having the most difficult or time-consuming Fixtures counted first. These should be marked on your Fixture List.
Approval of Inventory Plans	10. Take Floor Plan, Fixture List(s) and Requisition to Store Manager or Divisional Manager for review and approval.
Stockkeeping	11. As soon as you can, tell each salesperson the Fixtures they are assigned for Inventory. The second person can be assigned to the salesperson when Inventory starts.
	12. Begin checking stock as early as possible for soiled and damaged mdse to be cleared by the Buyer.
	12a. Have any mdse without price tickets pulled and tickets made.
Vendor Return Mdse.	13. As soon as list or information about mdse to be returned to Vendor is received from the Buyer, pull and transfer to the location designated by the Buyer.
	14. When mdse is returned direct to a Vendor from your Store, make Claim and take to Wrapping Dept.
Customer Returns	15. Be sure all Call Pick-ups and Mail Returns are being handled promptly and that they clear before Inventory.
	15a. Check Credit and Refund Books and be sure all returns have cleared. If in doubt, check with Sales Audit.
Sales Books & Registers	16. Check all salespeople's books and Registers to be sure all work has cleared and to be certain that money and/or tickets are not caught in or back of the drawer.
Transfers	17. Pull and transfer mdse before Cut-off Dates.
	17a. Clear any exception first with your immediate Supervisor and then call the Inventory Coordinator for authorization and instructions.
Reports	18. Be sure all reports (Sales, Purchases, Transfers, and Distribution) are checked on a current basis and that corrections have been made.
Inventory Sheets	19. During scheduled time on Calendar, pick up Inventory Sheets from the Office.
	19a. Turn in approved Yellow copy of Fixture List when Inventory Sheets are issued.
	19b. Sign Inventory Check Sheet.
	19c. Verify number of Inventory Sheets received.
	20. Using Fixture List, post the Dept. Number and Fixture Number on all Inventory Sheets before they are put on Fixtures.
Mdse Out-of-Dept.	21. Just prior to the Physical Inventory, locate any mdse "Out-of-Dept." and if possible have it returned.
	21a. In Store 01, the Display people inventory the Windows and each Sales Manager copies the mdse from the Window Inventory Sheets in the General Office.

FIG. 19.   Continued.

Responsibility	Action
	21b. Inventory of mdse "Out-of-Dept." is taken on an Inventory Sheet assigned to "Display" the day before the Physical Inventory.
	21c. An Inventory Adjustment Sheet is used to list any mdse being repaired.
Price Changes	22. Make all Price Changes as soon as possible, avoiding last-minute changes.
	23. Give the next unused Price Change Report in each book to your General Office to be sent as a group to the General Accounting Office the day before the Physical Inventory is taken. Write "Inventory Cut-off" and the Dept. No(s). across the face of the form and only send the Yellow copy.
	23a. In Store 01, give reports to your Div. Sales Manager to be sent to General Accounting.
Hampers	24. Be certain all hampers have been emptied or shown as a Fixture to be inventoried.
Laying Inventory Sheet	25. Approval must be given by the Store Manager before any Inventory Sheets are put on Fixtures before the Store closes. If approved:
	25a. Be sure good customer service is maintained.
	25b. Lay sheets on Fixtures as inconspicuously as possible.
	26. A responsible person can be assigned to help lay Inventory Sheets.
	27. Lay the sheets in numerical sequence according to the Fixture List and Floor Plan.
	27a. Do not lay the sheets in batches. Put them on each shelf or bin, or in drawers of the Fixture.
To Start Inventory	28. Assign the Department closing to a responsible person so you are free to start the Inventory.
	29. Have a meeting and review Inventory team instructions and then assign extra people to work with salespeople.
	30. Check the weakest teams first and/or teams not familiar with your department.
	30a. Observe all teams as soon as possible to be sure mdse is being counted and listed accurately.
Instructions To Be Reviewed with Teams	31. Review the Inventory Sheet used in your Dept.
	32. Tell the teams to use either the Stroke count method or to post the actual number of units.
	32a. Be sure any additional teams assigned during Inventory know how your Dept. is being recorded.
	33. Dos and Don'ts for Inventory Teams.
	33a. Do check Fixture No. on Inventory Sheet with number on Fixture before starting.
	33b. Do NOT erase on an Inventory Sheet. Draw a line through and enter on next line or block.

FIG. 19. Continued.

Responsibility	Action

      33c. Do quickly check mdse on Fixture and if not in order to count, arrange before starting.
      33d. Do NOT take an Inventory Sheet away from the Fixture it is assigned to.
      33e. Do NOT destroy an Inventory Sheet.
      33f. Do ask the Supervisor when more sheets are needed.
      33g. Do ask the Supervisor when in doubt about anything.
      33h. Do print legibly; remember, someone has to extend the Inventory.
      33i. Do NOT mix Stroke Count and actual number listing.
  34. To actually count and list:
      34a. 1st person calls description (if to be entered on sheet), then gives price, class, and season, and counts number of units.
      34b. 2nd person enters the information on the Inventory Sheet.
      34c. When all mdse is listed, check to be sure price, class, season, and units are posted for each entry.
      34d. Enter names of both team members on sheet.
      34e. Place the sheet back on the Fixture and start the next part of the Fixture or next Fixture.

During Inventory

  35. The Control Representative(s) assigned to your department also will be checking the teams.
      35a. Any problems will be brought to your attention to be corrected.
  36. Let your Control Representative know:
      36a. If you need additional teams.
      36b. When you are satisfied and sheets can be pulled.
      36c. When Stockrooms are completed so sheets can be pulled after the Floor Inventory has started.
  37. When additional sheets are needed on a Fixture, post sheet number issued on Fixture List.
  38. If you should need more sheets, get them from the Office. Never change a Department Number on an Inventory Sheet.

When Inventory Is Finished

  39. The Control Representative helps pick up sheets and maintains control of them.
  40. After accounting for all sheets, the Control Representative turns them in to the Office.
      40a. Person responsible for the Inventory works with the Control Representative and completes any missing price, class, season, or units.

FIG. 19. Continued.

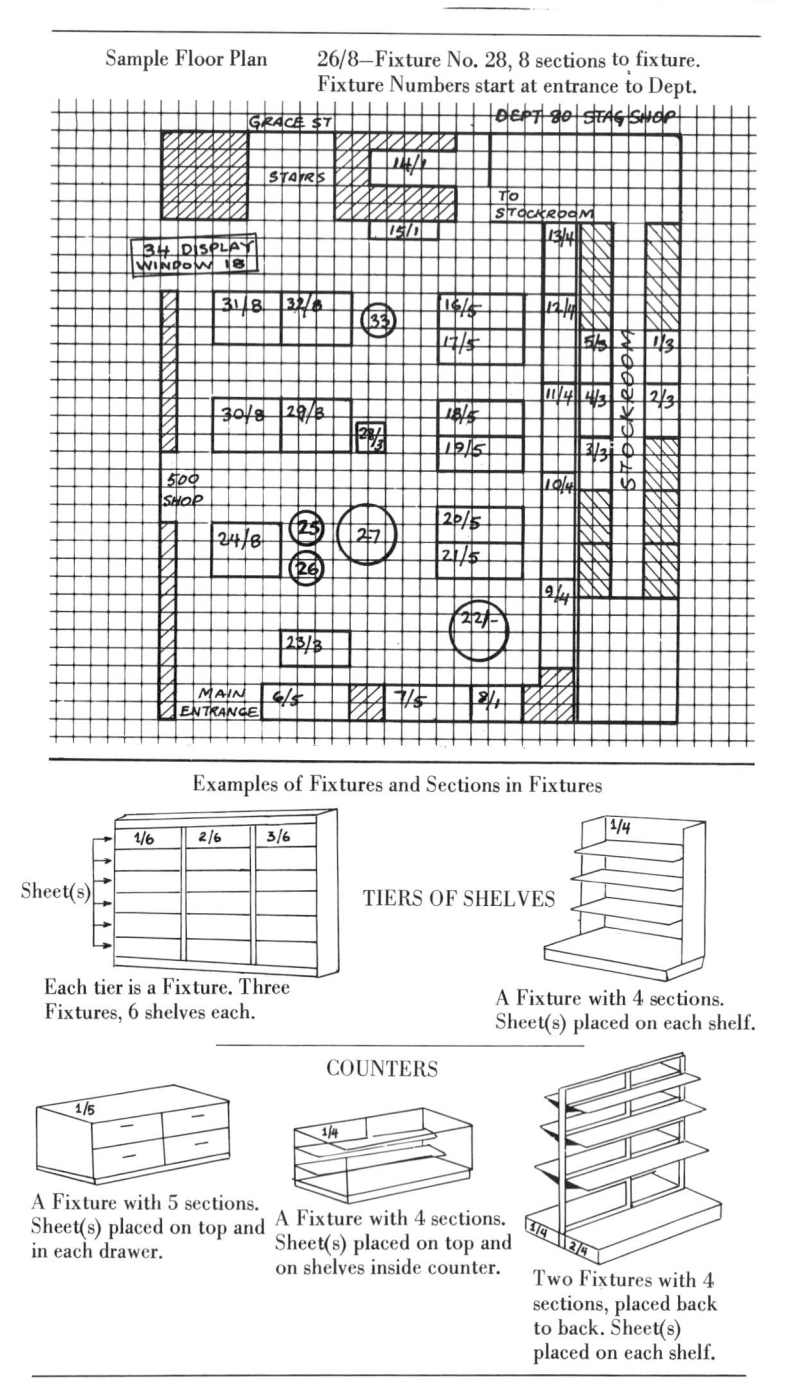

196 RETAIL ACCOUNTING AND FINANCIAL CONTROL Ch. 9

Sample Floor Plan — 26/8—Fixture No. 28, 8 sections to fixture. Fixture Numbers start at entrance to Dept.

Examples of Fixtures and Sections in Fixtures

Sheet(s)

TIERS OF SHELVES

Each tier is a Fixture. Three Fixtures, 6 shelves each.

A Fixture with 4 sections. Sheet(s) placed on each shelf.

COUNTERS

A Fixture with 5 sections. Sheet(s) placed on top and in each drawer.

A Fixture with 4 sections. Sheet(s) placed on top and on shelves inside counter.

Two Fixtures with 4 sections, placed back to back. Sheet(s) placed on each shelf.

FIG. 19. Continued.

Forms for the Inventory

The Controllers' Congress of National Retail Merchants Association has prepared an *Inventory Taking Manual* (2d ed., 1951), covering procedures and forms used in connection with the taking of physical inventories. The manual illustrates a number of forms that are in actual use and presents recommended forms of sheets and tags.

The recommended forms were developed after careful thought by the inventory committee, in an effort to present a composite picture of good practice in the use of inventory sheets, tags, and tallies. An inventory sheet is shown in Figure 20, an inventory tag in Figure 21, and an inventory tally in Figure 22. The inventory sheet is designed with two "Extension" columns which can be utilized for mathematical verification purposes. Extensions are initially entered in Column 2, and after the extensions are footed Column 2 is detached (note perforation). A second calculation of extensions is made, with entries noted in Column 1. For any one department the aggregate of Column 1 totals must agree with the aggregate of Column 2 totals. Any difference in overall totals can be traced to specific inventory sheets.

Many stores use both sheets and tags. Sheets are preferred where it is desired to limit the number of forms. Sheets are more easily controlled than tags; also, their use avoids repeating general information for each item, reduces manual handling, and facilitates computations as well as review. The tag has the advantage of flexibility. Counting and listing can be started in advance and can be interrupted without causing confusion. (It is to be noted, however, that the tags will be visible to customers, whereas sheets are usually kept in the background until official counting and listing begins.) "Spot" checking can be made largely a visual test of the presence of tags; a thorough check is readily made in the process of "pulling" the tags. Tags involve greater manual work in sorting to obtain analyses, but their use facilitates obtaining diverse data from a single record.

The inventory tally shown in Figure 22 has been designed for use by optical scanning equipment. The use of an optically scannable tally has the advantages of faster and more economical inventory summarization and improved accuracy through built-in controls in the data processing equipment. As indicated earlier,

IMPORTANT

1. Be accurate—write legibly.
2. Quantity and prices must be for the same unit.
3. Each and every sheet must be accounted for and returned.

INVENTORY SHEET

B 17059 | B 17059

Date ______________

Counted and Called By	Entered By	Location		Department	Department
Recounted and Called By	Entries Checked By	Fixture	Shelf	Class.	Class.

DESCRIPTION	TALLY	P or M √	Season Letter	Quan-tity	PRICE per unit Dollars	Cts.	EXTENSION Col. 1		EXTENSION Col. 2
							A		A
							B		B
							C		C
							D		D
							E		E
							F		F
							G		G
							H		H
							J		J
							K		K
							L		L
							M		M
							P		P
							S		S
							T		T
							W		W

DO NOT WRITE IN THIS SPACE ☞

BUYER'S APPROVAL	Figured By	Audited By		Figured By

FIG. 20. Inventory sheet.

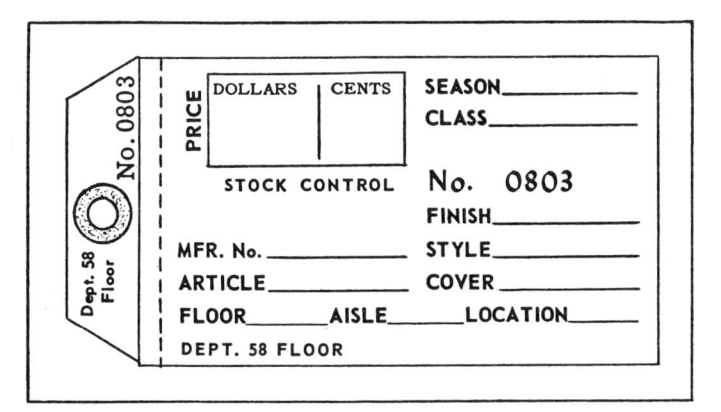

FIG. 21. Inventory tag.

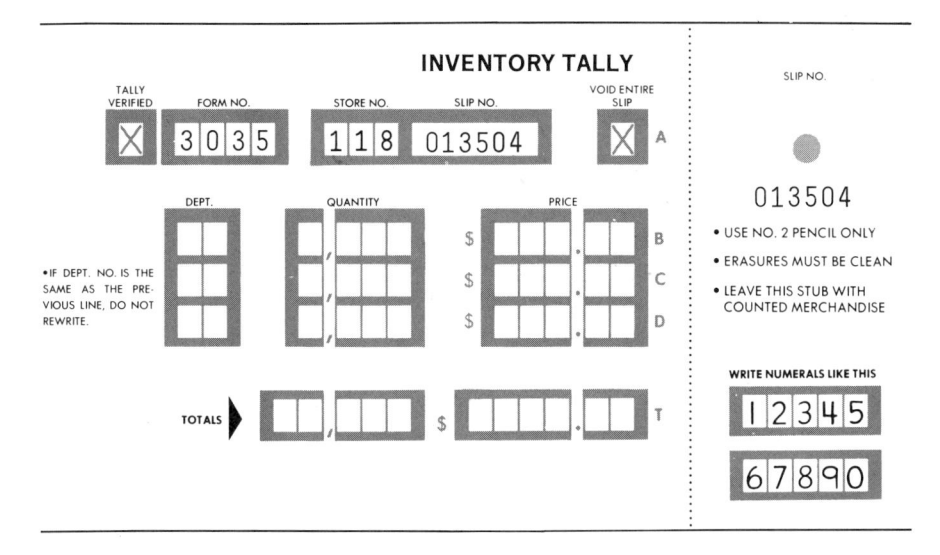

FIG. 22. Inventory tally.

the forms for the physical inventory taking can also be designed to summarize a variety of unit control data either manually or through the use of data processing equipment.

Aside from inventory sheets, tags, and tallies, there are a number of other forms used in recording the inventory. There are the forms required for summarizing inventory sheets and tags departmentally, and forms for controlling the sheet and tag numbers. Other forms are utilized for recording open transactions and the last transactions prior to inventory. Some of these data originate in accounting and control offices and some in selling departments. For example:

Sales audit office:
  Missing sales checks (not audited as sales)
  Missing sales returns (not audited as returns)
Receiving room: Last receiving report number
Warehouse: Last transfer number out of warehouse
Selling departments:
  Unfilled sales checks (sales passed but goods not delivered)
  Last price change numbers (price increase and reduction)
  Last charge-back issued for return of merchandise
  Number of last merchandise transfer issued

The information as to open transactions and last transactions is required by the Inventory Office in order to corroborate the propriety of the inventory cutoff. A final important form which has a bearing upon the cutoff is the inventory report from department buyers, which contains a certificate. An illustration of this form is shown in Figure 23.

Time of Inventories

The preponderance of retailers take an annual physical inventory on or about the fiscal year-end date. A large number take a supplementary semiannual inventory, and a limited number of retailers cycle the taking of physical inventories throughout the fiscal year. The taking of a complete semiannual or year-end physical inventory becomes a problem of organizing and coordinating the activities of the entire retail organization as of one date. Differences disclosed by such inventories are subject to study as of that date. The plan of spreading inventory taking throughout the entire fiscal period has the advantage of distributing the burden of work over the season, work ordinarily performed by a specialized crew of inventory takers. Admittedly, this plan provides merchandisers with current information on the status of individual departmental inventories, which may be useful. It does not, however, supply a complete analysis of total store inventory such as is provided when all departmental inventories are taken on the same date. Another difficulty in staggering or cycling physical inventories revolves about the collection and reconciliation of all related cut-off data, an

Inventory Certificate and Cut-Off Sheet

TO: DEPARTMENT MANAGERS

Re: Inventory January 31, 19___

Fill in all the blank spaces indicating that merchandise at locations other than warehouses, stockrooms, or forward stock has been accounted for. Write "None" if careful investigation discloses no merchandise. Return this sheet to the Inventory Office on (day) February 1, 19___ , with your inventory sheets or tickets.

USE A SEPARATE SHEET FOR EACH DEPARTMENT   Dept. No.___

Entered on Inventory Sheets Numbered		Entered on Inventory Sheets Numbered	
Displays-Own floor #___ to #___		Merchandise on Loan #___ to #___	
Displays-other flrs. ___ to ___		Advertising Office ___ to ___	
Receiving Room ___ to ___		Dry Cleaners ___ to ___	
Marking Room ___ to ___		Workrooms ___ to ___	
Alteration Room ___ to ___		Customer's Returns ___ to ___	
Window Display ___ to ___		Bargain Tables not ___ to ___	
Buyer's Office ___ to ___		Out on Repair-chgd. ___ to ___	
Dining Room ___ to ___		___ to ___	
Cold Storage ___ to ___		___ to ___	

Please fill in the last numbers used in the following forms which affect the Inventory as of January 31, 19___ .

	Last Number		Last Number
Charge Credit Form No. ___	___	Retail Price Change Form No. ___	___
Cash Credit Form No. ___	___	Vendor's Returns Form No. ___	___
Gift Exchange Form No. ___	___	Mdse. Transfer Form No. ___	___

This is to certify that I have personally checked into every factor pertaining to the Inventory and have found them in accordance with instructions. All the merchandise under my jurisdiction, wherever located, has been carefully counted and listed according to instructions. All merchandise was taken according to the prices shown on the price tickets.

Signature _____
Department Manager

(Used by permission of NRMA)

FIG. 23. Inventory certificate and cut-off sheet.

extremely difficult procedure when it is done on a departmental basis rather than on an all-store basis.

Some departments should be inventoried more frequently than others. Furniture and other house furnishings departments may have inventories taken only once or twice a season, whereas small wares, ready-to-wear, and shoes may be inventoried as often as once a month, or even more frequently. The frequency with which inventories are taken depends largely upon prior shortage experience. In ready-to-wear departments, weekly inventories of units in stock are frequently made as a key merchandising tool, and often with a view to testing the unit control systems and records. Such inventories are, however, taken quickly for this special purpose and are not computed in dollar amounts or for comparison with book dollar controls.

Under a plan of taking inventories with regular frequency throughout the fiscal year, a specific inventory may be taken as of a day that is not the closing day of a monthly or seasonal accounting period. This may be true also where all or practically all inventories are taken as of one date shortly before the last day of the fiscal year or other accounting period. This introduces the problem of "working forward" or "updating" the physical inventory by taking into account the transactions between the physical inventory date and the fiscal closing date. (Less frequently there is the problem of "working back" a physical inventory taken after the fiscal closing date. Whether worked forward or backward, however, the problems are similar.) Working an inventory forward simply involves accounting for the conventional stock ledger transactions (i.e., accounting for all increases and decreases in the dollars of departmental inventories). There are, however, two ways in which the working forward is accomplished. One method starts with the amount of the summarized physical inventory, adds the merchandise debits, and subtracts the merchandise deductions for the intervening days to the end of the fiscal period. This updated physical inventory is then compared with the corresponding book figure at the end of the fiscal period to arrive at the inventory shortage. The other method compares the physical inventory with the derived book inventory as of the physical inventory date to determine the shortage or overage. The book inventory as at the close of the fiscal period is then adjusted by the computed shortage or overage, and the result is considered to be physical inventory as at the close of the fiscal period.

Inventory Cutoff and Reconciliation

There have been several references thus far in this chapter to the "cutoff," or line of demarcation, between transactions before and after inventory, which must be recognized if there is to be a valid comparison between the accounting records and the physical inventory. For a correct cutoff, it is important that departmental purchases be charged with all invoices for goods included in inventory, or sold before inventory date, and be credited with chargebacks for goods returned to vendors or segregated from stock for such return. It is desirable that pending claims with vendors or other departments be cleared or be appropriately recorded before the inventory. Transfers between departments should be fully entered on the records. On the other hand, goods not charged to purchases, such as consignment or memorandum items, should be excluded from inventory; and goods not credited to purchases, such as stock out for repair, cleaning, or on loan or exhibition, should be included in inventory. With respect to departmental sales, the cutoff procedure calls for exclusion from inventory of items recorded as sold but undelivered at inventory date, and items returned by customers for which return credits have not been recorded at inventory date. On the other hand, goods should be included in inventory for which departments have received no credit as sales, such as items on loan or memorandum to customers and items for which sales checks are delayed and thus are "missing" to the sales audit office at time of inventory. These various distinctions are the essence of cutoff procedures. For accuracy in book controls of stock, such as the retail inventory method, it is important also that price changes (markups and markdowns) given effect in the inventory or on goods sold be fully recorded.

"Reconciliation" of inventory refers to the process whereby book control inventory figures and physical inventory figures are adjusted to a comparable basis, so that the difference will, in fact, represent the true shortage or overage. The word "reconciliation" is sometimes applied to the process of "working forward" or "working back" the physical inventory to the fiscal closing date. Figure 24 shows the reconciliation process of adjusting the book inventory to the date of the physical inventory to determine the shortage or overage as of that date.

Another form for use in the reconciling process is illustrated in Figure 25.

RECONCILIATION OF BOOK INVENTORY AND PHYSICAL INVENTORY

Dept. _____ Date of Inventory _____

Book stock as at _____ (last closing of stock
  ledger) $
Add: Charges for period from date of last book
  figure:
  Domestic purchases $
  Foreign purchases
  Markups
  Department transfers
  Invoices in transit
  Workroom bills
  Unaudited return sales checks
  *Undelivered sales where sales checks have been
    recorded

Deduct: Credits for period from date of last
    book figure:
  Net sales
  Markdowns
  Discounts
  Allowance for shortages
  Unaudited sales checks
  Unpassed charge-backs to vendors

  Adjusted book stock

Physical inventory
  Add: Items as follows:
  Memorandum sales to customers
  Merchandise out on exhibition
  Memorandum charges to workrooms
  Memorandum charges to vendors
  Merchandise loaned to other departments

  Deduct: Items as follows:
  Merchandise borrowed from other departments
    (if taken in inventory)
  *Undelivered sales where sales checks have
    been recorded
  Adjusted physical inventory
  Disclosed shortage (or overage)
  Shortage already allowed for and deducted
    from book figure
  Total actual shortage (or overage) $_____ †

*Which of these two procedures is to be followed depends in any specific case upon whether the transaction should at date be included as a sale, properly reflected, for example, in accounts receivable. If the transaction is at date properly treated as a sale, merchandise if on hand is to be excluded from physical inventory, credit already having been made to book stock. If the transaction is not at date properly treated as a sale, the merchandise is to be included in physical inventory as taken, but book stock should be increased accordingly to eliminate for the time being the sales credit made.

†Shortage already allowed for is increased by disclosed shortage (or decreased by disclosed overage) to determine total actual shortage.

FIG. 24. Reconciliation of book and physical inventories, at retail.

INVENTORY RECONCILIATION SHEET

EXHIBIT S

For "Building" up Book Stock
For "Cut-off" adjustment to be made to Book Stock
For "Stock-Taking" adjustment to be made to Book Stock

Dept. No.

Inventory Date as of _____

Transactions	From Mo.-Day	To Mo.-Day	Check Add or Deduct	At Retail Add	Deduct
Sales (Net)					
Markdowns, M/D Canc. (Net)					
Employees' Discount (Net)					
Markups, M/Up Canc. (Net)					
Purchases (Net)					
M. Invoices & Claims to be incl.					
N. Invoices & Claims NOT to be incl.					
O. Open on Rec'g Records to be incl.					
P. Open on Inv. Register to be incl.					
Q. No Invoice received Temporary Invoices to be incl.					
R. Sales, etc., open on Audit Records to be incl.					
TOTALS					
Net Amount to be used					
Book Stock as of _____					
Book Stock after adjustment					
Actual Physical Inventory as of _____					
BOOK ADJUSTMENT STOCK-TAKING DIFFERENCES OVER SHORT					

	This Year	Last Year
Overage		
Shortage		
Shortage previously charged off — ___% to Net Sales		
TOTAL OVER SHORT		
% to Net Sales		
Actual Net Sales for Period		

(Used by permission of NRMA)

FIG. 25. Inventory reconciliation sheet.

Shortages or Overages

Differences between book inventory control figures and physical inventory figures, as disclosed by the reconciliation process, are subject to explanation. They may be due to errors in deriving the book figures or to incorrect taking of the physical inventories. Errors in the book figures may be due to breakdowns in the operation of the store systems.

It is a duty of the inventory office to investigate and explain the differences. The first step is to recheck carefully the figures entering into the derivation of the book inventory. If a large unexplained shortage or overage remains after having established the reasonable correctness of the book inventory, the physical inventory should be retaken. If a second inventory results in a comparably large difference, there is an implication of negligence in the handling and marking of merchandise or of actual theft or dishonesty on the part of employees or public. Where unit controls are in use, they supply a valuable check on both physical inventories and book controls. Reference should be made to such records in investigating inventory differences.

The causes of inventory shortages and errors in the accounting records are numerous and may arise in the operations of the following offices or departments:

    Order and invoice office
    Receiving room
    Marking room
    Reserve stock rooms
    Selling departments
    Delivery departments
    Sales audit department
    Accounts payable office
    Statistical office
    Inventory taking

An extensive discussion of the causative factors of shortages is included in Chapter 12. In more condensed form, some of the principal causes of shortages or overages are as follows:

1. Lack of vendor's invoice for goods received.
2. Faulty checking of merchandise.
3. Incorrect charge-back of returns to vendors.

Ch. 9 TAKING PHYSICAL INVENTORIES 207

4. Inadequate check on invoices for errors in prices and calculations (including retail), and lack of safeguards against duplicate bills.
5. Defective controls over goods sent out to contractors, repair shops, engravers, etc., and also over goods sent out on memorandum to customers.
6. Poor layout of receiving and marking rooms with respect to exits, facilities, fixtures, etc.
7. Failure to make claims against shippers for shortages, breakage, etc.
8. Errors in marking and re-marking and in having the marked prices conform to pre-retailed prices on the purchase orders or price entries on the invoices.
9. Loss of merchandise before reaching the selling floors or while in transit to branch stores.
10. Failure to report breakage and damage.
11. Lack of controls on selling floors, at inspection and wrapping desks, and in fitting and alteration rooms.
12. Failure to report markdowns, whether taken in ordinary course or on lot sales; remnants; etc.
13. Loss on sample cutting of piece goods.
14. Incorrect handling of discount sales.
15. Improper methods in handling credits and refunds for merchandise returned and even exchanges.
16. Failure to account for all sales checks and to conduct correct sales audit.
17. Theft by customers or employees.
18. Faulty clerical work on sales checks, markdowns, etc.
19. Inefficiency in taking and listing the physical inventory.
20. Incorrect calculation and summarization of inventory.

Under the operation of the retail method of inventory, there is one important source of figures entering into the book records which is not subject to ordinary accounting control. The figures in question are the retail prices of purchases. The unit selling prices placed on merchandise should be the same as those placed on invoices. There is in the ordinary course of business no mathematical proof of the accuracy of these figures. Prevention of errors is largely a question of method. Likewise, in the accounting office the unit retail prices must be extended to obtain the total retail value of each invoice. There is also no mathematical proof of this work or control over totals in the same sense that such proof is obtained for total cost of purchases and for sales. Reliance must be placed on the original calculators and the recheck clerks and on any subsequent administrative review made by buyers of the details of invoices (cost and retail) comprising departmental purchases. The importance of this element in the book figures requires added care in the assignment of the calculation work and in the rechecking and examination for errors.

Inventory Summarization

A considerable variety of useful information and analyses may be obtained from inventory listings, in addition to determining departmental shortage or overage and departmental and store-wide results of operations. In planning for the physical inventory, the extent of information required for these useful reports should be kept in mind so that adequate provision is made in the listing forms and related instructions. Among the more important departmental and store-wide inventory reports prepared from physical listings are the following:

1. Age of merchandise by seasons, comparative with the preceding year.
2. Inventory shortages or overages.
3. Slow-moving merchandise.
4. Excess stock.
5. Comparison of stock by classifications.
6. Imported merchandise on hand, subdivided as to classification and season letter.
7. Consignment merchandise on hand.
8. Inventory turnover, departmentally and by classifications, price lines, styles, etc.

10

Determination of Purchases

Control of Purchase Orders

Under modern budgetary methods, allotments for merchandise purchases are established in advance. Purchases are kept under control by comparing the totals of orders placed against the predetermined purchase allotments.

To effect this control, all orders for merchandise purchases are approved by a budget office or a merchandising office before they are placed with vendors. In addition, control is maintained over acceptance of merchandise entering the store or warehouse. This is done by prohibiting the unpacking and stocking of any merchandise before it is determined that the invoice conforms to an order placed with the approval of the budget office or merchandising office and that the terms, quantities, and prices on the invoice coincide with those on the purchase order.

Checking, Marking, and Stocking

The receipt of merchandise in original packages is almost universally placed under the control of an operations division, which is independent of the merchandising division. The operations division is responsible for the expeditious flow of merchandise through the receiving and marking areas, which obviously involves responsibility for the quality of services provided and the productivity of these areas. The operations division enforces adherence to company control procedures, deals with the carriers, staffs the receiving and marking areas, and maintains effective interdepartmental relationships. In order to clearly assign these duties and to achieve the desired control, the operations function should be centralized, with all of its activities under one manager who is independent of the merchandising division. Any dispersion of responsibility for the process of receiving, checking, marking, and reserve stocking of goods is highly undesirable since it can lead to the relaxation of vital controls and to costly and inefficient operations.

Control of Merchandise Received

Accounting control of merchandise before and after being placed on sale presents two different problems. When goods are placed on sale, they are in fixed and known locations and their values are established and recorded. Control is maintained by means of inventory systems, sales checks, price-change reports, transfers, loan and return records, and inspection systems. However, while merchandise is being moved between the receiving door and the reserve stock rooms or selling floors, its value is not established or recorded in the accounting records. While merchandise is in this state of transition it is not subject to any control system which will automatically locate it and definitively fix its valuation for accounting purposes. In operations where it is geographically feasible, and for appropriate departments, it is desirable to centralize the receiving and marking operations either at the main store of a branch operation or at a central receiving location. Through this centralization, improved cost control can be achieved by eliminating functional duplication, with better control over merchandise as a further advantage. Where it is not feasible to effect this centralized operation, it is difficult to achieve accounting control. Centralization effectively facilitates the coordination of all physical movements of merchandise and synchronizes them with the required accounting controls. In effect, physical merchandise movements and accounting controls are closely interrelated until the goods are ready to be placed on sale. These control measures are outlined in the following paragraphs.

Outline of Purchasing and Invoice Procedure

Typical procedures for placing orders and checking and approving invoices may be generally described as follows.

1. Orders originate with buyers and are approved by the merchandise office and the budget office.

2. The budget office maintains records of orders placed, unfilled orders, and available purchasing allotment ("open-to-buy") for each selling department. If the purchasing allotment is adequate to cover the amounts of the orders, they are approved and mailed to vendors. When orders exceed the purchase limits, they are referred for investigation, leading either to revision of the orders or to revision of the purchase limits to permit placement of the orders. Copies of the orders are placed on file in the order-checking office, where invoices are compared with orders upon receipt of merchandise.

3. Many stores require a "pre-retailing" of orders in part or whole; that is, the retail prices at which the goods are to be sold are placed upon the copies of the orders that are retained in house. Where this is done, the merchandise office and the budget office can check orders for conformity with pre-established departmental markon ranges. The retail prices on the orders are placed on the goods unless buyers obtain permission for changes in prices before marking.

4. Merchandise received from local vendors is usually accompanied by invoices, with the receiving-door clerk placing identical (receiving) numbers on the invoices and the packages received. Invoices for shipments by freight, express, and mail are sent to the receiving door from the mail-opening room and are matched with the shipments as received. Identical (receiving) numbers are also placed on these invoices and packages.

5. In many stores a system of bill aprons is used. The aprons may be written at the time of registering invoices and stamped with the registration numbers, or they may be written upon receipt of merchandise and stamped with the receiving numbers. In the latter event, the same (receiving) number would appear on both the invoice apron and the package or packages received. A variation is to have apron sets prenumbered, with the receiving clerk maintaining numerical control over their sequence. The apron will then constitute the receiving record: the receiving clerk will retain one file copy, will attach one copy to the invoice as an apron, and will give a third copy (without the full detail of other copies) to the delivery agent as a receipt for the goods. A fourth copy, supplied for freight and express shipments, may be used in the subsequent

audit of freight and express charges. The principal features of a bill apron are shown in Figure 26, covering general classifications of merchandise. For ready-to-wear merchandise the apron often provides space for inserting additional descriptive information such as style, size, and color.

\multicolumn{6}{c}{PASTE on BILL and SEND to INVOICE OFFICE}						
THEIR TRUCK MESSENGER OUR TRUCK		CONDITION OF SHIPMENT		DATE	REG. NO.	
RECEIVED FROM:					AMOUNT OF INVOICE	
QUANTITY AND DESCRIPTION OF MERCHANDISE:						
ORDER NO.		ORDER CHECKED		DEPARTMENT	SENT TO FLOOR	
QUANTITY CHECKED		EXAMINED AND APPROVED			RECEIVING CLERK	
AMOUNT OF INVOICE		ANY RETURNS ON THIS BILL			TERMS	
OTHER COSTS		RETURN NO.			PRICE AND QUALITY CORRECT	
		DUE DATE				
TOTAL COST		RATE OF DISCOUNT		AMOUNT		BUYER
RETAIL PRICE					EXTENSIONS	
% MARKON		DAYS ANTICIPATION			CHECKED	RECHECKED

FIG. 26. Bill apron.

6. Invoices go from the receiving door to the order-checking office where they are checked against copies of orders. If invoices are in agreement with orders, they are entered on the invoice register and sent to the receiving area. If there are differences between an invoice and an order, the matter is investigated and a decision is made on how the transaction is to be handled. For example, upon receipt of a quantity of items that exceeds the quantity ordered, the excess may be retained or returned; upon receipt of less than the quantity ordered, the order may be processed or held open pending receipt of additional quantities. Differences as to other aspects of the purchase transaction, such as terms, specifications, and prices, are also investigated and resolved at this point, generally by contact with the department buyer or assistant buyer. After checking, the copies of orders are transferred from the open file to a closed file and a daily report is submitted to the budget office of

invoices received relative to orders placed. Utilizing these figures the amount of open orders is determined. The open order file is reviewed periodically to test the accuracy of the running tabulation of open orders.

7. Where pre-retailing is in use, the retail prices are copied on the invoices from the orders.

8. Removal of invoices from the receiving and marking rooms should not be permitted. They are frequently locked on file boards to prevent misplacement. If pre-retailing is not used, buyers must visit the marking or opening rooms to insert unit retail prices on the bills, a little used practice in current retailing.

9. As checking and marking are completed, the invoices are initialed by the various employees involved with this work and subsequently by the buyers.

10. The invoices are then cleared from the invoice register as completely checked and approved for payment. The invoice register serves as a controlling device. Making an entry when an invoice is received safeguards against loss, and open items on the register can be easily noted for follow-up. The register is useful for a ready determination of the invoices in transit, and as a record of all merchandise received.

These outlined procedures, when properly carried out, provide a measure of assurance against the passing of duplicate vendor bills. An invoice is not assigned a number at the point of receipt unless there are packages to be marked with the same number. An invoice does not pass to the receiving area unless there is a corresponding unfilled purchase order. An invoice is not initialed by the checkers and markers unless the specific goods required by the invoice have passed through their hands. Lastly, it is expected that buyers will exercise care in signing bills, to detect spurious ones that may have passed all the preceding checks and double-checks. The preparation of aprons at the receiving door is additional protection against the passing of duplicate bills.

There will naturally be adaptations and variations of the outlined procedures, especially in connection with the receipt of furniture and similar goods at remote warehouses. However, regardless of location, control over the receipt of merchandise should be centralized and the responsibility of operations personnel divorced from merchandising activities.

It should also be noted, as briefly discussed in Chapter 4, that given a requisite degree of computerization, systems can be developed which will not only integrate the accounting, open-to-buy, and unit control systems but also streamline the receiving and invoice processing functions. This can achieve operating economies and improve operating and accounting controls.

The Invoice Register

As previously noted, invoices may be recorded on an invoice register after having been checked against approved copies of the purchase orders. The invoice register may be a loose-leaf book with a sheet provided for each department (Figure 27).

INVOICE REGISTER

Month _____   Dept. No. _____

Date	Register Number	Date of Invoice	Vendor	Amount	Date Cleared

FIG. 27. Invoice register.

The amount column can be totaled daily to provide information for statistical compilations of preliminary figures for purchases. When invoices are completely checked and signed by buyers, the registration entry is closed by a date in the final column, and invoices are passed along for entry on the purchase record. Invoices not closed out represent invoices in transit. Amounts at cost of the invoices in transit can be determined from the invoice register by a tabulation of the "open" items.

An adaptation of the bill apron is sometimes used to eliminate the invoice register. An extra copy of the apron or a tear-off stub of the apron is prepared to form a loose-leaf file of invoices received. The copies of bill aprons or stubs are pulled from the file as invoices pass for entry on the purchase record; the aprons which remain in the file then represent invoices in transit.

Invoices can be registered and the information recorded for electronic data processing. A computerized system would contain information starting with the purchase order and including registered invoices and purchase journals. A listing of open items would be generated as an open registration listing as often as necessary.

The Purchase Record

There are a variety of forms of purchase record: handwritten, produced by means of mechanical bookkeeping, and printed out by electronic data processing equipment. The format and extent of information contained in this record will, of course, be governed by the accounting system and the information deemed desirable by management. The basic information required in the purchase record is indicated in Figure 28. Additional information could include the amount of loaded discounts and computation of the markon percentage on each invoice.

PURCHASE RECORD

Month _____   Dept. No. _____

Register Number	Invoice Date	Vendor	Cost	Retail	Discount

FIG. 28. Purchase record.

Invoices are entered on the purchase record after they are cleared through the required invoice procedures and are ready for payment. Returns to vendors, otherwise referred to as "chargebacks" or "claims," are entered as "negative" statistics so that departmental totals represent net purchases.

The purchase record represents the purchases charged to the individual selling departments. There may be one or several purchase records, as preferred. For example, one record may be used for entering domestic invoices and claims, foreign invoices, transportation costs, workroom bills, sundry items, departmental transfers, and markups of retail prices. From a single record of this kind, a total of purchases may be carried into a condensed form of stock ledger. On the other hand, there may be a separate record for each of the aforementioned elements of purchases. Totals from these records are then posted directly either to a detailed form of stock ledger, or to a record for accumulation of purchases figures, from which one total is posted to a condensed form of stock ledger.

The purchase record is generally prepared in duplicate, with one copy furnished to departmental buying personnel to corroborate the propriety of departmental purchase charges. There is always the possibility that invoices may, through error, be improperly charged to departmental accounts or incorrectly retailed. Accordingly, under all circumstances and systems, buyers should make it a practice to review the departmental purchase records.

Internal Control Over Payments for Purchases

The procedures described above have been predicated upon a system which separates the accounting distribution from the payment function, with the distribution function performed by an "invoice office" and the payment function by the accounts payable department. In many organizations the two functions are performed by the accounts payable department. Invoices are processed first by order clerks working under the jurisdiction of the receiving manager or controller (or even as an integral part of the accounts payable department). After this function is completed, invoices are turned over to the accounts payable department for processing, as part of a "unit run" type of operation. In utilizing this technique, there is a simultaneous preparation of the departmental purchase record and the voucher payment check. The most common approach is to process for payment (and distribution) only those invoices which have been finally approved for payment. The charge-out departmentally can be on the basis of either processed invoices or the combined total of processed invoices plus uncleared invoices. The latter will be represented by individual invoice aprons, the uncleared items on the invoice register sheet, or the open registration report furnished by data processing.

This "unit run" method of operation sacrifices some internal control over payments for purchases, since the same group of employees initiates the payments for merchandise and also provides the related accounting distribution. In some instances the accounts payable department completes and signs voucher checks and mails them directly to vendors, thereby eliminating even more of the conventional internal controls.

Where a store deems it necessary, for whatever purpose, to sacrifice conventional controls in this fashion, some alternative controls over merchandise payments are essential. These controls may take the form of a combination of "administrative review" and spot-checking by internal audit personnel. The administrative review should be made by supervisors who are in a position to judge the reasonableness of the accounting distributions and by the departmental buyers who should examine the copy of the purchase record to satisfy themselves as to the propriety and accuracy of the individual invoices charged to their respective departments. The retail stock ledger, which serves also as a departmental statement (see Chapter 6, Figure 14), offers buyers a unique opportunity to make an administrative review of the entire accounting for purchases and stocks because it sets forth the actual process of such accounting. Tests by the internal audit staff would consist of an examination of the purchase invoices supporting the paid voucher checks, with particular emphasis on evidence of approval by checkers, markers, and buyers.

Returns to Vendors

Goods to be returned to vendors are entered on prenumbered "chargeback" or "claim" forms after proper approval, and are shipped out through the vendor return goods room. This room operates along the lines of the delivery room wherein nothing is permitted to leave the store unless entered on a chargeback (some goods, of course, may go out on memo charges). Quantities and prices are verified before goods are passed for shipment. The completed chargebacks are forwarded to the accounts payable office, which maintains a numerical control over, and accountability for, all chargeback numbers.

The chargeback forms are prepared at least in duplicate, with one copy for the vendor and one copy retained by the store. There may be a third copy for inclusion with the package to facilitate handling by the vendor, and additional store copies for distribution to the statistical area, marking area files, and accounts payable. On the store's copy the retail value is shown. The retail value should be the same as was charged into stock when the merchandise was purchased. (If there have been any retail price changes, they should be canceled.) The chargebacks are entered on the purchase journal as negative amounts so as to reduce the purchases to net figures.

Given the clerical cost of processing vendor chargebacks and claims, it may be desirable to institute a policy pursuant to which claims under a specified minimum dollar amount are not processed. In any event, it may be advisable to keep statistics by vendor concerning the frequency of short shipments disclosed by checking orders. Such statistics can focus attention on vendors with a relatively high frequency of short shipments, thereby enabling the retailer to take corrective action.

Transportation Costs

Inward freight, express, and cartage are added to the cost of merchandise purchased. This may be done by making a departmental analysis of transportation invoices and cash vouchers for transportation costs. The distribution may be made weekly or monthly, with one total posted to the purchase journal or to the record for accumulation of purchase elements. It is not necessary to enter transportation costs on the specific invoices unless it is store practice to compute the markon on each purchase invoice.

Foreign Purchases

Invoices for imported merchandise are not handled under the ordinary routines outlined for domestic invoices. Foreign purchase orders are usually placed through commission merchants abroad or through a store's own foreign offices. These foreign agencies maintain accounts with the foreign vendors and receive merchandise locally for the purpose of assembling it into compact shipping cases which are forwarded to the purchasing store. Complete consular invoices are drawn up and insurance and freight paid. When the merchandise arrives at its destination, it passes through the custom house and duties are paid.

In some instances, a shipment may be for one department from a single vendor. If more than one department is involved, the consular invoice is divided into sections at the store for the respective selling departments. Each department's goods are then handled separately in accordance with the normal checking and marking routine. Each invoice or segment of invoice is translated from foreign to domestic money values and the insurance, freight, fees, and duties are applied. Also, an amount may be loaded on the invoice to cover outside buying office expenses or commission fees. This work is usually delegated to a capable person who has acquired experience in handling foreign invoices, and is conversant with such specialized tasks as translating currencies and verifying duty rates. The same person customarily keeps the foreign purchase journal and is able to answer questions of buyers and others regarding goods purchased abroad.

Consignment Purchases

The routine on consignment purchases is the same as on regular purchases, if no distinction is made between the two kinds of purchases. Some stores charge consignment purchases into the accounts just as though they were regular purchases, but mark the invoices suitably so that they will not be paid before the merchandise is sold. These stores consider consignment goods as much a part of stock as any other goods, and they apply consignment orders against planned purchases and include the invoices in purchases and inventories. Under these circumstances, the total departmental merchandise statistics include combined regular and consignment merchandise, with no distinction between them.

Some stores maintain a separate record of consignment merchandise, and no consignment merchandise is charged to purchases until it is sold. This may be done by means of a special invoice register, which may reflect the original consignment invoice amounts, whether still outstanding in their entirety or after portions of the goods have been sold; the related cost amounts are then passed for payment. The register is actually a control over consignment merchandise in the store and is supported by a file of invoices showing the items on consignment. Periodically, the store ascertains the consigned merchandise items sold, and vendors are requested to submit regular invoices (marked "sold from consignment"). These regular invoices are checked against the consignment invoices, and both are carefully marked with cross references so that the consignment records will reflect the items for which regular bills have been passed. The invoices for goods sold from consignment require signatures of departmental buyers and a representative of the controller's office. These invoices are then entered on the purchase journal in the regular manner, as if they were ordinary purchase invoices. In effect, under this system no entries are made in the purchase journal for consigned goods until there is a receipt of invoices for goods sold from consignment. As a double-check, it is desirable to have a representative of the accounts payable department inspect the underlying documentation, checking signatures on the original consignment invoices and on the invoices being passed for payment, with a view to checking overall propriety and adherence to store procedures.

The foregoing routines may be satisfactory when consignment purchases represent only a small proportion of total departmental purchases. Where a principal portion or all of the merchandise of one or more departments is purchased on consignment, or where large amounts of merchandise are purchased on consignment from a single vendor, a greater degree of control and more detailed recordkeeping may be required. The required difference in treatment principally would involve the manner of recording consignment stock and entering invoices for consignment goods sold. Formal ledgers may be required, listing for individual consignment vendors the details of each shipment and the related partial settlements made. Also, it may be necessary to segregate this merchandise in some fashion and to take physical inventories periodically as a test on book controls and as a basis for settlements.

Where merchandise on consignment is not charged into the records until sold, there is the obvious problem of not commingling consignment merchandise with regular merchandise when physical inventories are taken.

Workroom Bills

Workrooms "recover" their costs by means of charges to selling departments and to customers. Charges against departments are of two kinds: for workroom-made merchandise, and for alterations and repairs.

Bills for workroom-made merchandise pass through the checking and marking procedures required for regular invoices, and are charged to departmental stock accounts as purchases, at cost and retail. Workroom bills require the same handling as bills from outside vendors. They are controlled by an invoice register (perhaps a special one for this purpose) and passed to buyers for signature. They are entered on the records either through the purchase journal or by separate journal entry, charging departmental purchases accounts and crediting workroom cost accounts.

Alteration and repair bills are charged against any departmental gross margin, and are generally captioned "Alteration and workroom costs."

"No Retail" Bills

A number of invoices that are chargeable against departmental purchase costs carry no retail since there is no corresponding increase in the selling value of merchandise. Examples would comprise bills for cleaning, supplies, parts, and labor required to prepare or repair merchandise to render it salable, where there is no workroom to absorb these costs.

If charges of this nature can be billed to departments through workroom accounts, they would not be included in cost purchases from which markon is determined, but would be classified separately as alteration and workroom costs. Where possible, it seems desirable that these "no retail" bills charged directly to departments be included with the captioned alteration and workroom costs, rather than being designated as purchases. Separate tabulation of "no retail" bills on the purchase journal facilitates this treatment.

Department Merchandise Transfers

In department and chain stores it frequently becomes necessary to transfer merchandise from one department to another and to and from the main store and the branches. Departmental transfers also arise when there is a consolidation or split-up of departments, a shift of some classification of merchandise from one department to another, or a reclassification of sizes or price lines between departments. Also, it is often the practice to transfer to budget departments slow-selling merchandise of regular departments. In addi-

TRANSFER SHEET

To: ______

Order # ______ From ______ Filled by ______ No. ______

Dept. # ______ Date ______ Shipped by ______

	Season Ltr.	*Lot Number*	*Article*	*Description*	*Quantity*	*Retail Price*	*Total Retail*

FIG. 29. Merchandise transfer sheet.

tion, there are a great many transfers in small amounts between selling departments and workroom and expense accounts.

A distinctive form should be utilized for transfers (see Figure 29). Weekly or monthly, or at the end of a four- or five-week period, the transfers are summarized, at cost and retail, and appropriate distribution is made to the departmental purchases and workroom and expense accounts.

Determination of the appropriate cost and retail amounts is the main problem with respect to transfers. For ordinary transfers between departments or between stores, and to workroom and expense accounts, the retail amount used is the retail marked on the merchandise; cost may be determined by resorting to the average markon of the department disposing of the merchandise. For non-routine transfers of material amount, the prices to be applied may depend upon the specific circumstances. In some instances it may be satisfactory to price the transfers at retail and at cost based upon the average markon of the department disposing of the merchandise. In other instances, cost may have to be "negotiated" through agreement between the departments concerned. This would occur when the transfer is from a regular department to a budget department, or between departments having different price lines, or because of the condition of the merchandise being transferred.

When transfers are not made at the retail and cost of the department disposing of the goods, the retail amount credited to the disposing department must be adjusted in the retail ledger on the basis of the agreed-upon cost and the markon percentage of such department. Any difference between the adjusted (lower) retail and the retail before transfer would have to be recorded as a markdown by the disposing department. The department receiving the goods will set a retail based on the agreed-upon cost, comparable to a purchase from an outside vendor. This procedure avoids distorting the cumulative markon percentages of the departments involved in the transfers.

This methodology can be illustrated by the following transaction. A transfer of 20 suits is scheduled to be made from the regular men's clothing department to a corresponding budget department. The suits are marked to sell at retail at $90 in the regular department, but are to be sold for $65 in the budget department. The two departments agree that the cost of the transfer should be $840. The cumulative markon percentage of the regular department is

40 per cent; the adjusted retail for the regular department on the suits being transferred is $840 divided by 60 per cent (complement of the markon), or $1,400. On the transfer, cost is entered at $840, retail transferred from the regular department is entered at $1,400, and retail transferred to the budget department is entered at $1,300 (20 × $65). The regular department is required to take a markdown of $400, representing the difference between retail of $1,800 (marked on the suits before transfer) and $1,400, the retail at which transferred. In this transaction, the retail credited to the regular department on the transfer, $1,400, is greater than the retail of $1,300 charged to the budget department. This differential affects the total sheet of the stock ledger, but is of no consequence because markon percentages are only determined departmentally, and not by utilizing all store totals. For the individual departments the figures have been handled properly, with no distortion of the respective markon percentages. For a more detailed discussion of departmental merchandise transfers, see Chapter 7, pages 151 to 154.

For ordinary transfers, which are more numerous, the following procedures may be employed.

1. Transfer requests originate in the department, workroom, or office desiring to obtain merchandise, with the form prepared at that point, in duplicate, and approved by the buyer, workroom head or supervisor, office manager, or expense controller, as circumstances require.

2. The original and duplicate of the transfer are then forwarded to the department from which the goods are to be obtained. The transferring department should insert only the retail prices on the transfer form. If feasible, a representative of the marking department could be utilized to check the quantities and prices, verify the signatures, and initial approval on the transfer. Routine checks of an established percentage of transactions could be carried out at this point by proceeding to the receiving department and verifying the physical transfer of merchandise and the propriety of the retail ticketing. The original of the transfer is forwarded to the statistical office, or it may be transmitted via the marking department representative. The duplicate, which remains with the department releasing the merchandise, is useful in tracing a missing number or for subsequent follow-up to ensure that the proper credit has been received.

3. In the statistical office, transfers are computed at "cost" by use of departmental average markons and then entered in the accounts.

The transfer books should be kept under numerical control, with an accountability for each transfer number. For control purposes, the number of transfer books should be kept to a minimum, with their use strictly restricted to authorized users. Transfers in process which would not be included in stock ledger figures have to be taken into account when reconciling book and physical inventories.

Invoices in Transit

As previously noted, invoices are cleared from the invoice register to the purchase journal after they are checked and the merchandise is marked and placed either in reserve or forward stock. Under this procedure, there is some lapse of time between the physical entry of the merchandise at the receiving door and the recording of invoices as purchases in the purchase journal. During this interval invoices are said to be "in transit." It is customary to consider merchandise represented by in-transit invoices as part of the departmental merchandise stock, even though it has not been formally checked into stock and recorded on the purchase journal. This is appropriate since inventory at any particular date is considered to include everything that has been received by the store through that date. Also relevant is the consideration that, upon receipt, merchandise is deducted from the unfilled order totals and represents a reduction of the open-to-buy. The sum of inventory and unfilled orders represents total merchandise responsibility as of a particular date.

The total of invoices in transit can be determined from open items on the invoice register and charged on the departmental stock ledgers weekly, monthly, or for a four- or five-week period, or in accordance with any other basis on which the stock ledgers are kept. The amounts thus set up for closing purposes are reversed at the opening of the new period or continue to be carried until reversal at the next closing. In any case, at each closing a new total for merchandise in transit is reflected in the accounts.

Retail amounts of invoices in transit are usually estimated on the basis of the markon percentage of the bills which have cleared during the month or period. Such an estimate has to be made even when all registered invoices are initially charged to purchases. As actual retail on invoices in transit is subsequently determined, adjustment is made for differences between the actual and estimated amounts.

The foregoing discussion of invoices in transit refers to invoices covering merchandise received in the store up to a given date. These invoices are to be distinguished from invoices for merchandise which is en route or physically "in transit" to the store as of the same date, that is, merchandise which has been shipped by vendors prior to or on the closing date but has not yet reached the store. Such merchandise is commonly referred to as "merchandise in transit," without regard to whether it is F.O.B. shipping point or point of destination. In preparing a balance sheet, it is customary to reflect as a liability the total amount of merchandise in transit bearing an invoice date prior to the balance sheet date, with a corresponding increase in inventory. This is simply a balance sheet entry, with no effect on stock records or profits.

Merchandise on Memorandum and on Loan

There are occasions when merchandise, either customer- or store-owned, is sent out of the store "on memo," generally for repair or processing of some sort. In the interest of control, it is frequent practice to utilize chargeback forms for as many memo transactions as possible. Alternatively, numerically controlled "memo charges" can be used and followed up in the same manner as chargebacks. Where memo charges are used, and especially where memo transactions are sometimes put on chargebacks, care should be exercised in approving invoices from the repairers or processors for work performed. It is especially necessary to guard against being billed for the store's own merchandise which was merely delivered on memo to the repairers or processors. Careful follow-up on returns to vendors and shipments out on memo should be emphasized because it may be neglected in the face of the larger problem of receiving merchandise. The receipt of merchandise is generally surrounded with various procedural safeguards while memo charges are often the responsibility of a limited number of personnel and can become the source of inaccuracies and losses. Memo charges are not entered in the stock records, but they must be considered when reconciling book and physical inventories.

Closely akin to the memo charge is the "merchandise loan." Merchandise is frequently removed from the stocks of departments to be displayed in windows or in other departments or sections of the store, or exhibited out of the store. Merchandise items sent to store workrooms for repair or processing, while not on loan, sometimes come under this classification, because "memo charges" are generally limited to merchandise leaving the store premises. A simple accountability and control system over merchandise on loan is desirable to ensure that such merchandise safely finds its way back to the selling department. A suggested system is outlined as follows:

1. A prenumbered merchandise loan form should be prepared in duplicate by the department or office wishing to obtain the goods, and properly approved by some authorized supervisor.
2. The original and duplicate of the form should be presented to the department making the loan. Retail prices of the merchandise should be entered on the form at this point, and, if feasible, the store inspection service may be utilized to check the transaction and stamp both copies of the form.
3. The original of the form should be sent to the statistical office, through the inspection service, if feasible, with the duplicate retained by the lending department until the goods are returned. Upon receipt of the returned merchandise, the duplicate will be signed by the proper person in the lending department to acknowledge return of the merchandise, and the duplicate will then be forwarded directly to the statistical office.
4. At the statistical office the duplicate and original copies are matched, thus closing out the item. Unmatched loan slips in the files will supply details of merchandise out of departmental stocks on loan and the departments to which it is charged. There should be a periodic follow-up on all open loan slips, with an accountability of each numbered loan form by the statistical office.

The amounts of merchandise on loan are not entered in the departmental stock records, but must be taken into account when reconciling book and physical inventories. A problem commonly experienced is loss of or damage to goods loaned. Any such losses should be charged to the department that failed to protect the loaned merchandise.

Receiving

The clerk at the receiving door is responsible for making a record of all shipments received and the condition in which they are received, and for giving receipts for packages, cartons, and cases received. These packages, cartons, and cases are moved as expeditiously as possible to the opening areas, while the invoices, which the clerk either received with the shipment or received in advance of receipt of express, mail, and freight shipments, are sent to the appropriate office for order checking and registration. If there is no cause for delaying the invoices, they are forwarded promptly to the opening areas where the packages received have been distributed to tables, bins, or enclosed spaces (for the more valuable goods). When the merchandise and invoices have been brought together, the goods are opened and the merchandise is checked against the invoices for proper quality and, to the extent consistent with company policy, for proper quantity. In this regard, after having developed statistics as to frequency of shortages by vendor, a retailer may conclude that it is unnecessary to count or, alternatively, may make only periodic limited test counts of merchandise received from selected reliable vendors. Of course, such determination will be influenced by the value of the units received. Past history notwithstanding, with regard to high unit cost items, it will probably continue to be advisable to determine that the proper quantity has been received. Checking of quantities should be strictly supervised to see that there is adherence to established company policy and that counts are accurate. Checking of quality requires the ability to judge merchandise. Employees who do this work should know how to handle the merchandise they are checking or examining so that no spoilage or damage will result. In some instances a blind check is used: checkers who do not have the invoices make lists of the items found in shipments. These lists are later checked independently against the invoices. The blind check method is a costly one and is best restricted to departments where it would prove valuable. With competent and conscientious checkers under proper supervision, the check against invoices should suffice for most departments. The invoices should bear evidence (initials or signatures) that the goods have been counted and inspected by receiving personnel.

Marking

After checking, the goods, accompanied by the invoices, are moved to the marking tables. If buyers have put retail prices on the store copies of their orders, these prices will have been copied on the invoices by the order checkers, and will be on the invoices when they reach the marking tables. Otherwise, the buyers will have to visit the receiving and marking rooms in order to enter retail prices on the invoices. The invoice should bear evidence (initials or signatures) that the merchandise has been properly marked. Marking tickets are frequently prepared on machines, and usually show the season letter or number, manufacturer's number, style number, selling price, and, where required, size and color. In a number of stores a three-part ticket is often utilized for both marking and stock control. This ticket is separated at point of sale so that information that has been prepunched into the ticket can be readily converted into machine-readable form for updating of computerized inventory information.

Some retailers have found that by combining, to some extent, the checking and marking functions operating economies can be achieved without sacrificing control. For example, in the preponderance of situations where retail prices appear on the store copies of purchase orders, the preparation of a number of price tickets exactly equal to the invoiced quantity can combine the counting and marking functions in effective fashion. If after affixing the tickets to the merchandise, there are tickets left over, a shortage is indicated equal to the number of excess tickets. Conversely, an insufficient number of tickets would indicate an overage.

Earlier mention has been made that centralization of the responsibility for receiving, checking, and marking increases control and also speeds up the processing of merchandise, all of which is highly desirable. On the other hand, it must be borne in mind that a competent buyer may often find it helpful to refer to invoices for any one of several valid reasons. It may be advisable, therefore, to make invoices readily and easily available to buyers under proper safeguards or to photocopy invoices for the buyers' files, for constant reference in merchandising.

Reserve Stock

After being marked, the goods are moved into either forward or reserve stock. With respect to reserve stock, it is preferred practice to have a consolidated stock room under the supervision of the head of receiving and marking. This arrangement facilitates movement of goods from the marking tables to reserve stock. A consolidated room centrally directed also results in more efficient and economical handling of goods.

11

Determination of Net Sales

Net Sales

Net sales is undoubtedly the most important element of a store income account and of its stock ledger accounts and merchandise statistics. The problems associated with correct determination of net sales are many and varied. A number of these problems are discussed in this chapter.

The Sales Audit Office

Notwithstanding the advent of computers and the increasing use of highly sophisticated point-of-sale equipment, the equivalent of a sales audit function must be performed if a store is to obtain timely and accurate sales statistics. In this connection, the basic responsibilities of the sales audit office or function may be enumerated as follows:

1. Compilation of gross sales and returns departmentally and on an all-store basis.
2. Compilation of transactions departmentally and on an all-store basis.
3. Compilation of tax statistics and other miscellaneous data arising in connection with sales, such as discounts, parcel post and freight charges, and alteration charges.

4. Accumulation of salespersons' sales and returns for commission purposes.
5. Establishing accounts receivable control totals.
6. Establishing an accountability for cash sales, and balancing cash sales figures against the combined total of cash and "paper" accepted in lieu of cash.

Compilation of Gross Sales and Returns

The problem of compiling gross sales and returns revolves about the problem of summarizing the detailed sales and credit media. In the conventional retail environment the sales media are represented by sales checks and register tapes, or are encoded directly at the registers, covering the different kinds of sales; the credit media are represented by credit checks. In more detailed terms, these media comprise:

Sales checks:
  Charge sales
  C.O.D. sales
  Cash sales (normally recorded on cash registers; where registers are nonexistent or inadequate, or where tube-room cashiers are used, cash sales checks are normally utilized)
Credit checks:
  Call credits (return merchandise is called for by store's delivery service or by common carrier)
  Express and mail credits (merchandise is returned via express and parcel post)
  Floor credits (merchandise is personally returned by customers)
  Merchandise allowance credits (a special allowance which does not involve the physical return of merchandise)

Some stores use different types of sales books for cash, C.O.D., and charge sales, and for accommodation deliveries. Other stores use two books, one for C.O.D.'s and one for all other transactions; or, a single sales book may be used to cover sales of all kinds. The use of a single book tends to simplify the control problem involved in the issuance of sales books. Where one sales check is used to cover all types of sales, there should be a conspicuous earmarking of all C.O.D. sales checks. This need arises because of the more involved procedures associated with the accounting for C.O.D. sales.

In addition to regular sales deliveries, formal checks or memoranda should be used to authorize the movement of merchandise taken from the store. Checks or memoranda should be used to record and authorize the following deliveries:

Customers' own goods for which a service or repair charge is made.
Customers' own goods for which no service or repair charge is made.
Accommodation deliveries.
Memorandum sales or deliveries.

Outline of Audit Procedures

In the light of advanced techniques and computerization that have been adopted in recent years, no one particular system of audit procedure can be offered as typical. The large-scale acceptance of the cycle billing of accounts receivable has played a dominant role in shaping the audit procedures ultimately evolved. Audit procedures are normally subdivided into two broad categories: preaudit and post-audit. "Preaudit" means the audit of charge sales checks before posting to customers' ledgers. Under this plan, the audit office determines the total of charge sales and ascertains accounts receivable control totals. "Post-audit" means that charge checks are posted to customers' ledgers before audit and the posted checks, together with control totals, are passed to the audit office for verification. With the widespread adoption by retailers of cycle billing of customers, often accompanied by nondescriptive billing and the mailing of sales checks to customers, the only type of audit utilized becomes preaudit. However, the advent of point-of-sale equipment and the related direct encoding of sales at the registers has led to the adoption of descriptive billing by retailers, with no sales media forwarded to customers.

With preaudit established as a common practice, two approaches have achieved perhaps the most popular acceptance: tally audit and floor audit. Each has been adapted to individual stores with numerous variations. A generalized description follows, but it should not be considered all-inclusive.

Tally Audit

As the name implies, a tally envelope is filled out daily by the salesperson. The amount of each sales check written in the course of the day is recorded opposite the sales check number. At the close of each business day, the listing of sales check amounts, exclusive of cash sales checks, is totaled. The total of charge and C.O.D. sales checks, together with the day's receipts of cash and cash-equivalent paper, are noted on the tally envelope and serve as the basis for the department's flash sales report. The tally envelopes for the department are then banded and turned over to sales audit for subsequent processing.

After accounting for the sequence number of sales checks, departmental charge and C.O.D. sales are determined by adding charge and C.O.D. sales checks. Cash sales for the department are determined by reference to cash register readings, and these readings are balanced against salespersons' and cashiers' cash reports. Where register coverage is inadequate or nonexistent, cash sales checks are added in the same fashion as charge and C.O.D. sales checks. The aggregate of charge, C.O.D., and cash sales constitutes the department's gross sales.

While the use of cash registers in department stores has been traditional, a few stores have experimented with their complete elimination, with the obvious intent of eliminating the necessity for a large capital investment. However, this has been tried only in those situations where cash sales comprise a relatively small percentage of total sales. Under these circumstances, it is envisioned that the writing of sales checks on the small percentage of cash sales which would not otherwise be written will not act as a selling or customer service deterrent.

Floor Audit

Floor audit essentially involves the utilization on the selling floor of cash registers, or point-of-sale equipment, as audit devices at the point of sale. Proper register capacity and adequate register or point-of-sale terminal coverage are prime requisites. Floor audit envisions that every sale (cash, charge, layaway, C.O.D., budget) occurring on the selling floor will be recorded on the cash register or point-of-sale terminal. A cash–take sale does not require the writing of a sales check, the register receipt being considered sufficient. All other sales require a written sales check which is validated (register imprinted) by the cash register or provided directly by the point-of-sale terminal. Since all sales are rung on the register or point-of-sale terminal, sales totals are provided by department and by salesperson (and often by merchandise classifications or sub-classifications). The balancing consists of balancing cash receipts plus sales checks against the total sales statistic provided via the register or point-of-sale terminal.

In order to ascertain sales by type of sale where registers are used, there must be a tabulation of the individual sales checks by type of sale (i.e., charge, C.O.D., layaway, etc.). The difference between total departmental sales and sales checks written, exclusive of cash sales checks, represents cash sales. As with tally audit, control is exercised over sales checks by accounting for the numerical sequence of sales checks. Where point-of-sale equipment is used, sales by type of sale are obtained as an automatic by-product of the processing by the computer to which the point-of-sale terminals are connected.

Sales Check Number Control

The common practice is to account for the numerical sequence of sales checks. The underlying theory is that the custody and physical issuance of sales books is under strict control, with individual salespersons accountable for each sales check number. The subsequent verification of sales check sequence number is an extension of this control. Its ultimate aim is to prevent the spurious writing of sales checks which would permit the unauthorized movement of merchandise from the store premises. Supplementary safeguards are the store's security department and outside shopping and investigation services. Chief reliance, however, must be placed upon the basic integrity of sales personnel and upon the conscientious discharge of duties by the inspection and delivery department personnel.

Despite the control features inherent in numerical sales check verification, some stores, after the installation of floor audit, have abandoned it. As already noted, under floor audit all sales, regardless of type of sale, must be recorded on the cash register. Sales checks are normally written for all sales except cash–takes, and there must be register certification (register imprint) of all sales checks written. No packages are accepted by the inspection or delivery departments unless they bear the register certification.

With the register imprint a requisite for merchandise delivery, some stores have abandoned the missing sales check verification, reasoning that the possible misuse of sales checks and unauthorized movement of merchandise via the normal delivery channels are substantially minimized. Since the cash register is used for recording all sales, missing sales checks would be reflected as shortages. However, the exact reason for a shortage would still remain unknown. Many factors could contribute to shortages, including missing sales checks, unrecorded register voided transactions, and actual cash shortages. No follow-up investigatory reference could be made to the original sales checks since they would have been forwarded to accounts receivable for processing.

An adaptation of floor audit, referred to as register receipt audit, is an even greater departure from sales check control. Under this plan, either the sales check is eliminated completely and replaced by a receipt ejected by the register, or a simplified, one-part, unnumbered sales check is used. In either event, the danger would lie in the loss of an original sales check, and the impossibility of reconstructing a customer charge.

Cycle Billing and Accounts Receivable Control Totals

The cycle billing plan has come into widespread usage, particularly by organizations which characteristically have a large number of accounts, such as retailers and public utilities. Under this system, designated groupings of customers' accounts, generally alphabetically arranged, are termed "cycles," and each cycle is billed on the same predetermined date (generally other than month-end) each month. This procedure of billing the various cycles monthly on the same dates is known as "cycle billing."

In those retail organizations where separate controls are maintained for the individual cycles, generally termed "multiple cycle controls," sales checks and other source media such as remittance advices and credit slips are accumulated each day and sorted by cycles, with the respective daily totals by cycle recorded in cycle controls. The source media are then forwarded to the accounts receivable department daily, and are filed in customer account trays until the next billing date for the respective cycles. At the billing date the customers' statements and a proof-sheet trial balance are prepared simultaneously with the posting of the media to the customers' ledger cards. The original media generally are mailed to the customers together with the monthly statements; microfilm copies of the media are retained as the store's supporting detail since generally only amounts, without the corresponding merchandise descriptions, are posted to the accounts.

Using multiple cycle controls, it is possible to make a comparison of cycle control totals with the sum of customers' account balances rendered each billing date, and any differences can be readily determined. In addition to this comparison, a reconciliation of all the cycle control totals with the general ledger balance at the end of the month (or four- or five-week period) is usually made. Figure 30 illustrates a reconciliation of cycle control totals with the general ledger control account as of a month end or period end.

Frequently, only a single, overall control account is maintained, rather than the multiple cycle controls previously described. Under this method the comparison of the general ledger control and the supporting detail of customers' accounts at the end of the month or period involves much more work than with multiple controls. Various methods may be used to make this comparison, as outlined below.

1. A complete inventory of all unbilled media may be made in the form of tape listings. This inventory, together with totals of billed amounts at the last respective billing dates, is compared with the month-end (or period-end) general ledger control. The tabulation of unbilled media under this method is also usually done on the balance sheet date. Since this procedure requires considerable time and a temporary halt in filing the account media in the trays, particularly where there is a large number of accounts, this method may be impractical except in the smaller stores.

2. Another method of taking the complete trial balance, generally during the last month of the year, is as follows:

   a. Cycles billed during the latter half of the month are "frozen"; that is, the posting media are not filed in the trays but set aside, with tape listings made of the respective media. Year-end balances of these cycles thus consist of the amounts shown on the billing date trial balances plus totals of unfiled media.
   b. Cycles usually billed within two days of the end of the month are billed as at the month end; in this case, billing date trial balances are actual year-end balances.

238 RETAIL ACCOUNTING AND FINANCIAL CONTROL Ch. 11

ABC DEPARTMENT STORE
ANALYSIS OF ACCOUNTS RECEIVABLE CONTROL
January 28, 19—

Cycle Letter	Latest Cycle Billing Date	Billed Balance at Billing Date[1]	Detail Accounts Over (Under) Control at Indicated Billing Dates	Totals of Transactions Since Billing Date, Per Individual Cycle Controls					Balance at End of Year 1/28/—
				Add		Deduct			
				Charge Sales	Journal Entries	Cash Remittances	Returns	Journal Entries	
A	1/1	$ 318,701.65	$ 174.16	$ 109,263.62	$ 898.86	$ 95,572.10	$ 27,133.42	$ 4,145.53	$ 302,013.08
B	1/2	992,413.42	1,059.49	339,952.90	3,251.93	237,866.04	83,086.56	15,390.53	999,275.12
C	1/5	700,201.00	(5,308.35)	217,359.56	1,028.97	99,056.50	37,479.85	9,500.53	772,552.65
D	1/7	468,299.66	1,411.87	127,110.51	869.07	31,946.59	21,588.17	5,202.36	537,542.12
...									
W–Z	12/28	762,498.32	(1,718.93)	300,034.23	5,010.16	270,956.93	73,139.41	12,570.80	710,875.57
		$10,777,160.94	($7,000.45)	$5,138,624.40	$250,060.22	$4,004,981.63	$1,212,159.88	$213,815.53	$10,734,888.52

Add: Amount detail under controls   7,000.45[2]

Balance per general ledger $10,741,888.97

[1] Totals of billed balances at cycle billing dates are obtained from trial balances prepared simultaneously with customers' statements.
[2] The actual difference as at year end (or at the end of a calendar month or accounting period) is unknown. The reconciling figure represents the aggregate difference between the cycle control totals and the detailed billed amounts as at the indicated cycle billing dates. Any differences which have arisen since the respective cycle billing dates and the end of the year (or month or accounting period) would not be known, and consequently would not be reflected in this reconciling figure.

FIG. 30. Reconciliation of cycle controls with general ledger control.

c. Cycles billed during the first half of the month are not "frozen," but the media are filed and taped while they are in the trays. These media totals are added to the balances shown by trial balances on the last billing dates.
d. The aggregate of items (a), (b), and (c), effectively comprising amounts previously billed to customers and the total of all unposted media, is then compared with the corresponding general ledger balance.

Instead of making this detailed tie-in of trial balances of billed amounts and unbilled media to the ledger control, some retailers make periodic procedural tests of the agreement of media amounts billed for a cycle period with the corresponding previously tabulated totals of the same media. This can be accomplished as follows:

For a selected cycle or cycles, media totals of sales slips, credit slips, and remittances for the cycle period are respectively established in advance of posting to the accounts.
The totals of the respective media subsequently billed are then compared with these previously established tape totals.

The use of a single control eliminates a great many corrections or transfers of incorrectly sorted source media which would otherwise be required under multiple controls. Under a multiple control system such erroneously sorted media would have been included in daily media totals posted to the individual controls, thereby necessitating transfer postings to correct the controls. However, the use of a single control has a very basic disadvantage. Having determined, by one of the methods previously outlined, that a significant difference exists between the detail customers' accounts and the general ledger control, the localization of the difference is extremely difficult, if not impossible. After approval, unresolved differences between the detail customers' accounts and the general ledger control (normally the detail is less than the control) should be charged off to income.

A variation of the single, overall control is often referred to as the two-cycle control. Two approaches are possible:

1. *Billed and Unbilled.* Daily, in summarizing all media (sales, credits, payments, and journal entries), the sales audit department must distinguish between media which will be billed *before* the month end or period end ("billed") and media which will be

billed *after* the month end or period end ("unbilled"). The totals of billed and unbilled media are separately posted to accounts receivable controls. At month end or period end, the aggregate of all customer billings (trial balances) for the month, plus the aggregate of the daily unbilled control amounts for the month (or period), is compared with the general ledger control account.

2. *Post-listing of Media.* The important feature of this technique is the daily imprinting of the month (or period) of origin on all media. After a cycle has been billed, the media are separately analyzed (sales, credits, payments, and journal entries) and summarized by month (or period) of origin. These cycle media totals are maintained for all cycles billed during the month and are subsequently compared with the general ledger control account. Since most cycles straddle two calendar months (or periods), the reconciliation of media with general ledger control is not possible until the end of the subsequent month. Thus, a comparison of the aggregate of the January billed media with the January 31 general ledger control account is not possible until the end of February.

There is no unanimity of opinion regarding the selection of the single-control, two-control, or multiple-cycle control over retail receivables. While the use of multiple-cycle controls is believed to achieve the greatest measure of control, in the interests of economy and simplicity many department stores have adopted the one- or two-control approach. In arriving at the control system desirable for a particular retail establishment, the advantages and disadvantages of the respective control systems should be weighed in the light of such factors as number of customer accounts, previous experience with receivable shortages, availability of equipment, physical or other accounting controls, and personnel capability.

Quality of Accounts Receivable

No discussion of accounts receivable would be complete without considering the quality of the receivables. It can be generalized that the quality of accounts receivable is dependent in part upon the store's sales and credit policies and in part upon the effectiveness of the collection procedures employed. It is axiomatic that an aggressive selling policy abetted by a liberal credit policy will produce more overdue and uncollectible accounts than will a selective selling program with more restrictive credit terms. However, the former may be more desirable if the policy generates a sufficient volume of sales and if effective collection procedures are employed to encourage prompt payment and reduce uncollectibility. Furthermore, efficient collection procedures designed to discourage customer delinquencies effectively will result in a higher volume of credit sales.

The second phase of the problem of managing accounts receivable is control of the costs of carrying customers' credit accounts. Since the carrying of customers' accounts represents an investment of funds which might be otherwise invested, it is logical to assume that there should be considered as a cost of carrying these accounts an amount representing the return which might have been obtained if such funds were alternatively invested. At a minimum this cost comprises interest on funds borrowed to carry customers' accounts and the various costs associated with maintaining a credit and collection department. The collection of delinquent accounts becomes correspondingly more difficult and expensive as the receivables become increasingly older. Therefore, efficient expense control must be predicated on prudent credit policies and upon early and active collection procedures once delinquency is determined. A third consideration, less determinable but equally important, is the reduction in future sales to delinquent accounts. Statistical evidence exists to indicate that purchases drop sharply with the increasing age of delinquent accounts. While delinquent balances are, of course, undesirable, the retention of the customers may be desirable. As a practical matter, many credit managers make special efforts to retain as customers those with delinquent balances as long as such balances are being paid. When the aggregate of credit costs becomes excessive, these costs will reduce and may eliminate the profitability of sales. Every reduction of the cost of carrying customers' accounts or of collection expense obviously will be reflected in the overall profitability of the business.

Aging of Accounts Receivable

The credit department must employ tools and techniques for measuring the efficiency of its policies and the effect of these policies upon the viability of the overall corporate operation. Perhaps the most widely recognized tool is the aging of accounts receivable, which may be defined as an analysis of amounts due from customers, distinguishing between amounts not yet due and amounts past due, with the latter being analyzed as to the length of time past due. Supplementary techniques include the use of ratios and statistical data such as the number of days of credit sales represented by the balance of accounts receivable, monthly collection percentages in absolute terms and in terms of a trend (i.e., cash collections of a month or four- or five-week period related to the balance of accounts receivable at the beginning of the month or period), bad debt loss ratio, delinquency ratio, and collections of past due accounts.

In the past it was general practice for businesses to prepare aging schedules, usually in columnar form, showing past due accounts grouped by periods for which they were delinquent. These schedules, when prepared on a monthly basis, gave immediate indication of delinquent accounts. Given the tremendous growth of credit sales in more recent years, this practice had fallen into some degree of disuse. In some instances, credit management found it sufficient to have problem or delinquent customers' ledger cards tabbed, using different colors for each period of delinquency. Alternatively, some credit managers developed the practice of aging a portion of accounts receivable on a rotating basis, completing the cycle over a period of a year or more. In other companies, it was not uncommon to find that the only aging schedule prepared was for the independent accountants in connection with their annual audit examination. However, the upsurge in computerization of the billing and receivables function in more recent years has seen a significant re-emergence of periodic agings. Many computer systems provide aging data, or identification of problem accounts, as by-products of the monthly cycle billing operation.

The effectiveness of aging as a primary tool of credit management is undeniable. Aging provides a list of delinquent customers who will become the target of more vigorous collection procedures although admittedly the essence of good collection practice is the consistency of efforts applied across the board. In targeting the potential problem accounts, aging provides the basis for a concentrated analysis of the quality of a retailer's accounts receivable. It constitutes an effective measurement of the efficiency of credit department policies and procedures and provides the credit manager with an opportunity to control the cost of credit operations by indicating what steps should be taken to tighten credit policies and emphasize collection procedures.

Some credit managers have challenged the use of aging schedules as a measure of collection performance. They feel that it is too broad and transitory and includes traditionally slow paying accounts such as governmental agencies and similar organizations. However, these objections can be met simply by segregating those accounts which introduce bias into the aging schedule. A more valid objection focuses on the cost of aging accounts receivable, and it must be admitted that the manual preparation of an aging schedule is an expensive and time-consuming operation. However, practical alternatives are available. The use of a rotating aging plan designed to review all accounts in a specified period, supplemented by the results of comparative ratios, will in most instances be sufficient to enable the credit manager to maintain adequate control of customer receivables. Moreover, as noted earlier, the introduction of card punch and electronic data processing equipment has enabled the production of aging schedules quickly and efficiently as a by-product of the monthly billing procedures, without substantial increases in cost.

It should also be recognized that schedules of aged receivables are useful for other than credit management purposes. They are an important factor in the preparation of budgets and projections of cash flow. Also, they will represent an important requirement in connection with financing of accounts receivable or in other financial dealings involving institutional lenders.

In the preparation of aging schedules, consideration should be given to their multipurpose uses. The criteria for the determination of when and in what amounts customers' accounts are past due should be satisfactory from the points of view of management, the credit department, institutional lenders, and factoring houses. For certain types of accounts, the basis for determining the timing and amount of past due accounts may be particularly troublesome. Although regular or thirty-day charge accounts present no unusual problems in this respect, the method of aging installment accounts, revolving credit accounts, and option accounts is subject to wide variations in current practice.

The aging of individually tailored installment accounts ranges from designation of only the unpaid installment as past due to recognition of the entire unpaid balance as past due at the due date of the unpaid installment. Variations include the designation of only the unpaid installment as past due until several installments remain unpaid, at which time the entire balance is considered to be past due. However, for collection purposes, the passing of an installment payment does not necessarily constitute a delinquency. Many credit managers do not consider an account to be delinquent until several months after the due date of the unpaid installment. Nevertheless, the existence of an unpaid installment cannot be overlooked. Failure to pay an amount when due generates the first evidence for doubt as to its eventual collectibility, and the older an account, the more difficult a successful collection effort. Failure to pay an installment when due also means an increase in the cost of carrying the account and a related increase in collection expense. Furthermore, a prompt, effective collection policy at this point may discourage the customer from failing to make future payments.

The problems of aging revolving credit accounts are similar to those of installment accounts and a similar variety of current practices exists. Whereas the terms of an installment sale may extend for several years, the term of a revolving account generally may be six, ten, or twelve months; i.e., one-sixth, one-tenth, or one-twelfth of the customer purchase is due each month. Furthermore, since maximum credit limitations are imposed on revolving accounts, an additional problem arises in the aging of "overbuys," the amount by which purchases exceed credit limitations. One method of aging revolving accounts (using the six-month account as an example) is to compare payments made over the previous six months with the total of required payments for that period, and consider the payment shortage as past due. The disadvantage of such a method is that it fails to give recognition to past due amounts at the beginning of the period. A common practice is to consider the entire unpaid balance of a revolving account past due when a limited number of payments are missed, usually not exceeding six. As to overbuys, current billing practice is varied. Some retailers spread the amount of overbuy over the customary term (i.e., six, ten, twelve months, etc.) of the revolving account, whereas others consider it as billable in the full amount at the next billing cycle.

The optional charge account, a more recent innovation in credit accounts, combines the features of the regular or thirty-day account with those of the revolving credit account. By making full or partial payment, the customer respectively indicates a desire to have the account treated as either a regular or a time account. As with revolving credit accounts, the entire unpaid balance should be considered past due either when the initial payment due is missed or when a limited number of payments are missed.

In summary, the aging of receivables is a multipurpose tool which enables the credit department to exercise efficient control over accounts receivable, enables top management to measure the efficiency of the credit department, and provides institutional lenders and others with a basis for evaluating the quality of accounts receivable. The comprehensive aging schedule should be prepared on the basis of sound principles acceptable to all potential users. The entire unpaid amount of any account should be considered past due when any scheduled payment, or a limited number of consecutively scheduled payments, has not been made. The introduction of machine and electronic data processing equipment has greatly facilitated the speed and frequency of the preparation of aging schedules, with little change in cost. This has enabled the credit department to increase its control over accounts receivable, to detect early indications of delinquency, and effectively to implement its credit and collection policies, thereby increasing the efficiency and profitability of the credit operation.

Accumulation of Sales by Sales Clerks

In connection with the customary procedure of paying selling commissions, it is necessary to compile sales by salespersons. Under floor audit, the information on gross sales is readily available from register tapes or from computer runs. Under tally audit, the data listed on the tally envelopes are often used in compiling gross sales. Often the figures utilized are the reported gross sales figures supplied by the individual sales clerks, and no detailed daily check by employees is made. In reducing gross sales to a net sales basis (the basis for most commission calculation), returns and allowances are applied either specifically against the sales clerk making the related sale or on some pro rata basis.

C.O.D. Sales

There are three general methods of handling C.O.D. sales.

1. C.O.D.'s are not recorded as sales until collected. The delivery department or outside carrier employed may require perhaps three days to effect delivery (with longer periods for parcel post,

freight, and express C.O.D.'s), and during this time uncollected C.O.D.'s are open items on the records of the sales audit office. As collections are made, the related amounts are credited to sales and the items are cleared from the audit office control records. Undelivered items are cleared upon return to stock, but no credit slips are issued. Under this plan, there are no C.O.D. accounts receivable, and a minimum of C.O.D. returned sales (those returned by customers subsequent to acceptance and settlement). Uncollected items as of any given date are considered part of stock, rather than merchandise sold.

2. C.O.D. sales checks are audited daily and charged to C.O.D. accounts receivable. Credits to C.O.D. accounts receivable comprise cash collections or returns to stock. For the latter, shipping copies of sales checks which have been utilized as address labels will be employed as credit slips once the merchandise is signed back into stock. Under this plan, C.O.D.'s are treated like charge sales and carried as accounts receivable until collected.

3. C.O.D. sales checks, other than parcel post, freight, and express C.O.D.'s, are "sold" to the outside delivery carrier. Remittance is made to the store by the carrier on the basis of receipt of sales checks properly validated by the store's delivery department. Remittances received from the carrier, representing the aggregate amount of C.O.D. sales checks turned over to the carrier, are credited directly to sales. Sales are subsequently reduced for undelivered items, with the amount of returns being offset against subsequent carrier remittances.

Under the first method there will be a number of checks carried over from day to day, thereby resulting in differences between daily audited sales figures and the corresponding departmental reported totals. The second method is likely to ensure that all C.O.D. sales checks clear through the sales audit daily, but credits for nondeliverable items may be numerous. The third method may require that some checking be made to ensure that all C.O.D. sales checks written in the selling departments are accounted for, either as cash receipts or customer cancellations.

Deposit Sales

Similar to C.O.D.'s are sales where deposits are accepted on account. Such deposits are received as partial payments against goods on hand or goods on order, the balances to be paid by additional deposits or upon delivery of merchandise. There are two usual methods for recording these sales.

Under the first method these transactions are treated as incomplete until delivery of the goods, or at least until the goods are ready for delivery, if full payment has been made in the interim. Under this method the deposits as received are recorded as liabilities, with such liabilities canceled upon completion of the sales recognition transactions. This method is applicable also where deposits are received on orders for merchandise not in stock. A deposit is entered on a deposit check, a portion of which is given to the customer as a receipt. When the merchandise is ready for delivery, a regular sales check is written for the full amount and notation is made thereon of the deposit number and amount and of the net balance due. The sales checks are audited for the gross amounts, with appropriate transfers being made to offset and cancel the related deposit liabilities. Details of the deposits are usually kept on records maintained by the sales audit office. A control account in the general ledger reflects the total amount of outstanding deposits.

Under the second method, the transaction is regarded as a completed sale at the time the deposit is received. A sales check is written at this time for the full amount and the deposit is deducted on the face of the check. The deposits are recorded as cash sales and the balances due on the transactions are recorded as C.O.D. sales. The C.O.D.'s arising in this manner are included with the regular C.O.D. receivables and are closed out in the usual manner when collected. When this method is used, care should be exercised to prevent inclusion in physical inventory of goods already sold under the deposit plan. This is best done by actual segregation of the goods.

If this second method is used, great care should be exercised in recognizing as sales any orders for goods not in stock. Generally speaking, such orders should not be treated as sales.

Will-Call or Layaway Sales

These sales comprise a special type of deposit sales, and are similar to installment sales except that merchandise is not released to customers until the full amount is paid. The general procedure is to set aside an article for a definite period of time during which payments are to be made which will aggregate the total sales price at the close of the "layaway" period. If the article is not taken up at the close of the period it may be returned to stock.

As in the case of other deposit sales, the sale is considered complete either when taken up at the end of the layaway period (a cash sale), or at the time of the first payment (a charge sale). In the latter case, the charge sales check is for the full amount of the sale, the initial payment being treated as a collection on an open account, with the excess of selling price over the first payment as an open account receivable. Under the first method, where recognition of the sale is delayed, deposits are recorded as liabilities to customers. Under the second method, the merchandise should be definitely segregated in will-call rooms so that it will not be confused with departmental inventories.

The file of active will-call accounts should be reviewed frequently to ascertain delinquent accounts. Missed payments should be followed up promptly, and the merchandise returned to stock as soon as possible. There is a constant specter of markdowns in an operation of this type.

Merchandise and Gift Certificates

These certificates are issued either in exchange for cash or as charges to accounts of customers, with all such amounts reflected as liabilities on the books of account. From time to time the certificates are used by holders to apply in whole or in part on purchases made from the store. If used in its entirety, a certificate is surrendered to the store cashier in lieu of cash, and the transaction is recorded as a cash sale. If the holder wishes to use only part of a certificate, a voucher is obtained from the accounting office for the amount desired, and an entry of such amount is made on the face of the certificate. Such vouchers are accepted by cashiers in lieu of cash and the transactions are entered as cash sales. The sales audit office receives the used certificates and vouchers to verify the cash sales totals and advises the accounting office as to the amounts to be transferred from the certificate liability account to cash sales. The general ledger account reflecting the amount of unused certificates outstanding should be supported by a detailed record of all certificate numbers and corresponding amounts outstanding.

Memorandum Sales

Occasions often arise that require stores to send merchandise out for demonstration or exhibition. Store rules usually require that no merchandise can leave the store premises unless a form of sales check is affixed to the merchandise. Deliveries of this kind are not definitely chargeable to any account, and are therefore covered by memorandum records. If goods are returned, the memorandum record is closed. If merchandise is retained—that is, purchased by the holder—a sale should be recognized, with appropriate transfer made from memorandum records. Goods sent out on approval may also sometimes be included on the memorandum record, although in most cases approval merchandise is likely to be billed directly as a charge sale and credited if returned. As long as charges remain on the memorandum record, the merchandise is out of the departmental physical stocks but not removed from the stock ledgers. Such merchandise should, of course, be considered in reconciling book and physical inventories at the time physical inventories are taken.

Discount Sales

Included under this heading may be sales to institutions, clergy, dressmakers, business houses, interior decorators, and special customers. Many stores still allow discounts to all or some of these classes of customers even though it is a generally waning practice.

When discount customers purchase for cash, the discount is deducted from the sales checks and accounted for in the sales audit office. Discounts on charge sales may be deducted from sales checks, or they may be subtracted in totals from monthly statements either as rendered or as settled. The first method renders departmental analysis easier and also eliminates the need for providing for allowable discounts at the close of accounting periods. The second method does not initially require as much time as the first, but it does not meet all requirements without supplementary work.

These discounts represent a loss in retail value, similar to markdowns, and accordingly, they must be reflected in the departmental stock accounts. When discounts are deducted from sales checks, the discounts are tabulated and entered in the stock records as credits to stock in the same manner as sales. Where sales checks are audited gross and the discounts are deducted from customers' bills, the stock records do not require credit entries for such discounts in order to reflect the proper closing stock status. However, sales will be overstated and discounts understated unless adjustments are made to the respective totals for the aggregates of discounts deducted from customers' account. The usual practice is to deduct the amount of discounts from sales and enter that total as a discount credit to stock.

Sales to employees are also discount sales. The most common practice is to write a sales check for all employees' sales, whether cash or charge, deducting the discount at the point of sale. Thereafter, the audit office tabulates departmentally the employees' discount amounts listed on all such sales checks.

A store utilizing the retail method of inventory control and doing a considerable amount of business with the public on discount terms may find it expedient to exclude such business from regular retail operations. Under such circumstances, a separate discount or contract department sometimes is established to handle all discount operations, other than sales to employees. In this situation, the merchandise sold at a discount is transferred from the regular selling departments at the normally established retail and cost prices. However, transfers into the discount or contract department reflect the cost of the transferring department but utilize the discounted retail figures since those figures are the amounts that will be charged to customers. The gross margin of the discount department is, of course, the excess of discounted retail over the computed costs transferred into the department. In some instances the sales and departmental profits of the discount or contract departments remain segregated, consistent with the treatment of other selling departments; in other instances the sales and profits of these departments are allocated to the departments that originally supplied the merchandise for sale to customers.

Installment, Time, or Deferred Payment Sales

These sales are usually made on a conditional basis whereby full title does not pass until final payment is made. When one uniform price is placed on merchandise and adhered to regardless of terms of sale, the usual practice is to charge interest or include carrying charges in addition to the merchandise price and to arrange equal monthly installments covering the total of selling price and carrying charges.

A special accounting problem connected with this class of sales is that of repossession of merchandise when accounts become uncollectible. If at all possible, retailers desire to avoid repossession. Repossessed merchandise is difficult to resell, and the handling of such merchandise is likely to conflict with store policies. Moreover, the expense of repossession and reconditioning often consumes all profit on the transaction. Nevertheless, repossession is often necessary as a matter of principle and to uphold the credit policy of the store. A preferred method of accounting is to place a selling price on the repossessed goods and take them into stock at this selling price, "as is," that is, without inclusion of retail of reconditioning expense, with "cost" or mercantile obtained by deduction of the average departmental markon percentage. Mercantile, as determined, is credited to the customer's account. If the account balance exceeds the credit, the difference is charged to bad debts. If, as may happen occasionally, the account is less than the credit, the difference is treated as a bad debt recovery or as miscellaneous income, unless by agreement the customer is allowed a specified amount, or any credit balance standing open is refunded. This accounting would similarly apply to defaulted layaway accounts.

The interest or carrying charge that is added to the merchandise price in installment selling is not to be recorded as part of sales. Rather, it should be treated as interest earned or sundry income. Customers' installment accounts usually are charged with the full carrying charges at the time the sales are recorded and sundry income is credited. At fiscal closings a computation is made of the amount of carrying charges included in the outstanding installment accounts receivable, and that amount of sundry income is deferred to future periods. In effect, the carrying charges are taken into income ratably as the installments are collected, rather than in full as the sale is recorded.

Forward Sales Orders and Special Orders

In the retail trade the volume of sales orders for future delivery is relatively small, and such orders usually do not have the same firm character as in some other lines of business. However, "will notify" and "special order" transactions cannot be ignored in a discussion of retail sales. The related problems are sometimes perplexing and involve accounts receivable, book inventories, and detailed stock records, as well as periodic gross margin statements.

In this book we are concerned with the practical accounting problems involved, including such questions as at what times and under what conditions sales orders should be taken up into sales account, how the inventory recordkeeping is affected, and in what periods gross profits on such transactions should be reflected in the accounts, either in whole or in part. The problems are more significant in some lines or departments than in others. Retail furniture merchants, for example, are definitely concerned with such questions.

In retailing, except for "take-withs," sales are normally delivered to an address supplied by the customer. The basic problem at issue is when may a sale be considered as legally completed before delivery (as, for example, when held at the store pursuant to customer's instructions). In *Gunther v. McGoldrick* (N.Y. Sup. Ct., App. Div., 1st Dept., June 24, 1938), the question at issue was whether sales of furs during the summer months, for delivery later in the year outside of New York City, with free storage meanwhile, were subject to the city sales tax. The following is from the Court's opinion:

> The transactions in question involving future delivery outside of the City of New York were not taxable as they were not consummated until the merchandise was delivered to the petitioner's customers outside the territorial limits of the city.

The opinion also quotes Section 100 of the New York State Personal Property Law, Rule 5, namely:

> If the contract to sell requires the seller to deliver the goods to the buyer, as at a particular place, or to pay the freight or cost of transportation to the buyer, or to a particular place, the property does not pass until the goods have been delivered to the buyer or reached the place agreed upon.

Apart from the legal concept of the time at which a sales transaction is considered to be completed, it is important that there be no indiscriminate recording of orders as sales. A test of admissibility as a sale is whether the customer may be billed for the merchandise at once, regardless of delivery date; also, there should at least be constructive delivery by segregation of the goods from regular stock. Unless merchandise can be billed, the transaction can scarcely be considered a completed sale. Only when the charge becomes a real account receivable is it proper to exclude the merchandise from inventory. In retailing it is well known that even after delivery there is a large percentage of returned sales. There is even greater likelihood of cancellations where delivery of merchandise has not been completed.

There are different problems with respect to special orders, that is, orders for merchandise not in stock or to be made up from goods in stock, as, for example, draperies, curtains, and upholstery. Before delivery can even constructively be made, there are materials to be purchased or labor and production costs to be incurred. Clearly it would be incorrect to enter this type of order as a sale until all related costs have been charged into purchases. Ordinarily, no sale should be recognized until delivery is made, but, in any event, such recognition should definitely be delayed until all costs have been incurred and the merchandise is ready for delivery. Any other course will erroneously inflate profits and also, where a dollar control of inventory is operated, misstate the book inventory figures. In some cases departmental stock records can be kept current by transfers to workrooms of goods to be used toward the filling of orders. Such merchandise will then be in workroom stocks while the orders are in process of being completed.

Will-Notify Transactions

With respect to furniture and similar household merchandise, it is a common practice for customers to place orders well in advance of desired delivery dates. This may be done to take advantage of special prices being offered temporarily or seasonally, or to allow for time required to obtain merchandise similar to that in stock, but different in details such as shades of fabric, size, or finish, or to assemble and prepare goods for delivery. In many instances a store is requested to hold the goods until notification by the customer as to time and place for delivery.

Many furniture stores withhold recording of such sales until actual delivery, meanwhile including held merchandise as part of stock and carrying any deposits received as liabilities. In a comparatively small operation this procedure may prove reasonably satisfactory. However, a considerable amount of "will-notify" business is likely to cause complications. If such merchandise is physically segregated from other stock without being deducted as sales on stock records, confusion may result as to the quantity and amount of merchandise on hand for present business. Without segregation, there is likely to be even more confusion as to available stock. There is the further consideration that the recording of "will-notify" sales on a "deliver" basis may cause a disproportionate amount of sales in certain months generally preferred for delivery, with relatively small sales in months when orders are actually taken. This will add to the difficulties inherent in any planning of stocks, advertising, and other expenses in relation to sales.

Storage Charges

Questions of accounting procedure arise where storage charges, such as for fur storage, are made to customers. It is common practice for storage charges to cover the period from the date goods are received until, say, the close of the calendar year. While charges may be made on various bases, a common basis is a charge related to declared or appraised value, with no regard to the length of the storage period, provided it is within the calendar year. If storage is continued into the new year, the customer ordinarily becomes liable for a storage fee for the second year. Some goods are received early in the season and remain in storage until near the end of the year. Other articles may come in late and be taken out early, without, however, affecting the amount charged.

The full storage charge should not be recorded as income upon receipt of the goods. In many cases no amount of storage income is recorded until the goods are taken from storage. In operations of the latter kind, practically all the storage sales as recorded are realized in the months well toward the end of the storage year. The result is that a disproportionate amount of the storage revenue is realized in those months in which the bulk of items is withdrawn, regardless of the fact that storage expense continues throughout the year and is exceptionally heavy at the time that garments are first placed in the vaults. An alternative accounting practice widely used is to defer all expenses of storage until such time as the garments are withdrawn, recognizing at such time both the storage expenses and the storage revenue. This is preferable to charging off all expenses as incurred but deferring the revenue pending withdrawal of the garments. However, it has the disadvantage of excluding storage operations from the accounts throughout most of the year, and then suddenly recognizing all storage activity in a relatively brief period.

A more appropriate procedure is to absorb the storage expenses as they arise and to allocate storage revenue on a pro rata basis over the period in which the garments remain in the vaults. Under this plan, the full charge for the year is made against the customer when the goods are received, with the offsetting credit being to a deferred storage sales account. Since it is rarely the practice to bill the customer for storage charges before the articles are withdrawn, or before the end of the storage year, the sales checks as written are retained in house. As garments are withdrawn from storage, or at the end of the storage year if not withdrawn, the sales checks are removed from file and the customers are billed.

Transfers from the deferred storage sales account to sales are made monthly (or for each four- or five-week period) on a pro rata basis. Any remaining balances in the deferred sales account related to goods taken from storage may be transferred to sales in the respective months or periods of removal. Sometimes these procedures will be applied only in the fall months, when there are large withdrawals from storage.

Repair Charges

Charges for repairs to customers' own goods or for cleaning, where the goods are delivered when finished or are held for customers to call, should present no problem in accounting for sales. Charge customers may be billed and amounts recorded as sales when the work has been completed. For cash customers amounts will be treated as cash sales when customers call for their goods and pay the charges. If payments have been made when goods are left for repair, the amounts paid can be recorded as deposit liabilities which are later transferred to revenue when the repair work is completed.

Where repair or cleaning is done on customers' goods placed in storage, it is the usual practice not to bill the charges until the articles are withdrawn from storage or until the end of the storage year. This is done as a practical matter since the customer normally would not make payment until there has been an inspection, by the customer, of the repair work. The problem remains, however, of getting such charges into sales when the work is completed, because cost and expense are incurred long before the items are withdrawn or before the close of the storage period.

Two extreme practices appear to be followed in some stores: (1) to record the charge at once as a sale, regardless of when the costs are incurred, and (2) to record the sale only when the charge is billed. Under the first practice, the charge against the customer is included as an additional item on the sales check written to cover storage charges. However, it is not billed to the customer until the articles are withdrawn from storage or until the end of the storage year. The method is to be criticized for recording a sale before related costs are incurred and recorded. It is customary to spread the work of repairing and cleaning of stored goods throughout the less active months of the storage period. Operating results are inaccurately stated where sales income is recorded in advance of the entry of cost of sales. The inaccuracy may be material if large amounts of repair and cleaning charges are involved.

Under the second practice, there is also inaccuracy because costs are recorded, but sales income is deferred. A modification is to defer the costs along with the revenue until the charges are billed, and at that time to recognize both costs incurred and related revenues for accounting purposes.

Customers' Credits

Three varieties of credits arise from the return of merchandise:

1. Call credits—written to enable the store's own delivery department or outside carrier to pick up merchandise at customers' homes. Once the order to pick up merchandise is executed and the merchandise is signed back into departmental stocks it becomes a valid credit. Such credits cover cash or charge business.
2. Express and mail credits—written upon the receipt of goods by express or parcel post and covering both cash and charge business.
3. Floor credits—for merchandise returned personally by customers. Two forms are used, one for cash credits and one for charge credits.

With respect to call credits and express and mail credits, the merchandise is routed through the return goods room for checking and inspection. The credit forms are signed by representatives of the selling departments who note retail price on the forms, as well as by representatives of the return goods room. Prior to submission to sales audit, some stores make it a practice to investigate the legitimacy of credits covering furniture and bulk items and those credits involving a customer request for reimbursement. Sales audit then processes these credits as return sales, reducing departmental gross sales.

On all floor credits the merchandise is received and the credit signed in the selling department, or alternatively at service desks if the latter are maintained. Countersignature by the floor manager is recommended. Cash credits can be surrendered by customers in exchange for cash or applied on new purchases.

All credits are basically either charge or cash credits. Charge credits are summarized and forwarded, together with control totals, to the accounts receivable department for application against the individual charge accounts affected. Cash credits are summarized, with control totals being forwarded either to the accounts receivable or the accounting department. It is sometimes the practice to keep a detailed "log" or listing of cash credits by number and amount. However, the detail entailed by such recordkeeping has discouraged its use by some retailers. As payment is made to the customer or as the cash credit is used for cash sales, the particular credit number and amount is stamped off. In effect, the log represents the detail in support of a liability to customers.

It is also sometimes the practice to keep a log on call credits. These are the credits which, because of delay in the pick-up and eventual return to stock, give rise to customer complaints. Since a large percentage of customer complaints is attributable to credits, this log is utilized to substantiate the issuance of a credit. It will disclose whether a particular credit is open, or it may serve as an indicator that a credit was posted to the wrong customer's account.

In addition to credits representing the return of merchandise, there are credits which represent special allowances to customers. These credits are written essentially by the bill and merchandise adjustment departments, although floor authorities also are often permitted to write this type of credit. These customer adjustments are often discretionary in nature. Credits which represent purely policy adjustments should be charged off to expenses. Credits representing a true merchandise allowance should serve to reduce departmental gross margins.

While it may be impractical and costly to account for the serial numbers of every credit issued, it is desirable that the volume of missing credits be kept to a minimum. As heretofore noted, logs may be maintained, and as each credit is used a notation may be made, opposite the credit number and amount, of the date audited. Such a record will provide the serial numbers of all open credits, and will also alert the store as to any unauthorized re-submission of credits.

Items Not Recorded as Sales

There are some items charged to customers or collected from them that for obvious reasons are not classified as sales. For example, excise taxes or local sales taxes payable by customers are not sales. A store is simply the collecting agent. The amounts of such taxes, whether collected in cash at the time of sale or entered together with the merchandise item on a customer's charge account, should not be recorded as sales but as a liability to the taxing authority. Parcel post, express, and freight charges to customers should be credited to the respective expense accounts, rather than to sales. Proceeds from sales of supplies, waste, etc., should be credited to expense accounts (or supply inventory accounts if maintained) or sundry income, and not to sales.

These items differ from alteration and workroom charges to customers. Charges by workrooms classified as subsidiary service workrooms are, in fact, sales. However, although entered on sales checks, so that the amounts may be collected from customers, such charges are usually credited to alteration or workroom cost accounts rather than to sales. They are thus applied to reduce alteration and workroom costs which are included net in total merchandise costs. This procedure is followed in the accounts and merchandise statements so that there will be shown the ratio of gross margin to sales of merchandise only and also the ratio of service workroom net costs in relation to merchandise sales. If a store wishes to include such items solely for its statistical tabulation of sales, so that sales reflect total charges to customers, this may be done by transfer without affecting the procedure recommended for merchandise statements.

Frequently obsolete, damaged, or otherwise unsalable merchandise is removed from departmental stocks for disposition in lots at salvage prices. A good procedure in such instances is to make a transfer to a salvage account. With reference to Figure 14, "Merchandise Statement and Stock Ledger (Combined)" (page 109), this would be effected as follows.

Credit would be given to the department for the estimated salvage value of the merchandise on line 5, Transfers (net). Utilizing the departmental gross markon percentage, the retail price corresponding to this salvage value would be developed and entered on line 12, Transfers (net). The difference between the marked selling price (prior to removal from stock) and the aforementioned mathematically developed retail figure would be taken as a markdown, and entered on line 24, Markdowns. Upon sale of the salvage goods the salvage account will be credited and should show a gain or loss, depending upon whether the amount realized is greater or less than the salvage estimate made at the time of transfer. The gain or loss is reflected as a credit or charge to miscellaneous income.

An alternative, but not recommended, procedure is to transfer the salvage goods out of the regular department at a complete loss and, when the goods are later sold, credit sundry income, not sales, with whatever proceeds are received.

Trading Stamps

Trading stamp plans were one of the more significant post-war developments in retailing, although the practice has been curtailed in more recent years primarily because of cost. The greatest impetus to the acceptance of trading stamp plans was their adoption by food supermarkets. Essentially trading stamps constitute a promotional device intended to associate in the minds of the ultimate consumer a trading stamp with a particular store or group of stores.

Trading stamp plans are operated either by an independent trading stamp company or are controlled by the retailer. The independent trading stamp company customarily enters into a licensing agreement with a retailer whereby the retailer becomes a member of a particular trading stamp system. The stamp company provides the retailer with the stamps (and such auxiliary supplies as catalogs and stamp collecting books) which are distributed to the customers of the retailer. The consumer accumulates the stamps and upon making the proper accumulation exchanges such stamps, ordinarily at a redemption center, for merchandise items shown in the catalog. When the stamps are purchased on the normal "nonredemption" basis, the retailer sets up an "inventory" of stamps which is customarily treated as a deferred charge. As such stamps are distributed to the consumers, the ordinary charge is to advertising and sales promotion expenses, with a corresponding credit to the deferred charge. Any balance of stamps remaining at year end would constitute an unamortized deferred charge.

Whether independently operated or controlled by the retailer, the trading stamp company derives its revenue from the sale of stamps to retailers. Its basic expenses, in addition to the normal general administrative expenses, would comprise the cost of merchandise used in making redemptions, cost of operating the redemption centers and warehouses, printing expenses, and promotional expenses which are designed to associate in the minds of the consumers a particular trading stamp with a particular store or group of stores. This last point is fundamental to the operation of a trading stamp system since it acts as an inducement for the consumer to patronize a particular retailer.

The important accounting problem to be faced by the trading stamp company is the determination of the number of stamps expected to be returned for redemption. A book of accumulated stamps with a certain exchange value can be converted into the corresponding cost of merchandise items offered as premiums. Accordingly, for purposes of costing out the estimated stamp redemptions a reserve on anticipated stamp returns is set up, with an offsetting charge to some cost of redemption account. This reserve is established on some historical basis related to prior stamp returns. As the stamps are redeemed, the reserve for redemption is charged, and the merchandise account (inventory) is credited.

12

Shortages and Shortage Control

Introduction

Inventory shortages or shrinkage, the difference between book and physical inventory at retail, is a term that is easy to define but, as most retailers will attest, difficult to control. The increase in inventory shortages over the years has reached alarming proportions. Whereas retailers in the past were concerned with shortages normally running between 0.5 per cent and 1 per cent of net sales, present figures are between 2 per cent and 5 per cent, and there is concern that these figures may continue to rise in the coming years. The problem can be said to be widespread throughout the retail trade, with the experience of the discount retailers generally being poorer in this regard than the more conventional retailers.

Contributory Factors

The dramatic growth in retail organizations, particularly in recent decades, has been a significant factor in the increase in inventory shortage. To a great extent, this growth has been achieved via the geographical dispersion of new units and new warehouses. Any such growth is inevitably accompanied by a certain dilution of headquarters control and by the necessity to delegate executive responsibilities. The delegation of such responsibilities and the corresponding increase in local branch store autonomy are not necessarily accompanied by a deterioration in operations. However, the mere existence of 10 or 100 branch stores effectively means the existence of 10 or 100 different levels of leadership, of competency, of experience, and of motivation. Moreover, the problems of geographic dispersion of units and delegation of executive responsibility are compounded by the greater difficulties in effective communication over these far-flung networks.

The more extensive the network of stores and warehouses, the greater the reliance on paperwork and controls, and the greater will be the potential for breakdowns in basic store and warehouse disciplines and corresponding increases in recordkeeping errors, many of which lose their identity in the final shortage statistic. These problems may be further aggravated by certain cost-cutting efforts which are achieved at the expense of weakened internal and operating controls and curtailed training programs. Under these circumstances, certain short-term cost reductions may be realized, but long-term deterioration, in terms of service to customers and control over operations, is inevitable.

As a corollary factor, the increase in branch store operations has been accompanied by an increase in the number of hours, and days, during which stores are open. Often, this has involved a smaller degree of store coverage with a greater percentage of part-time or contingent, less experienced personnel, with reduced or minimal supervision. The extreme illustration in this regard is the typical discount, self-service, check-out type store with large selling areas manned by a minimum of selling or stock personnel. The increased opportunities for shoplifting are obvious under these circumstances.

A marked trend toward more visibly displayed and more easily accessible merchandise has afforded easier access to the shoplifter. Simply stated, merchandise on tables and racks is easier to steal than merchandise displayed in display cases. Moreover, it is an unfortunate fact but statistics reflect a significant increase in the incidence of crime, particularly among amateur criminals.

A further significant factor bearing upon the internal aspects of shortage is the overall personnel problem. Too often the unrecognized causes of shortage are rooted in the store's inadequate practices involving the selection of personnel; the training of personnel in store practices, procedures, and controls; the establishment of satisfactory career development programs; the effective communication, by management, of anticipated standards of performance; and the monitoring of employee and supervisory performance. Stated differently, retailers have not always been successful in communicating to employees their keen interest and concern with the shortage problem and in having employees identify their personal economic well being with the viability of the retailer's operation.

Classification of Shortages

Shortages probably can best be classified by source of origin: those relating to "paperwork" errors, which result from breakdowns in controls attributable to employee negligence and carelessness or to deliberate commissions or omissions in any one or more steps in the recordkeeping process; and those due to theft, by employees or non-employees. Retailers are constantly debating the extent to which each type of shortage contributes to the overall problem. The estimates are at best conjectural, although the non-employee contributory factor is generally deemed to represent less than 50 per cent of the overall problem. Aside from the exact relationships of the causative factors, the most important deterrent is management's acknowledgment of the severity of the problem and the communication to all employees of an intense concern and keen desire to implement a remedial program. Thereafter, it becomes a continuing training, education, and monitoring program that must focus on all the related accounting, physical, and operational controls, particularly the weak links in the operation. Accordingly, this chapter will focus on certain of the how's and why's of inventory shortage, with particular emphasis on the deviations from sound practices and controls that contribute to the enormity of the problem.

Loss Prevention

Whether termed loss prevention, shrinkage control, or shortage control, most retail organizations have recognized that preplanned preventive action is critical to the success of any remedial shortage program. This current philosophy represents a change from the past, when the semiannual or annual physical inventory disclosed a shortage of untenable proportions and galvanized the retailer into massive—and generally inconclusive—efforts to ascertain the underlying rationales.

The preventive program is initiated by the manifestation of management's intense concern with the problem, and the communication of this concern to all executive, supervisory, and individual subordinate employee levels. Obviously, the controller's responsibility for shortage differs from that of a buyer, sales clerk, porter, or night watchman; however, the shortage problem and management's dedication to resolving it should be imparted to all levels of employees. Staff training programs and oral and written communications to all employees must comprise a continuing program as overt manifestations of management's concern.

Staff training programs are vital since they provide the foundation for indoctrination in prescribed company practices and controls. New merchandising personnel should be provided with written procedures setting forth all merchandise systems and procedures, complete with sample illustrations of forms such as purchase orders, receiving reports, price change reports, and chargebacks. These employees must also become familiar with security and other operational procedures so that they may have an overall grasp of the company's operations. The written procedures should be supplemented by staff training sessions which concentrate on actual problems and instruction in the preparation and utilization of merchandise-related reports. Periodic sessions can be utilized to remind older employees of store procedures and to stress problem areas.

Emphasis should also be placed on training sales register personnel. This group of employees can play a vital part in curtailing shortages. The proper training of such personnel in initially recording sales or sales returns is obviously critical, but the alertness of these employees can prove even more important as an excellent deterrent to both non-employee and employee thefts.

Depending on the size of the organization, the establishment of a separate shrinkage control department may well be warranted. The size of the department may vary, depending on the store's needs, from a single shortage controller and an assistant, to the utilization of a much larger staff. Whatever its size, this group should have the primary responsibility of coordinating the efforts of the various loss prevention units in the organization—the controller's department, the security department, the internal audit group, the operations group, and others. Conventionally, the individual heading the shortage control department generally should report to the controller or chief financial officer in the organization. A well-defined organizational alignment and clearly defined responsibilities are prerequisites to an effective loss prevention program. Although one unit may have prime responsibility for inventory and physical plant protection, its efforts must be integrated with those other departments whose efforts all combine to determine the effectiveness of combating shrinkages. Many retailers have established shortage committees to great advantage. Usually such a committee consists of a cross section of employees representing merchandising and nonmerchandising functions, bringing to bear a wide spectrum of executive experience and expertise within the organization on the shortage problem. The greater the manifestation of management concern and the greater the involvement of various disciplines and executive levels within the organization, the more successful will be the shortage reduction effort.

A properly functioning security department is obviously critical to the success of any shortage control program. However, its activities should more strongly emphasize loss prevention, as opposed to the apprehending of shoplifters. In the past many retailers have viewed their security departments almost exclusively as apprehenders of shoplifters and performers of special fraud investigations. This definition of a security department's responsibilities must be significantly expanded if this department is to function effectively in the overall shortage prevention program. Since employee theft has increased significantly over the years, security personnel must become heavily involved in this aspect of the theft problem. The security department's responsibility should be expanded to include not only the selling floors but also the stock and reserve rooms, warehouses, and any other nonselling areas where merchandise is received or stored and subsequently issued. The department should include a well balanced staff of both uniformed and nonuniformed personnel who are knowledgeable in the details of retail operations and in the related prospective theft problems. Moreover, security personnel should be consulted in the construction of new stores and in prospective modifications in the physical layout of existing units so that their views on the related security implications of all such changes will be considered.

Another department that should be used to the fullest extent in combating shortages is the internal audit group. Given the overriding importance of inventories in any retail environment, there should be a continuing review of all the procedures and controls surrounding the receipt, storage, and movement of inventories. The internal audit group should utilize well defined, written programs in focusing on the major problem areas. When deficiencies in operations and controls, or failures to adhere to established company procedures, are disclosed by the reviews made by this department, they should be discussed in detail with the line executives directly responsible and followed up by written reports submitted to management. While this group will be emphasizing deviations from prescribed procedures and controls, it should also be alert to prospective changes and modifications that will improve the operational efficiency of any department or function under review.

It is essential that management follow up on the operating and control problems cited by the internal auditors, satisfying itself that remedial action has been taken by the line executives within a reasonable period of time. An internal audit group can only be as effective as the support it receives from top management, and its stature and effectiveness will be determined by the emphasis that top management places on its findings and recommendations.

Paperwork Errors and Human Error

The conventional recordkeeping surrounding the flow of merchandise, the marking and re-marking of merchandise, and the sale of merchandise can literally involve tens and probably hundreds of thousands of individual transactions. These involve books of original entry such as the purchase journal or register and the retail ledger, and supporting records and documents such as vendor invoices, price change reports, receiving reports, and sales slips. At every point in the flow of merchandise where an entry is made or a document prepared, a potential source of inventory shortage or shrinkage exists. Errors, and the resulting shortage, can occur either by a deliberate manipulation of records or by negligence or carelessness on the part of an employee.

In the area of recordkeeping, retailers continuously debate whether the "cost" of maintaining stocks by store is worth the additional control over shortages that it affords. It is the authors' opinion that the additional costs of recordkeeping on a recurring basis, which are attributable to the control required over interstore transfers, are justifiable when compared to the resultant benefits.

Separate store records provide branch store and top management personnel with a clear picture of the problem departments and problem stores within the organization. This obviously localizes and pinpoints responsibility for shortages, thereby making it possible to knowledgeably direct the retailer's efforts toward the resolution of the problem. In addition to improved shortage control, separate store records should furnish useful insights into the merchandising operations of branch stores. Obviously a change from a common pool stock to stock maintained by individual store represents a significant effort, but difficulties of transition can be minimized by a fully documented and well planned conversion program.

The determination of a shortage statistic is, of course, based upon the taking of a reasonably accurate physical inventory. Reference should be made to Chapter 9, which sets forth the procedures and guidelines for ensuring that a proper physical inventory is taken, including the reconciliation, if necessary, from the physical inventory data to the book inventory data. One aspect of taking a physical inventory that must be stressed when discussing shortages is consigned stock inventory. In some notable instances, inventory shortages were deliberately obscured by including vendor-consigned stock in the company's physical inventory amounts. To avoid any such problem, the consigned stock should be physically inventoried at the same time the company's merchandise is counted. The maintenance of separate inventory control accounts for consigned stock will also enhance control over this inventory.

In the following sections, there are set forth certain basic internal control and check procedures surrounding the flow of merchandise that are critical to shortage control. Violations of these safeguards, whether deliberate or through carelessness or negligence, will ultimately be translated into a larger shortage statistic. It will also be evident that in some instances cited errors in paperwork and employee carelessness may encourage or obscure employee and/or non-employee thefts.

Purchase Orders

One of the most important control requirements, about which management should be most insistent, is that purchase orders be prepared for all merchandise purchased. Abuse of this control not only poses potentially serious shortage control problems, but also has adverse operational and financial ramifications. In more specific terms, the failure to prepare purchase orders on a timely basis can create a series of interrelated problems, as follows:

1. It can render ineffective the retailer's "open to buy" system (see Chapter 4).
2. It creates difficulties in knowledgeably scheduling the timing of vendor deliveries, with the related inefficient scheduling of receiving and marking personnel, thereby resulting in higher payroll costs.
3. It can create a backlog and bottleneck in receiving, occasioned by the delays required to obtain purchase orders from departmental buyers, and in the entire paper work processing.
4. It increases susceptibility to pilferage in the receiving department, because of the backlog that is created.
5. It will increase vendor complaints and the related clerical effort to investigate and resolve such complaints.
6. It can make meaningless the measurement and evaluation of departmental and company-wide commitments.
7. It can inhibit the intelligent evaluation of buyer and departmental performance.

Accordingly, adherence to this requirement should be closely monitored by receiving personnel, and any abuses should be reported to management without delay.

When merchandise is received for which no corresponding purchase order is on hand, it should obviously be placed under control. Shortages can be masked when merchandising personnel, aware of control weaknesses in the receiving and marking departments, are successful in having merchandise transferred to the selling floor without going through the formal processing routines.

Further, adequate controls should be maintained over prenumbered purchase order forms, with only authorized personnel given access to such forms. Weak control over purchase order forms could result in the diversion of merchandise to unauthorized receiving or other locations. Finally, incorrect, incomplete, or illegible purchase orders can result in shortages even before the merchandise is received by the store or warehouse. For example, an illegible purchase order can result in one price being reflected on the books of account and another on the price tag, e.g., merchandise booked as $9.99 each which is being sold at two for $9.99.

Receiving

All merchandise should be received at a central receiving area, whether it be a platform, room, or separate section off the selling floor. Merchandise should never be received directly on the selling floor; the potentials for control abuses or errors in checking, marking, and recording of the shipment are too extensive. Adequate procedures should exist to ensure that merchandise is delivered to the receiving area promptly once it has been received by the store. Needless to say, only receiving personnel or those otherwise authorized should have access to the receiving area.

Many receiving departments require that preliminary claim reports be prepared when merchandise is initially inspected. This practice provides better documentation and improved control over potential claims, and ultimately expedites collections of claims. Claims should be closely scrutinized by responsible employees to ascertain whether there is a consistent pattern of claims filed against certain designated vendors or carriers. This prospective identification of problem vendors or carriers is a good example of the integration of shortage control with other operational activities (principally traffic and merchandising, in this instance) to improve overall profitability.

Occasionally, merchandise is paid for prior to its receipt. This practice definitely should be discouraged, but where it is permitted adequate control must be maintained over such invoices so that they can be properly accounted for at any given date. If such invoices are included in book figures and not otherwise adjusted as of the physical inventory date, an apparent shortage will result. On the other hand, an apparent overage will result when merchandise is released to the selling department prior to its being compared and checked to a vendor's invoice or "dummy" invoice.

The order-checking department should receive all invoices directly from vendors; in no instance should invoices be directed to merchandise or store managers or other personnel.

Marking

As in the receiving operation, the ideal approach to marking is centralization. Centralizing the operation will result in generally closer supervision over this important function and will eliminate certain weaknesses inherent in a dispersed operation.

One of the most important practices to be followed in the marking department is to have only authorized personnel in the area. Not only does this eliminate the potential possibility for theft, but perhaps more importantly, it reduces the confusion and eventual errors that sometimes result when too many people are attempting to get merchandise moved to the selling floor, stockroom, or warehouse. In no event should marking room personnel allow merchandise that has not been completely marked and checked, as prescribed by company procedures, to be removed from the area. To abdicate the marking function to merchandising personnel, as is unfortunately done at peak selling seasons such as Christmas, presumably in response to emergency selling requirements, is to invite shortages.

Marking room procedures should be clearly defined, with supervisory personnel constantly checking adherence to these procedures. Spot checks can be made to determine that quantities marked and invoiced agree; that department numbers are correct, especially where similar merchandise could be sold in more than one department; and that the proper type price tag is being used. Preticketed merchandise requires special attention to ensure that the retail prices per invoices, which are used in posting to the retail ledger, agree with the ticketed prices.

Some retailers employ outside services to perform the marking function. Procedures should be established to review merchandise received from such sources. The procedures followed by these agents also must be reviewed since the retailer generally is required to pay for merchandise presumably shipped to the marking agent.

Re-Marking

Good control over re-marking merchandise generally embraces the same controls as those over the initial marking, with the single most important factor being centralized re-marking. Perhaps the best deterrent to shortages is to have only authorized personnel do the re-marking. In addition, they would be the only ones to have access to new tickets or special pens required for re-marking. Controls are seriously weakened, and shortages invited, when the re-marking is left to sales or merchandising personnel. More and more retailers are getting away from the red pens or pencils that were once prevalent in re-marking merchandise. This practice opened the door to unrecorded markdowns, and certain enterprising customers were quick to recognize how they could get merchandise at reduced prices. The re-marking should be initiated by a preprinted, numerically controlled price change report. Accounting or statistical department control over the issuance and subsequent accountability for such forms will focus on a potential shortage situation by identifying a missing price change report.

Shortages can result when marking personnel do not re-mark price tags (principally quantities, prices, or department numbers) in accordance with changes as authorized by the price change report. Accordingly, the selling department initiating the price changes should check to see that the merchandise subsequently returned has been re-marked pursuant to instructions.

It is widely recognized that one source of shortage is the unrecorded markdown, and allowing merchandise personnel to re-mark merchandise on the selling floor increases the likelihood of unrecorded markdowns. In addition, this manipulation is sometimes fostered by the strict budgeting of markdowns. When confronted with an inflexible budgeted markdown policy on one hand, and the necessity to reduce selling prices to move merchandise on the other hand, buyers have been known to bypass prescribed re-marking procedures. Markdown budgets must be viewed as guides and goals; they cannot dictate merchandising policy which must be responsive to the practical requirements of the marketplace. From a financial and operational standpoint, the retailer is much better off aware of the impact of markdowns on a timely basis, as opposed to the delayed recognition of a shortage. The inevitable result effectively is the "delayed" recognition of a markdown masked as an increase in the shortage statistic.

Transfers to the Selling Floor, Stockroom, or Warehouse

As noted earlier, there should be an absolute prohibition on merchandise being received directly from a vendor by the selling department or stockroom. Prescribed receiving and marking procedures should never be bypassed. Moreover, in transferring merchandise throughout the store, carts, baskets, hampers, etc., should be covered and locked whenever possible, and never left unattended. In addition, service elevators, rather than customer elevators, should be used in transporting the merchandise.

Merchandising personnel receiving merchandise in the selling area should, for many classifications of merchandise, carefully check deliveries as to quantity and prices. This control is sometimes relaxed in peak selling periods when receiving personnel do not give selling departments ample time to schedule staff to check incoming shipments. At the very time when controls should be at their strongest, many retailers find prescribed procedures being weakened.

Reserve stockrooms left unlocked and accessible to unauthorized personnel are invitations to employee and non-employee theft. The expansion of branch store operations over the years has resulted in interstore transfers becoming a prime source of shortages. Accordingly, proper control over interstore transfers requires stringent adherence to physical controls and paperwork procedures. Wherever possible, merchandise should be secured in some type of locked container. Store receiving personnel must be alert to containers which appear to have been tampered with or opened without authorization. Interstore transfer forms should be used, and checked to merchandise and manifests by the receiving store as soon as the merchandise is received. The lack of numerical control over transfer forms is another potential source of paperwork shortage or indirectly of theft.

Warehouse and stockroom security cannot be overemphasized. It is imperative that only authorized personnel have access to designated areas, and that merchandise be removed only upon proper authorization. Additional locked areas should be provided for valuable merchandise.

Stock on the Selling Floor

Shortages will occur when sales personnel make errors in the handling and recording of merchandise sold. Generally, many of these errors result from inexperience or ignorance on the part of sales employees, and the monitoring of performance together with some form of continuing training program are key factors in keeping shortages in this area to a minimum.

Sales clerks should be constantly concerned with the accurate entering of sales prices and quantities on sales checks and cash registers. Sales clerks should be alert to prices which appear to be out of line with others in the department, and there should be a periodic review of the prices of stock on hand, including legibility of price tickets.

Cash register instructions distributed to all sales personnel should eliminate misunderstanding as to the operation of the register. Sales personnel should, of course, be familiar with the register key assigned to their respective selling departments. Department heads periodically should review sales checks to satisfy themselves that there is constant adherence to prescribed procedures by sales personnel. Many times merchandising and sales personnel minimize the necessity of recording sales in the proper department if the departments are related or possibly under one buyer, e.g., men's furnishings and men's ready-to-wear. Accordingly, management must emphasize to sales personnel involved in interselling between departments that, from a merchandising and financial control standpoint, it is essential to know the correct shrinkage figures by department.

Adequate care and controls should be maintained over all merchandise leaving the department, exclusive of sales to customers. This would include merchandise on loan for display or advertising, interdepartment transfers for subsequent sale to customers, merchandise out for repairs, and returns to vendors. Of particular importance is merchandise designated for return to vendors. It should be adequately documented, and selling personnel should receive a signed receipt from the shipping department or vendor return room. This merchandise should be stored in a separate area to avoid commingling with merchandise received from vendors in the normal course of business.

In past years only "big-ticket" items, e.g., furniture and appliances, were delivered to customers' homes. However, with the growth of cities and the resulting traffic congestion, an ever increasing number of customers are having merchandise sent directly to their homes or places of business. Since this service obviously requires additional handling of merchandise before it gets to the customer, it presents another potential shortage problem. The delivery department must be made responsible for all merchandise received and must maintain adequate records of receipts and shipments. In this area, improper documentation of damaged or lost merchandise, which ultimately results in incorrect or no recording, could result in a shortage. All reductions must be recorded if the book records are to reflect properly the inventory status.

Merchandise is frequently returned from customers with price tickets removed or mutilated. Re-marking of such merchandise should be under the same controls as for any other merchandise received.

Employee and Non-Employee Thefts

It is apparent from the situations described above that paperwork errors and human error can lead to or at least be conducive to employee thefts. The potentially dishonest employee, observing the lack of discipline within the organization, may be encouraged to attempt the misappropriation of merchandise. Experience has shown that dishonest employees will take advantage of operational weaknesses or control breakdowns to secure merchandise within a store, and then determine the best way of removing it from the premises.

The initial guideline in preventing employee dishonesty is to learn as much as possible about the potential employee before hiring. Accordingly, all employees should be screened and checked as to their past history. Once hired, the emphasis must be on adequate supervision. Many retailers also use outside "shopping" services to deter or discover employee and non-employee theft. "Shopping" consists of having an outside service organization shop certain departments, concentrating on the cash register and the checking out of merchandise.

Employee theft can also occur in connection with employee discounts. Abuses by employees for fellow employees and friends is a serious problem. A continual review of employee discounts by management will usually spot any unusual occurrences which might indicate that unauthorized discounts are being taken.

The methods used by employees for removing merchandise from a store are as varied as the employees. A common technique is the purchase by an employee of a large, inexpensive merchandise item; the bag and stamped receipt are then utilized to subsequently remove more expensive merchandise from the store. One possible deterrent is to have the security department require employees as they leave the store to open packages on a spot-check basis. This prospective deterrent presupposes that the retailer has established the requirement that employees use designated entrances and exits at all times, a highly desirable practice. Ladies' handbags have been used effectively in pilfering merchandise and cash. Accordingly, store policy should deal with the question as to whether women employees can bring handbags to the cash register area. Practices in this regard have ranged from a prohibition on bags to limitations on the size of the bags and even to the requirement that they be made of transparent plastic.

These examples of the unauthorized removal of merchandise from a store do not include the important situations where an employee steals merchandise by taking advantage of procedural and control weaknesses. Examples of potential vulnerability would comprise poor receiving and checking procedures relating to the receipt of merchandise by the store, warehouse, and selling departments, and poor control over transfers from store to store or warehouse to store. In this regard, while outside shopping services can be useful, the best deterrents to employee theft are sound systems of internal control and check that are rigidly and continuously enforced by management.

The severity of the shoplifting problem has grown to alarming proportions in a rather short period of time. Experts in this area attribute the increase in shortage to the increase of "amateur" shoplifters—those adults and teenagers who steal for psychological reasons, i.e., "a thrill," "get something for nothing," or desire to "own something," or drug addicts in serious need of funds. In addition, there is the professional shoplifter. Usually much more cautious and with greater planning effort, this type of individual generally steals more expensive merchandise.

Unfortunately, it is not easy to spot the potential shoplifter, since such individual can be of either sex, any age, rich or poor, and of any ethnic background. However, certain actions or appearances may at least give some preliminary indications of potential hazard. Generally, a shoplifter will be carrying or wearing something that will aid in concealing the merchandise being pilfered. A shopping bag, briefcase, or loose overcoat provides good cover for a potential theft. Further, for obvious reasons the shoplifter is generally most active at the busiest hours of the day and during peak selling seasons such as pre-Christmas or back-to-school. The shoplifter will also utilize the layout of the store and nonselling areas to advantage. Lack of control over garments taken into fitting rooms can result in a dress or other clothing being worn under a person's own garments. Merchandise readily accessible on a counter near an exit is an invitation to the shoplifter.

The following are known methods which have been employed by shoplifters to pilfer merchandise, although it should be emphasized that shoplifters are continually using great creativity in the misappropriation of merchandise:

1. The use of a false box. A box is tied or wrapped to give the appearance of a closed package. One section of the box can be opened and then closed to its original position without disturbing its outward appearance. This permits merchandise, easily moved from counter tops, to be placed in the box.
2. The use of loose fitting undergarments. Loose bloomers, fitted tightly at the knee and worn under a skirt, can be used to hide merchandise.
3. The use of a belt with hooks has been used by male shoplifters to hide stolen merchandise under a coat.
4. The use of coats with slit pockets provides another excellent means of getting merchandise from a counter or a rack to a concealed place without creating unnecessary attention.

The following are certain general guidelines sales and other store personnel should follow in either deterring successful shoplifting or rendering it more difficult:

1. Keeping the counters and other sales areas neat and clear, and never leaving anything around that can be stolen.
2. Knowing the physical layout of the department, particularly the weak and strong points relating to control over the merchandise.
3. Never leaving the selling department unattended.
4. Keeping the fitting rooms clear, and, if store procedures do not provide for a formal check-in system, being aware of the number of garments taken into a fitting room. Moreover, a customer spending an inordinate length of time in a fitting room should not be ignored.
5. Whenever possible, never turning one's back on a customer at a counter.
6. Knowing where assistance can be obtained from security employees once a potential or suspected shoplifter has been spotted.
7. Being alert to customers and watching for suspicious appearances, equipment, or behavior.

This last point is perhaps the most important and best means of discouraging the potential shoplifter.

While employees certainly play a significant role in deterring the shoplifter, management can play an important role in designing the physical layout of the store with security in mind. Stockrooms which are readily accessible from the selling floor will certainly not help a company's shortage program. Aisles should be set up in such a way that there is a minimum number of blind spots where shoplifters can operate undetected. Registers should be so situated that salespeople, in addition to recording sales, can have a good view of the aisles. An accepted merchandising practice has been to display expensive merchandise in locked security cases, and it appears that this practice will expand in the future, including less expensive merchandise as well. In this regard, it is recommended that employees be reminded periodically that security cases should be locked when not in use, with keys in possession of only authorized sales personnel.

As shortage percentages have increased, retailers have turned increasingly toward the use of various mechanical and electronic devices in attempting to reduce shortages. Such devices include closed-circuit television, alarm systems, radio and pocket transmitters, and sensitized merchandise tags. The latter item is used principally in ready-to-wear departments and in conjunction with alarm systems which are triggered once merchandise is removed from a designated area.

13

Branch Store Operations

Introduction

Although the first branch of a department store was opened in the mid-1920's, branch selling was not an immediate success. Most branch store units built prior to the early 1950's were small specialty shops located in selected suburban shopping areas. Department stores were concentrated in the downtown areas. It appeared that the outstanding stores had already been established; in fact, some stores were experiencing difficulties in maintaining positions of prominence that had been established over the years. Branch stores had not yet achieved their later status as stores in suburban or low-rent districts, with ample parking areas. Moreover, the impact of the "big-ticket" business of mail-order houses and other retailers had not yet been recognized.

While many of the outstanding department stores were growing, there was much talk of "profitless prosperity," and it did not appear that the economic and mercantile conditions of the times were conducive to the establishment of new independent department stores. In fact, it appeared increasingly that the growing competition being encountered by department stores was not from comparable retailers, but rather from specialty stores, including chain stores.

During the period following World War II, retailers awakened to the fact that for some time department stores had been generating a new form of intensive competition by establishing branch stores of several types. In this same period, another form of mass merchandising, known as the discount store, began to gain general acceptance. The appeal of the early discounters was wholly lower prices, often of brand merchandise. The shopper generally was willing to accept fewer or reduced services, in a less elegant environment, in exchange for the "bargain" which was often sold on a cash-and-carry basis. As with the conventional department stores, in time the discounters followed the consumers in the great exodus to the suburbs.

Independent Department Stores and Groups of Such Stores

Department stores that had become prominent by the 1920's and 1930's had for the most part been developed by outstanding merchants, either operating as individual proprietors or in partnership. As the founders or partners retired or died, the trend was to expand in corporate form. Some stores became large and important corporate units. In other instances, corporations acquired, at opportune times, several similar and affiliated units. The result was the creation of large independent stores and also of groups of stores owned or controlled by holding or operating companies.

For years the various stores of a group, even though affiliated, often operated with a great deal of autonomy. Each store determined its own merchandising policies, including its own markons, markdowns, discounts, shrinkages, and workroom costs.

While the purchasing of merchandise was done independently, the stores did interchange key information, and at times joined in obtaining market data or cooperated in the buying of certain staple merchandise and of some supplies. Also, in an effort to control costs, certain activities were consolidated, such as deliveries or common warehousing. However, aside from the interchange of information and a limited number of coordinated activities, to a large extent each store operated as if it were an independent unit. In fact, it was not unusual to find some stores in the same group operated under different policies, whether in the same city or the same general geographic area of the country.

Over the years some members of these groups opened a limited number of branches. However, the branches were not very large in size, and almost invariably were operated as part of the corresponding departments in the main store.

Occasionally, two neighboring affiliates of a group of stores attempted, with limited success, to operate selected selling departments with common buyers. Even though buyers directed departments in two or more stores, separate stock records were usually maintained, complete with a record of transfers in and out. Also, each store had its own markons, markdowns, discounts, and shortages, and the selling departments of the two stores were separately charged with the expenses deemed applicable to such departments.

Opening of Branches

The 1950's saw the rapid development of numerous suburban communities outside the major cities. This movement was generally accompanied by an improvement in the standard of living of the suburbanites. Also, transportation facilities were improving, and this added significantly to consumer mobility. As the number of automobiles increased, adequate parking soon became an essential ingredient for a successful store. All of these factors were influential in the rapid development of shopping centers which provided customers with facilities to do "one-stop shopping." The opening of branch stores accompanied this development as, effectively, the city department stores moved to the suburbs. However, this same suburban movement was also true of the discount and specialty stores and chain store retailers.

Most major downtown department stores had a number of objectives in their rapid expansion of branch operations, including:

1. Increasing their share of the market and market penetration in new areas and in those areas that were not adequately served by the main store.
2. Following the customers of the main store in their movement to the suburbs in order to preserve this share of market.
3. Becoming the dominant store in a preselected new trading area that was considered to have good potentials for growth and profitability.

These and other motives have generally led to the establishment of attractively furnished branch stores, in new buildings, with ample convenient parking facilities. Additionally, to simplify shopping, several types of retail outlets are usually located in the same immediate area in order to provide one-stop shopping. The inevitable result has been the ever increasing segment of retail sales, and related profits, accounted for by branch store sales of all types of retail operations. This has been achieved in spite of the complex operating, merchandising, and administrative problems which inevitably accompany the increase in the number of units comprising the retail company.

It is noteworthy that during this period of expansion retailing establishments began to combine more than one type of business. Apparel chains went into the discount business, as did large department and variety chains. Also, variety chains opened units that were in the nature of department stores. Often conventional retailing and discounting were conducted under one roof. Supermarkets began to carry software, hardware, and toys. Generally, it can be said that the distinctions between types of retailing have been clouded by these developments.

Dependent Suburban Branches

Retailers with large downtown stores continue to invest in branch stores at an increasing rate. More suburban branches are opened as retailers follow their customers to the suburbs in the effort to retain existing customers and to seek new customers in the ever expanding adjacent suburban areas. In this type of branch expansion the main stores do not establish branches in distant places but in new extensions of their own natural selling areas. This type of suburban store represents its respective city or central store. These stores are within reasonable distances from the parent stores and are generally merchandised, promoted, and directed from the central store. Even if they are merchandised commonly with the parent, separate merchandise stock records, at least at retail, may be maintained.

An almost ideal situation appears to be reached when a store opens a few large branches in similar suburban areas which represent expansions of the natural area of the central store. A well-organized, well-located group of this type can probably handle a large aggregate total of sales under common merchandising, common advertising, and other common expenses. However, when a branch operates outside the main store's natural trading area, it will probably be operated semiautonomously, adhering to policies set by top executives of the central store.

Branches in Shopping Centers

Another widespread development has been the large branch unit located in a shopping center. The center often contains comparatively large units of several department stores, a supermarket, and a great variety of small stores, including some that are local in character and others that represent regional or national chains.

At some point in the expansion of branch stores, particularly in situations involving big branch stores, it becomes infeasible to operate all units out of a central headquarters. The grouping of branch stores by divisions then becomes almost a practical necessity. Whether the common management is located centrally or in the various divisions, it is generally desirable to maintain accurate unit control and merchandise stock records separately, by store.

Organization of a Branch Store

Retailers have found that there is no single correct organizational setup for a branch store. Some stores have a local manager for each divisional merchandise manager. Others have lead salespersons who act as department managers for each of the buyers or groups of buyers. Figure 31 shows the organization charts of three branch stores.

Most retailers would agree that the most important executive of a branch operation is the store manager. The person selected for this vital position must possess executive and leadership abilities, with the full authority and ultimate responsibility for running the branch, and with all branch personnel subordinate to his or her authority. A thorough knowledge of the four functional specialties of retailing—merchandising, sales promotion, operations, and control—is essential. The manager must also serve as a liaison with the main store. The larger the number of branch stores and the greater their geographic dispersion, the greater will be the dilution of executive control from headquarters or division and the more important will be the branch manager.

Just as there may be diversity in the manner in which a branch is organized, there also may be differing views as to the person to whom the branch manager reports. Some retailers have the branch manager report to a Director or Vice President of Branches, whereas others have the branch manager report directly to the company's general merchandise manager.

Organization of Small Branch Store

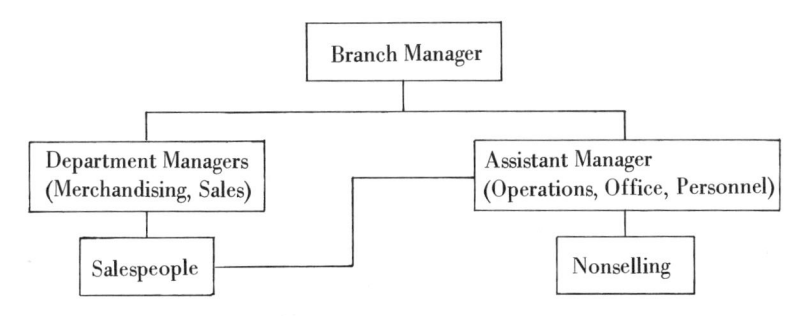

```
                    Branch Manager
                   /              \
   Department Managers        Assistant Manager
   (Merchandising, Sales)     (Operations, Office, Personnel)
           |                            |
       Salespeople                  Nonselling
```

Organization of Medium-Sized Branch Store

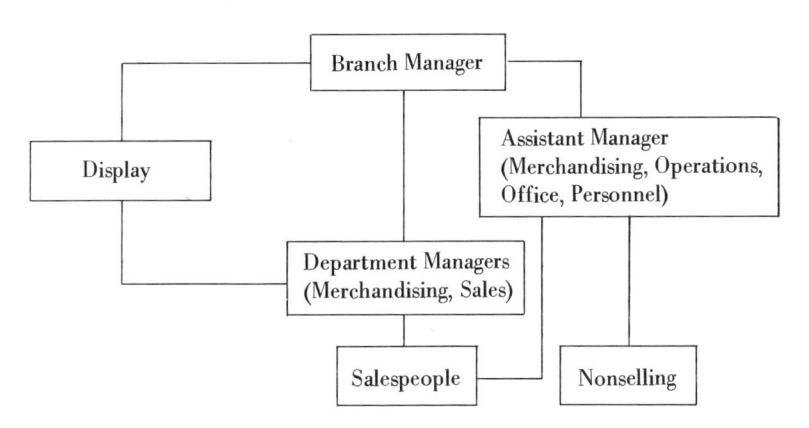

```
                    Branch Manager
                 /                  \
          Display              Assistant Manager
                               (Merchandising, Operations,
                                Office, Personnel)
                    |
            Department Managers
            (Merchandising, Sales)
             /            \
        Salespeople     Nonselling
```

Organization of Larger Branch Store

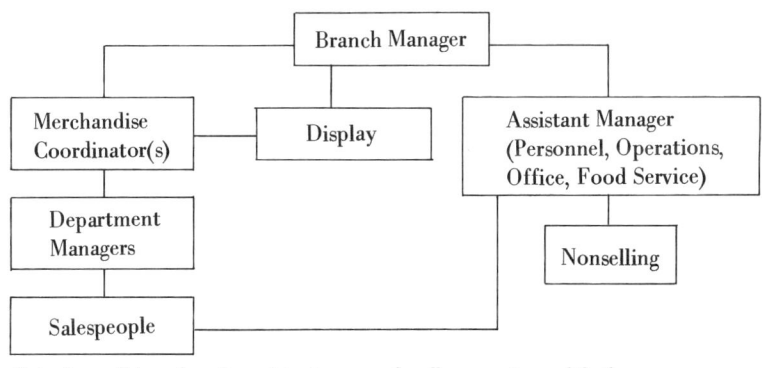

```
                      Branch Manager
            /              |             \
   Merchandise         Display      Assistant Manager
   Coordinator(s)                   (Personnel, Operations,
        |                            Office, Food Service)
   Department                              |
   Managers                            Nonselling
        |
   Salespeople
```

Note: In small branches, the assistant manager handles operations while the manager supervises merchandising and sales. In medium-sized branches, the assistant manager helps the branch manager with some of the merchandising responsibilities. In larger branches, merchandise coordinators supervise merchandising.

FIG. 31. Branch store organization. (*Source:* Branch Managers Manual, NRMA Operations Division)

Financial and Operating Procedures at Branch Stores

As a general rule, detail accounting records are not maintained at the branch store. The recording of transactions is generally performed at the main store or at centrally located accounting centers, based on data summarized and submitted by the branch. However, various reports prepared from these data, which are essential for day-to-day operations, are provided to the branch.

Cash

During the years much thought has been given to safeguarding cash through internal controls. Cash funds at branches are usually limited to cash register change funds, an imprest petty cash fund and/or bank account, and daily cash receipts. If payroll is paid locally, an imprest payroll bank account may also be maintained.

Cash register change funds should be maintained in separate individual containers. When such funds are not in the cash register, they should be locked in a safe. No cash should be left in registers overnight. The register should be read daily by someone other than the sales clerk. Each salesperson should tally his or her drawer daily. The results of the reading and the tally should be posted to a cash report. Periodically, the contents of the drawer should be counted by a responsible employee other than the sales clerk. All "surplus" cash from registers should be picked up during the day on a regular but non-routine basis; locked receptacles should be utilized for the collection of these funds. Cash receipts should be deposited at least once each day in a local bank. Arrangements should also be made for night depository privileges. Such deposits should be made into an account which is subject to withdrawal only by the home office. Moreover, banks should be instructed not to cash checks or money orders drawn to the order of the company and not to accept such checks for deposit in special accounts. The amount of all deposits should be reconciled daily with the amount of reported sales and cash register read-outs, as shown in Figure 32.

The amount of cash in change funds can be substantial, especially if the amount of the funds is maintained at constant levels throughout the year. In order to minimize the amount of these funds, critical reviews should be made of permanent change funds,

BRANCH _____

DAILY REPORT OF REGISTER _____

Gross own dept. sales [a]	$	
Gross leased dept. sales[a]		
Total		
Less: Sales returns[a]		
Net sales		
Sales taxes		
Excise taxes		
Total		
Less:		
Charge sales[a]	$	
Layaway deposits applied[c]		
Add:		
Layaway deposits accepted[c]		
Charge sales returns[b]		
Charge sales payments[b]		
Net cash receipts	$	(1)
Actual cash count	$	
Bank cards		
Other		
		(2)
Cash over (short)	$	(1 − 2)
Store Number _____ Manager _____ Date _____		

[a]Total obtained from tape of register reading (not included herein).
[b]Obtained from detailed listing (not included herein).
[c]Assumes that accounting for layaways is controlled by the branch store.

FIG. 32. Daily report of branch.

with a view toward budgeting balances on a monthly or seasonal basis.

Generally, disbursements for all merchandise and all significant branch expenses are made centrally. Thus, there is no need to maintain a general checking account at the branch. Disbursements made by the branch should be limited to minor expenses which must be paid immediately, e.g., supper money, miscellaneous maintenance supplies, certain freight charges, local travel and entertainment expenses. Such disbursements should be made through an imprest petty cash fund. The fund, preferably fixed in amount, should be reimbursed by the central accounting center at regular intervals, based upon approved petty cash vouchers submitted by the branch. If the amount of petty cash funds is significant, the procedure of reviewing balances carefully should also be applied to these funds.

It is common to maintain locally a separate imprest payroll bank account when payroll is paid by the branch. Time records can be forwarded from the branch to the main store or accounting center, or payrolls can be computed at the branch. If the payroll is prepared at the branch, it will be necessary to forward copies of the payroll register and payroll distribution to the location responsible for maintaining accounting records. If the branch pays its payroll in cash, payroll envelopes must be prepared; however, at many locations arrangements can be made to have the local bank fill the individual payroll envelopes. Clerical aspects are simplified if salaries are paid by check, with payroll check-cashing privileges for employees arranged at the local bank. The procedure of paying employees from daily receipts or petty cash funds, while used by some retailers, is generally not desirable from an internal control standpoint. Bank accounts should be reconciled monthly at the central accounting location.

Retailers generally follow the practice of transferring funds from local branch bank accounts to home office bank accounts by drawing checks on the local account and depositing them in home office accounts. In practice this is done either on a formal scheduled basis, or whenever funds in local banks appear excessive, or when home office accounts are low. Since data are usually forwarded by mail, a time lag of at least three or more business days exists between the date funds are deposited locally and the awareness of such deposits by the central accounting office. As a result, unless the company anticipates these branch deposits, or utilizes faster communication such as telephone or telex, there is the same approximate three-day lag in the initiation of any transfer of funds by the home office. To expedite and simplify the preparation of cash transfers, some retailers have adopted the practice of having branch offices use multi-part deposit/transfer checks. Under this system, for each day's deposit a combination deposit slip and transfer check is prepared simultaneously by store personnel. One part of this form is used as the deposit slip, the other part as the transfer check. Alternatively, retailers have made use of wire transfers of funds in order to accelerate cash transfers. Another practice used to transfer cash funds is to instruct local banks to automatically wire transfer funds to a home office bank account whenever the local bank balance exceeds a predetermined balance.

In order to expedite the processing of cash transfers from local depositories to main banks, some retailers have adopted a regional collection plan whereby certain regional banks are authorized to receive transfer checks for immediate processing directly from local depositories through post office lock boxes. These regional banks furnish the company with media for control and recordkeeping purposes. Funds are immediately transferred from the regional banks to the main bank. As a result, the time required to convert cash received into "available" cash is reduced. This "one-way" regional bank account should be reconciled monthly, preferably at the head office. The amount of funds collected in certain regional banks is often sufficient to enable the use of these banks as both regional depositories and main banks, thereby eliminating the final transfer. Finally, the periodic development of tight money and the high interest rates experienced in recent years have resulted in the development of a myriad of creative approaches to reduce both the time span between the original deposit of funds and their emergence as "available cash," and the productive utilization of temporary excess cash balances.

Credit Control and Accounts Receivable

Credit control at the branch is generally limited to soliciting charge accounts, accepting charge account applications, and checking on the credit status of customers. Although general charge account solicitation campaigns are usually designed by the main store or the head office, there is much room for collaboration with the branch manager in considering local conditions in any campaign. In addition, salespeople should exert a continuing effort to interest cash and bank charge account customers in opening a store charge account. The credit facilities of the branch should be prominently displayed to all customers. Some retailers place blank credit application forms in high traffic areas or may even drop applications into customers' shopping bags. Charge account applications taken at the branch store should be reviewed to determine that they are complete and then sent to a central location for review prior to approval. Credit-granting authority of the branch store manager is usually limited to approving an individual's request to charge and take merchandise on the day of application.

Before making a credit sale all salespeople should be instructed to contact the central credit location in order to obtain authorization for the sale. Such authorization is granted based on predetermined credit limits and the current status of the account. In addition, the employee checking the detail records should review for lost, missing, or spurious charge cards. Credit control checking can be accomplished by phone or by various other automated inquiry systems involving terminals hooked up to computers.

A practice which is sometimes used to reduce the amount of central checking is to supply cashiers with lists of lost or stolen charge cards and to set a reasonable sales dollar limit under which checking with the central files is not required. The cashier would review for unauthorized cards and ascertain whether the amount of the transaction exceeds maximum allowable limits, prior to ringing up the sale. Another method used to guard against sales in excess of an authorized credit limit is to code the limit into the charge account number.

Since most branch stores do not bill customers or maintain their own accounts receivable detail, it will be necessary to forward media for posting detail records to the location responsible for maintaining such records. The media supplied can be copies of sales and credit slips and listings of cash collected at the branch store. Customers' charge account numbers should preferably be noted on the cash listings, or the listings may comprise copies of preprinted forms utilized as customer receipts when the cash was collected at the branch.

Customers' monthly statements should include a notation that all remittances should be forwarded directly to the regional or central location responsible for maintaining accounts receivable detail records, in order to accelerate the flow of cash receipts and improve internal control.

A fairly recent innovation in retailing has been the introduction of point-of-sale recording equipment. Using this sophisticated equipment tied into a computer it is possible electronically to obtain credit authorization for sales and to update accounts receivable master files from data captured on the selling floor.

Inventory

Branch inventory policies and control procedures are a direct outgrowth of interrelated executive policy decisions. A number of branch inventory decisions should be made by management based upon answers to questions such as the following:

Is a good system of unit control to be maintained as a merchandising aid?

Are separate merchandise stocks to be maintained by individual branch stores, or will pooled (i.e., combined) stocks data be adequate?

If an overall (pooled) stock ledger is maintained, is the stock ledger to have a columnar layout, so that some approximation of stocks at branches is possible?

Are markdowns, discounts, shortages and workroom costs to be on a common basis, with the same percentages applicable to the central store and all branches?

Do all stores carry common merchandise at the same initial retail price?

Do branch stores have significant autonomy in initiating merchandise orders?

Is there a common, centrally controlled markdown policy?

What is to be the policy with respect to direct shipments to branches?

What is the policy regarding receipt of merchandise?

Are all deliveries to be made directly to the central store and then broken down for distribution to the branches?

The foregoing and related questions cannot be answered with any degree of finality since they are, in fact, dependent upon executive policies and relative costs in specific situations. The key debatable question in this regard is whether control over branch store merchandising necessitates maintaining full inventory control records for the individual branches.

A number of retailers have accepted the departmental pool concept. This concept envisions the existence of merchandise departments, regardless of location, with common departmental gross markons, common markdowns, common discounts and allowances, and common shrinkages. In short, common gross profits on departmental bases for the main store and branches are developed and allocated among the participating units on the basis of net sales.

No attempt is made to ascertain dollar inventories by location except at physical inventory time.

To a great extent, this approach has logically developed from, and normally visualizes, main store domination of merchandising policies. The original assortment of merchandise for the branch will ordinarily be established by the main store buyer, acting in conjunction with the merchandise manager. The main store buyer and merchandise manager will ordinarily establish and control price lines of the original merchandise assortment. This control is modified by branch personnel to the extent necessary to meet local competitive requirements. While the responsibility for maintaining stocks in the branch rests with branch personnel to a large degree, replacement of stocks is effected via a requisition which is acted upon by the main store buyer. While branch personnel are empowered to mark down merchandise to meet local competition, all other markdowns are the responsibility of and are authorized by the main store buyer.

Thus, although it can be seen that branch personnel do exercise some degree of discretion, dominance in establishing and maintaining overall merchandise policies resides in the main store. This practice is more pronounced in those operations where the branch personnel are viewed essentially as a merchandise handling and selling group, rather than as merchants exercising judgmental responsibilities. In effect, the handling of merchandise from the time it is purchased until it is sold, rather than the actual selection of merchandise, is viewed as the particular responsibility of branch personnel. The merchandise-related duties of branch personnel would include:

1. Keeping stocks complete.
2. Informing the main-store buyer of fast-selling and slow-moving items, staples that need balancing, and out-of-stock items requested by customers.
3. Following up on merchandise ordered for delivery to the branch.
4. Planning and supervising physical inventories.
5. Overseeing selling personnel and the clerical end of departmental operations.

A corollary benefit often cited in support of the pooled departmental approach is the significantly reduced clerical costs. A large amount of detail recordkeeping is required to maintain separate store stocks, particularly in accounting for all interstore transfers of merchandise. An important disadvantage, however, of using a pooled inventory control is the inability to determine departmental shortages by store location. For all practical purposes, the accountability for units and dollars of merchandise inventories is so diffused as to be nonexistent.

There is, however, another school of thought that insists that separate location inventories, by departments, are a prime requisite to successful branch store operation. The underlying theory is that the branch should not be viewed as an annex to the main store, but as an entity exercising discretion and responding to local needs with which it is most conversant. This would be particularly appropriate in those situations where the selling departments in the main store and in the branches have different mixes of merchandise, classifications, and price lines. While there may be a centralized buying office, the market requirements are established by branch store personnel. The main store will offer a "suggested" retail price, but the ultimate decision resides in the branch. All price change reports, whether markups or markdowns, emanate from and are the responsibility of the branch, and the shrinkage problem is a purely local one. Unit control and merchandise assortments, except for generalized main store supervision, are the prime responsibility of the branch.

Recognizing the near independence of the above type of merchandise operation is a prelude to establishing a separate location accountability of merchandise stocks and of merchandise gross margins. Of necessity this will involve a more extensive and more elaborate bookkeeping system.

There are also instances where separate stock ledgers, at retail, are maintained by store solely with a view to providing stock status by individual store location. In these situations common gross margins are computed and utilized for determining branch operating results, except for shortages which are developed on an individual store basis.

Financial Reporting

It is axiomatic that if there is to be an improvement in the profit performance of the total organization, there must be an improvement in the operating results of the individual segments of the business. Objectives must be clearly defined, and the responsibility for attaining such objectives must be delegated to specific executives. Moreover, methods must be developed that will objectively measure the performance of the designated executives. The basic financial report that is available to management to measure and monitor performance is the branch operating statement.

In the past, a great deal of controversy existed with respect to the appropriate approach to measuring operating results of branch stores. At the center of the controversy was the question of location performance versus individual (i.e., branch store management) performance. In essence, the matter becomes one of including or excluding various categories of expenses in evaluating branch store performance.

With respect to location performance, expenses incurred as a result of the existence and/or operation of that location are taken into account. These expense items would include, among others, selling payroll, branch store management, receiving and distribution costs, equipment depreciation, rents, and utilities.

However, in considering individual performance, a distinction is made between the so-called "controllable" and "noncontrollable" expenses, and only controllable expenses are taken into account. The theory is that, since individual branch managers have no control over such costs as rents, utilities, fringe benefit costs, and fixture and equipment costs and related depreciation, such items should not be considered in evaluating the performance of such managers.

In its preparation of the revised retail accounting manual, the Financial Executives Division of the NRMA attempted to come to grips with this question of measuring the performance of individual store locations. Depending upon the degree of refinement a particular organization desires, the NRMA espouses the concept of developing individual location *contribution* as a first level of measurement for all stores. Thereafter, if warranted, operating income by location can be developed.

In developing these levels of measurement, expenses have to be identified as direct, assignable, or allocable. Direct expenses, commonly referred to as "four-wall expenses," are those expenses that are incurred by or within a specific location, without regard to whether they are controllable. These expenses should be charged directly to each individual store location.

There are other items of expense that, notwithstanding the fact that they are incurred outside the "four walls" of a specific location, can be identified with the operation of that location. Examples of such items would be centralized mailing, shuttle service, delivery, and advertising. If this degree of refinement is desirable, those expenses which can be identified with specific locations should be assigned based on work load, usage, benefit, or some other logical basis. These expenses are initially accumulated in the expense center where they are generated, and then assigned periodically depending upon the reporting practice of the organization. Here again, no distinction should be made between controllable and noncontrollable expenses. Furthermore, in presenting the operating statement no distinction should be made between direct or assigned expenses.

In the third category are expenses which are not identifiable with any given location and are incurred for the benefit of the total organization. These expenses, commonly referred to as "central organization expenses," would include such items as company management, accounting, data processing, and public relations. To arrive at an operating income level, some stores may wish to allocate central organization expenses to all store locations. These expenses are initially accumulated in the central organization expense centers, and then allocated based on the proportion of the net sales of each location to the total net sales. (See Figure 33.)

Once an organization has determined the level at which performance should be measured, the question of controllable and noncontrollable expenses can be addressed. Controllable expenses

Expenses		
Direct "Four-Wall"	*Assignable* Identifiable	*Allocated* "Central Organization"
Direct Contribution		
Location Contribution		
Operating Income		

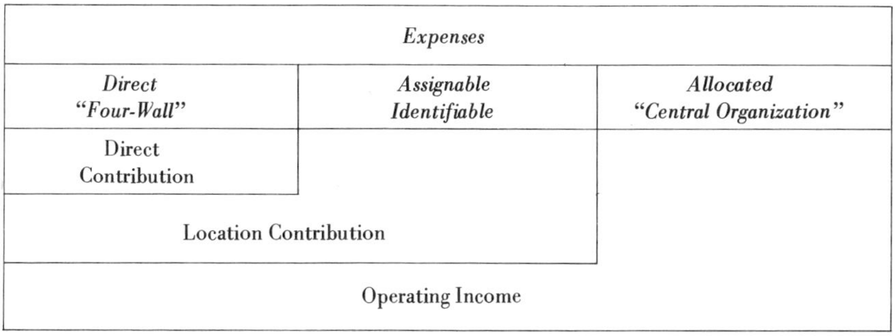

FIG. 33. Types of expenses in branch store operation. (*Source:* Retail Accounting Manual, NRMA)

OPERATING STATEMENT

Month _____   Store _____

		Month						Year to Date					
Net Sales													
Department		Current Month		Budget		Variance		Last Year		This Year		Budget		Variance		Last Year
No.	Description	Amount	%	Amount	%	Amount	%	Amount	%	Amount	%	Amount	%	Amount	%	Amount	%
1																		
2																		
4																		
7																		
.																		
.																		

Gross Margin
Controllable expenses:
  Selling salaries
  Branch management
  Service and operations
  Merchandise receiving
    and distribution
  Sales promotion
    Total
Controllable contribution
Noncontrollable expenses:
  Property and equipment
  Service and operations
  Personnel
    Total
Contribution
Allocation of central office
Operating income

FIG. 34. Individual store location operating statement.

would encompass both direct and assignable items of expense. By definition, central organization expense is noncontrollable. In making this distinction, the items of expense that will be considered controllable will vary with each organization. These variances are caused by the type of organization and by the degree of autonomy exercised by branch store managers.

Figure 34 presents a sample report which gives recognition to the above concepts. This sample is shown solely for illustrative purposes, and may be modified according to the needs of any given organization.

As shown, results are presented by month and year to date. Some organizations prefer to use season to date in lieu of, or in addition to, year to date. On the sample report, operating results are compared with budget for both the month and year to date. Some organizations also prefer to show the variance between the current period and the same period last year. These modifications can be made by expanding or contracting the form as desired.

Elements of revenue or expense which are shown below the operating income line for the total organization should not normally be allocated to individual store locations. These elements would include such items as interest expense, interest income, and taxes based on income.

The gross margin data shown in Figure 34 should be obtained from stock ledger data. If individual stock ledgers are not maintained by store, by department, the gross margin should be computed using the net sales of the location, by department, multiplied by the all-store gross margin percentage for that particular department. These departmental amounts should then be accumulated, and the total for a store entered on this form.

The use of a total all-store gross margin percentage, combining all departments within a store, should be avoided as distortive of periodic reporting. The range of departmental markons can be so wide, and the mix of merchandise on hand at any one date can be so unrepresentative of purchases made during a period ending on that date, that an "average" all-store gross margin basically derived from such markon data could be meaningless, if not misleading.

In support of the net sales amounts, a sales report for each individual store should also be prepared. A sample of such a report is shown in Figure 35. As indicated by the form, the upper portion of the report would disclose the net sales of each department within

SALES REPORT

Month _____ Store _____

Net Sales		Month							Year to Date						
Department		Current Month		Budget		Variance		Last Year		This Year		Budget		Variance		Last Year
No.	Description	Amount	%	Amount	%	Amount	%	Amount	%	Amount	%	Amount	%	Amount	%	Amount
1																
2																
4																
7																

Gross Sales:
Cash sales
Credit sales
Bank card
COD
Layaway
    Total
Returns and allowances
Net sales
Number of transactions
Average sale per transaction

FIG. 35. Individual store location sales report.

a particular store location. Directly below these departmental net sales data is an analysis of gross sales, by type of sale, with an aggregate deduction for returns and allowances. The final portion of the report shows the number of transactions and the average sales dollars per transaction. These last two statistics are becoming increasingly important, especially in times of spiraling operating costs and inflationary sales price increases. They provide some excellent insight into the impact of inflation on selling prices of merchandise offered for sale and into the productivity of sales personnel.

14

Non-Retail Operations (Workrooms)

Role of Non-Retail Operations in Retail Stores

Many stores engage in operations apart from the conventional retail selling departments. These operations are designed to provide convenient, store-controlled services with a view to maintaining the store's standards and customer goodwill. In addition, these operations may produce distinctive and exclusive articles of merchandise on special orders or for sale by the store's regular retail departments. Even though the various services provided by these operations may be obtained outside the store, the general belief is that the store customers are likely to be better served when workers are located on the store premises and are directed by store executives.

The efficiency of these non-retail operations has long been a problem to store executives, partially occasioned by a lack of standardized procedure in organizing and managing these types of operations and by a lack of uniformity in the accounting systems for allocation of costs. Accounting for non-retail operations has been included as a separate chapter in the 1976 edition of the "Retail Accounting Manual—Revised" ("RAM") published by the National Retail Merchants Association. This manual stresses standardization and simplicity, both of which are important in accounting for non-retail operations.

Categories of Non-Retail Operations

RAM proposes four categories of non-retail operations on the basis of the relationship to departments or to customers:

1. Cost selling departments.
2. Merchandise service workrooms.
3. Indirect manufacturing departments.
4. Expense service departments.

Some non-retail operations may combine characteristics of two or more of these classifications. The distinguishing characteristics of these hybrid departments are included with the following explanations of the various classifications of non-retail operations. As a general rule, however, an operation should be classified according to its primary purpose or function. Multiple accounting records should not be maintained for any given operation solely because it possesses characteristics of more than one classification.

Cost Selling Departments. Cost selling departments differ from retail selling departments in that inventories are determined from cost, rather than from retail, figures. Accordingly, RAM recommends that the cost selling departments be treated as separate and independent departments, with separate departmental operating results, in the same fashion as retail selling departments. Depreciation of inventories should be recognized as may be applicable. These cost departments are designed to generate profits, and their sales are included in total store sales.

Departments in this classification deal primarily and directly with the customer, and may manufacture finished products which are sold directly to customers. A markup on goods and services is taken with a view to generating a profit. Service departments such as those dealing in appliance repairs are included in this classification. Charges for repairs made by these service departments normally include a profit factor.

Merchandise Service Workrooms. Workrooms of this type are principally concerned with alterations and repairs, and their primary purpose is to provide customer services, rather than generate income. Although charges to customers include some markup on services, most retailers would be satisfied with an approximate break-even on the operations of these workrooms.

The losses of merchandise service workrooms should be transferred, as net workroom costs, to the cost or retail selling departments served by the workrooms. Sales of these workrooms, comprising charges to customers, are applied as a partial offset against the workroom costs, and consequently are excluded from total store sales.

Earlier mention was made of the mixed character of certain workrooms. If a repair department deals principally with customers, it may be treated as a cost selling department. On the other hand, if it principally repairs or conditions merchandise after sale by a selling department, it operates as a merchandise service workroom, and the resultant profit or loss on sales is transferred to the cost or retail selling department served. The authors prefer to treat workrooms as merchandise service workrooms where feasible, with the net workroom gain or loss transferred to the selling department as workroom costs. Under this procedure, workroom costs do not affect selling department markon percentages.

Indirect Manufacturing Departments. These operations produce goods for sale to customers of retail or cost selling departments. In some instances, these operations are part of another cost selling department, as for example, a bakery as part of a restaurant, with no separate accounts maintained for the bakery. However, when an indirect manufacturing operation is established as a separate department, it should be accounted for in the same manner as a merchandise service workroom.

Some operations are mixed in character in that they may include both manufacturing and service functions or they may deal both with customers and with selling departments. For example, a millinery workroom may produce new hats for stock and also alter hats in stock or hats sold. Accordingly, it would be classified as an indirect manufacturing department with respect to production and as a merchandise service workroom with regard to alterations. A workroom manufacturing for customers' special orders may also produce goods for departmental stocks, as, for example, the drapery and upholstery workrooms, or the custom tailoring workroom. These operations would be classified as cost selling departments where production on customers' special orders predominates but as indirect manufacturing departments if production of goods for departmental stocks is the major activity. Although a workroom may handle customers' special orders almost exclusively, it may deal with a selling department, rather than directly with customers. As an illustration, orders for stationery engraving may be treated as departmental sales rather than workroom sales; thus, the stationery engraving workroom would be treated as an indirect manufacturing department, rather than as a merchandise service workroom. Theoretically, two separate sets of accounts can be maintained for those operations that are mixed in character. However, RAM recommends that the non-retail classification assigned is that category which is representative of the functions which constitute the majority of the work performed by the operation in terms of the time involved and the revenue generated.

Expense Service Departments. Examples of expense service departments would comprise those serving expense centers and those serving employees. Gains or losses of such operations generally are transferred to reduce or increase related expense elements. By way of illustration, the gain or loss arising from the operation of an employees' cafeteria becomes an element of allocated fringe benefits; the net operating results of a print shop are transferred to the departments served by the shop.

Cost-No-Retail

Similar elements of cost having no corresponding retail value may arise from different sources. Merchandise service workroom charges may represent one such item. Such charges (less revenue from customers), representing net workroom costs, appear in cost of sales of the applicable selling department as a cost (with no corresponding retail). These charges do not enter into purchases and do not affect markon; they are captioned "Workroom costs." An example would include the charge from a merchandise service workroom for dyeing and/or cleaning a piece of merchandise, whether in stock or before delivery under a sale. In the event the merchandise is sent to an outside dyer or cleaner, the vendor's invoice should be charged in the accounts in the same manner as the corresponding entry for work performed in the store. In effect, the invoice should not be classified as purchases in the ordinary course of business, but as a category of workroom costs. RAM uses two separate captions for cost-no-retail items: "Other cost of sales" and "Workroom costs."

The manual recommends that cost-no-retail items be classified as "Other cost of sales" or as "Workroom costs" depending upon whether the charge is to make merchandise ready for sale or to make merchandise ready for customers after it is sold. In the authors' opinion this is a theoretical distinction. There is little, if any, practical advantage to this distinction since both classifications of items should not be included in ordinary purchases, and thus will have no effect on the selling department's markon percentage.

Principle of Workroom Operation

Earlier reference has been made to the manual's position that cost selling departments are to be treated as independent departments, whereas the results of operations of service workrooms represent net workroom costs which are to be transferred to the respective selling or other departments. The method of operation followed by a particular store will govern the classification of the particular operation. For example, in one store a unit which manufactures on special orders may deal directly with the customer and thus have its own selling department income account; in another store the finished product may be transferred to a selling department for sale to the customer, in which event the producing unit would be classified as an indirect manufacturing department.

A good general principle to follow with respect to non-retail operations is to establish a schedule of charges based upon the expectation of efficient operations, with aggregate revenue designed to practically offset costs. The non-retail sales volume is comparatively small, and the related overhead usually is so great that any schedule of customer charges designed to exceed operating costs probably would render prices prohibitive. However, it should be recognized that service units such as fur storage, rug cleaning and storage, and repair departments, which deal directly with customers, as well as some of the departments or workrooms handling special orders, are not subject to this practical limitation.

Recordkeeping

To the extent feasible and in the interests of economy, the recordkeeping for non-retail operations preferably should be centralized. Much of the accounting can be done in the general accounting and statistical office, based upon the accumulation of data in the non-retail operations. Effectively, the compilations of accounting and production data and the generation of operating reports and other pertinent statistics should be the responsibility of the controller's office. In this regard, it is important that the detailed records maintained for the non-retail operations provide the operating profit or loss realized by the individual operations.

Accounting Procedures for Cost Selling Departments

Restaurants, fur storage, rug cleaning and storage, and beauty parlor, which primarily deal directly with customers, generally operate as cost selling departments. Inventories, if any, are carried at cost. Sales are credited to the operations and are considered to be part of total sales of the store.

Costs basically comprise materials, labor, supplies, services purchased from outside sources, occupancy costs, insurance, depreciation, and any other direct expenses. These workrooms will have a net gain or loss, depending upon the ability (or desire of management) to reflect operating costs in selling prices to customers or in charges made to departments or expense accounts. Work performed on behalf of selling departments or for store decoration and upkeep is usually chargeable at cost without a profit margin.

Accounting Procedures for Service Workrooms

The accounting for service workrooms should consider that such operations principally serve individual selling departments.

The elements of cost of operation include materials, findings, payroll, and direct overhead, with the latter including appropriate charges for utilities, insurance, housekeeping, repairs, depreciation on equipment, and rent. Operating costs generally should not include charges for any allocation of administrative, publicity, buying, or selling expenses.

Workrooms operating principally for selling departments bill their net profit or loss to the departments with which they are associated. Examples are furniture finishing, piano renovating, and men's clothing busheling rooms. When work is performed on behalf of a number of selling departments, the billing is somewhat complicated. Frequently, under these circumstances, an established price list for the various categories of work performed serves as a basis for billing.

For garment alterations (except sometimes for men's clothing), the prices to customers are established by fitters who represent the workrooms. The price is an estimate of the cost. As explained in RAM, "Any revenue received from customers is used as an offset against the workroom cost in determining the workroom's net profit or loss to be transferred to the retail departments which it serves. Sales of merchandise service workrooms are to be excluded from total owned and total store sales."

Generally, there are three bases for billing charges imposed by alteration workrooms:

1. Customers' paid work—charged to customers and credited to sales of the workroom.
2. Customers' work assumed by the selling department and charged to such department as alteration and workroom cost. The customers' work assumed by the selling department represents the excess of the workroom cost estimate over the corresponding amount charged to the customer; stated differently, it is the portion of the cost assumed by the department as a matter of sales policy.
3. Department stock work—charged to the department as alteration and workroom cost.

Since all these charges are based upon estimates of actual cost, there should be a continual awareness of workroom operating costs and of the correlation of such costs with related billings. Often, it is necessary to make detailed studies of particular jobs and fitters in order to ascertain rationales for fluctuations and differences in cost and to uncover inefficient operations, as described in some detail later in this chapter.

Accounting Procedures for Manufacturing Workrooms

The accounting for manufacturing workrooms is relatively simple. Costs include materials, labor, and direct overhead. Allocation of general store overhead to workrooms is not recommended except that a rental charge for space, charges for utilities used in operations, insurance, repairs, and depreciation of production equipment should be made in order to obtain fair costs for comparison with outside producers. These costs, together with statistics as to the number of units produced, ordinarily provide sufficient data for interpreting workroom results. Occasional detailed studies (for example, costs of individual jobs and comparison with charges by outside manufacturers) provide useful supplementary information for control purposes.

A general form for reporting workroom operations is shown in Figure 36. The form may be used for all workrooms although each captioned item of information obviously may not apply to every workroom. (RAM illustrates a cost department operating statement which is somewhat similar to the workroom operating statement given in Figure 36.)

Controlling Alteration and Other Workroom Costs

Many stores report that alteration costs have become a very significant item of expense in the merchandising of clothing. The fact is that most store executives do not scrutinize their workroom costs as carefully as the other statistics included in the store and departmental operating statements. The net charge for workroom operations is frequently viewed as a necessary evil. As long as there is no significant increase from the prior period's actual figures or as compared to the current period's budgeted figures, little further attention is paid to workrooms. This attitude evolved because most retail store executives lack technical or operating knowledge of workrooms, particularly of the alteration workroom. For this reason, they have permitted and rely upon the alteration department to set its own policies and standards, with little monitoring of performance by top management.

Focusing on alteration workrooms, many retail executives are convinced that significant cost savings can be achieved by identifying problem areas and introducing effective controls, establishing, at the same time, an acceptable alteration policy. Alteration workroom deficiencies have been defined as falling within two broad categories, those arising on the selling floor and those related to the operation of the workroom. In more specific terms, these deficiencies include:

Inadequate supervisory control in the workroom.
Less than acceptable output by workroom employees as measured by any realistic standards of performance.
Resistance to change, particularly in the introduction of new cost-saving machinery in the workroom.
Selection of incorrect sizes, models, or styles by sales personnel on

WORKROOM OPERATING STATEMENT

	Month of		Season to Date	
	This Year	Last Year	This Year	Last Year
Cost and expenses:				
Inventory, beginning:				
Materials and supplies				
Materials in work in process...				
Labor in work in process.....				
Total inventory beginning ...				
Materials and supplies purchased				
Labor...................				
Inventory, ending:				
Materials and supplies				
Materials in work in process...				
Labor in work in process.....				
Total inventory, ending....				
Materials and supplies used....				
Labor used................				
Material and labor cost.....				
Management supervision				
Clerical salaries				
Rental charge				
Current and power				
Insurance				
Depreciation				
Miscellaneous.............				
Overhead cost...........				
Total workroom cost.......				
Revenue:				
Customers				
Other revenue				
Discounts received				
Total revenue				
Profit or (loss)				
Statistics:				
Number of units completed.....				
Average cost per unit				
Average number of employees...				
Average weekly payroll.......				

FIG. 36. Workroom operating statement.

behalf of customers, thereby requiring excessive alterations.
"Overfitting" of garments by fitters.
Charges not levied on customers on a knowledgeable, cost accounting basis.

However, before embarking on a remedial and cost reduction program, appropriate consideration will have to be given to the store's overall alteration policy. Since clothing departments differ significantly from one another, alteration policies must similarly differ. Stores that promote better merchandise to attract customers who like fine, well-fitted clothing will not restrict the fitter as to the amount of alterations permitted. The fitter will be instructed to produce as near a perfect fit as possible. On the other hand, stores selling low-priced clothing, appealing to customers whose purchasing power is somewhat limited, will not emphasize the fitting characteristics of the clothing, but rather the reasonableness of price. These stores have lower unit sales and lower markon, necessitating a restriction on the amount of alteration work that can be performed without charge. Usually such alterations will be limited to simple operations such as adjusting sleeve length and side seams on coats and the waist and length of trousers. To summarize, the alteration policy must be set in a manner which will provide the best fit possible, consistent with the customer demands and the overall store image that is being fostered.

The policy of charging customers for alterations varies from one extreme of charging for all alterations to the other of charging for none. Trends in men's and women's clothing departments are in opposite directions. The majority of women's clothing departments charge for all alterations, whereas many men's clothing departments do not charge for necessary alterations. A common policy in many men's departments is to charge for any alterations other than those normally expected to be incurred on men's clothing such as putting cuffs on trousers, adjusting sleeve length of coats, moving buttons, and adjusting the waist on trousers. Any program designed to control alteration costs should involve charging customers for major or unusual alterations they have requested.

Closely associated with the alteration "sales" policy is the cost which reasonably can be incurred by a viable retail operation. One approach, which utilizes anticipated sales volume, budgeted alteration costs, and budgeted production volumes in the form of number of garments by categories, involves the development of supportable per-garment alteration costs. These per-garment costs can be translated into the number of permissible hours per garment, thereby effectively limiting the extent of alterations allowable.

The amount of permissible alterations can be used as a control device by requiring a supervisory approval for any alteration job which exceeds the limit specified. This control is useful in restrictting salespeople who attempt to sell incorrect sizes or models and also in inhibiting the overzealous fitter.

Improved Productivity and Cost Control in the Workrooms

To effectively control the workroom operations, a system must be capable of determining costs and productivity with a reasonable degree of accuracy. The more effective systems have as their basis units of measurement referred to as work units. Such work units or units of productivity are subdivisions of every normal operation that can be performed in the alteration of clothing in a realistic time frame. In effect, realistic standards of performance are established in order to more effectively control productivity. Utilizing these production standards in conjunction with backlog data makes possible the assignment of work to employees with some reasonable expectation of when such work will be performed. Thereafter, it becomes a matter for supervisors to follow up on and to eliminate or mitigate those factors that contribute to substandard performance.

The knowledgeable use of these standards also will enable management to determine whether fitters are pricing alterations properly. In addition, a basis is provided for distributing the expense of alteration services to the associated selling departments, with each such department bearing its proportionate share of unrecovered alteration costs on the basis of the services used.

From the technical aspect, modern machinery has made a significant contribution toward increased productivity in workrooms, with no decline in the quality of alterations. In addition, in large alteration workrooms, efficiency can be improved by creating specialists for the various alteration operations, rather than having one tailor do all of the alterations on a particular garment. This enables workers to be placed in areas best suited to their capabilities. For example, less skilled workers can be assigned to such operations as ripping seams, adjusting sleeves, and putting cuffs on trousers, and more skilled tailors utilized for major alterations such as lowering a collar.

Some stores have found it advantageous to combine the men's and women's alteration workrooms. This has permitted greater flexibility in employee assignments and in scheduling the overall workload, with a consequent realization of economies.

To summarize, the productivity problem can best be solved by adopting every modern method and technique that will produce the most work in the least time and by establishing realistic production goals that are continually monitored. While a good system will identify problem areas, no system can automatically correct the problems. Efficiencies will be instituted and economies realized only when the designated responsible executives take action to correct the problems uncovered by the system.

Losses at the Point of Sale

Unnecessary alterations can be as significant a factor as workroom inefficiency in causing alteration losses. The selection of a correct size and an appropriate style or model will keep required alterations to a minimum. On the other hand, an improper selection will invariably result in major alterations.

In an effort to achieve maximum sales volume, salespeople are frequent offenders in this selection process. Although alterations can be minimized by instructing sales personnel in good selection techniques, controls must be implemented which will provide a means of continually monitoring their performance. The initial control lies with the fitter. Sales personnel should recognize that the opinion of the fitter is final regarding the selection of a correct size or model. A fitter cannot be challenged in the expression of an opinion that a garment cannot be altered to fit a particular customer.

The capabilities of fitters have a direct effect on alteration costs. These capabilities vary considerably, from an exceptional fitter who can produce a good fit with a minimum of alterations to a fitter who carves up a garment unnecessarily, causing high alteration costs. To make matters worse, fitters in the latter category frequently ruin the style of a garment in the process. Records of alterations, maintained by fitter, will quickly point out the fitters who effectively are attempting to restyle garments, rather than making only those alterations necessary for a proper fit, with consequent excessive alteration costs. Another control over the quality of work produced by fitters is exercised by the store's customers. A record of re-alterations required as a result of customers' complaints will quickly point out incompetent fitters.

Fitters have an effect on more areas than cost controls; they obviously have a direct effect on customer satisfaction. A poor fitting creates an irate customer, whereas a skillful fitter can do a great deal to enhance the job done by a salesman in developing and maintaining a loyal customer.

Most selling departments relate their net alteration costs to total sales, rather than to the sales of the garments altered. Alteration charges should be compared to the sales price of garments altered, and should be analyzed by salesperson.

15

Leased Departments

Introduction

The term "leased department" describes a retail operation, involving merchandising or service activities, which is conducted within a department of a specialty, department, or discount store by a company or individual independent of the one which operates the store itself. Such an arrangement is governed by an agreement between the store and the leased department operator setting forth particulars as to space allocated, methods of operation, responsibilities of the parties, allocation of expenses, and the portion of sales revenue which the store shall receive as consideration for permitting the outside interest to conduct business in its establishment and perhaps to sell under its name. The nature of these arrangements is such that they may be looked upon as leases of store space and privileges, the basis for the term "leased department." The store confines itself to operations other than the department's merchandising or service activities and obtains, in lieu of ordinary mercantile profits, rental income of fixed amounts or percentages of the sales of the leased department.

Leased departments have been present in conventional department stores for some time and have been used to broaden the store's merchandising and service activities and to provide specialized talent which the store might be lacking. Such leased departments account for only a small percentage of department store volume. The use of leased departments in discount stores, however, has contributed to the phenomenal growth of such stores since the mid-1950's.

The operators of leased departments are specialists in their lines of business. They provide the merchandise inventory, and sometimes the fixtures, and incur specific operating liabilities. Their compensation is their net operating profit, which is largely dependent upon their merchandising ability.

Selection and buying of merchandise, pricing, inventory control, and sales promotion are the responsibility of the lessee, unless restrictions are imposed by agreement. The lessee likewise controls the sales force and most other employees in the department and pays their salaries. The store usually requires, however, that the lessee's employees be satisfactory to the store management, conform to the store rules, and recognize floor managers as representatives of the store.

Organization and Theory of Department Leasing

In the ordinary organization of a department store, there are two major operating divisions: one concerned with merchandising and the other with store management, operations, and service. Purchase and sale of merchandise and merchandising policies, including the maintenance of sufficient gross margins and sales volume, are the major problems of one division, while the problem of efficient, economical service is the concern of the other division. Under leasing arrangements, the retailing operation is divided into two functions which are the responsibility of specialists who strive for maximum profit by effectively performing their individual functions, as follows:

> The lessee provides the inventory, does the merchandise planning and purchasing, operates the selling department, sometimes provides the fixtures, and pays all salaries and direct expenses (in some cases directly to the store for services such as advertising).
>
> The lessor provides the store name and premises, establishes operating policies, makes deliveries, provides for supervision, housekeeping and other services, and does the required work on charge accounts (credit responsibility is usually assumed by the lessor).

A leased department operator specializing in a particular line of merchandise may be able to operate departments in a number of stores with greater success than each of these stores could attain on its own. Such an operator will usually have highly skilled merchandisers who are in close contact with market conditions and specialists who are capable of serving customers in an efficient manner. However, when a store leases an excessive number of departments, including some of the larger departments which should not entail special merchandising difficulties, it is likely that the company is weak financially or lacking in merchandising and operating skills.

Lessor–Lessee Relations

From the store's point of view, great importance attaches to the character of the lessees and, likewise, to the merchandising ability of those who own or manage its leased departments. To a great extent, a lessee depends on the store name and goodwill for its success; on the other hand, whatever good (or ill) will the lessee develops is reflected in the attitude of its customers toward the store as a whole. No matter how well managed a store may be, a lessee can hurt the store's reputation by unfair merchandising methods, by selling inferior merchandise, or by refusing to treat customers' complaints in a courteous manner.

It is important for the store to check the background and stability of any potential lessee to ensure that the enterprise is sufficiently well capitalized to maintain an operation on a par with that of the rest of the store. Because of the size of its departments, an individual department or discount store may be limited as to the amount of time it can devote to expert merchandising guidance in particular lines of goods. This is apt to be true more particularly for departments in which the problems differ from those of the store's major departments; however, it is important that the department fit within current customer acceptance and the desired image of the store. Alternatively, it is important that the lessee be associated with a store that has a place and an image in the community, with the lessee exercising a degree of leadership which fosters this overall standing of the store in the community.

Historically, there have been outstanding cases where the operators of leased departments were or became very able, efficient, and prosperous—so much so, in fact, that ultimately the lease operator came to control the whole store. However, these were unique circumstances where, by reason of death, illness, or retirement, the store urgently needed new management capable of continuing to operate successfully under new conditions. It may have been a happy circumstance for the store to have had an experienced leased department so closely connected with store management as to be able to meet changed conditions without large losses of business to competitors. On the other hand, there have been numerous cases where stores have taken over leased departments that were very viable operations. In effect, such takeovers were viewed by the stores as a form of "internal growth."

It may well be that incorporation of a leased department into the store will represent progress on the part of both the lessee and lessor. Also, some leased departments are operated on a more or less temporary basis, until the lessee can prove to the store that a department can be profitably operated. For example, a manufacturer may be willing to operate a leased department for a limited period only, with a view to demonstrating that its product lines can be profitably merchandised.

Advantages to the Store

Invariably, the basic reason for leasing departments of a store to outside interests is that management believes that greater profit or better service to the public can be obtained by leasing, rather than by directly operating these departments. This conclusion may be based on one or all of the following factors:

1. A store may hesitate to invest capital in new departments or additional lines of merchandise where, because of novelty or lack of experience in handling the particular merchandise, there cannot be definite assurance of success.
2. It may be that, for certain departments, a store does not have purchasing facilities which enable it to maintain a stock that is sufficiently complete to satisfy its clientele or that can be purchased at prices which permit a fair rate of gross margin. A multi-store leased department operator is likely to have the advantages of lower costs and retail prices, greater variety, and more exclusive styles. Lessees who are also manufacturers can offer a store greater leasing income than is likely to be earned by store operation of such departments, and at the same time assure the store of a more complete stock of merchandise and consequently better service to the public.

3. There may be a desire to obtain the services of skilled merchandisers or specialists who can achieve strength and dominance in an area important to the overall store image. Successful and profitable departmental operation rests on a thorough knowledge of what to buy and how to sell. If the merchandising staff of a store cannot successfully merchandise certain departments, it is necessary either to engage qualified individuals at adequate compensation or to lease the departments to specialists. It has often been found more advantageous to do the latter. This is especially true for such departments as optical, photographic, restaurant, and beauty parlor, where specialized or even technical knowledge is required, or for unusual merchandising departments such as flower shop, baked goods, and patterns.
4. A leased department can provide working capital since cash is available to a store which controls receipts but is not remitted until the end of specified accounting periods.
5. Perhaps the chief factor which influences a store to lease some of its departments is the desire to achieve the maximum overall profit for the store. If contribution to profit per square foot is enhanced by utilizing selected leased departments in certain sections of the store, it is consequently in the best interests of the store to take advantage of leasing.

In essence, a successful lessee–lessor arrangement depends on the willingness of the store management to acknowledge that an outside merchandiser or operator can do a better overall job of running a particular department as compared to the internal operation directed by management.

Advantages to the Lessee

A lessee has certain advantages in leasing departments rather than opening independent locations, including the following:

1. In most instances, the operator of a leased department is interested in obtaining a reasonable volume of business in a specialized line of merchandise or service where volume ordinarily might not be sufficient to warrant the expense of opening a separate store. Leasing a department may meet this requirement.
2. The goodwill and prestige of a department store and the volume of business transacted on the premises present an unusually favorable background for the development of the leased department.

3. An additional incentive in leasing departments is that, under leasing arrangements, a lessee is relieved of the extensive and intricate problems of store management. While a great deal of supervision is necessary in the operation of a store as a whole, the store premises represent a large unit which can be supervised and controlled without regard to departmental subdivisions. There is economy and efficiency in such a large-scale, specialized operation, just as there is in merchandising a particular line of goods in many places under lease arrangements.

Departments Usually Leased

Departments frequently leased involve those where personal service is a large factor, as well as merchandise departments.

The service group includes optical departments, photographic studios, restaurants, beauty parlors, repair departments, clothes cleaners, etc. The principal element in the operation of such departments is competent, experienced management and skilled labor, rather than merchandise stock. For this reason, store management will turn to the trained organizations of lessees rather than attempt to acquire the knowledge necessary to operate and control such departments. Since the store emphasizes customer service, a reasonable lease income will usually satisfy management, provided the lessee gives good service and builds up the store's goodwill. Another factor influencing leases of service departments is that these departments may require installation of specialized equipment and fixtures. In many instances it is advisable for a store to avoid investment in such fixtures, especially where (for example, in beauty parlors) a heavy outlay is required in what may be more or less an experimental venture or untried field. If the store abandons its department, the specialized equipment is practically a total loss. On the other hand, such equipment might have large value to a lessee who can move it to a new location.

The merchandise group includes, among others, hardlines, sporting goods, footwear, millinery, furs, fabrics, jewelry, appliances, health and beauty aids, cameras, records, books, stationery, and candy and cigarette (including vending machines) departments. Departments selling fashion merchandise (that is, shoes, millinery, furs, etc.) are sometimes leased to syndicates which operate a large number of such departments, and which in some cases own or control sources of production. Manufacturers will sometimes operate a chain of leased departments in order to promote a distinctive product in outlets reasonably protected against the competition of rival manufacturers. At times, household equipment manufacturers (radios, washers, sewing machines, refrigerators, oil burners, etc.) assume retail distribution by means of leased departments, especially during the introductory period when new products are being placed on the market. In some cases, the operation of a leased department by the manufacturer may be only a temporary expedient, until another lessee can be found or until the store is convinced that the line is one that can be profitably carried. In instances where technical knowledge in sales and service is required, leasing departments to specialists has often proved more satisfactory than direct store operation. Miscellaneous departments such as candy and books have special problems unlike those of ordinary departments. These problems and the relatively small sales volumes are inducements to leasing.

The Lease Agreement

Relations between the store and the lessee are governed by a lease agreement. The agreement covers all matters pertaining to the term of lease, rental basis, merchandise and customer relation policies, accounting and settlements, sales promotion, and the responsibilities and duties of the respective parties. As in all contracts of a similar nature, it is desirable that the provisions be set forth clearly and concisely so that possibilities for future misunderstanding or dispute are not needlessly left open. A lease agreement properly drafted will allow the store to enforce the various provisions. It is often advisable to insert a clause that provides, through arbitration or otherwise, a means for settlement of questions that may arise.

There are both ordinary problems to be considered and, in particular instances, special problems because of the kind of department leased. In the following outline of important lease provisions, no attempt is made to cover all of the subjects which may, from time to time, require attention; however, no lease can cover every facet of the operation or foresee all the problems. Cooperation between the store and the lessee is vital. A good leased department relationship is like a partnership. Finding the right partner may not always be easy, but it is certainly the most important step in developing a good leased operation within the store.

Term. The contract may be for a long or a short term. The longer-term contract may be advisable where extensive outlays are made for special fixtures or equipment. Ordinarily, the term of a lease contract is rather short since it requires both the store and the lessee to constantly make efforts to improve if the operation is to succeed. In many cases the term is for one year and may include a provision for early termination.

Location. The agreement should clearly describe the space which is to be leased and its location in the store. It should specify whether the area may be increased or decreased, or the location changed; and if so, on what basis.

Rental. Rental provisions vary. Usually, rental is a stated percentage of net sales; however, a minimum amount must be paid even though the percentage on sales falls below the guaranteed minimum. In some cases there may be a fixed monthly rental regardless of volume of sales, or a fixed monthly rental subject either to increase by a specified rate on excess, or to decrease by a specified rate on deficiency, of sales as compared with a stated volume. Minimum rentals at best are calculated to give stores a minimum return, and percentage clauses allow lessees to conduct their operation with less risk. Thus, the minimum-plus has become a way of life for many lessors and lessees. In addition, there may be charges for direct expenses and indirect expenses on a pro rata basis. Various other bases may be agreed upon, as, for instance, a fixed percentage on gross or net sales up to a certain total, with either a larger or a smaller percentage on sales in excess of that figure. Provisions of the latter kind are used where a store offers as an inducement to the lessee a lower ratio for large volume or where the lessee, in order to obtain a lease, offers extra rental in the event that the location exceeds the estimated business-producing possibilities. There may be special provisions for carrying forward deficiencies or excess of rentals from one season to another within the lease term with final settlement at specified intervals or at the end of the lease term. In some leases it may be provided that at the option of one or the other, or both parties, the lease may be terminated if sales fall below a certain minimum.

Payment and Hiring of Employees. It should be clearly stated which departmental employees or classes of employees are to be paid by the lessee and by the lessor, respectively, and which are to receive fringe benefits and be covered by pension plans. Ordinarily, the manager of the department and the sales and stock clerks are paid by the lessee. Cashiers, inspectors, and wrappers are usually paid by the store, as are employees of its housekeeping and service departments. Employees engaged in window display and in the receiving of merchandise are borderline situations, and the agreement should set forth clearly which party is to be responsible for the compensation of such employees. Leased department employees should be required to observe all store rules in order to avoid personality conflicts and to ensure that controls are uniformly enforced.

Payment for Deliveries. Delivery should be specifically covered in the agreement. Sometimes the lessee is charged with deliveries at a specified rate per parcel. In other instances the lessor delivers without charge.

Payment for Advertising. Probably the more common procedure is for the lessee to be charged with advertising. This advertising is incorporated with the general store advertising, but is charged by the store to the lessee. In such cases it is important that the basis for the charges be clearly set forth—for example, whether the charge is to be on a lineage basis for the space devoted to the leased department, or whether any part of the general institutional advertising of the store is to be allocated, as well as whether charge is to be made for services of the advertising department of the store. Another problem is whether the lessee is to receive credit for any reductions of advertising bills that the store may earn by reason of its aggregate lineage within a specified period. It is frequently provided that the leased department shall do a certain minimum amount of advertising. The minimum may be a dollar or a lineage minimum, or an amount equal to a stated percentage of annual gross or net receipts as defined, or some similar basis, with the understanding that any deficiency is to be collected by the lessor after the close of the annual period as additional rent.

Preparation of Monthly Statements. Ordinarily, the store controls the registers or the register tapes of the operator, collects the receipts, audits them, determines expenses and any other items chargeable, and renders detailed monthly statements to the lessee.

Responsibility for Charge Accounts. In most instances the store's credit department passes upon charge sales of leased departments and any resultant bad debt losses are assumed by the store. However, there may be exceptions to this procedure, particularly where a leased department is operated by a manufacturer or jobber interested in promoting sales and willing to assume responsibility for credits. In any event, the agreement should be specific.

Insurance Coverage. Presumably the lessee—that is, the owner of the merchandise of the leased department—is responsible for fire insurance coverage on such merchandise. Responsibility of the store, if any, for damage to merchandise through fire, water, theft, loss, or other cause should be clearly defined. Both parties to the agreement, particularly the store company, should be concerned with the adequacy of protection provided through compensation and public liability insurance policies. It is not unreasonable for the store to expect the lessee to carry adequate insurance to protect the store against any claims that might be lodged against the store by reason of the lessee's inability to satisfy such claims. Quite apart from this contingency, it is important that the respective liabilities of the respective parties be clearly defined and adequately covered by insurance.

Other Provisions. Various other provisions should be included in the lease agreement, but it is not feasible to discuss many of them in this chapter. A few are touched upon in the remainder of this section.

Every agreement should set forth definitely which party has the right of employment, irrespective of which party pays the employees. It is usual to provide that the lessee may hire the employees paid by it, but that the store has the right to compel discharge of any employee who is objectionable or who does not comply with its rules. In some instances the store's personnel director may be entrusted with the hiring of certain employees of the lessee.

Other subjects of agreement deal with who shall provide and pay for supplies, utilities, and other services, the quality of the merchandise or service of the lessee, the general range of prices to be charged, the nature of display advertising, and appearance of the department. In some instances the lease agreement may contain definite provisions as to the basis on which, or means by which, the contract may be canceled. In these cases, the agreement should include a non-competition provision prohibiting the operation of a similar department in the market area of the store.

The agreement should be specific with respect to the time and manner of periodic settlements and whether interest is to be accrued upon either debit or credit balances outstanding subsequent to settlement dates.

16

Statements Reporting Operating Results

Principal Operating Statement

The principal statement for reporting operating results may also be the official income statement of the business. The retail merchandising operations, when summarized in the income account, show sales, cost of sales, gross margin, store operating expenses, and operating income. Nonmerchandising and nonoperating elements of expense and income may be added to the statement after operating income in order to present in one statement the complete income account for the period.

Form of Income Statement

The Financial Executives Division of the National Retail Merchants Association (NRMA) over many years has developed and promoted the adoption of standard forms of statements. Reference is made specifically to the 1976 publication, "Retail Accounting Manual—Revised" ("RAM"). RAM devotes an entire section to the topic of "Management Reporting." Included therein are the following chapters:

> Merchandise Department Performance Statistics.
> Summaries of Expense Data.

Individual Store Location Accounting.
Executive Reporting.
Return on Investment.

Each of these chapters deals with the question of reporting results of operations in one form or another. RAM presents examples of report formats for each of these specific areas.

Figure 37 shows a condensed income statement which incorporates, with some slight modifications, most of the concepts reflected in these various RAM chapters. This income statement, which portrays the results of operations for retailing organizations, can be used effectively by management to measure overall performance and to monitor the company's progress against plan.

As constructed, the condensed income statement shows results for the current month (or four- or five-week period) and year to date. Some retail organizations, especially those involved with fashion goods, prefer to show "season to date" instead of "year to date." Conventionally, as noted earlier, the Spring and Fall "seasons" generally run from February 1 to July 31 and August 1 to January 31, respectively.

The condensed income statement shown compares this year's results with budget and also discloses the amount of variance from budget. Historically, some organizations prefer to compare this year with last year. However, it is the authors' belief that comparison to a realistic budget or plan based on an informed assessment of the market is a more realistic and meaningful measurement of current performance. Comparison with the prior year effectively establishes the prior year as the norm or standard of achievement for the current year. In fact, results of the prior year may, for varied reasons, represent a disappointing performance, or may reflect a failure to properly exploit an existing market, or may include the impact of abnormal, non-recurring favorable or unfavorable circumstances. Against the background of these various possibilities, it can be seen that the prior year's performance is not necessarily a fair measure of the current year's performance. As noted, measurement against a plan or budget presumes the existence of a realistic and attainable budget. The elements involved in the preparation of such a budget are discussed in Chapter 5.

CONDENSED INCOME STATEMENT

Month _____

| | Month ||| Year to Date |||
	This Year	Budget	Variance	Last Year	This Year	Budget	Variance	Last Year
Total sales								
Owned retail sales								
Less: Returns and allowances								
Net owned retail sales								
Cost of merchandise handled								
Gross margin—owned								
Commissions from leased departments								
Other cost of sales	( )		( )		( )		( )	
Gross margin								
Operating expenses								
Operating income (loss)								
Other income, net:								
Finance charge income								
Sundry revenue, net								
Interest income								
Interest expense								
Income (loss) before taxes								
Provision for taxes based on income:								
Federal								
State and local								
Net income								

FIG. 37. Comparative income statement.

Leased Department Sales

The use of leased departments as a means of providing a full line of merchandise to the consumer has become predominant in recent years, especially for such retail departments as millinery and shoes, and such cost selling departments as the operation of beauty shops, shoe repair, and similar operations (see Chapter 15). The choice of using a leased department versus operating a department depends on many factors, including in-house expertise, relative return on investment, and, in general, whether the department is deemed to be a necessary complement to the company's operations. In any event, most retailers believe that the total volume of the company is an important factor of comparability, and accordingly, all-store total sales are included in the sales statistics, including the sales of leased departments.

Since the retailer receives only a commission from the leased department operator, based generally on gross sales, the cost of merchandise handled and operating expenses of the operator are generally not known. Some retailers report the amount of commissions from leased departments as an element of other income, not to be included in gross margin. However, the NRMA accounting manual considers such commissions as an element of gross margin, and the authors are in full accord with this presentation. A discussion of the various aspects of leased department accounts is included in Chapter 15.

Some companies may wish to show the components of the income statement both in dollars and as a percentage of sales. Where the leased departments are significant, this percentage comparison is made using total sales, including leased departments. It is the authors' opinion that using total sales for percentage comparison can be misleading since the merchandise costs and certain critical operating expenses associated with leased departments, such as buying expenses and sales payroll expenses, are not included in the income statement. Percentage comparisons preferably should be made utilizing total net owned retail sales.

The elements of cost of sales and the other items which enter into the derivation of gross margin are discussed in the following paragraphs. Net sales, purchases, discounts earned, alteration and workroom costs, other costs of sales, and gross margin have already been defined or explained as retail merchandising terms in Chapter 3. These definitions and explanations are not repeated here; rather, attention is focused upon questions directly related to the determination of the respective amounts for income statement purposes.

Net Sales

In Chapter 3, net sales of a store are defined as "gross sales less returns and allowances (except policy adjustments) and less discounts to employees and others."

The amount of gross sales includes receipts from restaurants, barber and beauty shops, cold storage, and other service departments, but does not include receipts from customers for alterations, which are applied as reductions of workroom and alteration costs. For the sake of simplicity, workroom and alteration costs would be included in other costs of sales in the accompanying condensed income statement.

In some stores the service departments represent an important part of store operations. For this reason the results of operations may be reported separately from the conventional retail departments that sell merchandise at normal markons. Under these circumstances, frequently consolidation of the retail and service departments results in distorted relationships which are not comparable with figures of other stores.

Taxes collected on merchandise sold and installment carrying charges should be excluded from sales. Installment carrying charges are an element of other income, net, and are shown as finance charge income in the accompanying statement.

In the event contract and wholesale operations are a significant factor, the related sales and costs and expenses should be segregated from the more conventional retail operations. Contract or wholesale volume is typically obtained at lower profit margins than realized by the regular retail business. Consequently, consolidation of such diverse elements results in abnormal relationships in the total all-store combined figures. If this combination of wholesale and retail operations produces operating results deemed distortive, the store's income account should be broken down into two or more separate sections.

Cost of Merchandise Handled

The principal items that enter into the total cost of merchandise handled are shown in detail in Figure 38. These items are described in the following paragraphs.

Inventory, Beginning of Period. Inventory is to be entered at mercantile, less whatever provision is made for future markdowns, or at the amount (after depreciation) determined under the cost method, before deduction of allowance for cash discounts included in inventory. Supplies and other non-merchandise items should not be included.

Where unearned discounts are established at the close of a period, as appropriate, the adjustment may be made either through inventories or through discounts. While it may appear that selection of either method is of small importance, and while adjustment through inventories has the advantage of showing on the income account the same inventory figures as are reflected on a comparative balance sheet, adjustment through discounts is recommended. This latter procedure has the advantage of reflecting discounts earned in the income statement, with such discounts being stated in a more meaningful relationship to sales.

Merchandise Purchases. As set forth in Chapter 3, the term purchases as used in retailing includes merchandise purchased (net of trade discounts deducted by vendors from the face of invoices), less returns and less allowances by vendors; cost of goods produced in a store's own manufacturing workrooms, such as dresses, candy, millinery, and toilet preparations; and duties, freight, insurance, and other similar charges entering into total landed cost of imported merchandise.

This caption of the income account also includes payroll of kitchen help in restaurants, of barbers, manicurists, beauty parlor operators, and employees doing similar service or production work, as well as other production costs in such departments.

Imported (i.e., landed) merchandise costs sometimes may include a buying fee for the services of foreign buying agents abroad. A number of stores also include the foreign traveling expenses of buyers or a prorated amount to cover costs of a store's foreign buying office. However, this practice is not recommended since such

COMPARATIVE DEPARTMENTAL OPERATING STATEMENT
Month and Year to Date, Ended _____

Department _____

	\multicolumn{4}{c	}{}	\multicolumn{4}{c	}{Year to Date}
	\multicolumn{2}{c	}{This Year}	\multicolumn{2}{c	}{Plan}	\multicolumn{2}{c	}{Last Year}	\multicolumn{2}{c	}{This Year}	\multicolumn{2}{c	}{Plan}	\multicolumn{2}{c	}{Last Year}
	Amount	%	Amount	%	Amount	%	Amount	%	Amount	%	Amount	%
Sales	$13,428		$13,500		$ 9,771		$104,979		$104,000		$81,742	
Less: Returns and allowances	1,407	10.5	1,500	11.1	1,478	15.1	12,236	11.7	12,000	11.5	13,377	16.4
Net sales	$12,021	100.0	$12,000	100.0	$ 8,293	100.0	$ 92,743	100.0	$ 92,000	100.0	$68,365	100.0
Merchandise costs:												
Inventory, beginning of period	$17,019		$18,500		$18,898		$20,880		$20,000		$24,136	
Merchandise purchases	5,914		4,000		3,088		50,886		50,000		36,095	
Transportation inward	110		100		82		908		900		705	
	23,043		22,600		22,068		72,674		70,900		60,936	
Inventory, close of period	15,322		15,000		16,800		15,322		15,000		16,800	
	7,721	64.2	7,600	63.3	5,268	63.5	57,352	61.8	55,900	60.8	44,136	64.5
Discounts earned	409	3.4	400	3.3	311	3.7	3,852	4.2	3,500	3.8	2,465	3.6
	7,312	60.8	7,200	60.0	4,957	59.8	53,500	57.6	52,400	57.0	41,671	60.9
*Workroom and alteration costs (net)	82	.7	80	.7	54	.6	612	.7	400	.4	437	.6
Total merchandise costs	$ 7,394	61.5	$ 7,280	60.7	$ 5,011	60.4	$ 54,112	58.3	$ 52,800	57.4	$42,108	61.5
Gross margin	$ 4,627	38.5	$ 4,720	39.3	$ 3,282	39.6	$ 38,631	41.7	$ 39,200	42.6	$26,257	38.5
Direct expenses:												
Payroll	$ 1,083	9.0	$ 1,080	9.0	$ 1,017	12.3	$ 7,281	7.9	$ 7,250	7.8	$ 5,880	8.6
Travel	125	1.0	120	1.0	103	1.2	1,050	1.1	1,250	1.4	1,020	1.5
Advertising	465	3.9	350	2.9	250	3.0	2,716	2.9	2,500	2.7	2,440	3.6
Total direct expenses	$ 1,673	13.9	$ 1,550	12.9	$ 1,370	16.5	$ 11,047	11.9	$ 11,000	11.9	$ 9,340	13.7
Department contribution	$ 2,954	24.6	$ 3,170	26.4	$ 1,912	23.1	$ 27,584	29.8	$ 28,200	30.7	$16,917	24.8

Statistics								
Retail inventory, first of period	$29,704		$29,082		$32,743		$35,975		$41,721
Retail purchases, plus markups	10,075		8,000		5,206		87,387		63,259
Total merchandise handled	39,779		37,082		37,949		123,362		104,980
Less: Retail inventory, end of period	26,675		24,002		28,940		24,002		28,940
Retail sales and reductions	$13,104		$13,080		$ 9,009		$ 99,360		$ 76,040
Made up of:									
Sales	$12,021		$12,000		$ 8,293		$ 92,000		$68,365
Markdowns	615	5.1	600	5.0	665	8.0	4,600	5.0	6,675	9.8
Sales discounts	100	.8	120	1.0	51	.6	920	1.0	1,000	1.5
Shrinkages	368	3.1	360	3.0			1,840	2.0	
Markon, month's purchases		40.2		48.7		39.1			
Cumulative markon for year to date								43.8		42.0
Markon first of season								42.0		42.1
Number of sales	8,715		8,750		5,306		60,000		36,142
Average gross sales	1.54		1.54		1.84		1.53		2.26
Percent of department sales to total sales		.8		.7		.5		1.0		.8
Sales per square foot selling area	7.97		7.90		5.85		58.90		48.21
Turnover		6.1						4.8		3.3			3.2
Percent of discounts to merchandise purchases		6.9		10.0		10.1		7.1		6.8

*If alteration charges to customers are included in departmental sales, the workroom and alteration costs will be stated gross and the amount of alteration sales to customers shown under statistics. If such charges are, as in the above illustration, credited to income of workrooms, the departmental figures for workroom and alteration costs will be net charges to departments.

FIG. 38. Merchandise departmental operating statement.

expenses should be considered operating expenses rather than merchandise costs.

Some stores which maintain buying offices in domestic buying centers, or pay agents for representation in domestic buying centers, load an amount on domestic purchases to cover the costs of the offices or representation, although these items are classified as operating expenses in RAM. Loading of this kind is done in the same way as loading for discounts, and for the same purpose: to "force" higher initial purchase markons since such markons would be based on "purchase" amounts which are higher than the underlying invoice costs. However, loading for buying costs and for discounts should not be included in merchandise values reflected on a store's balance sheet. Moreover, net income should not include loading applicable to unsold merchandise.

Freight, Express, and Truckage Inward. These elements include all charges for transportation of merchandise from manufacturer or wholesaler to store or warehouse.

Gross Cost of Merchandise Handled. This cost equals the sum of inventory at beginning of period, merchandise purchases, and freight, express, and truckage inward.

Inventory, Close of Period. Inventory is to be included on the basis stated under "Inventory, Beginning of Period."

Gross Cost of Merchandise Sold. Gross cost of merchandise handled, less inventory at close of period, gives the gross cost of the merchandise which has been sold during the period.

Discounts Earned. The discount amounts are on the earned basis. Detailed discussion of methods for determination of discounts earned is to be found in Chapter 8.

Cost of Merchandise Handled. Gross cost of merchandise handled, less discounts earned, gives net cost of the merchandise which has been sold during the period.

Gross Margin—Owned. Gross margin—owned is the remainder after deducting cost of merchandise handled from net owned retail sales.

Other Costs of Sales. For sake of simplicity, since in most operations the amount included is nominal, there has been included in this caption workroom and alteration costs and other costs of sales such as cost purchases. These would include relatively minor items and costs such as jewelry boxes, laundering, assembling, and restoration of merchandise. Those companies which incur significant alteration costs may wish to disclose these costs separately.

Ordinarily, the charges that are levied on customers for alterations and other services provided by workrooms should be deducted from net sales and shown as a credit against the workroom costs. See Chapter 14 for a further explanation of these items.

Gross Margin. Gross margin is the sum of gross margin—owned plus commissions from leased departments, minus other costs of sales.

Operating Expenses. Operating expenses are shown in total on the condensed income statement in Figure 37. Generally, as discussed later in this chapter, a separate statement is prepared showing the composition of such expenses. However, some companies may wish to include the detail in this statement if the key elements are not too numerous and would not make this statement too unwieldy to be used effectively.

Other Income, Net. Those items which do not enter into the determination of operating income should be shown separately. On the accompanying income statement four such items are shown. There may be others, for example, investment income, equity in subsidiaries not consolidated, and foreign exchange gains or losses, which likewise may be separately disclosed if deemed significant.

There has been a great deal of controversy surrounding the treatment of finance charge income. Some companies have maintained that this income should be treated as a credit against accounts receivable, credit and collection expense. Others maintain that this income should be shown as part of the gross revenues from operations. In the 1976 edition of RAM, the NRMA has taken the position that finance charge income should be treated below the operating income line as an element of other income.

Third-party credit cards are currently being accepted by many retailers. A charge, or discount from the sales price, is levied by these third-party companies for servicing the transaction. Again, a certain amount of controversy has surrounded the treatment of these charges. RAM states that these discounts should be treated as an expense item charged to accounts receivable, credit and collection as part of the company's operating expenses.

Sundry revenue, net, would include such items as revenue from telephone boxes, sale of waste, and rental of real estate not used in the business.

Interest income would include any income derived from investments in negotiable instruments, loans or receivables not created in the normal course of business, and similar investments.

As illustrated, interest income and interest expense should be shown separately. Effectively, these two items are not directly related and the principle of offset would be misleading.

The provision for taxes based on income should include federal, state, and local taxes based on income. State and local taxes which are based on capital assets employed, or some criterion other than income, should be included in operating expenses. It is sometimes difficult to segregate the portion of a jurisdiction's tax that is based on income when the tax is based on income or alternatively on some other factor when the income base is inapplicable. In those cases, the tax should be shown as either an operating expense or as an income tax, depending upon whether income or an alternative factor predominates in determining the tax liability.

Adaptation of the Standard Form to Everyday Use

Stores often find it necessary to make some modification of the standard form of income statement in preparing statements for the everyday use of their executives. These modifications frequently relate to the expense section of the statement, rather than to the elements entering into gross margin. With respect to the latter, however, variations are frequently found in the treatments of leased departments, manufacturing and alteration workrooms, wholesale and contract departments, restaurants, and service and storage departments. The variations generally occur when these elements of the business are deemed to be relatively significant. It is appropriate that stores adapt the standard form to their particular individual requirements, rather than limit the usefulness of their statements by strict adherence to a form designed largely for comparative purposes. Executives and merchandisers should have this in mind when making comparisons of their own statements with published statistics. The accounting office can always rearrange a store's figures so that they may be compared with published figures.

Operating Expenses

Over the years, retailers have focused increasing attention on controlling expenses as a means of improving profitability. The basic management organization of many retailers has been aligned with a view to fixing responsibilities for specific centers of activity with identifiable executives and managers. These individuals are then held responsible for controlling the expenses associated with their respective centers of activity.

As discussed in Chapter 5, operating expenses should be planned by functional groups and actual performance should be measured against plan on a periodic basis. Therefore, separate statistical statements showing the details of operating expenses are normally prepared in conjunction with the previously discussed income statement. The amount of detail any one company may wish to report will vary depending upon the size of the operation, the organizational structure, and the level to which responsibility can be reasonably fixed.

Since a considerable portion of RAM is devoted to the area of expense accounting and reporting, readers are encouraged to consult RAM for specific details; this chapter will consider only the basic concepts of expense reporting. In preparing RAM, the NRMA was faced with the problems of providing a chart of accounts for expense accumulation, summarization, and reporting that could be used by most retailers, regardless of size or type of operation, and at the same time of maintaining some degree of uniformity in reporting practices in order to make figure exchange feasible.

As a solution, RAM breaks down the various functions or centers of activity into 10 expense summaries, with 44 expense centers within these summaries. RAM suggests that the 10 expense summaries which follow can be used by even the smallest of retail operations:

    010 Property and equipment
    100 Company management
    200 Accounting and management information
    300 Credit and accounts receivable
    400 Sales promotion

500 Services and operations
600 Personnel
700 Merchandise receiving, storage, and distribution
800 Selling and supporting services
900 Merchandising

Companies that wish to show more detail can utilize the 44 expense centers provided within these expense summaries. For example, expense summary 400, sales promotion, has the following expense centers:

400 Sales promotion
    410 Sales promotion management
    420 Advertising
    430 Shows, special events, and exhibits
    440 Display

A company may use any or all of these expense centers, depending on its needs. However, if all the expense centers within an expense summary are not used, the expense elements pertaining to the unused expense centers should be included in the management expense center of each expense summary. Using as an example the 400 summary cited above, if a company did not wish to use the expense center 430—shows, special events, and exhibits—because the amount of expense incurred in this area was minimal and there was no one person assigned this responsibility, any expenses incurred for these types of activities would be included in 410, sales promotion management.

For those companies desiring an even finer breakdown of expenses, RAM also provides 22 subexpense centers for some of the expense centers. Again, each store can decide which, if any, of these subexpense centers it wishes to use. In effect, 66 expense areas of activity are provided (44 expense centers plus 22 subcenters). Using our example, sales promotion would comprise the following if all of the expense areas of activity were used:

400 Sales promotion
    410 Sales promotion management
    420 Advertising
        421 Newspaper
        425 Radio
        426 TV

427 Direct mail
428 Other
430 Shows, special events, and exhibits
431 Public relations
432 Merchandise shows
434 Special events and exhibits
440 Display
441 Display production
444 Sign shop

In addition to capturing expense by areas of activity, RAM also provides for classifying expenses by natural division which describes the type of expense. There are 17 basic natural divisions of expense as follows:

01 Payroll
03 Media costs
04 Taxes
06 Supplies
07 Services purchased
08 Unclassified
09 Travel
10 Communications
11 Pensions
12 Insurance
13 Depreciation
14 Professional services
16 Bad debts
17 Equipment rentals
18 Outside maintenance and equipment service contracts
20 Real property rentals
92 Credits and outside revenues

Provision is also made for the following three transfer accounts. Although not comprising basic natural divisions, they are used in addition to the natural divisions.

02 Allocated fringe benefits
90 Expense transfers—in
91 Expense transfers—out

A great deal of attention and emphasis has been brought to bear in planning and controlling expenses by area of responsibility.

COMPARATIVE STATEMENT OF OPERATING EXPENSES
BY EXPENSE SUMMARY

Period ________

Classification and Name of Expense	Month								Season to Date							
	This Year		Budget		Budget Var.		Last Year		This Year		Budget		Budget Var.		Last Year	
	Amt.	%	Amt.	%	Amt.	%	Amt.	%	Amt.	%	Amt.	%	Amt.	%	Amt.	%
010 Property and Equipment																
100 Company Management																
200 Accounting and Management Info.																
300 Credit and Accounts Receivable																
400 Sales Promotion																
500 Services and Operations																
600 Personnel																
700 Merchandise Receiving, Storage, and Distribution																
800 Selling and Supporting Services																
900 Merchandising																
Total Expense																

FIG. 39. Statement of operating expenses by expense summary. (*Source:* Retail Accounting Manual, NRMA)

Therefore, as an integral segment of the monthly (or four- or five-week) financial package, management should receive a statement similar to the one shown in Figure 39. This statement displays expenses by expense summary compared to budget, and to last year, and additionally shows variances from budget. These amounts are shown both for the current month (or four- or five-week period) and season or year to date. The statement as presented shows only the 10 expense summaries. Companies that use expense centers and/or subcenters may wish to display each center or subcenter that is used.

Management should also be provided with a monthly (or four- or five-week) statement of operating expenses by natural division. Figure 40 depicts the manner in which this information can be shown.

Each supervisor and manager would also want a breakdown of the expenses for his or her expense center. This can be done by displaying the natural divisions of expense applicable to each center for the current month (or four- or five-week period) versus budget, and season or year to date actual versus budget.

External Reporting Format of Income Statement

Most organizations prepare a monthly, quarterly, or annual report of operations which is used in reporting to such parties as shareholders, financial institutions, institutional lenders, and trade creditors. Over the years, retailers have adopted for use in external reporting a special form of income statement which attempts to reflect the cost of acquiring merchandise, and making it ready for sale, as part of cost of goods sold. Basically originating with an alternative permitted by the Securities and Exchange Commission in Regulation S–X, which governs the form and content of financial statements filed with the Commission, this special form has been adopted by many publicly held retailers. These retailers believe that this form presents more realistically the real costs incurred in making merchandise available to consumers at retail, thereby indirectly responding to criticisms sometimes directed toward the apparently large profit spread between retail prices and merchandise costs as reflected in published statements. Interpretations of published figures have tended to be unfair when comparison has been made between operations of retailers and of manufacturers

COMPARATIVE STATEMENT OF OPERATING EXPENSES
BY NATURAL DIVISIONS

Period _____

	Month								Season to Date							
	This Year		Budget		Budget Var.		Last Year		This Year		Budget		Budget Var.		Last Year	
Natural Divisions—Names	Amt.	%	Amt.	%	Amt.	%	Amt.	%	Amt.	%	Amt.	%	Amt.	%	Amt.	%
01 Payroll																
03 Media Costs																
04 Taxes																
06 Supplies																
07 Services Purchased																
08 Unclassified																
09 Travel																
10 Communications																
11 Pensions																
12 Insurance																
13 Depreciation																
14 Professional Services																
16 Bad Debts																
17 Equipment Rentals																
18 Outside Maintenance & Equip. Service Contracts																
20 Real Property Rentals																
92 Credits and Outside Revenues																
02 Allocated Fringe Benefits																

FIG. 40. Statement of operating expenses by natural divisions. *(Source: Retail Accounting Manual, NRMA)*

and wholesalers, where it has been pointed out that the latter two operate on what appear to be smaller profit spreads between selling and cost, with lower expense ratios. The conclusion has often been unfairly drawn that retailers exact from the public an undue profit margin in order to cover inefficiencies as expressed in high expense ratios.

Traditionally, this special form of income statement classified "occupancy and buying costs" as part of cost of goods sold. These costs could be obtained with reasonable ease when the NRMA's "Standard Expense Center Accounting Manual" (SECAM) (1954) grouped expenses into five major functional categories: Administration, Occupancy, Publicity, Buying, and Selling. However, with the 1962 revision, RAM replaced SECAM, and these five major groupings disappeared. Under the revised (1976) edition of RAM, it is a somewhat burdensome task to extract those elements of expense that traditionally were categorized as "occupancy and buying costs." Furthermore, since these elements of expenses are not specifically identified, there can be differences in interpretation and grouping as among companies, thereby losing some degree of comparability.

This, among other reasons, has caused some major retail companies to adopt a format for external reporting purposes which groups all costs and expenses together, exclusive of certain designated items (normally, maintenance and repairs, depreciation, taxes other than income taxes, rentals, retirement expense, and interest expense).

Some companies, while grouping all costs and expenses together, have chosen to show cost of goods sold as a separately captioned amount. In effect, there are three general schools of thought in presenting the costs and expenses for a company engaged in retailing:

1. *Traditional Method*
   Costs of goods sold, including occupancy and
     buying costs $xx xxx
   Selling, general, and administrative expenses   xx xxx
   Depreciation   x xxx
   Interest expense   xxx
2. *"Exclusive of" Method*
   Cost of goods sold and expenses, exclusive of items
     which follow: $xx xxx
       Maintenance and repairs   x xxx

Depreciation	x xxx
Taxes, other than those based on income	xxx
Rentals	xxx
Retirement expense	xxx
Interest expense	xxx

3. *Combination Method*

Costs and expenses of retail operations:	
Costs of goods sold	$xx xxx
Selling, general, and administrative expenses	x xxx
Maintenance and repairs	x xxx
Depreciation	x xxx
Taxes, other than those based on income	x xxx
Rentals	xxx
Retirement expense	xxx
Interest expense	xxx
Total costs and expenses	$xxx xxx

There can be many variations to meet specific situations. Although the authors continue to prefer seeing occupancy and buying costs classified as part of cost of goods sold, merit in the other forms of presentation is acknowledged. Whatever format is chosen, it should be consistent, period to period, to enable the readers to make appropriate comparisons.

It is apparent that the special forms of the income statement were designed largely as vehicles for the public presentation of operating statistics. For store executives they will present a new view of business operations, but will not add to the ability to control and conduct stores along profitable lines. It is apparently intended that the standard methods and formats shall be used to obtain operating and statistical information needed to manage the business and that the special forms shall be utilized only when preparing formal statements for public dissemination.

Merchandise Statistics

Up to this point the discussion has centered on the income statement, which is the formal and final summarization in condensed form of the operating results for a period or periods. Behind this statement there are the supporting details—the merchandise and expense statistics which are the real accounting tools for executive guidance and control. These statistics comprise that great body of statements, reports, and schedules by means of which executives and merchandisers acquaint themselves from day to day with conditions and operations of the business and which they use for guidance toward successful and profitable results.

First and foremost among these statistical statements is the report of selling department operations, variously referred to as Department Operating Statement, Buyer's or Department Manager's Report, Stock and Net Result Statement, etc. Basically this statement is a merchandise statistical statement, substantially devoted to disclosure of the elements and factors that have produced the merchandise profit "margins" or "spread" of the departments. The expense statistics usually incorporated in this statement will vary from company to company. Some companies believe that only controllable expenses should be included. These comprise those expenses which can be influenced and controlled by the merchant whose performance is being measured.

The NRMA in its 1976 revision advocates the use of "departmental contribution," as opposed to the full allocation of expense or the "net profit" concept that has been used by some companies in the past. An example of a departmental operating statement is shown in Figure 38.

At best, the problem of measuring performance and therefore the problem of assigning or allocating expenses is a difficult one. The role of the buyer or merchant has changed dramatically over the years. With most companies operating in multiple locations, the buyer is no longer directly responsible for selling activities or store operations. Performance of individual selling locations, as discussed in Chapter 13, has become as important as departmental performance. Furthermore, operating personnel are being measured by their performance, as previously discussed. In this framework, the authors concur with the approach of limiting expense measurement for departmental results to those elements which are direct controllable expenses.

In practice, the form of the department operating statement varies in different stores, from a very brief form to a voluminous one. A weekly statement is likely to be brief, containing only the principal statistical elements of merchandising operations. In some instances a brief form of monthly statement, showing the principal merchandise statistics, is prepared for buyers and a complete form is prepared for executives and merchandise managers. In this chapter the intent is to illustrate and discuss a fairly complete form, one not too heavily laden with items and yet not so brief as to omit important statistical features.

There are three basic sections of the department statement:

1. The merchandise section, showing sales, cost of sales, gross margin, and related elements.
2. The expense section, showing the operating expenses attributable to departments.
3. The statistical section, showing various statistics which assist in interpreting and explaining the statement.

While the form illustrated may seem a detailed presentation of departmental results, it contains less information than often appears on statements of this kind. On the other hand, it contains more information than some forms do, as, for example, the details relating to derivation of merchandise costs. Again, some statements do not include the items listed as statistics; but where they do, the retail statistics from the stock ledger are usually included.

Supplementary to the departmental statistical statements are numerous statements and reports of daily, weekly, or monthly merchandise and expense statistics, representing analyses of principal merchandise and expense elements. A list of the more important reports of this kind follows:

1. Sales:

   Daily report of departmental sales, showing comparison of day's sales with the same day of the previous year, as well as cumulative monthly (or four- or five-week) totals to date, this year compared with last year.

   Weekly report of departmental sales compared with the same week of the previous year.

   Comparative monthly (or four- or five-week) report of departmental sales, including cumulative totals to date (comparative with corresponding periods of last year).

   Comparative reports of merchandise classifications (comparative with corresponding periods of last year). (See Figures 41 and 42.)

   Report of sales analyzed by sales clerks.

   For unit control purposes:

   Analysis by classification, number of sales, and unit price.

COMPARATIVE CLASSIFICATION REPORT

Department: *Jewelry* Month of _____

Classification	Opening Stock		Purchases		Reductions		Net Sales		Closing Stock		
	This Year	Last Year	This Year	Last Year	This Year	Last Year	This Year	Plan	Last Year	This Year	Plan	Last Year
Diamonds												
Watches												
14 kt. gold jewelry												
10 kt. gold jewelry												
Semi-precious stone novelties												
14 kt. watch accessories												
10 kt. watch accessories												
Sterling silver hollow ware												
Sterling silver flat ware												
Sterling silver toilet goods												
Sterling silver bags & novelties												
Cutlery												
Plated hollow ware												
Plated flat ware												
Hygrade clocks												
Inexpensive clocks												

FIG. 41. Comparative classification report.

COMPARISON OF SALES AND STOCK REPORT

Department _____   Date _____

Merchandise Classification _____

Price Line	On Hand	On Order	Sales		
			Week	Month to Date	Season to Date
16.50					
19.50					
22.00					
25.00					
28.50					
34.00					
38.50					
45.00					
Totals.....					

FIG. 42. Comparison of sales and stock report.

 Analysis by classification, manufacturer, color, size, style, or lot number.
Return sales percentages, departmentally.
Percentages of each department's sales to total sales of store.
Sales per square foot of selling area of each department.
Number of sales transactions and average size of sale of each department.
Analysis by type of sale, that is, cash, C.O.D., charge, etc.
2. Inventories (statistics departmentally):
Excess stock report (classified between domestic and foreign).
Analysis of stock by classifications and season letters.
Comparison of inventory for several seasons, showing inventory markon percentages.
Merchandise in stock on memorandum.
Merchandise on loan to display and other departments.
Merchandise out on memorandum for repairs and to customers and manufacturers.
Inventory turnovers, departmentally and by classifications, price lines, styles, etc., and/or stock-to-sales ratios.
Division of stock between domestic and foreign merchandise, subdivided to show merchandise classifications and season letters.

Reports of shortages and overages.
Unit stock control reports.
3. Markdowns:
Analysis of markdowns by reasons.
Analysis by season letters.
Analysis by manufacturers of goods.
Comparison of markdowns for several seasons.
Percentages of markdowns to departmental sales.
4. Purchases:
Departmentally, showing markon percentages (daily, weekly, or monthly, and cumulative).
By classifications and manufacturers.
For unit control purposes: Analysis of purchases and returns by classification, unit price, quantity, etc.
Orders outstanding.
Open-to-buy balances.
5. Workrooms: Complete comparative operating report for each workroom, showing revenue, and operating costs such as wages, merchandise, supplies, etc. May also include statistical information as to number of units of work and average costs per unit.
6. Operating expenses:
Departmental expense analyses.
Analyses of amounts of the natural expense divisions, showing component elements making up the totals.
Summary of expenses by expense centers.
Production unit accounting reports.
7. Salaries:
Comparative monthly (or four- or five-week period) report in considerable detail showing salary expense of each department and office, grouped and summarized either along expense account classification lines or according to responsible executive divisions.
Weekly report showing number of persons and/or hours, regular hours and overtime, and total weekly salaries for each department and office. May be made comparative with previous year to show increases and decreases.
Selling cost percentages, departmentally and by sales clerks.
8. Advertising: Departmental report showing newspaper lineage used and cost thereof, with classification by media.
9. Delivery expense: Breakdown of delivery costs, tabulation of number and classes of deliveries, calculation of average costs of deliveries, and distribution departmentally.

Statements for Cost or Non-Retail Operations or Departments

The departmental statement illustrated and discussed earlier in this chapter (Figure 38) is a form primarily suitable for reporting on retail departments, that is, departments selling merchandise which can readily be controlled by the retail inventory method. It is not equally suitable for reporting on so-called cost departments, that is, departments selling service, or service and merchandise, or merchandise which cannot be controlled effectively under the retail method. Examples of such departments are restaurants, beauty shops, storage and cleaning, optical, and made-to-measure clothing. These departments customarily do not have problems of markdowns, shortages, and alteration costs as separate elements in the determination of gross margin. Likewise, they do not have inventories or purchases at retail and are not concerned with markons as an element of recordkeeping.

The method of deriving cost of sales for the various cost departments is not different in principle from that used for retail departments, but the elements of cost may be quite different. For example, as referred to earlier in the chapter, in a restaurant, cost of sales will include food materials purchased, salaries of kitchen help, water, gas, electricity, kitchen supplies, rental for the kitchen space, and depreciation of kitchen equipment. In beauty and barber shops, costs will include salaries of operators, supplies, depreciation of equipment, etc. Similarly, in other cost departments, there are apt to be salaries, supplies, and other items to be included in costs, in addition to purchases of material or merchandise. Some of these items of costs are of major importance in the operations and are best set forth separately, rather than included in a single figure for purchases.

Cost of sales for cost departments consists of opening inventory, plus purchases, salaries, supplies, and other items properly chargeable to costs, less closing inventory, and less any discounts earned. Where the cost department produces the merchandise it sells, the opening and closing inventories will include labor and materials in process as of the cutoff dates, as well as raw materials and finished products.

Direct expenses of cost departments differ somewhat in nature and importance from the direct expenses of retail departments. In this regard, a number of overhead items would not be deemed to apply or be allocable to cost departments. Expenses such as buying and merchandise management, sales promotion management, and sales training costs would apply to retail departments, but their allocation to cost departments would be inappropriate.

Obviously, the statement format used for any cost department will vary depending upon the nature and key control elements of any such department.

For further information regarding these types of operations, see Chapter 14.

17

Limitations in the Use of Percentages

Introduction

Throughout this book, in various chapters, much emphasis has been placed on operating and other percentages. Also, the derivations of a number of mathematical formulas have been shown, and illustrations have been presented with respect to percentage relationships, including the factors or elements to be taken into account in planning operations departmentally and on a broader scale. Comparative retail trade statistics, largely in percentages, are made available periodically, notably by the National Retail Merchants Association.

Recognizing the utilitarian value of all of the foregoing, a note of caution should be added. There are inherent limitations in the use of percentages, as compared with dollar amounts, in retail merchandise and expense accounting and control. Retailers have been well aware of these limitations, as witnessed by such concepts and studies as incremental sales and profits, contributed profits, and expense center and production unit accounting.

Another example is the retailers' concern with the troublesome problem of the best policy to follow with respect to so-called "big ticket" items with low markon percentages. On a percentage basis, the return realized from such sales could never be deemed satisfactory. However, the pool of profit dollars thereby contributed can have a significant beneficial impact on overall profitability. Moreover, the decision to carry such merchandise in stock may be a competitive necessity for the conventional department store in terms of establishing an image of aggressively competing on many fronts with discount houses, chain stores, mail-order houses, catalog stores, and similar promotionally minded retail organizations.

It certainly is not the purpose of this chapter to discuss the pros and cons of this particular question. However, it provides a good illustration of the type of problem that should be studied from the vantage point of dollars, as well as percentages.

Merchandise Management Accounting

In this connection, in recent years serious attention has been given to a retail accounting technique termed "merchandise management accounting." In its broadest sense it represents the application of cost accounting methods to retail operations in an effort to determine the profitability of individual items sold. Basically it represents a swing away from the traditional concepts, which viewed both gross margin and all expenses in terms of percentages of net sales. This technique presupposes that individual items sold have certain concomitant costs and expenses which can be estimated in advance of purchase. Proponents of merchandise management accounting therefore contemplate that as a tool it can be used to more effectively estimate and monitor the total profitability of individual merchandise items or lines. Equally important is the salutary effect of fostering a continuing sensitivity on the part of merchandise managers and buyers to the concomitant costs and expenses noted earlier. This envisions an improvement in profitability arising from the judicious selection of merchandise items, as well as from any reductions achieved through negotiations with vendors. To a certain extent this will require a shift of emphasis away from the automatic acceptance of certain pre-established departmental gross markon percentages as performance norms. Effectively, there must be a recognition of the fact that individual items sold within the same department do not necessarily incur all of the normal layers of cost, or in the same proportion. Accordingly, focusing attention on the nature and extent of such costs should prove highly beneficial.

Under the most detailed approach to merchandise management accounting, expenses are analyzed as between variable and fixed, with the most significant variable expenses normally being selling costs and markdowns. Gross margin, less variable expenses, is termed controllable profit. Through detailed cost accounting studies, cost patterns of variable expenses, by items within a selling department, are developed. Presumably, having established a selling price and gross margin, the controllable profit can be determined in advance of the purchase.

Under an intermediate approach to merchandise management accounting, the degree of refinement is appreciably reduced. Expenses are not refined as between fixed and variable; total expense center costs are used. Use is made of cost data currently available in many department stores which have adopted expense center and production unit accounting. Averages and unit costs per production unit are utilized with the idea of arriving at a departmental profit dollar contribution. This approach might be termed a departmental approach, as opposed to the item profitability approach described earlier. Thus, in connection with a specific, contemplated purchase in the open market, the original aggregate retail price is adjusted to give effect to the estimated retail reductions (markdowns, shortages, discounts, and allowances). From this "net sales" certain specified expenses (e.g., advertising, delivery, selling, etc.) are deducted to arrive at an estimated profit to be contributed by the specific purchase and its consequent resale.

The third and broadest approach to merchandise management accounting makes use of departmental expense percentages. Based upon prior-period statistics, departmental expense percentages are developed. As with the intermediate approach, the basis is departmental rather than per-item. In addition to considering markdowns, the controllable expenses which may be used are advertising costs, warehouse costs, delivery costs, and "other controllable expenses" [selling payroll, special commission payments (termed PM's), buying and merchandise management salaries, etc.].

Certain generalizations can be made with regard to merchandise management accounting. First, there is an element of fixed expense in many variable expenses and a variable element in many fixed expenses. Selling salaries are considered variable expenses. However, as long as a selling department is assigned a specific area, a minimum number of selling employees will be required to service the area regardless of sales volume. Depreciation is often viewed as a classical fixed expense. However, an expansion program designed to increase sales volume can be expected to increase significantly the annual depreciation charge.

Second, the two really significant variable expenses are selling salaries and markdowns. The averaging techniques employed in arriving at averages for a six-, twelve- or eighteen-month period fail to consider several significant factors. The rate of productivity of selling personnel will vary widely; the greater the urgency, the greater the productivity. A six- or twelve-month average will not necessarily be applicable to a special promotion. Further, while the purpose of markdowns is increased volume, in many instances, the markdowns are incurred when the purchase is initially made. Many retailers tabulate semiannual statistics which relate markdowns to specific vendor purchases, effectively recognizing the correlation of markdowns to purchases. Here again, the averaging technique may be dangerous, especially with respect to new items. Moreover, the average variable unit costs developed are based upon certain volumes and mixes of merchandise. Where there is a significant change in volume or in the mix of merchandise, the previously developed cost statistics become suspect.

In summation, it may be stated that the proposal that, when contemplating a purchase, buyers and merchandise managers think in terms of profit dollars contributed, rather than in the traditional terms of a minimum gross markon percentage, is highly desirable. This, however, envisions a major re-education program involving management and buying personnel. Measurement of profit dollars may be on either a per-item or a departmental basis. With respect to the per-item basis, there are practical considerations involving the cost and effort required to achieve the desired refinement. A departmental approach, while admittedly less refined, appears to offer a practical approach, especially when integrated with buyers' compensation to act as an inducement for improved profit performance.

18

Mathematics of Retail Merchandise Accounting

Introduction

This chapter addresses itself to some of the simpler phases of the mathematics of retail merchandise accounting, together with a few practical formulas and brief tables which can be expanded on the basis of the formulas. Since this chapter is intended to be of practical, day-to-day assistance to retailers, the theoretical or more complex phases of the subject have been omitted in the interests of practicality.

Expense Ratios Should Be Based Upon Sales

Cost of goods sold and many operating expenses fluctuate in a reasonably direct relationship with increases or decreases in sales volume. Moreover, the retailer's pricing policies must be adequate to cover all costs and expenses, both fixed and variable, and leave a residue of profit if the operation is to be viable. Consequently, the conventional practice is to measure expenses as percentages of sales, rather than as percentages of purchases or of cost of sales.

Percentages on Cost and on Selling Price, and Conversion from One Ratio to the Other

A buyer is aware of invoice cost and can readily obtain freight or other items that are included in the total cost of merchandise.

The buyer can therefore readily determine an amount to be added to such total cost of merchandise which, based on some predetermined percentage of cost, will constitute gross margin. Retailers, however, manage and control their operations on the basis of predetermined ratios on sales, not on total merchandise cost. Ignoring, for the moment, the question of what departmental gross margin is desired, the buyer obviously should be aware of the percentage to be added to cost to obtain the required corresponding markon percentage on sales.

The mathematics of determining such markon percentage are illustrated in the hypothetical example in which a department is assumed to require a markon of 40 per cent. What percentage must be added to cost?

Assume an original marked selling price of $100. If the markon ratio is 40 per cent, the markon was 40 per cent of $100, or $40. Cost was therefore $100 less $40, or $60. The amount added thereto was $40 or 66⅔ per cent. Consequently, in order to obtain a markon percentage of 40, 66⅔ per cent must be added to cost.

Conversely, we should be able to determine the markon percentage when we know what percentage has been added to cost of merchandise.

Assume a cost of $100, with a 60 per cent add-on, so that the original marked selling price is $160. Markon is $160 less $100 or $60; the percentage of markon is the ratio of $60 to $160, or 37½ per cent.

Tables I and II at the end of this chapter (page 371) show the percentages that must be added to cost to produce specified markon percentages, and conversely, the resultant markon percentages when various percentages are added to cost.

Each individual problem could be worked out along the lines of the preceding illustrations, or the formulas set forth in this chapter could be used. However, a short-cut method is available which gives results quickly where percentages can be reduced to fractions, as follows:

1. Where we wish to know what percentage to add to cost to obtain a specified markon percentage:
   a. Reduce the percentage of markon to a fraction.
   b. Keeping the numerator of the fraction as is, decrease the denominator by subtracting the numerator from the denominator.

c. Convert the resulting fraction back into a percentage; this will be the percentage to be added to cost to result in the specified markon percentage.

Illustration

QUESTION: What percentage must be added to cost to result in a 40 per cent markon?

PROCEDURE:

(a) 40 per cent = 4/10 or 2/5.

(b) Change 2/5, as stated above, into $\dfrac{2}{5-2}$ = 2/3.

(c) 2/3 equals 66⅔ per cent.

PROOF:

Cost	$100.00
Add: 66⅔ per cent	66.67
Marked selling price	$166.67

Ratio of markon (66.67) to marked selling price (166.67) = 66.67/166.67 = 2/5 = 40 per cent.

Summary of typical or common percentages converted in this manner:

Percentages of Markon			Added to Cost	
10 pct. = 1/10	$\dfrac{1}{10-1}$	= 1/9	= 11⅑ pct.
20 = 1/5	$\dfrac{1}{5-1}$	= 1/4	= 25
25 = 1/4	$\dfrac{1}{4-1}$	= 1/3	= 33⅓
30 = 3/10	$\dfrac{3}{10-3}$	= 3/7	= 42 6/7
35 = 7/20	$\dfrac{7}{20-7}$	= 7/13	= 53 11/13
40 = 2/5	$\dfrac{2}{5-2}$	= 2/3	= 66⅔
50 = 1/2	$\dfrac{1}{2-1}$	= 1	= 100
60 = 3/5	$\dfrac{3}{5-3}$	= 1½	= 150
75 = 3/4	$\dfrac{3}{4-3}$	= 3	= 300

This conversion can be reduced to a formula. If X equals the percentage of markon, and t equals the percentage added to cost, then:

$$t = \dfrac{X}{1-X}$$

Ch. 18   MATHEMATICS   355

2. Where we wish to know the markon percentages that result when various percentages are added to cost:
   a. Reduce the percentage added to cost to a fraction.
   b. Keeping the numerator of the fraction as is, increase the denominator by adding the numerator to the denominator.
   c. Convert the resulting fraction back into a percentage; this will be the markon percentage.

Illustration.
QUESTION: What markon percentage results from adding 80 per cent to cost?
PROCEDURE:
   (a) 80 per cent = $8/10$ or $4/5$.
   (b) Change $4/5$, as stated above, into $\dfrac{4}{5+4} = 4/9$.
   (c) $4/9$ equals $44\frac{4}{9}$ per cent.

ANSWER: Where 80 per cent is added to cost, markon percentage of $44\frac{4}{9}$ results.

PROOF:

Selling price	$100.00
Deduct: Markon	44.44
Cost	$ 55.56

Ratio of amount added to cost, $44.44/55.56 = 4/5 = 80$ per cent.

Summary of typical or common percentages converted in this manner:

Added to Cost   Percentages of Markon

10 pct. = $1/10$ $\dfrac{1}{10+1} = 1/11 = 9\frac{1}{11}$ pct.

20 = $1/5$ $\dfrac{1}{5+1} = 1/6 = 16\frac{2}{3}$

25 = $1/4$ $\dfrac{1}{4+1} = 1/5 = 20$

30 = $3/10$ $\dfrac{3}{10+3} = 3/13 = 23\frac{1}{13}$

35 = $7/20$ $\dfrac{7}{20+7} = 7/27 = 25\frac{25}{27}$

40 = $2/5$ $\dfrac{2}{5+2} = 2/7 = 28\frac{4}{7}$

50 = $1/2$ $\dfrac{1}{2+1} = 1/3 = 33\frac{1}{3}$

60 = $3/5$ $\dfrac{3}{5+3} = 3/8 = 37\frac{1}{2}$

70 = $7/10$ $\dfrac{7}{10+7} = 7/17 = 41\frac{3}{17}$

75 = $3/4$ $\dfrac{3}{4+3} = 3/7 = 42\frac{6}{7}$

Added to Cost		Percentages of Markon		
80	= 4/5	$\frac{4}{5+4}$	= 4/9	= 44 4/9
90	= 9/10	$\frac{9}{10+9}$	= 9/19	= 47 7/19
100	= 1/1	$\frac{1}{1+1}$	= 1/2	= 50
150	= 3/2	$\frac{3}{2+3}$	= 3/5	= 60

This conversion can also be reduced to a formula. If X equals the percentage of markon, and t equals the percentage added to cost, then:

$$X = \frac{t}{1+t}$$

Effect of Retail Stock Reductions

The two formulas just presented show relations between percentages added to cost and percentages of markon. As such they do not take into account retail stock reductions which principally comprise markdowns, shrinkages, discounts, and allowances. When no reductions are applied, the realized gross margin percentage is the same as the markon percentage. The application of retail stock reductions, however, results in a different situation. Departmental and storewide merchandise statistics reflect these reductions as a percentage of sales. Consequently, the practical question becomes the determination of the markon percentage that will result in a specified gross margin ratio after making allowance for all anticipated reductions. Logically, reductions relate to total merchandise in the departmental account; practically, they are stated in relation to sales.

Using:

1 as the original marked retail price,
x as the markon percentage,
y as the realized gross margin percentage, and
k as the ratio of total retail reductions to sales,

a formula may be developed based on the fact that the excess of markon percentage over the realized gross margin percentage equals the complement of the markon percentage times the percentage of reductions to sales. (Gross margin percentages in this chapter are before purchase discounts, unless otherwise stated.)

Using the symbols given above:

$$x - y = (1 - x)k$$
$$x - y = k - kx$$
$$x + kx = y + k$$
$$x(1 + k) = y + k$$
$$x = \frac{y + k}{1 + k}$$

Given this formula, a buyer can determine the initial markon that must be established to realize a gross margin which realistically gives effect to the subsequent retail reductions that can be expected to occur. As a typical example, what markon percentage must be used in order to realize a gross margin percentage of 35, after giving appropriate effect to the markdown, shrinkage, and allowance experience of 10 per cent on sales? The answer can readily be worked out from the formula, by inserting known percentages, as follows:

$$x = \frac{.35 + .10}{1 + .10} = \frac{.45}{1.10} = 40.91 \text{ per cent}$$

PROOF:

	Cost	Retail
Opening inventory and purchases	$118.18	$200.00
Sales		75.00
Reductions (10 per cent on sales)		7.50
		82.50
Closing inventory, retail		$117.50
Closing inventory, cost, 100 − 40.91 = 59.09 per cent of retail	$69.43	
Sales		$ 75.00
Cost of sales ($118.18 less closing inventory of $69.43)		48.75
Gross margin		$ 26.25

which is 35 per cent of sales of $75, as was assumed.

Table III (page 372) applies this formula to common gross margin percentages and percentages of reductions.

The buyer may decide that competitive conditions warrant the establishment of only a 40 per cent markon. Accordingly, the question may be the determination of the percentage of retail stock reductions that will permit a maintained gross margin of 36 per cent, given the 40 per cent markon.

This question also may be answered readily on the basis of the above formula. x and y are known, and k is the factor to be determined. So we recast the formula into:

$$x + xk = y + k$$
$$x - y = k - xk$$
$$x - y = k(1 - x)$$
$$k = \frac{x - y}{1 - x} = \frac{.40 - .36}{1 - .40} = \frac{.04}{.6} = 6\tfrac{2}{3} \text{ per cent}$$

PROOF:

	Cost	Retail
Opening inventory and purchases	$120.00	$200.00
Sales		75.00
Reductions (6⅔ per cent on sales)		5.00
		80.00
Closing inventory, retail		$120.00
Closing inventory, cost, 100 − 40 = 60 per cent of retail	$72.00	
Sales		$ 75.00
Cost of sales ($120 less $72)		48.00
Gross margin		$ 27.00

which is 36 per cent on sales, as was assumed.

Table IV (page 373) applies this formula to a range of markon and maintained gross margin percentages.

Effect of Workroom Loss or Expense

In addition to the problem of retail stock reductions, retailers must also consider departmental workroom expenses in determining realized gross margins. Workroom costs represent charges for service, repair, or alteration which effectively make merchandise ready for delivery. Retailers must provide for the absorption of these costs in calculating markon. The accounting for workrooms is discussed in Chapter 14.

The following example illustrates how adequate provision for workroom costs can be made in the determination of the departmental markon percentage.

Using:

w as the percentage of workroom costs to sales,
1 as the original marked retail price,
x as the markon percentage,
y as the realized gross margin percentage, and
k as the ratio of total retail reductions to sales,

the formula is:

$$x = \frac{w + y + k}{1 + k}$$

As a typical example, what percentage of markon must a buyer use in order to realize a gross margin percentage of 36, in a department where, based upon experience, retail reductions run 10 per cent on sales, and workroom costs run 2½ per cent on sales? On the basis of the preceding formula:

$$x = \frac{.025 + .36 + .10}{1 + .10} = \frac{.485}{1.10} = 44.09 \text{ per cent}$$

PROOF:

	Cost	Retail
Opening inventory plus purchases	$5,591.00 *	$10,000.00
Workroom costs, 2½ per cent of sales	125.00	
Sales		5,000.00
Reductions, 10 per cent on sales		500.00
		5,500.00
Closing inventory, at retail		$ 4,500.00
Closing inventory, at cost, 55.91 per cent of retail	$2,516.00	
Sales		$5,000.00
Cost of sales:		
Opening inventory plus purchases	5,591.00	
Less: Closing inventory	2,516.00	
	3,075.00	
Workroom costs	125.00	3,200.00
Gross margin		$1,800.00

which is 36 per cent on sales, as was assumed.

* (100 − 44.09) per cent of retail.

Table V (pages 374 and 375) applies this formula to a typical range of gross margins, workroom costs, and retail stock reductions.

In some instances, the problem at issue will be the determination of the maximum workroom expense (as a percentage of sales) that can be incurred given a reasonably definitive percentage of retail reductions to sales and a minimum predetermined gross margin percentage deemed acceptable by the retailer. The formula may then be recast as follows:

$$\frac{w + y + k}{1 + k} = x$$
$$w + y + k = x(1 + k)$$
$$w = x - y - k + kx$$
$$w = x - y - k(1 - x)$$

Assuming a gross markon of 39 per cent, and combined markdowns and stock shrinkages of 11 per cent of sales, what is the maximum allowable workroom expense, if 30 per cent gross margin is to be realized?

$$w = .39 - .30 - .11(1 - .39) = .0229$$

The answer, therefore, is 2.29 per cent of sales.

PROOF:

	Cost	Retail
Opening inventory plus purchases	$6,100.00	$10,000.00
Sales		5,000.00
Reductions		550.00
		5,550.00
Inventory at retail		$ 4,450.00
Inventory at cost, 61 per cent of inventory at retail	$2,714.50	
Sales		$ 5,000.00
Cost of sales:		
Opening inventory plus purchases	6,100.00	
Less: Closing inventory	2,714.50	
	3,385.50	
Add: Workroom expense, maximum 2.29 per cent of sales (2.29 per cent of $5,000)	114.50	3,500.00
Gross margin		$ 1,500.00

which is 30 per cent of sales, as was assumed.

Added Discounts and Loading

If a store applies added discounts to invoices (see Chapter 8), retailers have a further complication to consider in determining percentage or amount to add to prime cost. It also may be necessary to include as an element of cost a percentage or an amount of loading for duty, freight, insurance, or other costs and expenses.

Let

- a = percentage of added discount to be added to prime cost
- s = percentage to be added to prime cost to produce desired percentage of gross margin to be realized, including both prime cost and added discount as elements of cost
- b = percentage of loading for duty, freight, insurance, or other costs and expenses to be added to prime cost
- r = percentage to be added to prime cost to produce desired percentage of gross margin to be realized, including both prime cost and loading as elements of cost

It should be noted that these four symbols are expressed as percentages of prime cost, whereas symbols used previously in this chapter were percentages of sales.

A problem involving both added discounts and loading, as well as workroom expense, will be worked out later in this chapter; simpler problems involving the elements separately are illustrated first.

Added Discounts. The percentage to be added to prime cost to produce a desired percentage of gross margin to be realized, including both added discount and prime cost as elements of cost, equals markon percentage divided by cost, which equals 1 minus markon percentage (where 1 is original marked retail price), plus added discount percentage (on prime cost), also divided by cost (or 1 minus markon percentage). Expressed in a formula the relation is:

$$s = \frac{x}{1-x} + \frac{a}{1-x} = \frac{x+a}{1-x}$$

If there are reductions, we can substitute for x its equivalent, $\frac{y+k}{1+k}$:

$$s = \frac{\frac{y+k}{1+k} + a}{1 - \frac{(y+k)}{(1+k)}}$$

362　RETAIL ACCOUNTING AND FINANCIAL CONTROL　Ch. 18

QUESTION: What percentage must be added to prime cost so that, with an added discount of 5 per cent on prime cost, and retail stock reductions of 10 per cent on sales, gross margin of 40 per cent may be realized?

$$s = \frac{\frac{.40 + .10}{1 + .10} + .05}{1 - \frac{(.40 + .10)}{(1 + .10)}} = \frac{.50 + .055}{1.10 - .50} = \frac{.555}{.60} = .925$$

ANSWER: 92½ per cent must be added to prime cost if, after inclusion of a 5 per cent added discount (on prime cost) as part of cost, and after reductions of 10 per cent on sales, 40 per cent gross margin is to be realized.

PROOF:

	Cost	Retail
Opening inventory and purchases, at prime cost	$1,000.00	$1,925.00
Added discounts	50.00	
	$1,050.00	1,925.00
Sales		600.00
Reductions		60.00
		660.00
Closing inventory at retail		$1,265.00

Closing inventory at cost:

$\frac{1,050}{1,925} \times \$1,265 =$　　　　　$690.00

Sales		$ 600.00
Cost of sales:		
Opening inventory plus purchases and added discounts	$1,050.00	
Less: Closing inventory	690.00	360.00
Gross margin		$ 240.00

which is 40 per cent, as was assumed.

Loading. Now assume a store which does not use added discounts but has a department where foreign purchases require that prime cost be loaded for duty, freight, insurance, and other expenses.

QUESTION: Assuming a loading factor of 30 per cent on prime cost and retail stock reductions of 12½ per cent on sales, what percentage must be added to prime cost to realize a 40 per cent gross margin?

Using the formula:

$$r = \frac{\frac{y+k}{1+k}+b}{1-\frac{(y+k)}{(1+k)}} = \frac{\frac{.40+.125}{1+.125}+.30}{1-\frac{(.40+.125)}{(1+.125)}} = \frac{.525+.3375}{1.125-.525} = \frac{.8625}{.60} = 1.4375$$

ANSWER: 143¾ per cent must be added to prime cost.

PROOF:

	Cost	Retail
Opening inventory plus purchases at prime cost	$1,000.00	$2,437.50
Loading	300.00	
	$1,300.00	2,437.50
Sales		1,000.00
Reductions		125.00
		1,125.00
Closing inventory at retail		$1,312.50

Closing inventory at cost:

$\frac{1{,}300.00}{2{,}437.50} \times \$1{,}312.50 =$ $ 700.00

Sales $1,000.00

Cost of sales:
Opening inventory plus purchases
and loading $1,300.00
Less: Closing inventory   700.00   600.00

Gross margin $ 400.00

which is 40 per cent on sales, as was assumed.

See Table VI (pages 376 and 377) for application of this formula to a range of common gross margin, loading, and retail stock reduction percentages.

All Factors Previously Mentioned

At this point, let us take one final problem which involves all the factors previously mentioned.

Assume loading of 30 per cent on prime cost; added discount of 5 per cent on prime cost plus loading; retail stock reductions of 10 per cent on sales; and workroom costs and expenses equal to 4 per cent on sales. What percentage must be added to prime cost in order to realize gross margin of 36 per cent?

$$r = \frac{\dfrac{w+y+k}{1+k} + b + a(1+b)}{1 - \dfrac{w+y+k}{1+k}} = \frac{\dfrac{.04+.36+.10}{1+.10} + .30 + .05(1+.30)}{1 - \dfrac{(.04+.36+.10)}{(1+.10)}}$$

$$= \frac{.50 + 1.10(.30+.065)}{1.10-.50} = \frac{.50+1.10(.365)}{.60} = \frac{.9015}{.60} = 1.5025$$

Answer: 150¼ per cent must be added to prime cost, in order that, after loading of 30 per cent, and added discount of 5 per cent on prime cost plus loading, and retail stock reductions and workroom costs of 10 and 4 per cent, respectively, on sales, 36 per cent gross margin may be realized.

Proof:

	Cost	Retail
Opening inventory plus purchases at prime cost	$10,000.00	$25,025.00
Loading	3,000.00	
	13,000.00	
Added discounts	650.00	
	$13,650.00	25,025.00
Sales		15,000.00
Reductions		1,500.00
		16,500.00
Closing inventory at retail		$ 8,525.00
Closing inventory at cost $\left(\dfrac{13,650}{25,025} \times \$8,525\right)$	$ 4,650.00	
Sales		$15,000.00
Cost of sales:		
Opening inventory plus purchases, plus loading and added discounts	$13,650.00	
Less: Closing inventory	4,650.00	
	9,000.00	
Workroom costs and expenses (4 per cent on sales)	600.00	9,600.00
Gross margin		$ 5,400.00

which is 36 per cent on sales, as was assumed.

If the store in the foregoing illustration does not use added discounts, the formula becomes:

$$r = \frac{\dfrac{w+y+k}{1+k} + b}{1 - \dfrac{w+y+k}{1+k}}$$

Using the same data, except as to added discounts, i.e., $b = 30$ per cent, $k = 10$ per cent, $y = 36$ per cent, $w = 4$ per cent, then

$$r = \frac{\dfrac{.04 + .36 + .10}{1 + .10} + .30}{1 - \dfrac{.04 + .36 + .10}{1 + .10}} = \frac{.50 + .33}{1.10 - .50} = \frac{.83}{.60} = 1.3833\tfrac{1}{3}$$

ANSWER: 138⅓ per cent must be added to prime cost.
PROOF:

	Cost	Retail
Prime cost	$10,000.00	$23,833.33
Loading	3,000.00	
	$13,000.00	23,833.33
Sales		15,000.00
Reductions		1,500.00
		16,500.00
Closing inventory at retail		$ 7,333.33
Closing inventory at cost $\left(\dfrac{13,000.00}{23,833.33} \times \$7,333.33\right)$	$ 4,000.00	
Sales		$15,000.00
Cost of sales:		
Prime cost plus loading	$13,000.00	
Less: Closing inventory	4,000.00	
	9,000.00	
Workroom costs and expenses (4 per cent on sales)	600.00	9,600.00
Gross margin		$ 5,400.00

which is 36 per cent on sales, as was assumed.

Use of Table To Cover Workroom Costs

Table VI (pages 376 and 377) may also be used if net workroom cost, expressed as a percentage of sales, is a factor in determining the original pricing. Under these circumstances, the percentage of net workroom costs is added to the percentage of gross margin to be maintained and the table is used as before. For example, if a retailer desires to know the percentage to add to cost to realize 30 per cent gross margin in a situation where 10 per cent is to be added to invoice cost to cover foreign buying expense and where merchandise reductions average 8 per cent of sales, Table VI, opposite 30 per cent (first column) and 10 per cent (second column) and under 8 per cent merchandise reductions, supplies the answer: 69.71 per cent. If, in addition, net workroom costs average 2 per cent of sales, this is added to the gross margin of 30 per cent to be maintained, and the answer appears opposite 32 per cent (first column) and 10 per cent (second column) and under 8 per cent merchandise reductions, or 74.71 per cent.

If the problem is one of determining the markon percentage (assuming that cost includes prime cost, plus loading, plus added discounts, on a base of prime cost plus loading), the formula is as follows:

$$x = \frac{r - a - ab - b}{1 + r}$$

Using the data from the example on page 364:

$$x = \frac{1.5025 - .05 - .015 - .30}{2.5025} = \frac{1.1375}{2.5025} = 45.45 \text{ per cent}$$

This is in accord with the example on page 364, as follows:

$$\text{Markon percentage} = \frac{\$25,025 - \$13,650}{\$25,025} = 45.45 \text{ per cent}$$

as developed above.

Other Formulas

Gross Margin. Certain gross margin and other relationships and ratios, discussed elsewhere in this book, are set forth below for ease of reference. With respect to gross margin, a distinction should be made between (1) gross margin before discounts; and (2) gross margin including discounts.

1. Gross margin before discounts is the difference between net sales and total merchandise costs, with the latter comprising purchases including transportation inward and net alteration and workroom costs, less any increase in inventories or plus any decrease in inventories.

The percentage of gross margin before discounts equals the cumulative markon percentage before discounts, less the complement of the cumulative markon percentage (i.e., cost multiplier) times the retail stock reduction percentage, less the net workroom and alteration costs percentage.

2. Gross margin including discounts is the difference between net sales and total merchandise costs, with the latter comprising

purchases including transportation inward, and net alteration and workroom costs, less any increase in inventories or plus any decrease in inventories, and less discounts earned on merchandise sold.

The percentage of gross margin including discounts equals the cumulative markon percentage, plus the percentage of earned discounts, less the complement of the cumulative markon percentage (i.e., cost multiplier) times the retail stock reduction percentage, less the net workroom and alteration costs percentage.

Illustration. Let

x = markon percentage before discounts
y = gross margin percentage before discounts
d = percentage of discounts earned
z = gross margin including discounts = $y + d$
k = percentage of retail stock reductions
w = percentage of net workroom and alteration costs

Let $x = 41.5$ per cent, $d = 3.5$ per cent, $k = 6.5$ per cent, and $w = 1.2$ per cent.

CASE 1.

y (gross margin percentage before discounts) $= x - (1 - x)k - w$
$y = 41.5 - (58.5)(6.5) - 1.2$
$ = 41.5 - 3.8025 - 1.2$
$ = 36.4975$

Gross margin before discounts $= 36.4975$ per cent
Discounts earned $= 3.5000$
Gross margin including discounts $= 39.9975$ per cent

CASE 2.

$z = y + d = x + d - (1 - x)k - w$
$z = y + 3.5 = 41.5 + 3.5 - (58.5)(6.5) - 1.2$
$z = y + 3.5 = 45. - 3.8025 - 1.2 = 45. - 5.0025$
$ = 39.9975$

Gross margin including discounts $= 39.9975$ per cent

PROOF: Assume sales of $10,000,000 and opening inventory and purchases of $12,000,000 at retail.

	At Mercantile	At Retail
Opening inventory and purchases	$7,020,000	$12,000,000
Sales		10,000,000
Reductions		650,000
		10,650,000
Closing inventory at retail		$ 1,350,000
Closing inventory at mercantile, 58.5 per cent of $1,350,000	$ 789,750	
Sales		$10,000,000
Cost of sales:		
Opening inventory and purchases	$7,020,000	
Less: Closing inventory	789,750	
	6,230,250	
Workroom and alteration costs, net	120,000	6,350,250
Gross margin, before discounts		3,649,750
Discounts earned		350,000
Gross margin, including discounts		$ 3,999,750

which is 39.9975 per cent on sales.

Merchandise Turnover. To derive merchandise turnover, divide sales by the average inventory at retail. (See Chapter 7.)

Purchase Markon. Planned markon, either in dollars or as a percentage, should be not less than the quotient of the sum of planned markdowns, shrinkages, and sales discounts, plus planned expenses and planned profit, divided by the sum of planned sales, markdowns, shrinkages, and sales discounts. (See Chapter 5.)

In effect, the aggregate of markdowns, shrinkages, and sales discounts comprises the retail stock reductions.

Assume sales of $10,000,000; retail stock reductions of 6.5 per cent, or $650,000; expenses of 30 per cent, or $3,000,000 (including therein net alteration and workroom costs); planned profit of 7 per cent, or $700,000. Purchase markon required may be worked out as follows in percentages and in dollars.

	In Percentages		In Dollars	
Retail stock reductions	6.5%		$ 650,000	
Expenses	30.0		3,000,000	
Profit	7.0	43.5%	700,000	$ 4,350,000
Divided by:				
Sales	100.0		10,000,000	
Retail stock reductions	6.5	106.5	650,000	$10,650,000
Equals purchase markon		40.845%		$ 4,084,500

PROOF:
Gross margin (before discounts) as per preceding formula = 40.845 − (59.155 × 6.5) = 40.845 − 3.845
= 37 per cent

Sales	$10,000,000
Gross margin (37 per cent)	$ 3,700,000
Expenses (30 per cent)	3,000,000
Income (7 per cent, as assumed)	$ 700,000

Loaded or Added Discounts. Where loaded or added discounts are used, the amount to be loaded on cost equals gross cost times a percentage rate obtained by dividing the department discount rate minus the invoice discount rate, by 1 minus the department discount rate. (See Chapter 8.)

Let

a = percentage of cost to be loaded on cost
j = department discount rate
d = invoice discount rate

$$a = \frac{j - d}{1 - j}$$

Conversion of Discount Ratios from Sales to Purchases. On a gross margin statement, discounts earned appear in relation to sales, but one naturally thinks of discounts as related to purchases.

The approximate ratio of discounts earned to purchases may be derived by first deriving the percentage of original retail to sales—that is, the percentage of sales plus retail stock reductions to sales—and then dividing the discount percentage on sales by this percentage of sales plus retail stock reductions to sales, and then dividing the result by the complement of the markon percentage (i.e., the cost multiplier). (See Chapter 8.)

Tables

Utilizing the previously cited formulas, Tables I–VI have been prepared, expressed to the nearest one-hundredth of one per cent. While not complete, these tables are sufficiently representative to be of practical assistance to prospective users. The symbols utilized in these tables are explained on the following page.

x = markon percentage
t = percentage added to cost
y = percentage of gross margin to be realized (before discounts)
k = percentage of retail stock reductions (markdowns, shrinkages, discounts, and allowances) to sales
w = percentage of workroom costs (exclusive of charges included with purchases) to sales
a = percentage of added discount to be added to prime cost, or to be added to prime cost plus loading when loading is used
s = percentage to be added to prime cost to produce desired percentage of gross margin to be realized, including both prime cost and added discount as elements of cost
b = percentage of loading for duty, freight, insurance, or other costs and expenses to be added to prime cost
r = percentage to be added to prime cost to produce desired percentage of gross margin to be realized, including both prime cost and loading (and also added discount if used) as elements of cost.

TABLE I. Percentages of Cost To Be Added To Produce Specified Percentages of Markon

Formula: $t = \dfrac{x}{1-x}$

Desired Percentages of Markon	Percentages of Cost to be Added	Desired Percentages of Markon	Percentages of Cost to be Added
25%	33.33%	38%	61.29%
26	35.14	39	63.93
27	36.99	40	66.67
28	38.89	41	69.49
29	40.85	42	72.41
30	42.86	43	75.44
31	44.93	44	78.57
32	47.06	45	81.82
33	49.25	46	85.19
33⅓	50.00	47	88.68
34	51.52	48	92.31
35	53.85	49	96.08
36	56.25	50	100.00
37	58.73	60	150.00

TABLE II. Percentages of Markon Produced from Addition of Specified Percentages to Cost

Formula: $x = \dfrac{t}{1+t}$

Percentages Added to Cost	Resulting Percentages of Markon	Percentages Added to Cost	Resulting Percentages of Markon
30%	23.08%	65%	39.39%
32½	24.53	66⅔	40.00
33⅓	25.00	67½	40.30
35	25.93	70	41.18
36	26.47	72½	42.03
37½	27.27	75	42.86
40	28.57	77½	43.66
41⅔	29.41	80	44.44
42½	29.82	82½	45.21
45	31.03	83⅓	45.45
47½	32.20	85	45.95
50	33.33	87½	46.67
52½	34.43	90	47.37
55	35.48	92½	48.05
57½	36.51	95	48.72
60	37.50	97½	49.37
62½	38.46	100	50.00

TABLE III. Percentages of Markon Required To Produce Specified Percentages of Gross Margin Where Retail Merchandise Reductions Are Stated as Percentages of Net Sales

Formula: $x = \dfrac{y+k}{1+k}$

Percentages of Gross Margin to be Realized	\multicolumn{8}{c}{Percentages of Retail Merchandise Reductions to Net Sales}
	5%	6%	7%	8%	9%	10%	11%	12%
	\multicolumn{8}{c}{Percentages of Markon Required}
25%	28.57	29.25	29.91	30.56	31.19	31.82	32.43	33.04
26	29.52	30.19	30.84	31.48	32.11	32.73	33.33	33.93
27	30.48	31.13	31.78	32.41	33.03	33.64	34.23	34.82
28	31.43	32.08	32.71	33.33	33.94	34.55	35.14	35.71
29	32.38	33.02	33.64	34.26	34.86	35.45	36.04	36.61
30	33.33	33.96	34.58	35.19	35.78	36.36	36.94	37.50
31	34.29	34.91	35.51	36.11	36.70	37.27	37.84	38.39
32	35.24	35.85	36.45	37.04	37.61	38.18	38.74	39.29
33	36.19	36.79	37.38	37.96	38.53	39.09	39.64	40.18
34	37.14	37.74	38.32	38.89	39.45	40.00	40.54	41.07
35	38.10	38.68	39.25	39.81	40.37	40.91	41.44	41.96
36	39.05	39.62	40.19	40.74	41.28	41.82	42.34	42.86
37	40.00	40.57	41.12	41.67	42.20	42.73	43.24	43.75
38	40.95	41.51	42.06	42.59	43.12	43.64	44.14	44.64
39	41.90	42.45	42.99	43.52	44.04	44.55	45.05	45.54
40	42.86	43.40	43.93	44.44	44.95	45.45	45.95	46.43
41	43.81	44.34	44.86	45.37	45.87	46.36	46.85	47.32
42	44.76	45.28	45.79	46.30	46.79	47.27	47.75	48.21
43	45.71	46.23	46.73	47.22	47.71	48.18	48.65	49.11
44	46.66	47.17	47.66	48.15	48.62	49.09	49.55	50.00
45	47.62	48.11	48.60	49.07	49.54	50.00	50.45	50.89

TABLE IV. Maximum Allowable Percentages of Retail Merchandise Reductions To Net Sales To Maintain Specified Percentages of Gross Margin on Given Percentages of Markon

Formula: $k = \dfrac{x - y}{1 - x}$

Percentages of Markon	\multicolumn{8}{c}{Percentages of Gross Margin to be Maintained}
	23%	24%	25%	26%	27%	28%	29%	30%
	\multicolumn{8}{c}{Maximum Allowable Percentages of Retail Merchandise Reductions to Net Sales}
30%	10.00	8.57	7.14	5.71	4.29	2.86	1.43	—
31	11.59	10.14	8.70	7.25	5.80	4.35	2.90	1.45
32	13.24	11.76	10.29	8.82	7.35	5.88	4.41	2.94
33	14.93	13.43	11.94	10.45	8.96	7.46	5.97	4.48
34	16.67	15.15	13.64	12.12	10.61	9.09	7.58	6.06

	29%	30%	31%	32%	33%	34%	35%	36%
	\multicolumn{8}{c}{Percentages of Gross Margin to be Maintained}
	\multicolumn{8}{c}{Maximum Allowable Percentages of Retail Merchandise Reductions to Net Sales}
35	9.23	7.69	6.15	4.62	3.08	1.54	—	—
36	10.94	9.38	7.81	6.25	4.69	3.13	1.56	—
37	12.70	11.11	9.52	7.94	6.35	4.76	3.17	1.59
38	14.52	12.90	11.29	9.68	8.06	6.45	4.84	3.23
39	16.39	14.75	13.11	11.48	9.84	8.20	6.56	4.92
40	18.33	16.67	15.00	13.33	11.67	10.00	8.33	6.67

	35%	36%	37%	38%	39%	40%	41%	42%
	\multicolumn{8}{c}{Percentages of Gross Margin to be Maintained}
	\multicolumn{8}{c}{Maximum Allowable Percentages of Retail Merchandise Reductions to Net Sales}
41	10.17	8.47	6.78	5.08	3.39	1.70	—	—
42	12.07	10.34	8.62	6.90	5.17	3.45	1.72	—
43	14.04	12.28	10.53	8.77	7.02	5.26	3.51	1.75
44	16.07	14.29	12.50	10.71	8.93	7.14	5.36	3.57
45	18.18	16.36	14.55	12.73	10.91	9.09	7.28	5.45

	40%	41%	42%	43%	44%	45%	46%	47%
	\multicolumn{8}{c}{Percentages of Gross Margin to be Maintained}
	\multicolumn{8}{c}{Maximum Allowable Percentages of Retail Merchandise Reductions to Net Sales}
46	11.11	9.26	7.41	5.56	3.70	1.85	—	—
47	13.21	11.33	9.43	7.55	5.66	3.77	1.89	—
48	15.38	13.46	11.54	9.62	7.69	5.77	3.85	1.92
49	17.65	15.69	13.73	11.76	9.80	7.84	5.88	3.92
50	20.00	18.00	16.00	14.00	12.00	10.00	8.00	6.00

TABLE V. Percentages of Markon Required To Produce Specified Percentages of Gross Margin Where Total Retail Merchandise Reductions and Net Workroom Costs Are Stated as Percentages of Net Sales

Formula: $x = \dfrac{w + y + k}{1 + k}$

Percentages of Gross Margin to be Maintained	Percentages of Net Workroom Costs to Sales	5%	6%	7%	8%	9%	10%	11%	12%
						Percentages of Markon Required			
26%	½	30.00	30.66	31.31	31.94	32.57	33.18	33.78	34.38
	1	30.48	31.13	31.78	32.41	33.03	33.64	34.23	34.82
	1½	30.95	31.60	32.24	32.87	33.49	34.09	34.68	35.27
	2	31.43	32.08	32.71	33.33	33.94	34.55	35.14	35.71
27	½	30.95	31.60	32.24	32.87	33.49	34.09	34.68	35.27
	1	31.43	32.08	32.71	33.33	33.94	34.55	35.14	35.71
	1½	31.90	32.55	33.18	33.80	34.40	35.00	35.59	36.16
	2	32.38	33.02	33.64	34.26	34.86	35.45	36.04	36.61
28	½	31.90	32.55	33.18	33.80	34.40	35.00	35.59	36.16
	1	32.38	33.02	33.64	34.26	34.86	35.45	36.04	36.61
	1½	32.86	33.49	34.11	34.72	35.32	35.91	36.49	37.05
	2	33.33	33.96	34.58	35.19	35.78	36.36	36.94	37.50
29	½	32.86	33.49	34.11	34.72	35.32	35.91	36.49	37.05
	1	33.33	33.96	34.58	35.19	35.78	36.36	36.94	37.50
	1½	33.81	34.43	35.05	35.65	36.24	36.82	37.39	37.95
	2	34.29	34.91	35.51	36.11	36.70	37.27	37.84	38.39
30	½	33.81	34.43	35.05	35.65	36.24	36.82	37.39	37.95
	1	34.29	34.91	35.51	36.11	36.70	37.27	37.84	38.39
	1½	34.76	35.38	35.98	36.57	37.16	37.73	38.29	38.84
	2	35.24	35.85	36.45	37.04	37.61	38.18	38.74	39.29
31	½	34.76	35.38	35.98	36.57	37.16	37.73	38.29	38.84
	1	35.24	35.85	36.45	37.04	37.61	38.18	38.74	39.29
	1½	35.71	36.32	36.92	37.50	38.07	38.64	39.19	39.73
	2	36.19	36.79	37.38	37.96	38.53	39.09	39.64	40.18

		5%	6%	7%	8%	9%	10%	11%	12%
32	½	35.71	36.32	36.92	37.50	38.07	38.64	39.19	39.73
	1	36.19	36.79	37.38	37.96	38.53	39.09	39.64	40.18
	1½	36.67	37.26	37.85	38.43	38.99	39.55	40.09	40.63
	2	37.14	37.74	38.32	38.89	39.45	40.00	40.54	41.07
33	½	36.67	37.26	37.85	38.43	38.99	39.55	40.09	40.63
	1	37.14	37.74	38.32	38.89	39.45	40.00	40.54	41.07
	1½	37.62	38.21	38.79	39.35	39.91	40.45	40.99	41.52
	2	38.10	38.68	39.25	39.81	40.37	40.91	41.44	41.96
34	½	37.62	38.21	38.79	39.35	39.91	40.45	40.99	41.52
	1	38.10	38.68	39.25	39.81	40.37	40.91	41.44	41.96
	1½	38.57	39.15	39.72	40.28	40.83	41.36	41.89	42.41
	2	39.05	39.62	40.19	40.74	41.28	41.82	42.34	42.86
35	½	38.57	39.15	39.72	40.28	40.83	41.36	41.89	42.41
	1	39.05	39.62	40.19	40.74	41.28	41.82	42.34	42.86
	1½	39.52	40.09	40.65	41.20	41.74	42.27	42.79	43.30
	2	40.00	40.57	41.12	41.67	42.20	42.73	43.24	43.75
36	½	39.52	40.09	40.65	41.20	41.74	42.27	42.79	43.30
	1	40.00	40.57	41.12	41.67	42.20	42.73	43.24	43.75
	1½	40.48	41.04	41.59	42.13	42.66	43.18	43.69	44.20
	2	40.95	41.51	42.06	42.59	43.12	43.64	44.14	44.64
37	½	40.48	41.04	41.59	42.13	42.66	43.18	43.69	44.20
	1	40.95	41.51	42.06	42.59	43.12	43.64	44.14	44.64
	1½	41.43	41.98	42.52	43.06	43.58	44.09	44.59	45.09
	2	41.90	42.45	42.99	43.52	44.04	44.55	45.05	45.54
38	½	41.43	41.98	42.52	43.06	43.58	44.09	44.59	45.09
	1	41.90	42.45	42.99	43.52	44.04	44.55	45.05	45.54
	1½	42.38	42.92	43.46	43.98	44.50	45.00	45.50	45.98
	2	42.86	43.40	43.93	44.44	44.95	45.45	45.95	46.43
39	½	42.38	42.92	43.46	43.98	44.50	45.00	45.50	45.98
	1	42.86	43.40	43.93	44.44	44.95	45.45	45.95	46.43
	1½	43.33	43.87	44.39	44.91	45.41	45.91	46.40	46.88
	2	43.81	44.34	44.86	45.37	45.87	46.36	46.85	47.32
40	½	43.33	43.87	44.39	44.91	45.41	45.91	46.40	46.88
	1	43.81	44.34	44.86	45.37	45.87	46.36	46.85	47.32
	1½	44.29	44.81	45.33	45.83	46.33	46.82	47.30	47.77
	2	44.76	45.28	45.79	46.30	46.79	47.27	47.75	48.21

TABLE VI. Percentages To Be Added to Prime Cost To Produce Specified Percentages of Gross Margin, Including in Cost Loading Percentages on Prime Cost for Duty, Buying Expense, Etc., Where Retail Merchandise Reductions Are Stated as Percentages of Net Sales

Formula: $r = \dfrac{\dfrac{(y+k)}{(1+k)} + b}{1 - \dfrac{(y+k)}{(1+k)}}$

Percentages of Gross Margin to be Maintained	Percentages of Loading on Prime Cost	5%	6%	7%	8%	9%	10%	11%	12%
					Percentages of Merchandise Reductions to Sales				
				Percentages to be Added to Prime Cost					
29%	10%	62.68	64.23	65.77	67.32	68.87	70.42	71.97	73.52
	20	77.46	79.15	80.85	82.54	84.23	85.92	87.61	89.30
	25	84.86	86.62	88.38	90.14	91.90	93.66	95.42	97.18
	33⅓	97.18	99.06	100.94	102.82	104.69	106.57	108.45	110.33
	40	107.04	109.01	110.99	112.96	114.93	116.90	118.87	120.85
	50	121.83	123.94	126.06	128.17	130.28	132.39	134.51	136.62
30	10	65.00	66.57	68.14	69.71	71.29	72.86	74.43	76.00
	20	80.00	81.71	83.43	85.14	86.86	88.57	90.29	92.00
	25	87.50	89.29	91.07	92.86	94.64	96.43	98.21	100.00
	33⅓	100.00	101.90	103.81	105.71	107.62	109.52	111.43	113.33
	40	110.00	112.00	114.00	116.00	118.00	120.00	122.00	124.00
	50	125.00	127.14	129.29	131.43	133.57	135.71	137.86	140.00
31	10	67.39	68.99	70.58	72.17	73.77	75.36	76.96	78.55
	20	82.61	84.35	86.09	87.83	89.57	91.30	93.04	94.78
	25	90.22	92.03	93.84	95.65	97.46	99.28	101.09	102.90
	33⅓	102.90	104.83	106.76	108.70	110.63	112.56	114.49	116.43
	40	113.04	115.07	117.10	119.13	121.16	123.19	125.22	127.25
	50	128.26	130.43	132.61	134.78	136.96	139.13	141.30	143.48
32	10	69.85	71.47	73.09	74.71	76.32	77.94	79.56	81.18
	20	85.29	87.06	88.82	90.59	92.35	94.12	95.88	97.65
	25	93.01	94.85	96.69	98.53	100.37	102.21	104.04	105.88
	33⅓	105.88	107.84	109.80	111.76	113.73	115.69	117.65	119.61
	40	116.18	118.24	120.29	122.35	124.41	126.47	128.53	130.59
	50	131.62	133.82	136.03	138.24	140.44	142.65	144.85	147.06

		5%	6%	7%	8%	9%	10%	11%	12%
33	10	72.39	74.03	75.67	77.31	78.96	80.60	82.24	83.88
	20	88.06	89.85	91.64	93.43	95.22	97.01	98.81	100.60
	25	95.90	97.76	99.63	101.49	103.36	105.22	107.09	108.96
	33⅓	108.96	110.95	112.94	114.93	116.92	118.91	120.90	122.89
	40	119.40	121.49	123.58	125.67	127.76	129.85	131.94	134.03
	50	135.07	137.31	139.55	141.79	144.03	146.27	148.51	150.75
34	10	75.00	76.67	78.33	80.00	81.67	83.33	85.00	86.67
	20	90.91	92.73	94.55	96.36	98.18	100.00	101.82	103.64
	25	98.86	100.76	102.65	104.55	106.44	108.33	110.23	112.12
	33⅓	112.12	114.14	116.16	118.18	120.20	122.22	124.24	126.26
	40	122.73	124.85	126.97	129.09	131.21	133.33	135.45	137.58
	50	138.64	140.91	143.18	145.45	147.73	150.00	152.27	154.55
35	10	77.69	79.38	81.08	82.77	84.46	86.15	87.85	89.54
	20	93.85	95.69	97.54	99.38	101.23	103.08	104.92	106.77
	25	101.92	103.85	105.77	107.69	109.62	111.54	113.46	115.38
	33⅓	115.38	117.44	119.49	121.54	123.59	125.64	127.69	129.74
	40	126.15	128.31	130.46	132.62	134.77	136.92	139.08	141.23
	50	142.31	144.62	146.92	149.23	151.54	153.85	156.15	158.46
36	10	80.47	82.19	83.91	85.63	87.34	89.06	90.78	92.50
	20	96.88	98.75	100.63	102.50	104.38	106.25	108.13	110.00
	25	105.08	107.03	108.98	110.94	112.89	114.84	116.80	118.75
	33⅓	118.75	120.83	122.92	125.00	127.08	129.17	131.25	133.33
	40	129.69	131.88	134.06	136.25	138.44	140.63	142.81	145.00
	50	146.09	148.44	150.78	153.13	155.47	157.81	160.16	162.50
37	10	83.33	85.08	86.83	88.57	90.32	92.06	93.81	95.56
	20	100.00	101.90	103.81	105.71	107.62	109.52	111.43	113.33
	25	108.33	110.32	112.30	114.29	116.27	118.25	120.24	122.22
	33⅓	122.22	124.34	126.46	128.57	130.69	132.80	134.92	137.04
	40	133.33	135.56	137.78	140.00	142.22	144.44	146.67	148.89
	50	150.00	152.38	154.76	157.14	159.52	161.90	164.29	166.67
38	10	86.29	88.06	89.84	91.61	93.39	95.16	96.94	98.71
	20	103.23	105.16	107.10	109.03	110.97	112.90	114.84	116.77
	25	111.69	113.71	115.73	117.74	119.76	121.77	123.79	125.81
	33⅓	125.81	127.96	130.11	132.26	134.41	136.56	138.71	140.86
	40	137.10	139.35	141.61	143.87	146.13	148.39	150.65	152.90
	50	154.03	156.45	158.87	161.29	163.71	166.13	168.55	170.97

19

Development of LIFO for Retailers

Introduction

A sound basis of determining inventory valuation is one of the most important factors in arriving at a company's financial position and operating results. Prior to the inception of the last-in, first-out (LIFO) method of inventory accounting, acceptable retail inventory valuation methods reflected losses realized, or expected to be realized, but did not reflect inflationary and deflationary changes in price levels. Rising price levels, coupled with increasing effective income tax rates, have been experienced during most of this century. This upward movement of price levels and income tax rates has forced retailers to re-evaluate their methods of inventory measurement.

Until the late 1940's, the only practicable inventory pricing methods available to retailers were based principally on a form of average cost (retail method) and, to a lesser extent, on specific identification. The practical effect of using the retail method during a period of rising prices is to increase reported, but not real, earnings, with a corresponding increase in income taxes payable. On the other hand, there are certain tangible economic advantages that may accrue to a company from the utilization of LIFO. However, before adopting LIFO a company should satisfy itself that, over the long term, it will be affected by continued inflation and that future inventory prices will not fall below the corresponding prices in the base year (i.e., opening inventory in the year LIFO is elected). In addition, the economic benefits are maximized if inventory levels (in terms of units) will at least remain stable or will increase with the passage of years, although, even with some decline in inventory levels, the benefits still may be substantial.

Improvement in Cash Flow

Assuming the validity and applicability of these assumptions and other considerations (see Chapter 23), the economic advantages of adopting LIFO are directly and indirectly linked to the inherent potential tax savings. The benefits of electing LIFO are realized essentially in improved cash flow arising from reduced federal and state income taxes in the year the method is adopted. Further improvements in cash flow may be realizable in the following year from reduced estimated federal and state income tax payments, since these payments can be based on the prior year's actual tax liability. Additional cash-flow benefits will be realizable in future years as costs continue to increase; essentially these benefits are measured by the tax effect on the difference between LIFO cost and replacement cost of year-end inventories.

Stated differently, the payment of higher taxes on a non-LIFO basis effectively results in the depletion of cash that otherwise would be available for a company's projected capital reinvestment program and dividend distributions to shareholders. In effect, many companies have found that the payment of income taxes on transitory inventory profits, as well as the necessity to replace inventories at ever rising, higher prices, has necessitated additional borrowings, and, practically speaking, no company's borrowing capacity is unlimited. Borrowing obviously involves the payment of interest, and companies have been made painfully aware of the future adverse impact on earnings and cash flow of high interest rates. Moreover, at some point, these increased borrowings place such demands on credit lines that some companies may find their credit rating downgraded, a factor that quickly translates into still higher interest rates.

In summary, the positive cash-flow implications of LIFO, rooted in reduced current and future tax payments, should normally translate into reduced requirements for outside borrowings and lower interest costs, which, in turn, will beneficially affect the earnings and cash flow of future years. Under these circumstances, economic considerations may dictate the business judgment of electing LIFO, notwithstanding that, since book and tax reporting must be on the same basis, there will be a conflict between the desire for improved cash flow on one hand, and higher reported earnings and a balance sheet that reflects improved working capital and stockholders' equity positions on the other. Accordingly, any decision to adopt LIFO should be preceded by a projection of its impact on company earnings, balance sheet, and cash flow over, say, three to five years.

In addition to the economic advantages mentioned above, from the financial reporting point of view the use of LIFO more closely matches current inventory replacement costs with current sales. In the opinion of many financial analysts, the more direct association of costs with sales under LIFO significantly improves the quality of a company's earning report. Moreover, use of the LIFO method will mitigate the prospectively adverse impact on earnings of future price declines which could lead to the incurrence of heavy losses upon disposition of the inventories.

Disadvantages of LIFO

Because of income tax requirements, the LIFO method cannot be used for some financial reporting purposes and not others; thus, the greater the cash-flow advantages of LIFO, the more depressing the impact on reported earnings. In effect, a company's reported working capital and stockholders' equity are reduced by the amount by which LIFO reduces the valuation of inventories, net of the related tax effect. In absolute dollar and per-share terms and in terms of a trend, a pattern of annual earnings growth has been the expectation and demand of the marketplace and the conventional measurement of management performance. The adoption of LIFO can upset this reported earnings pattern. While the marketplace may discount earnings during some inflationary period of years, there is no assurance that higher price/earnings multiples will not be applied to earnings of future years.

Moreover, a company adopting LIFO must take into consideration the fact that a comparison of relative performance with other companies in the same industry that may not be on LIFO is not always easily understood or appreciated by readers of financial statements. In addition, a prospective sale of securities may well militate against this depression of earnings. The possible adverse impact of LIFO on the conventional application of a multiplier to earnings, or on the ratio of earnings to fixed charges, should be carefully evaluated both by a prospective registrant and by the underwriter.

Loan indentures and other credit agreements frequently restrict the amount of retained earnings available for payment of cash dividends and reacquisitions of stock, and impose borrowing and other restrictions based on balance sheet and/or income statement formulas. Given the depressing impact of LIFO on net income, inventory valuations, and retained earnings, it may be necessary to modify or waive these various restrictive covenants before LIFO can be adopted. Under certain conditions, the penalties or premiums demanded by the institutional lenders as the offsetting costs of granting such modifications or waivers may be unacceptable. The prospective impact of LIFO on existing bonus and profit-sharing plans should also be taken into account, particularly as it may affect management incentive and performance.

Inception of LIFO

Against a background of dramatic inflation, followed by deflation, the LIFO method was considered by a variety of industries during the 1930's. LIFO was developed initially by the extractive industries and was used later by other industry groups, including retailers. It is an outgrowth of the base, or minimum, stock method infrequently used solely for financial reporting purposes and not permitted for income tax determination.

The Revenue Act of 1938 permitted producers and processors of certain nonferrous metals and tanners to elect the LIFO method for specific raw materials. The Revenue Act of 1939 extended the right to use LIFO to all taxpayers and permitted it to be applied to merchandise inventories. The method was, however, limited by regulation to the comparison of narrowly defined "like" merchandise. For example, a specific line of men's shoes was deemed to be like merchandise. Comparison was made of quantities at the beginning and end of the year. If the quantity was greater at the end of the year, the units at the beginning of the year would be priced at beginning-of-the-year prices. The excess over the beginning-of-the-year quantities was multiplied by either the first prices of purchases equivalent to such excess during the year (LIFO), or the last prices (FIFO), or the average price for the year, in accordance with the retailer's election. If fewer units were on hand at the end of the year, the inventory was valued at the unit prices of like goods at the beginning of the year. (T.D. 5504, 1946–1 C.B. 52.)

The Treasury's Early Position Toward LIFO for Retailers

The LIFO relief provisions of the 1939 Revenue Act were, however, of inconsequential benefit to retailers inasmuch as the large number of diverse items in retailers' inventories effectively precludes the application of the unit method. For example, a supermarket maintains many varieties of canned foods, assortments of household supplies, fruits, vegetables, and meats. Obviously, it is impossible to combine these various items in one inventory pool and arrive at a common natural unit of measurement. At the same time, it is impracticable to establish a separate inventory pool for each type of item in the inventory. Under the more suitable retail and dollar-value methods (see Chapters 22 and 23), the dollar serves as the common denominator and price indexes are utilized to eliminate changes in prices. Thus, with the aid of price indexes, retailers' heterogeneous inventories are adaptable to application of the LIFO method.

While the Treasury appeared somewhat unenthusiastic about permitting the practical application of LIFO for retailers, it was definitely opposed to the use of price indexes. Several retailers who filed their returns on a LIFO basis, using for the most part departmental price indexes adapted to the retail method, were assessed deficiencies. The practical result was that some retailers abandoned the use of price indexes, while others were discouraged from using price indexes from the outset. Despite the increasing confusion and the number of deficiencies assessed by the Treasury, some retailers continued on the LIFO method, utilizing price indexes. Such retailers were convinced that the Treasury's position was inequitable and arbitrary in effectively denying the use of LIFO to retailers.

Resolution of the Use of Price Indexes

The Treasury's limitation on the use of LIFO to the application of units of like merchandise was rejected by the Tax Court in the landmark decision of *Hutzler Brothers Co.,* 8 T.C. 14 (1947). The Court ruled in favor of the department store and held that:

Specific identification of goods was not required,
The inventory unit could be expressed in terms of a department's total dollars, i.e., the dollar-value method, and
The use of indexes of price changes and departmental pooling were permissible under LIFO.

The question of which particular price indexes should be used by retailers was not ruled on by the Tax Court, but was left to the discretion of the Commissioner of Internal Revenue.

Treasury's Position After *Hutzler* Decision

The Commissioner accepted the principles of the *Hutzler* decision and amended Regulations 103 and 111 under the 1939 Code. (T.D. 5605, 1948–1 C.B. 16; Reg. §§ 1.472–1(k) and 1.472–8 under the 1954 Code.) The Treasury provided in Mimeograph 6244, 1948–1 C.B. 21 (superseded by Rev. Proc. 72–21, 1972–1 C.B. 745), additional conditions for the use of LIFO in conjunction with the retail method and, in I.T. 3904, 1948–1 C.B. 18, acceptable price indexes and data published by the Bureau of Labor Statistics.

The Treasury's approval of the *Hutzler* principles was not, however, a total capitulation. An important clause in T.D. 5605 states:

A taxpayer using the elective inventory method in conjunction with retail computations must adjust retail selling prices for markdowns as well as markups, in order that there may be reflected the approximate cost of the goods on hand at the end of the year, regardless of market values.

The practical effect of the Treasury's requirement that retail selling prices must be adjusted for markdowns is to state inventories at cost under LIFO, rather than at the lower of cost or market under the retail method. This occurs because the effect of recognizing markdowns is to lower the percentage of markon and automatically increase the cost multiplier which is applied to the inventory price at retail. This is demonstrated by the following example illustrating the difference in inventory valuation, LIFO versus retail method, when markdowns have been recognized.

	Cost	Retail	Cost Multiplier
Retail method:			
Opening inventory plus purchases	$60,000	$100,000	60%
Deduct: Markdowns		10,000	
		$ 90,000	
Inventory valuation (60% × $90,000)	$54,000		
LIFO method:			
Opening inventory plus purchases	$60,000	$100,000	
Deduct: Markdowns		10,000	
	$60,000	$ 90,000	66⅔%
Inventory valuation (66⅔% × $90,000)	$60,000		

As indicated, use of the retail method effectively reduces the inventory valuation (to $54,000) in recognition of the inherent loss of value. Moreover, under the retail method, the ultimate sale of the merchandise will result in the realization of the normal departmental gross profit of 40% (i.e., $36,000 on $90,000).

However, as noted, the use of the net markon method which is obligatory for retail LIFO purposes preserves the initial cost of the inventories. In effect, any reduction of LIFO inventory below cost is not recognized for tax purposes [IRC § 472(b)(2) and Regulations §§ 1.472-2(b) and 1.472-8(a)(1)].

The *Hutzler* decision resulted in the sanctioning of the use of Bureau of Labor Statistics price indexes for department stores. Retailers other than department or specialty stores were not permitted, however, to use price indexes in conjunction with LIFO until the adjudication of two cases in 1949. Since that time dollar-value LIFO (see Chapters 22 and 23) has been a permissible and widely used method.

Specialty Stores. Revenue Ruling 53-23, 1953-1 C.B. 34, generally permits "specialty stores" on the retail method to qualify as department stores, and thereby use the department store inventory price indexes published by the Bureau of Labor Statistics (BLS). To use BLS indexes, a specialty store does not have to have as many, or as elaborate, departments as a department store, but it must have a fairly broad variety of a complete product line. For example, a men's or women's clothing and furnishings store or a furniture store can be recognized as a specialty store for purposes of using the BLS department store index.

Retailers who do not qualify as department or specialty stores may still use departmental BLS indexes, provided their goods are reasonably similar to those carried in the corresponding departments of a department store and they can independently demonstrate the accuracy, reliability, and suitability of the use of such indexes to the satisfaction of the district director. (T.I.R. 1342, January 28, 1975.) However, a jewelry store, for example, carrying primarily higher-priced jewelry such as precious stones and gold, would be precluded from using the department store jewelry index which is skewed toward inexpensive "costume" jewelry. In such a case, the retailer must compute his or her own index from the records under dollar-value LIFO (see Chapter 23). As in any case where the propriety of a tax accounting method is in question, the burden is on the taxpayer to show that the method used clearly reflects income. [Reg. § 1.446–1(a)(2).]

Variety Stores. Variety stores are retail stores engaged primarily in selling a wide range of merchandise in the lower and middle price levels, for example, "5 and 10 cent stores." For a short time the BLS prepared retail price indexes for variety stores. The publication of these indexes has been terminated and variety stores must now use indexes prepared from their own data to value LIFO inventories. Revenue Ruling 54–63, 1954–1 C.B. 33, and Rev. Rul. 55–220, 1955–1 C.B. 247, should be reviewed to determine the requirements for indexes prepared from the variety store's own data.

20

Election, Carryovers, Revisions, and Termination of LIFO

Introduction

Subject to the requirement of certain conditions, the LIFO inventory method may be adopted at the unilateral election of the taxpayer. Advance permission of the Treasury is not required. A number of factors should be considered in order to determine whether adoption of LIFO is desirable, and there are income tax requirements which must be satisfied in order to make a valid election.

Considerations Before Adopting LIFO

The following factors should be carefully evaluated:

Price level trends of departmental inventories.
Past experience with respect to the significance of markdowns and the likelihood of substantial markdowns in selling prices in the future.
Quantity changes, particularly prospective increases in volume or liquidation of items.
Technological changes which should be anticipated.

Tax adjustments required and the corresponding effect of adopting LIFO on the financial statements, particularly in connection with the use of the net markon method (see Chapter 22).

Special situations such as bargain purchases.

Although these factors may be interrelated, the LIFO election decision requires that each factor be considered individually. Sophisticated statistical techniques may be employed to assign values to each consideration.

Price Trends

One of the most important factors to be considered is the anticipated price levels of goods in the retailer's inventory. Despite the significant rise in general price levels since the use of LIFO was sanctioned for retailers, any consideration of trends must include the possibility that retail prices may decline sharply during recessionary periods.

In contrast with generally accepted accounting principles, IRC § 472(b)(2) and Reg. § 1.472-2(b) require that LIFO inventories must be carried at cost, and writedowns to market are not deductible for tax purposes. If prices decline sufficiently, the taxpayer may be carrying a LIFO inventory which is in excess of market values, thereby resulting in a correspondingly higher taxable income. This distortion of inventory values and taxable income is avoided under the conventional retail method which permits the inventories to be carried at the lower of cost or market for both financial and tax reporting purposes. Accordingly, if substantial annual markdowns are anticipated, the conventional retail method may well be preferable to LIFO.

The benefit of reduced taxes derived from LIFO obviously will be greatest if LIFO is adopted at the lowest point in a trend of rising prices. If adoption of LIFO is being considered after a long period of rising prices, the probability that this trend will continue must be evaluated carefully to determine whether LIFO will still be beneficial.

If the retailer anticipates that the price level of most inventory items will increase over succeeding years, while a few items may have some permanent or temporary decrease in price, or if the retailer is unable to exclude certain inventories from the LIFO election, the use of dollar-value pools as described in Chapter 23 should be considered. The use of a limited number of broad pools, or a single pool, or a grouping of selling departments resulting in the averaging of minor price decreases with overall increases in inventory prices, is generally preferable.

Quantity Changes

LIFO should be adopted preferably when physical inventory quantities are at, or near, normal amounts. If it is anticipated that large quantities of inventory will be added in years after LIFO is adopted, the lower price levels of the base year inventory will not be as significant, and the increments during years of inflated prices may be carried indefinitely. Any benefit from the adoption of LIFO would be realized only after the level of current inventory has stabilized and there are further increases in prices. Conversely, if inventory quantities at the time LIFO is adopted are in excess of future expected levels, subsequent reductions in inventories during periods of rising prices would result in the liquidation of lower-cost LIFO layers, and an increase in taxable income.

Even if the reduction in inventory is temporary, there is no provision in the law whereby replacement in the subsequent year would avoid the increase in taxable income. Similarly, even though the temporary reduction is caused by events beyond the taxpayer's control, such as strikes, floods, or embargoes, no relief is permitted. (However, special legislative relief was provided for involuntary liquidations of inventory occurring during World War II and the Korean Conflict.)

It is particularly important to adopt LIFO when quantities are at normal levels for goods whose price level changes are cyclical. If, however, the price level is expected to move primarily upward for some period of time, and current quantities are not deemed to be substantially in excess of future levels, LIFO should be adopted as soon as the upward price trend is determined.

Technological Changes

Changes in technology may result in the reduction of the cost of manufactured items through the substitution of materials and improved production techniques. When substitutions occur, there is the danger that the low-cost base year inventory layers will be liquidated and increased taxable income will result. Frequently, the price of new materials or processes may be higher in their first few years of use, but as demand increases, or as there is further refinement of a process, the price will drop considerably over several years. If such a situation is foreseeable, LIFO should not be adopted for that particular inventory until the price has stabilized and then begins to rise.

The effects of future technological changes on the composition of the inventory are usually of minimal concern to retailers since the effects of price changes can be minimized through the use of price indexes available for department stores, or by adopting a limited number of dollar-value pools. See Chapters 22 and 23.

Tax Requirements and Financial Statements

The limitations imposed by federal income tax requirements are also significant factors which must be considered. The Internal Revenue Code requirements are as follows.

1. Income for the taxable year preceding the year of election must be recomputed. The ending inventory for the year preceding the adoption of LIFO must be redetermined *at cost* and it will become the opening LIFO inventory. Applying this to retailers involves the use of departmental net markon cost multipliers to give effect to markdowns (see Chapter 22). This recomputation would normally result in an increase in taxable income for that year to the extent that items had been valued at market prices which were lower than cost.

Taxpayers may have valued a portion of their inventories at selling price less direct cost of disposition because the goods were unsalable at normal prices. The reasons could have been style changes, damage, imperfections, odd or broken lots, or other similar causes. The Internal Revenue Service effectively addressed this particular situation in Rev. Rul. 76–282:

> . . . the taxpayer's right to select the class or classes of goods to be covered by the LIFO election (or extension) goes to the nature of the goods and not to their condition, salability or other characteristics. Therefore, when the LIFO method is elected (or extended) for a particular class of goods, the election must include all goods within that class regardless of whether they are normal goods or goods that are unsalable at normal prices or unusable in the normal way. It is further held that the adjustment required under section 472(d) of the Code must include any write-down from actual cost with respect to goods

that are unsalable at normal prices or unusable in the normal way, as well as normal goods that have been written down to market value under section 1.471–4.

In summary, all taxpayers, including retailers, must restate to cost all inventories for which the LIFO election has been made and which have previously been marked down or written down for whatever reason. This restoration to cost effectively would apply to the opening and closing inventory in the year LIFO is adopted and to all applicable subsequent year-end inventories. Accordingly, it would be desirable to dispose of any such inventories in the taxable year preceding the adoption of LIFO and prior to each subsequent year-end date.

If a taxpayer has previously been using an unauthorized cost method (e.g., reflecting inadequate overhead in the cost of goods manufactured, or a standard cost system which does not properly reflect current costs), the Treasury will not be bound by the costs shown on the taxpayer's books. [Reg. § 1.472–2(d).] This may result in a substantial increase in taxable income which will cause a significant cash outflow and a higher LIFO base for the inventory. Manufacturers, rather than retailers, would be affected most seriously by this problem.

2. Once the LIFO method is adopted, it is irrevocable and the Commissioner's advance approval must be obtained to change to another method. [IRC § 472(e).] In the absence of a tax avoidance motive, there should be little difficulty in obtaining permission to change. The Treasury may not readily approve a change from LIFO where a taxpayer has expiring net operating losses or unused investment or foreign tax credits and wishes to offset them against the income resulting from the change. If the acceptability of a change from LIFO might be in question, it is advisable to contact the national office of the Internal Revenue Service in advance, or possibly to request a Ruling.

3. Beginning with the taxable year for which LIFO is adopted, all annual reports issued for credit purposes and financial statements prepared for shareholders or partners or publicly disseminated in any way must employ the LIFO inventory method consistent with the method used for tax purposes. For the year of change only, the company may report the impact of the change on the earnings for that year. However, the reduction of LIFO valuation to a lower market value, or the issuance to stockholders or

creditors of financial reports covering a period of operations less than the whole of the taxable year is not deemed to be at variance with the above requirements. [Reg. § 1.472–2(e).]

4. The Internal Revenue Service permits an important exception to the general rule that the LIFO method used for tax return purposes must be applied consistently on financial reports. Certain business combinations such as stock or asset acquisitions may be treated differently for accounting and tax purposes. Opinion No. 16 of the Accounting Principles Board of the American Institute of Certified Public Accountants may require that a certain type of acquisition be treated as a purchase, whereas for tax purposes the same transaction may be tax-free. Conversely, certain types of taxable acquisitions must be accounted for as "pooling of interests" under the aforementioned Opinion. The acquired corporation's historical cost bases of assets, including LIFO inventory layers, must be assumed by the transferee when a transaction is treated for accounting purposes as a "pooling of interests" and for tax purposes where it is tax-free. When a purchase or taxable transaction occurs, current fair market values, rather than historical cost bases, are determinative.

5. If an acquiring corporation continues to use the LIFO method to account for inventories acquired from a corporation which also used LIFO and the transaction is accounted for differently for financial reporting and federal income tax purposes, there will be a difference between financial accounting and taxable income. These resulting book and tax differences in costs, LIFO layers, and income will not be deemed to be a violation of the general reporting rules provided in IRC § 472 (c) and (e). The dollar amount and the reasons for the difference must be disclosed on both financial reports and tax returns, without regard to the materiality of such differences and without regard to whether separate or consolidated financial statements are prepared. These rules apply to all statements issued and tax returns filed after July 14, 1973. (Rev. Proc. 72–29, 1972–1 C.B. 757.)

6. The effect of the LIFO election on the financial statements prepared for stockholders is particularly relevant to retailers whose securities are traded publicly. Although a higher cost of goods sold will reduce taxable income and cash outflow, the adverse effect of LIFO on earnings per share may be an overriding consideration. The market price of the company's shares, dividend policy, working

capital provisions of loan agreements, incentive compensation, and profit-sharing plans are some of the important factors that could be affected by an adverse change in the basis of reporting earnings.

7. Many retailers use the Bureau of Labor Statistics (BLS) indexes in order to value ending inventories at base-year cost under the dollar-value method (see Chapter 22). [Reg. § 1.472–1(k).] The applicable BLS index showing the price changes for January is issued during the first week in March and it therefore provides the minimum delay for determining LIFO inventory for January 31 fiscal closings. Retailers whose fiscal year ends in July will use the BLS index for July, which is issued early in September.

Taxpayers other than retailers who use the LIFO method but do not maintain perpetual inventory records can avoid a delay in the preparation of the year-end financial statements. Such taxpayers have been allowed by the Internal Revenue Service to compute their closing inventories on the basis of a physical count one month before the year end by making appropriate adjustments for the twelfth month to ascertain the year-end inventory. This technique will also alert taxpayers as to the necessity to restore LIFO inventory pools that may have fallen below prior-year levels.

Scope and Timing of the LIFO Election

The LIFO election is subject to the Treasury's approval and possible modification. The LIFO method need not be elected for a taxpayer's entire inventory. If certain types of inventories or goods in a department are not suitable for LIFO, the taxpayer may be allowed to exclude those goods from his LIFO election. Factors such as dollar-value LIFO pools and the range of goods comprising a department, discussed in Chapters 22 and 23, strongly affect the consideration of which inventories may be excluded from the LIFO election.

A taxpayer who is engaged in more than one trade or business and who elects the LIFO method for one business may be required by the Treasury to value similar goods in all businesses under the LIFO method. [Reg. § 1.472–2(i).] This rule will not necessarily apply if each business is set up in a separate corporation, provided a valid business purpose can be established for separate corporations.

The LIFO election does not have to be filed with the Treasury until after the close of the year for which LIFO is under consideration. Consequently, the immediate effect of the election on the taxpayer's liability and on the financial statements for the year of adoption (and any tax impact for the prior year) can be readily ascertained.

Special Situations—Bargain Purchases

Where assets of a business are acquired in a bargain purchase for a lump-sum amount, the taxpayer's assigned values to the inventory may be disputed by the tax authorities. If a cost method such as first-in, first-out (FIFO) is adopted, any reduction in the assigned inventory value by the tax authorities effectively would be subject to tax in the year the inventory was sold. By creating a new corporation for the acquisition and then adopting the LIFO method the taxpayer would be protected from such an adjustment. Acquisitions of inventory would be treated as current purchases and not as "opening" inventory even if acquired on the first day of a newly formed corporation's existence. If the prices of subsequent purchases are higher than the initial purchase, the current purchases for the year would be valued most advantageously on a last-in, first-out basis. The closing inventory at the end of the first year would become the base-year LIFO inventory.

Mechanics of Making the LIFO Election—Form 970

The taxpayer must file a statement of a LIFO election on Form 970, in duplicate, with the tax return for the first taxable year for which the new method is used. In addition to the information requested on the form, in the case of manufacturers, the cost systems for raw materials, goods in process, and finished goods for each major product group must be explained in detail. [Reg. § 1.472-3(a).]

The use of broad, imprecise language on the form may result in future problems. Although the Regulations (§ 472) provide guidelines for inventory pools and the definition of what is a department (see Chapter 23), future borderline inventory classifications can create uncertainty and possible conflict with the Internal Revenue Service. Consequently, the taxpayer should specify precisely which inventories will be placed on the LIFO method.

Goods in transit may be included in the merchandise inventories specified on Form 970 as stock to be included on the LIFO basis.

Inclusion of merchandise in transit increases the size of the base-year inventory, thereby reducing the exposure to liquidation. Despite the advantages of including merchandise in transit, the practical problems of departmental classification, accurate computation of cost multipliers, and other time-consuming operations have forced a number of retailers to exclude in-transit goods from the election. The frequency and size of orders, number of suppliers, and stability of price levels are among the factors to be considered in determining whether the administrative expense of including goods-in-transit in the LIFO election is outweighed by the advantages. Regardless of the taxpayer's decision, the treatment of merchandise in transit should be indicated on Form 970.

The taxpayer's Form 970 may be rejected if it includes conditions or terms unacceptable to the Commissioner. If an election of LIFO must be accompanied by conditions, it is advisable to attempt resolution of uncertain areas in advance with the Internal Revenue Service.

Exclusions from the LIFO Election

A new store or, under certain circumstances, even a new department may be excluded from a previously made LIFO election by organizing the operation as a separate corporation. The consideration of whether to form a new corporation is also affected by whether the taxpayer files a consolidated income tax return and can show a business purpose for the separate corporation.

Carryover of Inventory Methods in Nontaxable Transactions

Inventory that is transferred from one corporation to another in certain types of tax-free transactions generally carries with it the inventory method and other tax accounting attributes used by the transferor corporation. Section 381(c)(5) provides:

> In any case in which inventories are received by the acquiring corporation, such inventories shall be taken by such corporation (in determining its income) on the same basis on which such inventories were taken by the distributor or transferor corporation, unless different methods were used by several distributor or transferor corporations or by a distributor or transferor corporation and the acquiring corporation. If different methods were used, the acquiring corporation shall use the method or combination of methods of taking inventory adopted pursuant to regulations prescribed by the Secretary or his delegate.

This provision of section 381 applies to the transactions enumerated in section 381(a). Broadly stated, they include distributions received in complete liquidations of an 80% or more controlled subsidiary under sections 332 and 334(b)(1), and a transfer of assets in a tax-free reorganization such as a merger (except a spin-off or similar type D reorganization) to which section 361 applies.

The applicability of the carryover rules is subject to the transferee corporation's being deemed to be the "acquiring corporation." The question of which company is the "acquiring corporation" is to be determined from all the facts and circumstances. Only a single corporation may be an "acquiring corporation." A parent corporation which receives the assets upon complete liquidation of its subsidiary will be deemed to be the "acquiring corporation." In nontaxable reorganizations, such as statutory mergers, the corporation which, pursuant to the plan of reorganization, ultimately acquires, directly or indirectly, the assets of the transferor corporation will be considered to be the "acquiring corporation." [Reg. § 1.381(a)–1(b)(2)(i).] Under the consolidated return regulations, in cases such as a reverse acquisition, where the dominant–acquiring corporation is reorganized or merged into the passive–acquired corporation, it is not always easy to identify the "acquiring corporation" and the transferee corporation. It seems from Reg. § 1.502–75(d)(3) that the larger and dominant corporation would be deemed to be the "acquiring corporation."

A tax-free acquisition, however, can be structured to preclude the application of the inventory carryover rules of section 381(c)(5). If the parent corporation is deemed to be the "acquiring corporation" under Reg. § 1.381(a)–1(b)(2)(i) and the inventories of the transferor corporation are transferred tax-free (after the acquisition) to a subsidiary of the parent, as permitted under section 368(a)(2)(C), or in the transaction under section 368(a)(2)(D) then the subsidiary will be entitled to adopt any permissible inventory method. [Reg. § 1.381(a)–1(3)(ii).]

Special carryover rules apply to the use of LIFO after an acquisition, depending on the accounting methods of each corporation, although in each case application may be made to the Commissioner to use a different method of inventory valuation. In the absence of such permission to change, the following rules apply.

1. If all the parties to the transaction used the same inventory method prior to the transaction, the acquiring company is required

to continue the same method, whether or not it integrates the businesses or continues to operate them separately. For this purpose, a corporation will be deemed to be on LIFO at the time of the acquisition if it makes a timely LIFO election for the taxable year in which the transaction occurs. [Reg. § 1.381(c)(5)–1(b)(1).]

If both companies in a two-company transaction are on FIFO and lower of cost or market, and the acquiring company makes a LIFO election for that year, the LIFO election will apply back to the beginning of that taxable year. Similarly, if both companies are on the same LIFO method, the election will apply back to the beginning of the year. On the other hand, if the LIFO methods are not the same, for example, if one company uses the natural business unit and the other uses multiple pools, rule 4 below will apply.

2. If, immediately after the transfer of assets, one (or more) of the trades or businesses is operated as a separate and distinct trade or business, the method used by that trade or business must be continued by the acquiring business. The Commissioner, however, has the right to require that the inventory method in any one trade or business be used in another trade or business if that is required for a clear reflection of income. [Reg. § 1.381(c)(5)–1(b)(2).] One of the essential conditions in establishing that there are two separate businesses is the maintenance of separate books and records for each business. [Reg. § 1.446–1(d)(2).]

3. If, immediately after the transfer of assets, the businesses are integrated, then to the extent that the same methods of inventory valuation were employed for particular types of goods, the same methods must be employed by the acquiring company, again subject to the Commissioner's right to require another method for a clear reflection of income. [Reg. § 1.381(c)(5)–1(b)(3)(i).]

4. If, immediately after the transfer of assets, the businesses are integrated, then to the extent that the inventory methods differ, the acquiring corporation must use the principal method being used for each particular type of goods, provided that such method will clearly reflect the income of the acquiring corporation after the transfer. [Reg. § 1.381(c)(5)–1(b)(3)(ii).] The principal method for each particular type of goods is determined by measuring the fair value of comparable types of goods under each method. For purposes of this determination, as in rule 1 above, a corporation that is not on LIFO will be deemed to be on LIFO if it makes a LIFO

election for the taxable year in which the transfer occurred. [Reg. § 1.381(c)(5)-1(c).]

An illustration of this last rule, as set forth in the Regulations, is contained in the Appendix of this chapter.

The carryover provisions apply also to other LIFO inventory attributes, such as cost, date of acquisition, and treatment of LIFO layers. These attributes are discussed in detail in Chapters 22 and 23. Regulations section 1.381(c)(5)-1(e)(i) provide that where the acquiring corporation is using LIFO, it must integrate its layers of inventories and make adjustments in accordance with various rules, depending on whether the acquiring corporation is on the dollar-value or specific goods method and whether the transferor corporation is on LIFO or FIFO.

As a general rule, a change from the principal method, or from an inventory method that is required to be continued, may be made only after permission of the Commissioner has been received. If an inventory method employed on the date of the transaction is continued, the acquiring corporation will be bound by the previously made elections. It will not be necessary for the acquiring corporation to renew any elections for an inventory method that is continued. [Reg. § 1.381(c)(5)-(1)(b)(4).] Any transferor corporation that is not using a continued method or the principal method on the date of the section 381 transaction is deemed to have automatically initiated a change in accounting method for purposes of the income adjustments required by section 481. The Commissioner's prior consent to the change is not necessary for the adoption of any method which, under the inventory rules of sections 471 and 472, does not require his consent. Any income or loss generated by the change in accounting method must be recognized by the acquiring corporation under section 481(c).

If the transfer of inventories occurred in a year which is barred by the statute of limitations, no change in inventory method may be made by the Commissioner by reason of Reg. § 1.381(c)(5). Also, if the year of transfer is not statute-barred, the inventory method will not be changed if the acquiring corporation has adopted a method consistent with the final Regulations, was given permission to use a method, or has adopted a method not requiring the Commissioner's consent. These rules do not prevent a taxpayer or the Commissioner from requesting or requiring a change in method in accordance with the Regulations. [Reg. § 1.381(c)(5)-1(g).]

Nontaxable Transfers of LIFO Inventory to a Subsidiary

If a LIFO inventory is transferred by a parent to a newly organized subsidiary in a tax-free transaction under section 351, and the new subsidiary wishes to adopt the LIFO method, it must file its own Form 970. The cost of its opening inventory will be determined as the average cost to the parent, aggregating all layers into one to determine average cost. Similarly, if the acquiring subsidiary is an existing subsidiary that is not using LIFO, the same rules apply. [Rev. Rul. 70–564, 1970–2 C.B. 109, relying on *Textile Apron Co., Inc.*, 21 T.C. 147 (1953) (Acq.).]

On the other hand, if the transferee is an existing subsidiary that is already using LIFO, the average cost rule does not apply. Instead, it must integrate the acquired inventories, maintaining the original LIFO layers and acquisition dates and costs into its own LIFO layers. [Rev. Rul. 70–565, 1970–2 C.B. 110, citing *Joseph E. Seagram and Sons, Inc.*, 394 F.2d 738 (CA–2, 1968).]

Revisions of the LIFO Method

Revisions of an existing LIFO method are usually deemed to be changes in accounting method requiring the permission of the Commissioner. Requests for permission to change are filed on Form 3115 with the Internal Revenue Service within the first 180 days of the year of change. As with nearly all IRS filing dates, there must be strict adherence to the 180-day period. Upon the showing of good cause, the filing of the application may be extended an additional 90 days.

Examples of revisions requiring permission include:

1. Change from specific identification to the dollar-value method, except if no changes in inventory pools are made. [Reg. § 1.472–8 (f)(1).]
2. Alteration of the method of computing values of a LIFO dollar-value pool or of the method of valuing LIFO increments, such as changing from the double-extension to the link-chain method (see Chapter 23) or valuing increments on the basis of the average cost of purchases, instead of most recent costs. [Reg. § 1.472–8 (e)(1).]
3. Change in the method of pooling, for example, the combination of similar but distinctive departments such as men's clothing with men's furnishings. [Reg. § 1.472–8(g)(1).]

Termination of LIFO

A taxpayer may not terminate the use of the LIFO method before receiving the permission of the Commissioner. The Commissioner may force a taxpayer to go off the LIFO method involuntarily if the taxpayer violates a provision of IRC section 472, or if the Commissioner determines that the LIFO method does not properly reflect income in accordance with IRC section 472(a).

The LIFO method may be discontinued at the taxpayer's initiative only by filing Form 3115 within the required first 180 days of the taxable year of change. The taxpayer must attach a schedule to Form 3115 showing the inventories to be affected by the change, valued under both LIFO and FIFO, and a statement that the proposed method conforms to the inventory method currently used for non-LIFO inventories, if any, or that the proposed method is otherwise consistent with the provisions of Reg. § 1.472–6. [Reg. § 1.446–1(e)(3); Rev. Proc. 70–27, 1970–2 C.B. 509.]

Typically, when LIFO is terminated, the value of the inventory at the beginning of the year of change under the new method will be greater than the value of the opening inventory for the same period as determined under LIFO. This excess is termed the "positive adjustment" which must be included in taxable income. The Internal Revenue Service has adopted an administrative procedure to mitigate the impact of the positive adjustment resulting from the discontinuance of the LIFO method by allowing taxpayers to spread the positive adjustment ratably over a period of years; depending upon the number of years LIFO was employed, this period may extend up to 10 taxable years.

The taxpayer may be allowed to spread the adjustment over a period longer than 10 years if the LIFO method has been used for six years or more prior to the year of change. The period over which the positive adjustment may be prorated by the IRS depends on the relationship of the taxpayer's LIFO reserve at the beginning of the taxable year of change to the average taxable income of the taxpayer for the three preceding taxable years. To arrive at the latter amount, the high year and the low year of the five taxable years immediately preceding the taxable year of change must be eliminated, and the taxable incomes of the remaining three years are added together and divided by three. The resulting amount is the average taxable income to be used. For this computation, the net operating loss is disregarded but certain special deductions (e.g., dividend-received deduction) are included.

If the LIFO reserve at the beginning of the taxable year of change exceeds the average taxable income as determined above, the positive adjustment will be spread over a period equal to twice the number of taxable years the taxpayer has been continuously using the LIFO method, up to 20 taxable years. If a taxpayer's LIFO reserve is equal to or less than the average taxable income, then the positive adjustment must be spread ratably over a period of 10 years. (Rev. Proc. 71–16, 1971–1 C.B. 682; amplified by Amendment #1, 1971–2 C.B. 527.) The allocation of the positive adjustment is elective with the taxpayer and must be requested by attaching a statement to Form 3115.

Where a taxpayer changes from LIFO to FIFO, either voluntarily or involuntarily, the new inventory is taken as stated in Reg. § 1.472–6:

(a) In conformity with the method used by the taxpayer under section 471 in inventorying goods not included in his LIFO inventory computations; or

(b) If the LIFO inventory method was used by the taxpayer with respect to all of his goods subject to the inventory, then in conformity with the inventory method used by the taxpayer prior to his adoption of LIFO inventory method; or

(c) If the taxpayer had not used inventories prior to his adoption of the LIFO inventory method and had no goods currently subject to inventory by a method other than the LIFO inventory method, then in conformity with such inventory method as may be selected by the taxpayer and approved by the Commissioner as resulting in a clear reflection of income; or

(d) In any event, in conformity with any inventory method to which the taxpayer may change pursuant to application approved by the Commissioner.

APPENDIX: DETERMINING PRINCIPAL METHOD OF ACCOUNTING FOR TYPE OF GOODS PURSUANT TO CARRYOVER REGULATIONS FOR NONTAXABLE ACQUISITIONS—ILLUSTRATION OF METHOD

Reg. § 1.381(c)(5)–1(c)(3)

Example (1). (i) X, Y, and Z corporations are all engaged in the manufacture of sheet metal. In addition, Y and Z corporations are engaged in the manufacture of paper containers. X and Y corporations use the first-in, first-out method of identifying goods and the cost method of valuing all inventories while Z corporation uses the first-in, first-out method of identifying goods and the cost or market, whichever is lower, method of valuing all inventories. X, Y, and Z corporations enter into a transaction to which section 381 (a) applies, and the acquiring corporation integrates the sheet metal businesses formerly operated by X, Y, and Z corporations and also integrates the paper container businesses formerly operated by Y and Z corporations. Each corporation has the same types of goods in the inventories of its sheet metal business and Y and Z corporations have the same types of goods in the inventories of their paper container businesses. Immediately after the date of distribution or transfer the fair market values of the respective inventories are as follows:

	X	Y	Z
Sheet metal	$10,000	$7,000	$15,000
Paper container		6,000	7,000

(ii) Since X, Y, and Z corporations all used the first-in, first-out method of identifying their inventories as of the date of distribution or transfer, then, under the provisions of paragraph (b) (3) (1) of this section, the acquiring corporation shall continue to use the first-in, first-out method of identifying all goods unless, in accordance with paragraph (e) of § 1.446–1, consent of the Commissioner is obtained to change the method of accounting.

(iii) Since the acquired corporations used different methods of valuing inventories in their sheet metal business and their paper container business, when the businesses were integrated the acquiring corporation must, under the provisions of this paragraph, determine which method of inventory valuation used by the acquired corporations on the date of distribution or transfer is the principal method of inventory valuation for each of such businesses.

(a) In determining which is the principal method of valuing inventories for the sheet metal business pursuant to subparagraph (2) of this paragraph, the total fair market value of the sheet metal inventories of X and Y corporations, $17,000 (i.e., $10,000 + $7,000 = $17,000), is compared with the fair market value of the sheet metal inventory of Z corporation, $15,000. Since the total fair market value of the sheet metal inventories of X and Y corporations ($17,000) exceeds the fair market value of the sheet metal inventory of Z corporation ($15,000), the cost method of valuation used by X and Y corporations is the principal method of taking such inventories, and must be used by the acquiring corporation in valuing such inventories, if the conditions set forth in subparagraph (1) of this paragraph are satisfied.

(b) In determining which is the principal method of valuing inventories for the paper container business pursuant to subparagraph (2) of this paragraph, the fair market value of the paper container inventory of Y corporation ($6,000) is compared with the fair market value of the paper container inventory of Z corporation ($7,000). Since the fair market value of the paper container inventory of Z corporation ($7,000) exceeds the fair market value of the paper container inventory of Y corporation ($6,000), the cost or market, whichever is lower, method of valuation used by Z corporation is the principal method of taking such inventories, and must be used by the acquiring corporation in valuing such inventories, if the conditions set forth in subparagraph (1) of this paragraph are satisfied.

Example (2). (i) X, Y, and Z corporations are all engaged in the manufacture of electrical appliances. In addition, X and Z corporations are engaged in the manufacture of plastic containers. X corporation uses the first-in, first-out method of identifying goods and the cost method of valuing all inventories. Y and Z corporations use the last-in, first-out method of identifying goods and the cost method of valuing all inventories. In applying the last-in, first-out method, Y corporation uses the dollar value method, the double-extension method, and pools under the natural business unit method, while Z corporation uses the dollar value method, the double-extension method, and pools under the multiple pooling method for all inventories. X, Y, and Z corporations enter into a transaction to which section 381(a) applies, and the acquiring corporation integrates the electric appliance businesses formerly operated by X, Y, and Z corporations and also integrates the plastic container businesses formerly operated by X and Z corporations. Each corporation has the same types of goods in the inventories of its electric appliance business and X and Z corporations have the same types of goods in the inventories of their plastic container businesses. Immediately after the date of distribution or transfer, the fair market values of the respective inventories are as follows:

	X	Y	Z
Electric appliance	$13,000	$10,000	$5,000
Plastic container	7,000		6,000

(ii) Since X, Y, and Z corporations all used the cost method of valuing their inventories as of the date of distribution or transfer, then, under the provisions of paragraph (b) (3) (i) of this section, the acquiring corporation shall continue to use the cost method of valuing all goods unless, in accordance with paragraph (e) of § 1.446–1, consent of the Commissioner is obtained to change the method of accounting.

(iii) Since the acquired corporations used different methods of identifying inventories in their electric appliance business and their plastic container business, when the businesses were integrated the acquiring corporation must, under the provisions of this paragraph, determine which method of inventory identification used by the acquired corporations on the date of distribution or transfer is the principal method of inventory identification for each of such businesses.

(a) (1) In determining which is the principal method of identifying inventories for the electric appliance business pursuant to subparagraph (2) of this paragraph, the fair market value of the electric appliance inventory of X corporation, $13,000, is compared with the total fair market value of the electric appliance inventories of Y and Z corporations, $15,000 (i.e., $10,000 + $5,000 = $15,000). Since the total fair market value of the electric appliance inventories of Y and Z corporations ($15,000) exceeds the fair market value of the electric appliance inventory of X corporation ($13,000), the last-in, first-out method of identification is the principal method of taking the electric appliance inventories and must be used by the acquiring corporation, if the conditions set forth in subparagraph (1) of this paragraph are satisfied.

(2) Since Y and Z corporations used different pooling methods, in applying the last-in, first-out method, the acquiring corporation must, under the provisions of this paragraph, determine which pooling method as used by Y and Z corporations on the date of distribution or transfer is the principal method. In making such determination pursuant to subparagraph (2) of this paragraph, the fair market value of the electric appliance inventory of Y corporation ($10,000) is compared with the fair market value of the electric appliance inventory of Z corporation ($5,000). Since the fair market value of the electric appliance inventory of Y corporation ($10,000) exceeds the fair market value of the electric appliance inventory of Z corporation ($5,000), the natural business unit method is the principal method of pooling and must be used by the acquiring corporation in applying the last-in, first-out method with respect to the electric appliance business, if the conditions set forth in subparagraph (1) of this paragraph are satisfied.

In addition, under the provisions of paragraph (b)(3)(i) of this section, the acquiring corporation must use the dollar value method and the double-extension method for valuing goods in its electric appliance inventory since Y and Z corporations both used such methods in valuing their electric appliance inventories as of the date of distribution or transfer, unless, in accordance with paragraph (e) of § 1.446–1, consent of the Commissioner is obtained to change the method of accounting.

(b) In determining which is the principal method of identifying inventories for the plastic container business pursuant to subparagraph (2) of this paragraph, the fair market value of the plastic container inventory of X corporation ($7,000) is compared with the fair market value of the plastic container inventory of Z corporation ($6,000). Since the fair market value of the plastic container inventory of X corporation ($7,000) exceeds the fair market value of the plastic container inventory of Z corporation ($6,000) the first-in, first-out method of identification, as used by X corporation, is the principal method of taking the plastic container inventories and must be used by the acquiring corporation, if the conditions set forth in subparagraph (1) of this paragraph are satisfied.

21

Retail Price Indexes

Introduction

As discussed in Chapter 19, the Treasury did not accept the use of indexes on a dollar-value basis until after the *Hutzler* decision. However, the Treasury now accepts the Retail Price Indexes which are prepared semiannually by the Bureau of Labor Statistics based on January 15 and July 15 price levels.

Department Store Inventory Price Indexes

A Department of Labor release dated February 3, 1948, supplied inventory price indexes published by the Bureau of Labor Statistics (BLS) for nine departmental groups numbered I through IX, for the fiscal years ended in July and January, commencing with 1941 as the base year equaling 100 and continuing through the year ended in 1947.

As of July, 1948, a tenth group, Ladies' Accessories, was added. As of January, 1954, the number of groupings was expanded to twenty. Since that time there has been no further expansion, nor has there been any change in the total storewide index numbers for soft goods (Groups I–XV), for durable goods (Groups XVI–XX), and Store Total. The derivation of the Store Total includes most departments in a store, except those that sell food, candy, liquor, tobacco, wallpaper and paint, and similar products. Even though these departments are not included in the derivation of the store-wide index, since specific index groups are not applicable the storewide index should be used. The listing below supplies descriptions of the constituent selling departments that comprise Groups I through XX and the Store Total (Group XXI).

BLS Department Groups		Revised Controllers' Congress Departments—Coding	
No.	Name	No.	Name
I	Piece Goods	11-00	Piece Goods
II	Domestics and Draperies	15-00	Household Textiles
		64-11	Curtains, Draperies, and Decorator Fabrics
III	Women's and Children's Shoes	39-00	Women's and Children's Shoes
IV	Men's and Boys' Shoes	53-00	Men's and Boys' Shoes
V	Infants' Wear	44-12	Infants' Apparel and Furniture
VI	Women's Underwear	36-00	Corsets and Brassieres
		38-00	Underwear and Negligees
VII	Women's and Girls' Hosiery	37-00	Women's and Children's Hosiery
VIII	Women's and Girls' Accessories	32-00	Neckwear and Accessories
		33-00	Handbags and Small Leathers
		35-00	Women's and Children's Gloves and Mittens
IX	Women's Outerwear and Girls' Wear	34-00	Millinery
		41-00	Coats and Suits, Women's, Misses' and Juniors'
		42-00	Dresses, Women's, Misses' and Juniors'
		45-00	Housedresses, Aprons and Uniforms
		43-00	Blouses and Sportswear
		46-00	Furs
		44-11	Girls' and Teen-Age Apparel
X	Men's Clothing	51-11	Men's Clothing
		or	
		51-14	Men's Clothing
		and	
		51-26	Men's Sport Clothing
XI	Men's Furnishings	51-12	Men's Furnishings
		or	
		51-15	Men's Furnishings
		and	
		51-27	Men's Casual Furnishings
XII	Boys' Clothing and Furnishings	52-00	Boys' Clothing and Furnishings
XIII	Jewelry	24-00	Jewelry and Silverware
XIV	Notions	12-00	Patterns
		21-00	Notions, Laces, Trimmings and Ribbons
		25-00	Art Needlework
		31-00	Umbrellas
XV	Toilet Articles and Drugs	22-00	Toilet Articles and Drug Sundries
XVI	Furniture and Bedding	61-00	Furniture and Beds
XVII	Floor Coverings	62-00	Oriental Rugs
		63-00	Domestic Floor Covering

BLS Department Groups		Revised Controllers' Congress Departments—Coding	
No.	Name	No.	Name
XVIII	Housewares	65–00	China, Glassware and Gift Shop
		66–21	Housewares
		67–00	Pictures, Frames and Mirrors
XIX	Major Appliances	64–12	Lamps and Shades
		66–12	Major Appliances
XX	Radios and Television Sets	68–00	Radio, Television and Records
		69–00	Pianos and Musical Instruments
XXI	No Separate Index Computed	26–00	Books and Stationery
		66–22	Wallpaper and Paint
		71–00	Flower Shop
		72–00	Automobile Accessories
		73–00	Pet Accessories and Pet Shop
		74–00	Toys, Sporting Goods and Cameras
		75–00	Luggage
		76–00	Candy
		77–00	Foods and Groceries
		78–00	Fresh and Smoked Meats
		79–00	Liquor Shop
		81–00	Smoke Shop

Table VII, on pages 407–409, sets forth the index numbers corresponding to Groups I through XXI, the soft goods storewide total, and the durable goods storewide total for the period January, 1942, through January, 1976, with January, 1941, as 100 per cent. (A similar chart exists, with July index numbers, for the period July, 1942, through July, 1976.)

The Department Store Inventory Price Index as of January, 1973, published in Revenue Ruling 73–178, 1973–1 C.B. 217 is a revised classification of the Controllers' Congress departments and corresponding revised BLS index groups set forth elsewhere in this chapter.

Revenue Procedure 72–21, 1972–1 C.B. 745, superseding Mimeograph 6244, 1948–1 C.B. 21, permits the application of a given group index to a number of departments in a store. This application must, however, be done "logically," and it is therefore necessary to examine the markup percentage with respect to each operating department to be included in one Department Store Inventory Price Index group. If the markups vary considerably, it may be necessary to compute the LIFO inventory separately for each operating department. [Reg. § 1.471–8 (c); Rev. Proc. 72–21, *supra*.] If a department does not fit into any of the twenty BLS index groups,

> . . . an index should be employed which represents an average for the whole of the remainder of the store. For example, this index may be the store

TABLE VII. BLS Department Store Inventory Price Indexes, January, 1942 to January, 1976, Inclusive
(January, 1941 = 100)

January

	Department Groups	1942	1943	1944	1945	1946	1947	1948	1949	1950	1951	1952
I	Piece Goods	120.3	136.8	144.1	151.0	166.7	196.4	218.6	211.4	191.3	216.4	211.7
II	Domestics and Draperies	120.3	136.8	144.1	151.0	166.7	196.4	218.6	211.4	191.3	216.4	211.7
III	Women's and Children's Shoes	108.7	119.2	122.2	124.6	131.1	160.6	190.3	196.2	191.5	214.0	213.7
IV	Men's and Boys' Shoes	108.7	119.2	122.2	124.6	131.1	160.6	190.3	196.2	191.5	214.0	213.7
V	Infants' Wear	116.7	131.3	136.3	145.0	147.0	158.8	178.2	180.3	156.3	179.1	177.3
VI	Women's Underwear	116.7	131.3	136.3	145.0	147.0	158.8	178.2	180.3	166.3	179.1	177.3
VII	Women's and Girls' Hosiery	116.7	131.3	136.3	145.0	147.0	158.8	178.2	180.3	166.3	179.1	177.3
VIII	Women's and Girls' Accessories	114.8	124.9	131.5	138.9	145.7	163.6	180.5	171.2	163.5	166.2	170.5
IX	Women's Outerwear and Girls' Wear	117.9	128.7	141.3	147.7	155.8	164.7	181.3	182.8	169.7	174.2	180.2
X	Men's Clothing	112.9	129.8	139.4	144.7	151.1	178.9	190.0	189.5	133.4	197.1	207.5
XI	Men's Furnishings	112.9	129.8	139.4	144.7	151.1	178.9	190.0	189.5	133.4	197.1	207.5
XII	Boys' Clothing and Furnishings	112.9	129.8	139.4	144.7	151.1	178.9	190.0	189.5	133.4	197.1	207.5
XIII	Jewelry	110.2	112.7	113.7	121.2	120.5	124.6	140.5	142.1	142.2	157.9	159.0
XIV	Notions	110.2	112.7	113.7	121.2	120.5	124.6	140.5	142.1	142.2	157.9	159.0
XV	Toilet Articles and Drugs	110.2	112.7	113.7	121.2	120.5	124.6	140.5	142.1	142.2	157.9	159.0
XVI	Furniture and Bedding	121.0	126.2	128.7	143.0	150.2	168.9	184.9	192.3	184.6	204.2	203.4
XVII	Floor Coverings	109.0	113.7	118.2	123.2	131.6	148.4	162.5	170.7	168.6	194.0	192.2
XVIII	Housewares	109.0	113.7	118.2	123.2	131.6	148.4	162.5	170.7	168.6	194.0	192.2
XIX	Major Appliances	118.1	121.8	127.5	134.6	139.6	157.9	170.1	171.0	158.6	170.5	162.8
XX	Radios and TV Sets	118.1	121.8	127.5	134.6	139.6	157.9	170.1	171.0	158.6	170.5	162.8
	Total, Groups I–XV–Soft Goods	115.0	127.5	134.8	141.9	148.6	166.7	184.5	184.7	174.6	189.0	192.0
	Total, Groups XVI–XX–Durable Goods	114.4	119.1	123.0	131.4	138.9	156.7	171.0	177.2	171.0	191.7	189.5
	Store Total	114.8	124.9	131.5	138.9	145.7	163.6	180.5	182.3	173.5	189.6	191.1

TABLE VII. Continued

January

Department Groups	1953	1954	1955	1956	1957	1958	1959	1960	1961	1962	1963	1964
I Piece Goods	202.8	204.1	200.7	200.2	199.4	200.1	199.5	200.4	202.4	204.7	204.8	206.8
II Domestics and Draperies	202.8	197.0	189.6	189.3	194.2	194.7	194.9	194.5	198.1	199.4	201.9	203.9
III Women's and Children's Shoes	211.2	213.3	215.3	220.8	233.6	240.0	245.9	262.3	264.0	269.4	271.7	271.6
IV Men's and Boys' Shoes	211.2	213.1	213.0	217.5	228.3	231.1	233.1	252.7	253.2	257.5	260.5	261.0
V Infants' Wear	173.9	170.2	170.3	171.2	174.5	175.7	174.9	174.5	177.3	177.2	178.7	178.1
VI Women's Underwear	173.9	172.5	171.6	169.7	172.3	175.2	177.3	176.1	178.9	178.9	180.2	181.0
VII Women's and Girls' Hosiery	173.9	173.7	168.1	164.8	163.1	160.6	158.3	158.0	157.9	156.8	157.0	156.1
VIII Women's and Girls' Accessories	168.9	170.1	172.4	172.1	175.4	177.8	178.7	181.8	187.1	193.2	199.9	198.8
IX Women's Outerwear and Girls' Wear	179.2	180.1	177.7	179.1	180.4	181.3	182.7	184.6	184.7	183.4	188.1	188.5
X Men's Clothing	200.9	204.4	205.3	206.4	211.2	213.7	214.4	216.3	226.4	227.8	229.6	238.3
XI Men's Furnishings	200.9	201.3	197.9	197.3	199.9	199.6	198.9	198.7	201.2	198.6	199.2	199.8
XII Boys' Clothing and Furnishings	200.9	203.2	199.7	202.2	205.9	206.1	205.1	205.8	209.6	211.0	212.9	217.7
XIII Jewelry	161.7	164.3	163.6	165.6	168.9	173.3	171.6	175.7	179.7	180.4	185.1	189.2
XIV Notions	161.7	161.7	158.7	158.6	162.1	166.1	164.2	165.1	164.9	170.0	177.9	179.7
XV Toilet Articles and Drugs	161.7	164.0	166.1	172.1	178.6	184.0	192.6	196.6	195.7	200.5	203.1	207.4
XVI Furniture and Bedding	206.1	211.4	207.7	211.9	218.1	219.7	222.5	224.7	226.2	229.8	232.3	232.5
XVII Floor Coverings	193.7	192.9	188.9	189.9	192.0	195.7	191.0	192.9	194.0	193.4	195.2	197.1
XVIII Housewares	193.7	197.7	198.1	201.5	213.9	224.9	223.3	227.5	229.0	228.0	236.4	238.3
XIX Major Appliances	158.4	154.3	143.4	143.4	141.7	135.8	134.7	132.5	130.5	131.7	130.9	132.6
XX Radios and TV Sets	158.4	157.0	142.4	139.5	138.8	135.9	131.4	130.5	130.4	126.5	122.9	120.6
Total, Groups I–XV–Soft Goods	188.8	188.8	186.9	188.0	192.0	194.1	195.3	198.0	200.4	201.4	204.5	206.2
Total, Groups XVI–XX–Durable Goods	188.4	190.6	186.8	187.9	193.1	195.9	194.7	196.3	196.9	197.1	199.8	200.6
Store Total	188.6	189.2	186.8	187.9	192.3	194.6	195.2	197.7	199.7	200.6	203.6	205.0

TABLE VII. Continued

January

	Department Groups	1965	1966	1967	1968	1969	1970	1971	1972	1973	1974	1975	1976
I	Piece Goods	205.7	206.6	208.1	210.8	223.9	228.9	235.5	231.1	226.3	261.4	274.7	279.3
II	Domestics and Draperies	206.0	209.6	214.0	223.4	233.1	238.9	240.3	243.9	252.7	271.6	320.4	328.2
III	Women's and Children's Shoes	275.1	281.9	300.1	313.2	335.7	350.8	363.1	370.3	378.4	390.0	406.8	401.2
IV	Men's and Boys' Shoes	263.1	275.7	294.6	303.2	315.5	334.8	349.6	354.6	378.0	408.9	442.7	439.2
V	Infants' Wear	179.0	177.2	180.1	185.5	195.4	200.3	207.2	211.9	219.6	236.0	291.5	300.0
VI	Women's Underwear	182.0	182.5	190.6	194.9	203.4	211.3	215.6	220.8	222.3	230.8	247.6	257.9
VII	Women's and Girls' Hosiery	155.0	155.2	155.1	157.0	157.9	158.2	160.4	156.9	155.8	159.8	166.3	167.4
VIII	Women's and Girls' Accessories	202.0	207.9	214.9	221.3	233.0	242.0	254.7	263.3	267.3	290.4	318.1	327.8
IX	Women's Outerwear and Girls' Wear	189.9	192.4	198.5	207.6	222.0	234.2	240.9	254.0	256.3	276.7	295.1	302.5
X	Men's Clothing	241.8	252.5	258.2	269.7	294.8	313.4	326.1	329.2	345.6	351.6	367.9	370.4
XI	Men's Furnishings	202.4	205.5	212.2	219.4	232.4	240.4	248.5	255.0	255.9	271.5	303.2	304.7
XII	Boys' Clothing and Furnishings	220.9	221.2	228.0	237.4	246.7	260.0	267.3	274.0	275.9	285.3	302.9	307.2
XIII	Jewelry	195.2	198.1	202.8	213.5	232.7	244.2	249.2	258.3	271.6	312.4	397.1	416.6
XIV	Notions	184.3	186.0	194.0	198.7	209.7	221.2	233.0	238.7	252.5	269.2	302.1	315.6
XV	Toilet Articles and Drugs	206.7	211.2	217.7	223.6	231.4	243.6	256.3	262.7	269.9	281.4	314.1	339.4
XVI	Furniture and Bedding	234.0	237.1	249.1	262.6	275.0	289.8	299.2	302.7	307.4	325.6	354.7	368.4
XVII	Floor Coverings	198.7	199.5	200.4	204.2	207.7	207.8	210.3	212.0	211.7	237.4	257.2	277.3
XVIII	Housewares	242.3	246.7	256.7	270.9	283.9	301.3	308.2	319.4	334.0	351.3	411.8	445.7
XIX	Major Appliances	130.0	128.0	128.5	130.3	133.9	139.5	144.7	146.7	148.9	149.9	166.6	176.0
XX	Radios and TV Sets	118.2	111.6	109.8	110.6	109.2	109.3	109.3	108.5	107.2	106.8	110.8	112.6
	Total, Groups I–XV–Soft Goods	208.5	211.5	218.4	226.6	240.0	250.6	258.1	265.2	270.9	288.3	318.2	326.8
	Total, Groups XVI–XX–Durable Goods	201.5	202.2	208.2	216.8	224.4	234.2	239.6	243.9	249.1	261.2	290.8	307.5
	Store Total	206.8	209.4	216.0	224.2	235.5	245.6	252.6	258.6	263.7	279.6	310.2	321.1

total, as shown by the Bureau of Labor Statistics, or that shown for apparel, piece goods and notions combined (groups I, III, IV, VII, VIII, IX, X, XI, XII and XIV), whichever of these combinations more closely represents the coverage of the inventory stock carried by the store.

Application of Indexes to Different Stores and Departments

A company operating in more than one location must determine whether LIFO computations should be developed separately for each store or on a combined basis. The decision will depend to some extent on the manner in which the stores are run. There is no intrinsic reason why corresponding sections in the same store, or in two or more stores of the same company in the same state, cannot be treated as a single department. However, departmental classifications should be maintained. Also, if locations are in different states, it may be preferable to make computations separately, or at least according to state lines, in order to avoid complications in determining taxable incomes earned in the respective states. Where one department crosses a state line, an allocation of the effects of LIFO on income may be required for reporting to the separate states. The required allocation may be made on the basis of inventories computed under the retail method.

An instance not directly covered by Rev. Proc. 72–21 is that of a heterogeneous department which carries goods included in two or more BLS groups. Generally, it is not possible or practical to segregate the inventory in accordance with the separate BLS groups. In the absence of a ruling by the Treasury, the following resolutions would appear to be practical:

> If the heterogeneous department includes only soft goods (i.e., goods included in Groups I–XV), use the aggregate soft goods index;
> If the heterogeneous department includes only hard goods (i.e., goods included in Groups XVI–XX), use the aggregate durable goods index;
> If the heterogeneous department includes soft and hard goods, use the store total index.

Under the dollar-value method, taxpayers (other than retailers who use BLS indexes) must develop their own indexes for each pool (see discussion in Chapter 23).

Adjustment of BLS Index Numbers

The index numbers published by the BLS use January, 1941, as 100 per cent. When LIFO is adopted in a subsequent year, the current year's percentage must be adjusted to reflect only the percentage change in price levels between the *beginning* of the first year LIFO was adopted (i.e., the base year) and the current year. This is done by dividing the current year BLS departmental index numbers (based on the year 1941 = 100) by the BLS departmental index numbers as at the close of the year preceding LIFO. The following example, which assumes a retailer elected LIFO for the year ended January 31, 1954, illustrates the mathematical determination of the index to be used for the related LIFO computations in the current year ended January 31, 1973:

Index January 31, 1953 (i.e., base year)	168.9
Index January 31, 1973 (current year)	267.3
Index to be used for current year ended January 31, 1973 (267.3 ÷ 168.9)	158.3

In effect, the base year (in the above example, January 31, 1953) is the focal point of all subsequent years' computations, and effectively is 100 per cent.

Application of Index Numbers to Variety and Specialty Stores

For a short period of time, Treasury-approved BLS index numbers were published for variety stores. The method of establishing index groups followed for department stores was equally applicable to the special price indexes for variety stores. The published indexes included ten groups and a store total (Group XI) termed Miscellaneous. Departmental classifications, following the pattern set for department stores, were keyed with the index groups to facilitate selection of the proper index. The requirement for treatment of markdowns applied to variety stores as well as department stores. Since these indexes are no longer published, variety store taxpayers should refer to Rev. Rul. 55–220, 1955–1 C.B. 247, before a substitute or self-computed index is used.

Specialty stores using the retail method and carrying a single type of merchandise, such as men's and boys' shoes, men's clothing, or men's furnishings may elect LIFO and use the appropriate BLS index, subject to approval by the Commissioner. If several departments are carried, similar to department stores, obtaining such approval would appear to be more likely.

When a specialty store determines its inventories on an actual cost basis instead of on the retail method, price indexes may be derived from retail price indexes "by the use of appropriate ratios based on cost percentages for the respective departments." In two illustrations set forth by the Internal Revenue Service, the taxpayer is advised to use cost percentages which are complements of net markon percentages, or cost percentages which are complements of gross profit percentages. These cost price indexes are derived from retail price indexes for the appropriate group by multiplying the retail price index by the ratio-of-cost percentages (current year over base year). For further data on these cases refer to Rev. Rul. 54–49, 1954–1 C.B. 32, and Chapter 22.

22

Computation of LIFO Inventories on the Retail Method

Introduction

The retail inventory method has been discussed in detail in Chapters 6 and 7. Under this method, departmental merchandise inventories are controlled at retail prices, and at year end (or at the end of any accounting period) the cost multiplier is applied to the inventory at retail to determine the inventory at cost. The cost multiplier is the complement of the average gross markup for the year, or for the last six months, without reduction for markdowns. The practical effect of reducing the retail value to cost under the retail method is to state the inventory at the lower of cost or market for all financial reporting purposes.

Under LIFO, through the use of retail price indexes, retail inventories are effectively translated into equivalent physical units. Changes in the year-end quantities of inventory, comprising increments or decrements, are reflected at the costs determined on a LIFO basis attributable to each of the years affected by such changes. A more detailed discussion of the calculation of the LIFO value of an inventory computed under the retail method is set forth later in this chapter. However, fundamental to this discussion is an understanding of how the retail method computation is adapted to a LIFO inventory.

Adapting the Retail Method Computation to LIFO Inventories

The retail method of computation may be used for determination of LIFO inventories, provided certain required tax adjustments are made. As noted earlier, the retail method recognizes markups, but not markdowns, in the calculation of cost multipliers, thereby effectively resulting in the valuation of inventories at the lower of cost or market.

LIFO inventories, however, are required by IRC section 472(b)(2) to be valued at cost. To accomplish this result, the cost of the LIFO inventory using the retail method of computation must be adjusted for both markups and markdowns in the computation of cost multipliers. [Reg. § 1.471–8(g).] Also, the closing inventory for the year preceding the adoption of LIFO must be redetermined at cost, as provided by section 472(d).

Book and Tax Adjustments in the First LIFO Year

Typically, there is a difference between the opening inventory (i.e., base-year inventory), which must be priced at cost for LIFO purposes, and the same inventory when it has been priced at the lower of cost or market under the retail method. In the year of change from the retail method to LIFO, this difference would result in additional taxable income which must be reported via the filing of an amended federal income tax return for the year preceding the year of change. [Section 472(d).] The gross effect of adopting LIFO is accounted for as a charge to cost of goods sold in the year of change. This gross effect includes the reduction in income in the current period attributable to the use of the newly adopted LIFO method, less the step-up of the opening inventory in the base-year inventory occasioned by the change from the retail method to LIFO.

The following example, which assumes LIFO election made for the year ended January 31, 1974, illustrates this net adjustment:

Inventory under the retail method:
Opening inventory, January 31, 1973 $192,358
January 31, 1974   255,675

Inventory computed under the LIFO method:
Opening inventory, January 31, 1973 $200,000
                   January 31, 1974   230,225

Under these circumstances, there would have been:

A step-up of $7,642 ($200,000 − $192,358) in the base-year inventory, basically ascribable to the use of the required net markon method (see Chapter 19).

A cumulative net reduction in inventory and gross profit, for the year ended January 31, 1974, of $25,450 comprising the difference between retail method and LIFO inventories as of January 31, 1974 ($255,675 − $230,225).

An adjustment must be made to reduce the general ledger merchandise inventory account, which is stated at cost under the retail method, to the corresponding cost under LIFO. This is generally done by utilizing a valuation allowance account which, when deducted from the merchandise inventory account, produces the LIFO inventory valuation. The entry would be as follows:

Cost of merchandise sold—LIFO adjustment $25,450
    LIFO valuation allowance $25,450

If separate entries are used to show the effect of the changes in valuation of the opening and closing inventories, the entries would be as follows:

LIFO valuation allowance $ 7,642
    Cost of merchandise sold—LIFO adjustment $ 7,642
    (To adjust opening inventories to LIFO.)

Cost of merchandise sold—LIFO adjustment $33,092
    LIFO valuation allowance $33,092
    (To adjust closing inventories to LIFO.)

Data Sheets for Cost Multiplier and LIFO Calculations

A number of work sheets or data sheets have been developed to facilitate LIFO computations for retailers, generally on a departmental basis. Basically, all types of data sheets are similar and produce the same answers; variations depend on the individual taxpayer's business requirements. Following are specimen data sheets, and accompanying explanations, which are used for determining both the departmental cost multipliers (Exhibit A, pages 416–19) and the related valuations (Exhibits B and C, pages 420–22) of the LIFO inventories.

Exhibit A

DEPARTMENTAL INVENTORY DATA SHEET
FOR COMPUTATION OF COST MULTIPLIER

Department: Men's Shoes —BLS Group IV

Line No.		12/31/69(a)	12/31/70	12/31/71	12/31/72	12/31/73	12/31/74
1	Purchases at cost	$ 950,321 (c)	$ 823,909	$ 750,426	$ 793,529	$ 695,813	$ 874,629
2	Less: Factory inter-(intra-) company profit included in store purchases	815	429	281	387	382	453
3	Total purchases at cost (line 1 − line 2)	$ 949,506	$ 823,480	$ 750,145	$ 793,142	$ 695,431	$ 874,176
4	Purchases at retail, including markups	$2,090,611(c)	$1,703,141	$1,653,821	$1,722,941	$1,487,699	$1,869,130
5	Deduct: Markdowns applicable to purchases (exclusive of shrinkage and special discounts and allowances) (b)	83,624(d)	46,390	39,271	59,821	54,371	41,839
6	Net purchases at retail (line 4 − line 5)	$2,006,987	$1,656,751	$1,614,550	$1,663,120	$1,433,328	$1,827,291
7	Cost multiplier (line 3 ÷ line 6) (b)	47.31%	49.70%	46.46%	47.69%	48.52%	47.84%

See accompanying notes.

Ch. 22   COMPUTING LIFO INVENTORIES ON THE RETAIL METHOD

Notes to Exhibit A

(a) Represents base-year opening inventory.

(b) As discussed in Chapter 19, the deduction of markdowns (net of markdown cancellations) in arriving at the departmental cost multipliers for LIFO purposes is necessary and obligatory in order to state departmental inventories at cost. After the *Hutzler* decision, until some time in 1951, total departmental purchases at retail were reduced by all of the departmental markdowns taken during the year. This was an obvious inequity since markdowns taken on the opening inventory were included with markdowns taken on the current year's purchases.

In 1951, after informal conference with U. S. Treasury personnel, the following letter, dated June 27, 1951, was sent to members of the National Retail Dry Goods Association (now the National Retail Merchants Association) remedying this inequity:

Dear Member:

This letter is intended to clarify several matters in connection with the calculation of retail inventories under the last-in-first-out method. One of the requirements incident to the adoption of LIFO is that a "cost" basis rather than a "cost-or-market" basis be employed. In order that this be accomplished, the Bureau of Internal Revenue requires that the cost complement used in valuing LIFO inventories be adjusted for markdowns as well as markups. In adjusting closing inventories of the first year prior to the adoption of LIFO to a cost basis, the LIFO net markup complement should be based upon the ratio of total merchandise handled at cost to the total merchandise handled at retail (the latter amount having been adjusted for markdowns). In computing both the cost and retail amounts of merchandise handled, opening inventories at the beginning of the first prior year should be *included*.

In valuing LIFO inventories for all subsequent periods beginning with the closing inventory of the first LIFO year, the LIFO net markup used in valuing all increments in physical inventory should be computed with reference only to goods purchased during the accounting period in which the increase occurred and, in these cases, opening inventory on hand at the beginning of each accounting period should be *excluded*.

In those cases where opening inventories are not taken into consideration in computing the markup percentage, it is important, in adjusting the retail purchases for markdowns, that only those markdowns applicable to purchases during the year be netted against the retail amount. Otherwise the resulting cost valuation of the increase will be somewhat above true cost and profits from merchandising operations overstated. Ideally, a segregation of all markdowns should be made and only those markdowns taken on current year purchases netted against purchases at retail. In some instances, this procedure may prove to be impracticable from an accounting standpoint, and should this be the case, it is suggested as an alternative solution for this problem that total markdowns taken during the accounting period be prorated in accordance with the ratio which goods included in the opening inventory bear to total merchandise handled. Thus, if opening inventory accounted for 20% of total merchandise handled, only 80% of total markdowns would be netted against retail purchases.

Since the foregoing suggested method conforms with the intent of present Regulations, there is reason to believe that it would be acceptable to the Bureau of Internal Revenue for tax purposes at the present time.

June 27, 1951

In summary, agreement was reached that departmental cost multipliers would be derived as follows:

1. With respect to the base year, opening inventory plus purchases at cost and retail would be used, with 100 per cent of markdowns deducted from the combined opening inventory plus purchases at retail.
2. With respect to all subsequent years, only purchases at cost and retail would be used, and only those markdowns applicable to the current year's purchases would be deducted from the purchases at retail. In this connection, if feasible, the segregation of markdowns produces a better result than the prorating method referred to in the above letter, since the percentage of markdowns on opening inventory is generally a higher percentage than the percentage of markdowns taken on current year's purchases.

(c) Represents opening inventory as of December 31, 1968, plus purchases for the year 1969 [see note (b) above].

(d) Represents all markdowns taken in the year 1969 [see note (b) above].

EXPLANATION OF DEPARTMENTAL INVENTORY DATA SHEET FOR
COMPUTATION OF COST MULTIPLIER (EXHIBIT A)

Department _____   BLS Group No. _____

Line No.		
1	Purchases at cost	The amount of total purchases for the current year are shown. Freight and other direct costs entering into the determination of purchases are included.
2	Less: Factory profit included in store purchases (if the retailer also manufactures merchandise)	
3	Total purchases at cost (line 1 − line 2)	
4	Purchases at retail, including markups	The amount of total purchases at retail for the current year.
5	Deduct: Markdowns applicable to purchases (exclusive of shrinkage, and special discounts to employees, institutional, contract, etc.)	LIFO, as a cost method, must account for both markups and markdowns. Shrinkage and special discounts do not represent depreciation in the value of the goods and are, therefore, not included in the markdowns statistic.
6	Net purchases at retail (line 4 − line 5)	
7	Cost multiplier (line 3 ÷ line 6)	This cost multiplier percentage is the complement of the net markon percentage. In years subsequent to the base year, it is used in the LIFO computation only where there is an increment in inventory, and is used in pricing out such increment (see Exhibits B and C).

Exhibit B

VALUATION OF LIFO INVENTORIES UNDER THE RETAIL METHOD

Department: Men's Shoes—BLS Group IV

Line No.		(1) 12/31/69	(2) 12/31/70	(3) 12/31/71	(4) 12/31/72	(5) 12/31/73	(6) 12/31/74
	I. Determination of Dollar Change in Current Year's Inventory						
1	Cost multiplier (see Exhibit A)	47.31%	49.70%	46.46%	47.69%	48.52%	47.84%
2	Inventory at retail	$542,708	$673,829	$653,721	$578,753	$542,498	$798,330
3	Adjusted BLS index	100.0%	103.6%	104.1%	105.3%	106.2%	106.9%
4	Inventory at base-year prices (line 2 ÷ line 3)	542,708	650,414	627,974	549,623	510,827	746,801
5	Increment at base-year prices	542,708	107,706	85,266	6,915	510,827[a]	235,974
	II. Valuation of Dollar Change						
6	Increment year number	(1)	(2)	(2)	(2)	(1)	(6)
7	Increment at index price (line 5 × appropriate year BLS index)	542,708	111,583	88,336	7,164	510,827[a]	252,256
	III. Determination of LIFO Closing Inventory						
8	Increment at cost (line 7 × appropriate year cost multiplier)	256,755	55,457	43,903	3,561	241,672[a]	120,679
9	Prior LIFO basis inventory	-0-	256,755	256,755	256,755	-0-	241,672
10	Current LIFO basis inventory (line 8 + line 9)	$256,755	$312,212	$300,658	$260,316	$241,672	$362,351

[a]Represents base-year opening inventory. Alternatively, this can be shown as a decrement, at base-year prices, of $38,796 ($549,623 − $510,827), and priced out as follows:

	Decrement @ Base-Year Prices	Applicable BLS Index	Decrement @ Current-Year Prices	Applicable Cost Multiplier	Decrement @ LIFO Cost
	$ 6,915	103.6%	$ 7,164	49.70%	$ 3,561
	31,881	100.0	31,881	47.31	15,083
	$38,796				$18,644

Reconciliation:
LIFO cost, 12/31/72 $260,316
Deduct: Decrement, as above   18,644
LIFO cost, 12/31/73 $241,672

EXPLANATION OF DATA SHEET FOR VALUATION OF LIFO INVENTORIES UNDER THE RETAIL METHOD (EXHIBIT B)

Department _____   BLS Group No. _____

Line No.		
	I. Determination of Dollar Change in the Current Year's Inventory	
1	Cost multiplier	Determined on Departmental Inventory Data Sheet for Computation of Cost Multiplier (see line 7 of Exhibit A).
2	Inventory at retail	Retail value of the departmental inventory as taken from stock records (i.e., retail ledger).
3	Adjusted BLS Price Index	This is published semiannually by the Department of Labor, Bureau of Labor Statistics (BLS), as of January and July. Because the published BLS statistics use 1941 price levels as a base (100) and the company's base year is December 31, 1969, the company's index numbers require adjustment. (See discussion regarding conversion of index numbers in Chapter 21.)
4	Inventory at base-year prices (line 2 ÷ line 3)	
5	Increment (or decrement) at base-year prices (line 4 of current year as compared to the next lower line 4 of a preceding year)	Determination of changes in the dollar amount of the current year's inventory *at base-year prices.*
	II. Valuation of Dollar Change	
6	Year of increment column number	This ensures that an increment is matched with the appropriate cost multiplier, index number, and other data for the year of that increment.
7	Increment at appropriate year index prices (line 5 × line 3)	The current retail value of any increment is obtained by applying the appropriate year BLS index (line 3) to the increment at base-year prices (line 5). If there has been a decrement, it is applied to the most recent layer(s), in reverse chronological order, at the applicable index price and cost multiplier of such layer(s).
	III. Determination of the LIFO Closing Inventory	
8	Increment at cost (line 7 × line 1)	The current retail value of the increment on line 7 is reduced to current cost by application of the appropriate year cost multiplier on line 1.
9	Prior LIFO basis inventory	The appropriate LIFO cost inventory (i.e., LIFO inventory at year-end date preceding the year of increment) is added to the current year's increment at current year's cost.
10	Current LIFO basis inventory (line 8 + line 9)	This is the ending LIFO cost inventory.

Exhibit C

VALUATION OF LIFO INVENTORY

Department: _Men's Shoes_ _____BLS Group IV

Line No.		12/31/69	12/31/70	12/31/71	12/31/72	12/31/73	12/31/74
1	Inventory at retail	$542,708	$673,829	$653,721	$578,753	$542,498	$798,330
2	Adjusted BLS index	100.0%	103.6%	104.1%	105.3%	106.2%	106.9%
3	Inventory at base-year prices (line 1 ÷ line 2)	542,708	650,414	627,974	549,623	510,827	746,801
4a	Increase line 3 (current year minus preceding year)	542,708	107,706				235,974
4b	(Decrease) line 3 (preceding year minus current year)			(22,440)	(78,351)	(38,796)	
	Application of subsequent decreases A.		(22,440)				
	B.	(31,881)	(78,351)				
	C.		(6,915)				
	D.						
5	Calculation of (decrease) at cost:						
	A. (Decrease) above or portion thereof			(22,440)	(78,351)	(6,915)	
	B. Index for decrease (index of year to which applied)			103.6%	103.6%	103.6%	
	C. (Decrease) at year of application of index (A × B)			(23,247)	(81,172)	(7,164)	
	D. Cost multiplier for year of application			49.7%	49.7%	49.7%	
	E. LIFO (decrease) (C × D)			(11,554)	(40,342)	(3,561)	
	F. (Decrease) not used in preceding section					(31,881)	
	G. Index for this portion decrease					100.0%	
	H. (Decrease) at year of application of index					(31,881)	
	I. Cost multiplier for year of application					47.31%	
	J. LIFO (decrease) (H × I)					(15,083)	
	K. (Decrease) not used in preceding section						
	L. Index for this portion of decrease						
	M. (Decrease) at year of application of index (K × L)						
	N. Cost multiplier for year of application						
	O. LIFO (decrease) (M × N)						
6	LIFO increases at current prices (4a × 2)	542,708	111,583				252,256
7	LIFO cost multiplier for current year	47.31%	49.70%				47.84%
8	LIFO increase (decrease) at cost (6 × 7 or 5E + 5J + 50)	256,755	55,457	(11,554)	(40,342)	(18,644)	120,679
9	LIFO closing inventory	$256,755	$312,212	$300,658	$260,316	$241,672	$362,351

Detailed Explanations Related to the Computation of LIFO Inventory Under the Retail Method

The LIFO cost valuation of inventory under the retail method is generally computed as follows (see Exhibit B).

Determination of a Dollar Change in the Current Year's Inventory. The retail value of the departmental inventory at the end of the year must be reduced to the base-period price level. This is done by applying the appropriate BLS price index to such end-of-year inventory at retail. A comparison of such year-end closing inventory, expressed in terms of the base-year price level, with the base-period inventory, will show whether there has been an aggregate increment or decrement since the base year.

Valuation of a Dollar Change. Such aggregate increment or decrement must then be expressed at current retail prices. Assuming an aggregate increment, this is done by multiplying the individual layers (year-by-year basis) by the BLS index number for the year or years in which the increment or increments have occurred. A decrement in the inventory is always treated as a decrease in the most recent year(s) incremental layer(s), in reverse chronological sequence. In the event all increments are successively eliminated, the decrement is applied to the base-period opening inventory.

Determination of the LIFO Closing Inventory. The retail value of the aggregate increment or decrement must be reduced to LIFO cost by applying the cost multipliers applicable to each year. If there has been an increment over the preceding year, the cost multiplier for the current year is used. If a decrement has occurred, then the cost multiplier applied is the cost multiplier applicable to the layer(s) being reduced (or eliminated).

In order to arrive at the closing LIFO inventory for the current year, the current year's increment valued at LIFO cost is added to the closing LIFO inventory of the preceding year. Current year's decrements valued at LIFO cost are subtracted from the closing LIFO inventory cost of the preceding year.

As noted above, for LIFO inventory purposes, the cost multiplier is used to reduce the retail value of an increment to its cost. This percentage represents the ratio of the year's purchases at cost to purchases at retail value. As shown in Exhibit A, such ratio is determined by dividing purchases at cost by the sum of purchases at retail, plus markups (net of markup cancellations) minus markdowns (net of markdown cancellations).

Example of LIFO Calculations

Examples are shown in Exhibits A, B, and C of cost multiplier and LIFO data sheets covering five years of a retail men's shoe department, BLS Group IV. In these exhibits, LIFO was initially adopted for the year 1970. The computation of an increment is shown for 1970, and a decrement that reduced part of the 1970 increment is shown for 1971. In 1972 a decrement further reduced the 1970 increment. In 1973 a decrement eliminated the balance of the 1970 increment and even reduced a portion of the opening (1969) base-period layer. In 1974 a new layer of increment is shown which is added to the (reduced) 1969 base-period layer, and such incremental layer is priced out at 1974 prices.

See also Rev. Proc. 72–21, which illustrates the LIFO inventory method as applied to the retail method of pricing inventories. (Revenue Procedure 72–21 supersedes Mimeograph 6244, 1948–1 C.B. 21.)

Computation of Opening LIFO Inventory for Base Year and Increment for Year 1970. After the cost multiplier for the base year has been determined (see line 7, Exhibit A), it is inserted on line 1, column 1 on Exhibit B.

Reference to the final inventory control records shows that the inventory at retail as of December 31, 1969, is stated at $542,708. This amount was determined through an actual physical count of the departmental inventory, or by the maintenance of perpetual inventory records (retail ledgers) which are adjusted by physical counts during the year, and is shown on line 2.

The base-year opening inventory is the point of reference for subsequent years' LIFO computations and the BLS price index number is therefore stated at 100 per cent. The opening inventory at retail is converted to cost by applying the cost multiplier, resulting in an opening inventory on a LIFO cost basis of $256,755.

The next step is to determine the LIFO inventory at December 31, 1970. The cost multiplier for the year 1970 is 49.70 per cent. The inventory control records indicate that the closing inventory at retail of the men's shoes department was $673,829. Using the formula shown in Chapter 21, the adjusted BLS index number is computed to be 103.6 per cent as shown on line 3.

The year-end inventory, at retail, is divided by the BLS index number in order to state the inventory, at retail, at the base-year price level. The latter amount is compared with the opening base-year inventory in order to determine whether there was an increment (or decrement) in the dollar value of the base-year inventory, at the base-year price level.

The increment of $107,706 at the base-year price level must now be expressed at current price levels, at retail, which is determined to be $111,583. This increment must be converted to cost by applying the appropriate cost multiplier. By then adding the 1970 increment at cost ($55,457) to the base-year opening inventory ($256,755), the inventory at LIFO cost amounts to $312,212 at December 31, 1970.

The increment of $107,706 at base-year prices in 1970 is treated as a separate layer from the opening base-year inventory. Any decrement in inventory from the $312,212 LIFO cost level must first be applied against the entire 1970 layer before reducing the December 31, 1969, inventory.

Computation of Decrements for Years 1971 and 1972. To determine the amount of the decrement in inventory which occurred in 1971, the next preceding lower figure on line 4 is subtracted from the 1971 figure on line 4. The next preceding lower figure is $542,708 in the December 31, 1969, column. The difference between $627,974 and $542,708 represents a net increment of $85,266 since 1969. Despite this increment the December 31, 1970, layer was decreased, at base-year prices, by $22,440 ($650,414 − $627,974). Because the net increment of $85,266 is attributable solely to the 1970 inventory layer, the numeral 2, representing the December 31, 1970 (year of increment) column, is inserted on line 6. Future identification of the respective layers is thus facilitated.

To obtain the retail value of the increment, it must be multiplied by the appropriate adjusted BLS index (which in this case has been indicated as numeral 2) representing 103.6 per cent. Similarly, in order to determine the increment at cost, the cost multiplier of 49.70 per cent for December 31, 1970, is multiplied by the increment of $88,336 in order to arrive at the cost of $43,903. The closing LIFO inventory at December 31, 1971, is the sum of the net increment (line 8), and the LIFO value of the prior closing inventory (line 9), which in this case is December 31, 1969.

When there is an increment for a new layer, the prior LIFO basis inventory (line 9) is the same as the current LIFO basis inventory of the preceding year (line 10), as for 1970 and 1974. However, where a decrement has occurred, as in 1971 and 1972, part or the entire previous year's LIFO layer has been reduced. Accordingly, the current LIFO basis inventory is the sum of the net increment, valued at the cost of that increment, plus the current LIFO basis inventory for the year preceding the year in which the most recent increment occurred.

Computation of Decrement for Year 1973. In 1973 the remaining balance of the 1970 layer was eliminated and a portion of the December 31, 1969, base-year inventory was additionally reduced.

The numeral one is placed in line 6, column 5 (increment-year number) to indicate that the remaining layer is attributable solely to the base-year layer. The increment at index price, line 7, column 5, is equal to the amount shown as the increment in line 5 because the adjusted BLS index for the base year is 100 per cent. Similarly, the cost multiplier for the December 31, 1969, base layer of 47.31 per cent is applied to this increment of $510,827 to arrive at the LIFO cost of $241,672.

The effect of the 1973 inventory change may be analyzed as follows. In 1973 there has been a decrease of $38,796, stated at base-year prices, in the department inventory (line 4 of 1972 minus line 4 of 1973, or $549,623 minus $510,827). The 1973 decrement of $38,796 at base-year prices has not only eliminated the $6,915 remaining from the December 31, 1970, layer, but it has also reduced the base-year inventory by $31,881. The remaining LIFO inventory at base-year prices is attributable solely to the December 31, 1969, base year. (See Note a to Exhibit B.)

Computation of Increment for Year 1974. The computation for the year ended December 31, 1974, is comparable to the computation of the increment shown in column 2, for the year ended December 31, 1970. The increment for the year 1974 is treated separately from the (reduced) base-year inventory (LIFO cost basis) of $241,672, and is identified as number 6 for future reference.

Other LIFO Computation Formats. The LIFO work sheet illustrated in Exhibit B is designed to show the cumulative changes in inventory of one department. Shown in Exhibit C is an example of another type of data sheet using the same LIFO data. Except for the arrangement of the items on the work sheet, the two data sheets are virtually identical in years in which there is an increment. In years in which there is a decrement, Exhibit C shows more detail and, correspondingly, requires a greater number of entries. The closing LIFO inventory is determined in a decrement year in Exhibit C by subtracting the amount of the decrement from the prior appropriate closing LIFO inventory.

The annual LIFO computations are readily adaptable to electronic data processing. A number of retailers have found it feasible, in terms of economy, efficiency, and accuracy, to adapt these computations to the computer.

Purchase Discounts

Conventional retailers, as opposed to discount retailers (i.e., "mass merchandisers"), generally keep the retail stock ledger and related statistical merchandising records on the basis of purchases at gross invoice cost—that is, before deduction of discounts. In the valuation of year-end inventories under the retail method, appropriate recognition is given to the net invoice cost of merchandise purchased. In effect, discounts applicable to year-end inventories, which are deemed to be unearned at such date, are netted against departmental inventories (see Chapter 8). Trade practice varies in the manner in which such unearned discounts are computed. Some retailers determine discount rates (from purchase records) on an individual department basis, whereas other retailers develop and utilize an overall, storewide discount rate. The discount procedure utilized in connection with the retail method should be used in determining inventory valuation on the LIFO basis. If a retailer has both purchase and added (i.e., "loaded") discounts which are eliminated under the retail method, a comparable method should be followed on the LIFO basis.

Figure 43 shows the comparative computation of discounts in inventory under the retail and LIFO methods where discounts, both purchase and added, are computed on a storewide basis.

R COMPANY

COMPUTATION OF RESERVE FOR UNEARNED DISCOUNT AT COST
UNDER RETAIL METHOD AND ON LIFO BASIS

	Under Retail Method		On LIFO Basis	
Added discount:				
Inventory at cost	$2,539,839.86		$1,843,906.88	
Discount percentage	3.167		3.167	
Reserve		$ 80,436.73		$ 58,396.53
Cash discount:				
Inventory at cost	2,539,839.86		1,843,906.88	
Less: Added discounts	80,436.73		58,396.53	
	2,459,403.13		1,785,510.35	
Discount percentage reserve	4.208	103,491.68	4.208	75,134.28
		$ 183,928.41		$ 133,530.81
Inventory at cost		$2,539,839.86		$1,843,906.88
Less: Unearned discount		183,928.41		133,530.81
		$2,355,911.45		$1,710,376.07

FIG. 43. Computation of reserve for unearned discount at cost under retail method and on LIFO basis.

With respect to discount retailers, the purchase cost figures included in the retail stock ledger are reflected net of purchase discounts. Accordingly, no further adjustment is required in the valuation of year-end inventories either under the retail method or on the LIFO basis.

Theoretically, under the LIFO method, since the current year-end inventory comprises constituent layers of various years, the discount rates in such years should be applied to the corresponding layers. Consequently, if an inventory is made up of, say, a 19X1, 19X3, and 19X8 segment, the unearned discount percentage for each of those years should be applied separately to the individual segments. As a practical matter, however, departmental and/or storewide discount rates tend to vary little from year to year. Accordingly, most retailers apply the current year's discount rates to year-end LIFO inventory valuations, ignoring the minor imperfections that might result from applying different discount rates, as appropriate, to the layers of the various years.

Figure 44 shows a comparison of inventories under the retail method and LIFO basis, the resultant comparative reduction or LIFO reserve after adjustment for purchase discounts, and the re-

Ch. 22   COMPUTING LIFO INVENTORIES ON THE RETAIL METHOD   429

SUMMARY OF MERCHANDISE INVENTORY, RETAIL DEPARTMENTS, ON LIFO BASIS,
USING BLS INDEXES BEFORE AND AFTER ADJUSTMENTS FOR UNEARNED DISCOUNTS
Years Ended January 31, 19X1, 19X2, and 19X3

	Reduction in Merchandise Inventory, Retail Departments, Before Reserve for Unearned Discounts	Reserve for Unearned Discounts — Reserve Required	Reserve for Unearned Discounts — Reduction in Reserve	Reduction in Merchandise Inventory, Retail Departments, Net of Unearned Discounts as Adjusted
Year ended January 31, 19X1:				
Merchandise inventory, retail departments:				
As computed under the retail method	$2,957,326	$ 91,093		$2,866,233
As computed under net markon basis	3,105,545	98,407		3,007,138
(Increase) in inventory	($148,219)			
(Increase) in reserve for unearned discounts			($ 7,314)	
Net (increase) in inventory, January 31, 19X1				($140,905)
Year ended January 31, 19X2:				
Merchandise inventory, retail departments:				
As computed under the retail method	3,662,840	127,247		3,535,593
Add: Adjustment due to computation under net mark on basis as at January 31, 19X1, as above	148,219	7,314		140,905
	3,811,059	134,561		3,676,498
As computed on basis of last-in, first-out (BLS Indexes)	3,589,319	122,926		3,466,393
Reduction in inventory	221,740			
Reduction in reserve for unearned discounts			11,635	
Net reduction in inventory, January 31, 19X2				210,105
Total reduction in inventory as at January 31, 19X2	73,521	4,321		69,200
Year ended January 31, 19X3:				
Merchandise inventory, retail departments:				
As computed under the retail method	4,001,604	145,448		3,856,156
Less: Adjustments due to computation on basis of last-in, first-out, as at January 31, 19X1, and 19X2, as above	73,521	4,321		69,200
	3,928,083	141,127		3,786,956
As computed on basis of last-in, first-out (BLS Indexes)	3,775,671	137,436		3,638,235
Reduction in inventory	152,412			
Reduction in reserve for unearned discounts			3,691	
Net reduction in inventory, January 31, 19X3				148,721
Total reduction in inventory as at January 31, 19X3	$225,933	$8,012		$217,921

FIG. 44. Summary of merchandise inventory, retail departments, 'before and after unearned discounts.

lated effects on gross margin for fiscal years ended January 31, 19X1, 19X2, and 19X3.

Methods of Handling Split Departments

In a department store it is not uncommon for departments to be combined or split, or for new departments to be created or old ones terminated. From the point of view of LIFO computations, there are at least two types of changes of departments which require consideration: (1) where a department starts out as one department and splits into two or more departments in a later year; (2) where two or more departments are in existence in the base year and in subsequent years combine and become one. Treasury Regulations are silent with respect to split or combined departments.

For an example of a split situation, assume the following data for Department X, which existed as an independent department through January 31, 19X5. During the fiscal year ended January 31, 19X6—say, on August 7, 19X5—Department X split up into two departments, X (the old department) and Y:

Year Ended	Inventory at Retail	Inventory at Cost	Purchases at Retail Net of Markdowns	Purchases at Cost	Complement of Purchase Markon Percentage
Department X (BLS Group I)					
January 31, 19X1	$30,000	$20,000	$50,000	$25,000	56.25% *
19X2	40,000	30,000	75,000	35,000	46.67
19X3	35,000	25,000	80,000	60,000	75.00
19X4	27,000	20,000	70,000	50,000	71.43
19X5	30,000	22,000	60,000	45,000	75.00
19X6	20,000	15,000	30,000	25,000	—

Year Ended	Inventory at Retail	Inventory at Cost	Purchases at Retail Net of Markdowns	Purchases at Cost	Complement of Purchase Markon Percentage
Department Y (BLS Group I)					
From August 7, 19X5 to January 31, 19X6	$30,000	$20,000	$50,000	$20,000	—

* Cost multiplier is calculated taking into account opening inventories at cost and retail.

Ch. 22 COMPUTING LIFO INVENTORIES ON THE RETAIL METHOD 431

The easiest and most practical method is to continue to treat Departments X and Y as one department, as follows:

Combination of Departments X and Y (BLS Group I)

January 31, 19X6 $50,000 $35,000 $80,000 $45,000   56.25%

In the above illustration for the fiscal years ended January 31, 19X1, through January 31, 19X5, Department X figures are used. For the fiscal year ended January 31, 19X6, and thereafter, the combined figures would be used for the LIFO calculations.

As indicated, where departments are split, one method is to continue to treat the departments as one, even after the split. Another method is to ascertain the percentages that the inventories of the new departments bear to total inventory of the original department at the date of split, and apply these percentages retroactively, thereby allocating inventories at retail and the LIFO layers for each of the prior years.

Some retailers, when allocating the prior-year inventories at retail and the LIFO inventory layers to each of the departments, prefer to use as a basis of allocation the relation of inventory at retail for each of the new departments to the total of all the split departments at the year end in which the department was divided, rather than at the date of the split as indicated above. Their rationales are (1) no inventory may be readily available at the date of split, and to take one may be too burdensome; and (2) because inventories at an interim date may be larger or smaller for the different kinds of merchandise handled, the inventories at the year end bear a better relationship to year-end inventories of prior years.

The argument for recomputing LIFO on the basis of allocating the old department into each of its subdivisions is that the Treasury requires that LIFO must be computed separately for each department; to continue to treat the subdivided department as one may be a violation of the rule. The arguments for continuing to treat the subdivided department as one are as follows: (1) there is no definition of a department to serve as a guide, nor one which requires a determination that separating the inventory on the books, or even physically, creates two or more departments; (2) there is no way of knowing the actual physical inventory for subdivisions of the old department in the prior years, and an allocation based on the physical subdivision at a later date is arbitrary; and (3) if the same goods which were not segregated in the earlier years met the test of a unitary department, then for sake of consistency they should be similarly treated in later years, even though either (or both) the location of the goods has been changed or the statistical records show a subdivision. In the absence of an express directive to the contrary, the authors favor continuing the split departments as one departmental entity for LIFO computation purposes.

Methods of Handling Combined Departments

Combined departments present a more complicated problem. One method is based upon the theory that, as of any date, a LIFO inventory is made up of layers of purchases. Consequently, by adding together the LIFO layers for each of the combined departments, for the years prior to that within which the departments are combined, a combined LIFO inventory may be determined. On the other hand, some retailers adhere to the so-called "beginning-of-LIFO" basis. In effect, an attempt is made, in the years after the departments are combined, to split the departments in the same ratios as the departmental inventories at the end of the base year. Other reasonable ratios for splitting the departments may be available.

In the first of the two alternatives, the combined department is treated as one department. Under the so-called "beginning-of-LIFO" basis, separate LIFO computations are made for segments of the goods in the combined inventory. Under ordinary circumstances the authors prefer the former treatment. The absence of Treasury Regulations covering this problem would seem to permit the application of such practical methods as meet the test of reasonableness.

To illustrate the preferred procedure, an example is given of the combination of Departments 2 and 3. Both departments are independently operated until they are combined during the year ended January 31, 19X7. At January 31, 19X7, the inventory for the combined department will, of course, be one figure which is made up of inventory layers of Departments 2 and 3 from all prior years. Computations illustrating the theory of combining LIFO layers follow.

COMPUTATION OF INVENTORY AT COST ON LIFO BASIS USING LAYERS AT JANUARY 31, 19X6

January 31	(1) Index	(2) Inventories at Retail	(3) Inventories at Retail on 19X1 Basis (Col. 2 ÷ Col. 1)	(4) Retail Inventory Layers at 19X1 Prices	(5) Retail Inventory Layers at Current Prices (Col. 1 × Col. 4)	(6) Cost Multipliers	(7) LIFO Layers at Cost (Col. 5 × Col. 6)
			Department 2				
19X1	100.00	$16,901	$16,901	$12,327	$12,327	60.80	$7,495
19X2	111.08	15,965	14,373	—			
19X3	114.50	15,268	13,334	—			
19X4	126.28	15,566	12,327	—			
19X5	141.41	24,066	17,019	2,811	3,975	59.52	2,366
19X6	146.78	22,219	15,138	—			
				$15,138			$9,861
			Department 3				
19X1	100.00	$20,000	$20,000	$5,500	$5,500	70.30	$3,867
19X2	111.08	14,997	13,500				
19X3	114.50	6,299	5,500				
19X4	126.28	9,472	7,500	2,000	2,526	65.00	1,642
19X5	141.41	14,141	10,000	2,000	2,828	64.00	1,810
19X6	146.78	13,946	9,500				
				$9,500			$7,319

In order appropriately to combine the LIFO layers of Departments 2 and 3, it is necessary to (1) combine and aggregate the departmental retail inventory layers at 19X1 prices; and (2) recompute the combined cost multipliers, as follows:

1. The computation of combined departmental layers at 19X1 prices is taken from column 4, "Retail Inventory Layers at 19X1 Prices":

Department	19X1	19X4	19X5	Total
2	$12,327		$2,811	$15,138
3	5,500	$2,000	2,000	9,500
	$17,827	$2,000	$4,811	$24,638

Inventories at retail on 19X1 basis (column 3) for combined Departments 2 and 3 are then aggregated as follows:

Year Ended January 31	Combined Layers of Inventory at Retail at Base-Year Prices Not Liquidated at January 31, 19X6	
19X1		$17,827
19X2		—
19X3		—
19X4	($17,827 + $2,000 =)	19,827
19X5	($19,827 + $4,811 =)	24,638
19X6		—

2. Combined cost multipliers are recomputed as follows:

Department	Retail Inventory Layers at Current Prices (Col. 5)	January 31, 19X1, LIFO Layers at Cost (Col. 7)	Cost Multipliers (Col. 7 ÷ Col. 5)
2	$12,327	$ 7,495	60.80
3	5,500	3,867	70.30
	$17,827	$11,362	63.73 (as computed)

Department	Retail Inventory Layers at Current Prices (Col. 5)	January 31, 19X5, LIFO Layers at Cost (Col. 7)	Cost Multipliers (Col. 7 ÷ Col. 5)
2	$3,975	$2,366	59.52
3	2,828	1,810	64.00
	$6,803	$4,176	61.38 (as computed)

Year Ended January 31	Combined Cost Multipliers As Computed Above
19X1	63.73
19X4	65.00 (from Department 3)
19X5	61.38

Combining the LIFO layers of Departments 2 and 3:

		(1)	(2)	(3)	(4)	(5)	(6)	(7)
January 31	Index	Inventories at Retail *	Inventories at Retail on 19X1 Basis (Col. 2 ÷ Col. 1)	Retail Inventory Layers at 19X1 Prices	Retail Inventory Layers at Current Prices (Col. 1 × Col. 4)	Cost Multipliers	LIFO Layers at Cost (Col. 5 × Col. 6)
19X1	100.00		$17,827	$17,827	$17,827	63.73	$11,362
19X2	111.08		17,827				
19X3	114.50		17,827	—			
19X4	126.28		19,827	2,000	2,526	65.00	1,642
19X5	141.41		24,638	4,811	6,803	61.38	4,176
19X6	146.78		24,638	—			
				$24,638			$17,180

* No figures are supplied or required in column 2 because there is no relation between the recomputed LIFO layers at January 31, 19X6, and the combined annual inventories at retail for all years then ended.

Ch. 22 COMPUTING LIFO INVENTORIES ON THE RETAIL METHOD

The schedule above has all the data required for making a LIFO computation as at January 31, 19X7, of the single combined department.

If unearned discounts in inventory are computed in layers, it may be correct to compute a combined discount percentage for Departments 2 and 3 in very much the same manner as the combined cost multipliers are computed. One example will suffice to illustrate the methodology:

Year Ended January 31, 19X1

Department	(1) LIFO Layers at Cost	(2) Unearned Discount Percentage in Inventory	(3) Unearned Discount in Inventory (Col. 1 × Col. 2)
2	$ 7,495	3.0	$225
3	3,867	2.0	77
	$11,362	2.7 (or $302 ÷ $11,362)	$302

In this illustration, 2.7 per cent is the combined unearned discount percentage in inventory for the fiscal year ended January 31, 19X1.

It should be noted that Department 2 and Department 3 have the same BLS index numbers. In view of the fact that the BLS department groupings are limited in number, it appears probable that the index numbers for merged departments would be the same. However, there are instances in practice where departments having different index numbers are combined. An illustration of the combining of LIFO layers in such situation follows on the assumption that Departments 1 and 4 of X Company combined to form one department as at January 31, 19X7.

First, the two departmental LIFO inventories are set up showing their positive layers of LIFO inventory as follows:

	(1)	(2)	(3) Inventories at Retail on 19X1 Basis (Col. 2 ÷ Col. 1)	(4) Retail Inventory Layers at 19X1 Prices	(5) Retail Inventory Layers at Current Prices (Col. 1 × Col. 4)	(6) Cost Multipliers	(7) LIFO Layers at Cost (Col. 5 × Col. 6)
January 31	Index	Inventories at Retail					
			Department 1				
19X1	100.00	$27,263	$27,263	$27,263	$27,263	55.10	$15,022
19X2	117.18	39,385	33,611	6,348	7,439	54.73	4,071
19X3	122.65	41,642	33,952	341	418	53.71	225
19X4	131.28	73,173	55,738	7,182	9,429	52.19	4,921
19X5	134.23	55,214	41,134				
19X6	133.97	75,359	56,251	15,117	20,252	54.56	11,049
				$56,251			$35,288
			Department 4				
19X1	100.00	$41,438	$41,438	$39,878	$39,878	61.30	$24,445
19X2	113.27	45,170	39,878				
19X3	118.49	68,934	58,177	7,680	9,100	60.38	5,495
19X4	119.62	88,344	73,854				
19X5	120.40	91,900	76,329				
19X6	120.64	57,374	47,558				
				$47,558			$29,940
			Departments 1 and 4 Combined				
19X1	100.00		$ 67,141	$ 67,141	$67,141	58.78	$39,467
19X2	117.18		73,489	6,348	7,439	54.73	4,071
19X3	118.66		81,510	8,021	9,518	60.10	5,720
19X4	131.28		88,692	7,182	9,429	52.19	4,921
19X5	—		88,692	—			
19X6	133.97		103,809	15,117	20,252	54.56	11,049
				$103,809			$65,228

The combined cost multipliers in column 6 are obtained by dividing the combined figures in column 7 by those in column 5.

January 31	Col. 7		Col. 5		Col. 6
19X1	$39,467	÷	$67,141	=	58.78
19X2	4,071	÷	7,439	=	54.73
19X3	5,720	÷	9,518	=	60.10
19X4	4,921	÷	9,429	=	52.19
19X6	$11,049	÷	$20,252	=	54.56

The combined figures in column 3 are derived by cumulating at the end of each year the merged figures in column 4 as follows:

January 31		Col. 4		Col. 3
19X1		$67,141		$ 67,141
19X2	+	6,348	=	73,489
19X3	+	8,021	=	81,510
19X4	+	7,182	=	88,692
19X5	+	0	=	88,692
19X6	+	15,117	=	103,809

The index numbers in column 1 came from the department which is the source of the LIFO layer. For January 31, 19X2, 19X4, and 19X6, that department is number 1. For January 31, 19X1, there is a combination of LIFO layers from both Departments 1 and 4; since both departments have an index of 100.00, the merged department also uses 100.00. For the year ended January 31, 19X3, there is also a combining of LIFO inventory layers of Departments 1 and 4; the index number for Department 1 is 122.65, and for Department 4 it is 118.49. The index used in the combined department is 118.66 for the year ended January 31, 19X3, derived by applying the following formula:

$$\text{Index number} = \frac{\text{Retail inventory layer at current prices}}{\text{Retail inventory layer at 19X1 prices}}$$

For the combined department, the newly computed index number is determined by dividing $9,518 by $8,021, or 118.66.

At this point it should be mentioned that nowhere in Mimeograph 6244, or elsewhere, is there any reference as to whether the use of a derived index number is permitted. It would appear that, in the absence of definitive rules, the Treasury should accept an answer which is practical and reasonable. In the example above—for the year ended January 31, 19X3—it would appear that the use of the computed index of 118.66 should be allowed.

A corollary question that arises in the example is the appropriate index number to be used after the combination, say, for years ended January 31, 19X7, and subsequent. In the authors' opinion, since the merchandise included in the combined department falls into two index groups, use of the storewide index is reasonable.

Special Problems

In some instances parent and subsidiary corporations use one stock ledger for all locations, and the statistical data with respect to purchases at retail, purchases at cost, and markups (net) and markdowns (net) for similar departments at various locations are combined. In this situation similar departmental physical inventories at retail at the various locations are added together for purposes of determining shrinkage of inventory. Also, only one cost multiplier is computed, based on the inventory and purchases for all locations for similar departments. In such instances LIFO cost multipliers would also be the common cost multipliers, after adjustment for markdowns.

Certain retailers not only have retail operations but manufacture some categories of merchandise. A practice sometimes followed is to load the store purchases with so-called factory profits. This would be reflected in a transfer of manufactured goods from the owned factory to the store at a cost figure which includes factory profit. The store would then enter the loaded costs in the stock ledger. The inventory at cost computed under the retail method would later be reduced by the factory profit. Under LIFO computations, the correction factor should be reflected in the cost multipliers by eliminating from departmental purchases at cost the loaded factory profit.

Revenue Ruling 23 (1953-1 C.B. 34) extended the permissible use of BLS department store retail price index numbers to enable a specialty or other retail store using the retail method to use the BLS index numbers "if it has a reasonable number and variety of departments, though not necessarily all of the departments of the most elaborate department store, and if the goods carried in its various departments are reasonably similar to those carried in corresponding departments by a typical department store in its general locality." The LIFO computations would then be made in the same way and subject to the same rules as a department store. "It is not intended that an extremely specialized store carrying a single line . . . such as a shoe store, . . . which would use only a single group index as compiled by the BLS, could use such a single index without showing that such an index is adequately representative of its whole inventory."

In Rev. Rul. 54-49 (1954-1 C.B. 32) the Commissioner, recognizing that certain retailers do not employ the retail method, set up a method of computing LIFO by permitting the derivation of wholesale or cost price indexes from published BLS department store retail price index numbers. The basis for the ruling was advice requested in connection with a specialty store not employing the retail method. The authors see no reason why the ruling would not be applicable to other taxpayers (say, a department store) not using the retail method if they would qualify for use of BLS department store price indexes except for the fact that the retail method is not used.

Revenue Ruling 54–49 sets forth two methods of deriving cost or wholesale price indexes from the BLS department store retail price indexes suitable for LIFO computations. In the first instance, the Commissioner permits the application of the change in complement of departmental net markon percentage (see illustration which follows for Department A) against the retail price index to derive a cost price index. As noted earlier, the net markon percentage adjusts for markdowns on the year's purchases. In the second case, the Commissioner permits the application of the change in complement of departmental gross profit percentage to retail price index (see Department B illustration on page 440) to derive cost price indexes. With respect to use of the change in complement of markon percentage, the Commissioner reasons that "the difference between the movements of wholesale (or cost) and retail prices for any given year must be reflected in a change in the markon percentage, since cost and retail prices would necessarily change by the same relative amount if the markon were uniform."

The Commissioner recognizes that a specialty store may not use the retail method and therefore may not know its markon percentage (computed on purchases) though it does know its departmental gross profit (computed on sales). With respect to the use of changes in the complement of the departmental gross profit percentage, rather than the complement of the net markon percentage, and application of the respective changes to the BLS retail price index in order to determine a cost price index, the Commissioner observes that the only difference between the two is that one is computed on sales and the other on purchases; over the course of years, they will average out.

The ruling illustrates the derivation of a cost price index based on departmental markon percentage as follows:

Department A

Line No.		December 31 19X0	19X1	19X2
1	Retail price index (appropriate group index)	100.0	150.0	160.0
2	Net markon percentage *	40.2%	42.7%	38.5%
3	Cost percentage (complement of line 2)	59.8%	57.3%	61.5%
4	Ratio of cost percentages (current year over base year)	59.8/59.8	57.3/59.8	61.5/59.8
5	Cost price index (line 1 times line 4)	100.0	143.7	164.5

* To be determined by the taxpayer for each department on the basis of its own average for the taxable year.

The ruling also illustrates a second method of deriving a cost price index. The computations illustrated in Departments A (above) and B (below) may be used interchangeably, that is, whether there is available a net markon percentage or gross profit percentage. Department B calculations contained in the ruling are shown below.

Department B

Line No.		January 1 19X0	19X1	19X2
1	Retail price index (January 1, 19X1 = 100) (BLS Group I)	191.3	216.4	211.7
2	Gross profit percentage *	41.2%	40.7%	41.5%
3	Cost percentage (complement of line 2)	58.8%	59.3%	58.5%
4	Adjusted price index (line 1 multiplied by line 3)	112.4844	128.3252	123.8445
5	Cost price index (January 1, 19X0 = 100) (line 4 divided by 112.4844 and multiplied by 100)	100.0	114.1	110.1

* To be determined by the taxpayer for each department on the basis of its own average for the taxable year.

Revenue Ruling 54–49 also states:

> The use of derived cost price indexes, as described above, by specialty stores on the cost inventory method will be subject to all the conditions of Mimeograph 6244, C.B. 1948–1, 21, and Rev. Rul. 23, C.B. 1953–1, 34, except the condition that the taxpayer employ the retail inventory method.

The indexes in the LIFO illustration which follows show the application of the index numbers already computed and illustrated above for Department A in Rev. Rul. 54–49:

Ch. 22 COMPUTING LIFO INVENTORIES ON THE RETAIL METHOD 441

Year Ended December 31	(1) Inventory at Cost	(2) Cost Price Index *	(3) Inventory at Cost at Base-Year Prices (Col. 1 ÷ Col. 2)	(4) Inventory Cost Increment at Base-Year Prices (Increase of Figures in Col. 3 over Prior Year's Figures in Col. 3)	(5) Inventory Cost Increment at Respective Layer Prices (Col. 2 × Col. 4)	(6) LIFO Inventory at Cost Before Reduction for Discounts in Inventory (Addition of LIFO Layers in Col. 5)
19X0	$10,050	100.0	$10,050	$10,050	$10,050	$10,050
19X1	15,100	143.7	10,508	458	658	10,708
19X2	20,210	164.5	12,285	1,777	2,923	13,631
				$12,285	$13,631	

* See line 5 of the Department A illustration above.

The inventory in column 1 is stated at cost. Where departmental inventory is valued at the lower of cost or market or some other basis, the departmental inventory must, for LIFO purposes, be restated to cost.

The LIFO computations differ somewhat from the computations where the retail price index is used. The wholesale or cost price index is divided into a cost inventory, whereas under the retail method LIFO computations the first step is to divide the retail inventory by a retail price index. Under the above method, column 4 reflects a determination of LIFO cost layers at base-year prices which, multiplied by the appropriate index numbers, give the LIFO costs for each layer in column 5. Under the retail method the figures derived in column 5 would be the LIFO retail prices for each layer, requiring thereafter an application of a cost multiplier to reduce the LIFO retail (i.e., current price) layers to LIFO cost layers.

23

Dollar-Value LIFO

Introduction

A retail establishment which does not qualify as a department store or as a specialty store under Rev. Rul. 53-23, 1953-1 C.B. 34, or Rev. Rul. 54-59, 1954-1 C.B. 32, is required to use either the unit method or the dollar-value method in the determination of inventories under LIFO.

As discussed in Chapter 19, the use of the unit method by retailers is necessarily limited. The *Hutzler* decision (see Chapter 19), which permitted the use of the Bureau of Labor Statistics (BLS) price indexes in the computation of LIFO inventories, was limited to department and specialty stores. It was not until November, 1949, after two court decisions adverse to the Government [*Edgar A. Basse*, 10 T.C. 328 (acq. in part), and *Sweeney and Co., Inc.*, 7 T.C.M. 121], that the Treasury approved the use of the dollar-value method by retailers other than department stores. The Regulations were amended to permit the use of dollar-value LIFO retroactively for all taxable years beginning after December 31, 1938, and to make the LIFO method apply "to any other method of computation established to the satisfaction of the Commissioner as reasonably adaptable to the purpose and intent" of the statute.

The greater practical advantage of the dollar-value method is reflected by its adoption in new LIFO elections as well as in applications for change from the specific goods method.

General Discussion of Dollar-Value Method

The dollar-value LIFO method is similar in principle to the retail LIFO method used by department stores, except that instead of using price change indexes prepared and published by the Bureau of Labor Statistics (see Chapter 21), each taxpayer must compute specially developed, "in house" indexes. Since many retail establishments are not eligible for use of the Department Store Price Indexes, or have divisions, affiliates, or subsidiaries which are involved in manufacturing or processing, the discussion will not be limited to a retail operation. Regulations § 1.472–8, adopted January, 1961, define the dollar-value method and such related areas as the methods of computing dollar-value LIFO, establishing pools, natural business units, the treatment of finished goods and work in process, changes in method of pooling, election of the dollar-value method, and the change from another LIFO method to the dollar-value method.

Any taxpayer may elect to use the dollar-value LIFO method, provided that it is used consistently and clearly reflects income. Under this method, the inventories of the taxpayer are divided into one or more pools. Computations thereafter are made by pools. Base-year cost is defined as the aggregate of the cost (determined as of the beginning of the taxable year for which the LIFO method is first adopted, i.e., the base date) of all items in a pool. An increment occurs when the total of the ending inventory extended at its base-year cost exceeds the total of the opening inventory extended at base cost. Since the comparison is made of dollar totals, fluctuations may occur in the quantities of the items making up the pool, coupled with the introduction of new items and the disappearance of old items, without causing any decrements.

Pooling Arrangement

Reg. § 1.472–8(b). It is important for a taxpayer to consider carefully the election as to the number of pools. The method of pooling must be used for the year of adoption and for all subsequent taxable years unless a change is required by the Commissioner in order to reflect income clearly, or unless permission to change is granted by the Commissioner. A method of pooling is treated as a method of accounting [Reg. § 1.472–8(g)].

Natural-Business-Unit Pools

Reg. § 1.472–8(b)(1)(2). In the case of a manufacturer or processor, a pool ordinarily consists of all items entering into the entire inventory investment for a natural business unit unless the taxpayer elects to use multiple pools, as discussed below. There are no fixed rules for identifying a natural business unit; the facts and circumstances govern. The natural business divisions adopted for internal management purposes, the existence of separate production facilities and processes, and the maintenance of separate profit-and-loss records for separate operations (other than those separated merely because of differences in geographical location) are important factors to consider. A business enterprise may be composed of one or more natural business units. If it is composed of only one unit, only one pool is required, which is to be used for all its inventories, including raw materials, goods in process, and finished goods. Additional natural business units within the enterprise require additional pools. It is significant to note that where the natural-business-unit pool is availed of, all inventories within the unit must be included. Furthermore, a taxpayer may not change the treatment of inventories from the multi-pool, dollar-value LIFO method to the single-pool, dollar-value LIFO method if the labor and overhead costs entering into the entire inventory investment are not to be included in the proposed single pool.[1]

The natural-business-unit pool is generally preferred by taxpayers because the broader the pool, the less likelihood that a liquidation of low-cost inventory will occur. Generally, substitution of new materials can be accomplished without the loss of low-cost base inventory. Where similar types of goods are inventoried in two or more of a taxpayer's natural business units, the Commissioner may apportion or allocate those goods among the units if he determines that it is necessary to clearly reflect the taxpayer's income.

Multiple Pools

Reg. § 1.472–(8)(b)(3). Multiple pools may be established in preference to the natural-business-unit method of pooling or for inventory items not coming within a natural business unit that has

---

[1] Rev. Rul. 71–351, 1971–2 C.B. 216.

been adopted. All items included in each pool should be substantially similar. In determining this, consideration must be given to such factors as similarity in types of raw materials or processing operations, use of products, and whether the groupings follow industry custom and are used for internal management and accounting purposes. For example, raw materials of unlike nature may not be included in one pool even though each becomes a part of the finished product. Grouping of items held for sale should be by major lines, types, or classes of goods that conform to the customary business classifications used in the particular trade involved. The requirement that the pools be established by major types of materials, etc., does not bar establishing a miscellaneous pool for items relatively insignificant in dollar value by comparison with other inventory items. These items must not be properly includible as part of another pool. Also, the dollar-value method can be used in conjunction with the raw-material content method authorized in Reg. § 1.472-1. In such event, the rules of multiple pools would apply, whereby similar raw materials would be grouped in a particular pool.

Generally, the natural-business-unit method is used in connection with manufacturing or processing businesses, although the multiple-pool method might be elected, particularly if there are items in the natural business unit for which the taxpayer does not wish to elect LIFO. Wholesalers, retailers, jobbers, and distributors are required to classify their pools, similar to the rules for multiple pools, by major lines, types, or classes of goods, although, in appropriate cases, the natural-business-unit method may be used with permission of the Treasury [2] [Reg. § 1.472-8(c)].

At the time the return is examined, a determination will be made as to the appropriateness of the number of pools, grouping of items within the pools, and all computations [Reg. § 1.472-8(d)].

Authorized Methods of Computation

Reg. § 1.472-8(e). The dollar-value regulations provide that the double-extension method be used in computing LIFO values unless it is impractical. If so (many taxpayers have found it impractical), the index method or the link-chain method is permitted.

---

[2] Rev. Rul. 62-77, 1962-1 C.B. 80.

These basically are adaptations of the double-extension method. The three methods are discussed below.

Double-Extension Method

Reg. § 1.472–8(e)(2). Each item in the inventory pool at the close of the taxable year is extended at both base-year unit cost and current-year unit cost. The extensions at the two costs are then totaled. The first total gives the amount of current inventory in terms of base-year cost, and the second total gives the amount in terms of current-year cost.

If the inventory at the close of the taxable year expressed in base-year costs exceeds the opening inventory in terms of base-year costs, there is an increment for the year; an index of current-year costs to base-year costs must then be determined to value the increment. The index is computed by dividing the total of the year-end inventory extended at current costs by the total of the inventory extended at base costs. This index is applied to the current year's inventory increment at base-year costs to reflect that inventory increment or layer at current costs.

The current-year cost of items making up a pool may be determined by referring to the actual cost of the goods most recently purchased or produced; by referring to the actual cost of the goods purchased or produced during the taxable year in the order of acquisition; by applying an average unit cost equal to the aggregate cost of all the goods purchased or produced throughout the taxable year divided by the total number of units so purchased or produced; or according to any other method that, in the Commissioner's opinion, clearly reflects income. The election to use one of the above, made in the year of adoption, is binding for all future years and cannot be changed without Treasury permission.

If the closing inventory for the year extended at base is less than the opening inventory extended at base, there would be a decrement for the year. The decrement is reflected by reducing the most recent layer of increment, applying to the decrement at base the index established for that particular layer of inventory. If the amount of the liquidation exceeds the amount of the most recent layer of increment, the preceding layers of increment, in reverse chronological order, are to be successively reduced by the amount of the excess until all the excess is absorbed.

See pages 452–55 for illustrations of the application of the dollar-value, double-extension LIFO method.

Index Method

Reg. § 1.472–8(e)(1). The use of the double-extension method may be impractical because of technological changes, extensive variety of items, or extreme fluctuations in variety of items. In such cases, the valuation of the closing inventory at base prices may be accomplished by converting the closing inventory at current prices to a closing inventory valued at base prices by using an index number developed from an inventory sample. A representative cross-section of inventory is priced at both current and base prices, and an index of changes in price level is derived by dividing the valuation at current prices by the valuation at base prices. By applying this index number to the total closing inventory valued at current prices, the value of the closing inventory at base prices can be computed. This or other sound and consistent statistical methods may be used if it is demonstrated to the District Director's satisfaction that the method of computation is appropriate, and that the index developed is accurate, reliable, and suitable. A statement describing the method must be attached to the first return in which it is used and a copy filed with the Commissioner of Internal Revenue. If the taxpayer considers it desirable, advance approval may be requested for the first taxable year for which it is used. The request must be submitted within 90 days after the beginning of the taxable year.

Link-Chain Method

Reg. § 1.472–8(e)(1). In arriving at the amount of inventory increment in a particular year, it is first necessary to determine the increment in terms of base-period prices. It is not difficult to reprice the closing inventory of a particular year in terms of base-period prices if items contained in the inventory remain uniform from year to year. However, where there is a change in the items making up the inventory, it becomes necessary to reconstruct a base price for the new items. As the year involved becomes further removed from the base period and where a gradual change is being effected in the nature of the inventory, it becomes increasingly difficult to reconstruct realistic base prices. It is in this area that the use of a link-chain index to convert current inventory values back to base-period prices is particularly helpful.

Under the link-chain method, a taxpayer computes an index for each year, which measures the extent of price-level change for that year alone. This is accomplished by extending the year-end inventory at closing prices and at beginning-of-year prices. The total of the extensions at closing prices is then divided by the total of the extensions at opening prices to determine the index change for the year. This first step differs from the double-extension method, as discussed earlier, only in that the taxpayer extends the inventory at beginning-of-year prices, rather than at base prices. By multiplying each annual index by the prior cumulative index, it is possible to develop an index that, when divided into the closing inventory at closing prices, results in a determination of the closing inventory at base prices. To the extent that the inventory at base exceeds the prior year's closing inventory at base, an increment results that must be extended for LIFO purposes at current costs, depending upon the taxpayer's election for pricing increments.

An example of the dollar-value, link-chain LIFO method appears on pages 455–56. This example also illustrates the use of different indexes in determining LIFO values, each of which is separately determined. One index is used to deflate year-end inventories to base-year cost; the other is used to price the inventory increment at current cost.

In this example, the option used to price the increment at current cost is the earliest cost in the year of increment. Since adoption of LIFO presumes the continuation of inflation over the long term, use of this option should normally provide the maximum tax benefit from LIFO. It should be emphasized that both of the aforementioned indexes are typically developed from representative samples of inventories tested.

The link-chain method may be used only upon demonstrating that the use of either the index method (discussed above) or the double-extension method is impractical or unsuitable in view of the nature of the pool. If a link-chain index method is used, a descriptive statement must be attached to the income tax return for the first taxable year for which it is adopted and a copy of the statement must be filed with the Treasury. The determination as to whether the method is appropriate and acceptable is made when the Treasury examines the return. As in the case of the index method, advance approval can be requested of the Commissioner for the first year for which it is used. This request must be made within the first 90 days of such year.

Treatment of New Items

Reg. § 1.472–8(e)(2)(iii). It was pointed out earlier that the increment must be first determined in terms of base prices, and that an accepted step in the procedure is the pricing of the closing inventory quantities at base prices. The question then arises: What happens when an item (or items) in the closing inventory was not on hand at the beginning of the year? The current cost of a new item is considered the base-year cost unless a different amount can be reconstructed or established. If the item existed on the base date but was not stocked, a determination of what the cost would have been may be established from quotations or other available data. If the new item is a raw material or product that did not exist on the base date, a base-date cost may be reconstructed, using reasonable means and assumptions. For example, if the new item is closely related to the other items in the pool and represents a relatively small part of the total dollar value of such pool, it may be reasonably assumed that the price change with respect to that item was similar to the other items contained in the pool. If the pool is quite broad, the price relationship may be limited only to those items within the pool that are closely related.

If a base-year cost is not reconstructed or established, the earliest cost that is reconstructed or established in a year subsequent to the base year may be used. For example, the first purchase or production cost was employed by a taxpayer in a litigated case and the Tax Court did not object to its use.[3]

As previously stated, where a taxpayer is unable to determine base-year (or intermediate-year) cost for a new item, the current-year cost of an item is required to be used as the base-year cost. This approach creates obvious distortions in periods of changing price levels since both the amount of inventory change in terms of base-year costs and the relationship of base-year costs to current-year costs (LIFO index) will be improperly reflected. These distortions do not occur, or are minimized, under the link-chain method since new items entering the inventory can be restated at

---

[3] *Basse*, 10 T.C. 328 (1948) (acq.).

opening-of-year prices, which, using the cumulative index factor, effectively convert to base-year costs. Therefore, if a taxpayer anticipates that new items will be a significant element in the dollar-value LIFO inventory, permission to adopt the link-chain method should be sought.

Election To Use Dollar-Value Methods

Reg. § 1.472–8(f). Except in the case of a taxpayer electing to use the LIFO inventory method for the first time, in accordance with Reg. § 1.472–3, or in the case of a taxpayer changing to the dollar-value method and continuing to use the same pools as were used under another LIFO method, the Treasury's consent must be obtained in order to use this method. According to the Regulations, the taxpayer must file Form 3115 with the Treasury, ordinarily within 180 days after the beginning of the taxable year in which it is desired to make the change. [See Reg. § 1.446–1(e)(3) for the information required to be submitted.] In the year of the change from another LIFO method to the dollar-value method, the beginning inventory must be converted to the dollar-value method without change in the aggregate value. The layers of increment will remain unchanged except that when items formerly inventoried under the specific goods method are included in a single dollar-value pool, the layers of increment for each year will be combined.

Extent of Election

Reg. § 1.472–1. Except for mandatory inclusions in a natural business unit where the single-pool dollar-value method of pricing inventories has been adopted, the LIFO method may be applied to all or part of the inventory. It may be limited to specific classes or kinds of goods. In the case of a manufacturer, it may be limited to the stage in the manufacturing process when a product is first produced that is recognized as salable, or it may be applied to raw materials only, including raw materials in goods in process and finished goods. The latter may be desirable if the manufacturing processes are comparatively rapid, only small quantities of finished goods are retained on hand, and labor is a minor element in the total cost of the finished product. In industries where labor costs become an important part of the cost of the finished goods, it is usually desirable to use the LIFO method for valuing the manufacturing costs as well as material costs. One method of doing this is to establish separate pools for raw materials, work in process, and finished goods. A disadvantage of this method is that the taxpayer may suffer a liquidation in the raw-material pool, even though the raw material is still on hand as a component of increased stocks of work in process and finished goods. A possible alternative (about which the IRS is understood not to have taken a position) is the use of one pool for raw materials (including raw materials in work in process and in finished goods) and another for manufacturing costs (labor and overhead). A properly weighted single pool is another possibility, which appears to avoid possible IRS objections. Many exponents of LIFO maintain that this method will provide the most accurate results, and there appears to be strong support for that position. This breakdown eliminates the change in efficiency factor that can cause a distortion under the other methods (particularly where conversion costs are included).

Illustration. Assume that item A is included in the finished goods inventory of Company X on January 1, 1974, at $22.50 and that the breakdown, by cost components, is as follows:

Materials	$ 7.50
Labor, 1 hr.	5.00
Overhead (200% of labor)	10.00
Total cost	$22.50

Assume also that during the course of the year the company switched to a more efficient assembly arrangement and that the total cost of item A at the year end is $19.00. The cost components are as follows:

Materials	$ 8.50
Labor, ½ hr.	3.00
Overhead (250% of labor)	7.50
	$19.00

If Company X had item A on LIFO as part of its finished-goods category and compared opening and closing inventory costs, it would appear that there was a 15.6 per cent decrease in costs. Actually, material costs increased 13.3 per cent and labor costs increased 20 per cent.

Eliminating the efficiency factor, the cost of item A at opening inventory prices, for determining price-level change only, would be as follows:

Materials	$ 7.50
Labor, ½ hr. @ $5 per hour	2.50
Overhead (200% of labor)	5.00
Total reconstructed opening cost	$15.00

The $4.00 cost increase during the year represents a 26.7 per cent increase compared to a 15.6 per cent decrease without adjustment for the change in efficiency. It is the authors' opinion that the elimination of the efficiency factor should be considered irrespective of the method in use. An inventory classification by cost components—i.e., raw materials, labor, and overhead—simplifies the adjustment by eliminating the efficiency factor automatically. Thus, treating labor as an item would reflect the efficiencies realized throughout the years; similarly, efficiencies achieved in overhead costs could also be reflected.

It should be noted that the above illustration is greatly simplified, particularly as it relates to overhead. Overhead would usually be broken down into its constituent elements, e.g., indirect labor, power, supplies, etc., and the dollars of each element included in year-end inventory would be deflated by an appropriate price index. As examples, the price indexes could be developed by referring to average hourly labor rates for indirect labor, cost per kilowatt hour for power, and taxes per $100 of valuation for personal property taxes. The practical effect of the foregoing is one weighted index for overhead that, when combined with the corresponding indexes for raw materials and labor, will result in an overall weighted index for the year.

Illustrations of the Dollar-Value, Double-Extension LIFO Method

Example 1

a. A taxpayer elects, beginning with calendar year 1974, to compute inventories by using the LIFO inventory method under section 472, and further elects to use the dollar-value method in pricing such inventories as provided in Reg. § 1.472-8(a). The taxpayer continues to use the first-in, first-out method for day-to-day operational purposes, computing LIFO only at year end. For such LIFO purposes, Pool No. 1 is created for items A, B, and C. The composition of the inventory for Pool No. 1 at the base date, January 1, 1974, is as follows:

Item	Units	Unit Cost	Total Cost
A	1,000	$5.00	$ 5,000
B	2,000	4.00	8,000
C	500	2.00	1,000
Total base-year cost at January 1, 1974			$14,000

b. The closing inventory of Pool No. 1 at December 31, 1974, contains 3,000 units of A, 1,000 units of B, and 500 units of C. The taxpayer computes the current-year cost of the items making up the pool by reference to the actual cost of goods most recently purchased. The most recent purchases of items A, B, and C are as follows:

Item	Purchase Date	Quantity Purchased	Unit Cost
A	December 15, 1974	3,500	$6.00
B	December 10, 1974	2,000	5.00
C	November 1, 1974	500	2.50

c. The inventory of Pool No. 1 at December 31, 1974, shown at base-year and current-year costs, is as follows:

		December 31, 1974, Inventory at January 1, 1974, Base-Year Cost		December 31, 1974, Inventory at Current-Year Cost	
Item	Quantity	Unit Cost	Amount	Unit Cost	Amount
A	3,000	$5.00	$15,000	$6.00	$18,000
B	1,000	4.00	4,000	5.00	5,000
C	500	2.00	1,000	2.50	1,250
Total			$20,000		$24,250

d. If the amount of the December 31, 1974, inventory at the base-year cost were equal to, or less than, the base-year cost of $14,000 at January 1, 1974, such amount would be the closing LIFO inventory at December 31, 1974. However, since the base-year cost of the closing LIFO inventory at December 31, 1974, amounts to $20,000, and is in excess of the $14,000 base-year cost of the opening inventory for that year, there is a $6,000 increment in Pool No. 1 during that year. This increment must be valued at current-year cost, i.e., the ratio of 24,250/20,000, or 121.25 per cent. The LIFO value of the inventory in Pool No. 1 at December 31, 1974, is $21,275, computed as follows:

	December 31, 1974, Inventory at January 1, 1974, Base-Year Cost	Ratio of Total Current-Year Cost to Total Base-Year Cost	December 31, 1974, Inventory at LIFO Value
January 1, 1974, base cost	$14,000	100.00%	$14,000
December 31, 1974, increment	6,000	121.25	7,275
Total	$20,000		$21,275

Example 2

a. Assume that the taxpayer in Example 1, during the year 1975, completely disposes of item C and purchases item D. Assume further that item D is properly includible in Pool No. 1. The closing inventory on December 31, 1975, consists of quantities at current-year unit cost, as follows:

Item	Units	Current-Year Unit Cost, December 31, 1975
A	2,000	$6.50
B	1,500	6.00
D	1,000	5.00

b. The taxpayer establishes that the cost of item D, had it been acquired on January 1, 1974, would have been $2.00 per unit. Such cost shall be used as the base-year unit cost for item D, and the LIFO computations at December 31, 1975, are made as follows:

		December 31, 1975, Inventory at January 1, 1974, Base-Year Cost		December 31, 1975, Inventory at Current-Year Cost	
Item	Quantity	Unit Cost	Amount	Unit Cost	Amount
A	2,000	$5.00	$10,000	$6.50	$13,000
B	1,500	4.00	6,000	6.00	9,000
D	1,000	2.00	2,000	5.00	5,000
Total			$18,000		$27,000

c. Since the closing inventory at base-year cost, $18,000, is less than the 1975 opening inventory at base-year cost, $20,000, a liquidation of $2,000 has occurred during 1975. This liquidation is to be reflected by reducing the most recent layer of increment. The LIFO value of the inventory in Pool No. 1 at December 31, 1975, is $18,850, and is summarized as follows:

	December 31, 1975, Inventory at January 1, 1974, Base-Year Cost	Ratio of Total Current-Year Cost to Total Base-Year Cost	December 31, 1975, Inventory at LIFO Value
January 1, 1974, base cost	$14,000	100.00%	$14,000
December 31, 1974, increment	4,000	121.25	4,850
Total	$18,000		$18,850

The above examples utilize the most-recent-purchases method to value year-end inventory at current costs. In Example 1 that method is also used for valuing the increment. However, other methods such as earliest acquisition during the year or average cost are also available to value the increment, which could provide significant tax benefits.

Many taxpayers, with the apparent concurrence of the Internal Revenue Service, use a different method of determining current-year cost to develop an index to value increments (part d of

Example 1) than they use for determining increments (part c of Example 1). For instance, increments (at base-year cost) are commonly determined utilizing the taxpayer's normal accounting method, usually FIFO or average cost as reflected in the detailed year-end inventory records, whereas increments may be valued (at current cost) on the basis of earliest acquisition cost during the year, or latest acquisition cost. The use of the same method for both purposes should not be required, even though the example in the Regulations proceeds on the assumption that the same method will be used.

Illustration of the Dollar-Value, Link-Chain LIFO Method Using Different Cost Methods To Determine Base-Year Costs and LIFO Values

Facts: Assume that a taxpayer adopts LIFO for 1973, utilizes the link-chain method, and maintains its inventory cost records for management purposes on an average cost basis, the same basis previously used for tax purposes. Furthermore, assume that this taxpayer has elected to use the earliest cost method to value LIFO inventory increments. This rule would be applied as follows:

1973

1. Inventory at December 31, 1973 @ 1973 average cost — $1,500,000
2. Inventory at December 31, 1973 @ 1972 average cost — 1,200,000
3. Deflator index, 1973 to 1972 ($1,500,000 ÷ $1,200,000) — 125%
4. Inventory at December 31, 1973, at base-year costs $\left(\frac{1{,}500{,}000}{1.25}\right)$ — 1,200,000
5. Inventory at December 31, 1972, at base-year (i.e., LIFO) costs — 1,000,000

   1973 increment at base-year costs — 200,000
6. Index of earliest-year costs to December 31, 1972, costs. [This index establishes a relationship between prior-year (i.e., December 31, 1972) average cost to earliest costs in 1973, and could be determined based on valid statistical samples.] — 115%
7. LIFO increment at earliest-year costs ($200,000 × 115.0%) — 230,000

   Inventory at December 31, 1973, at LIFO ($1,000,000 + $230,000) — $1,230,000

1974

1. Inventory at December 31, 1974 @ 1974 average cost — $1,800,000
2. Inventory at December 31, 1974 @ 1973 average cost — 1,565,000
3. Deflator index, 1974 to 1973 ($1,800,000 ÷ $1,565,000) — 115%

4. December 31, 1974, inventory at base-year costs:

Index	Annual	Cumulative
1973	125.00%	125.00%
1974	115.00	143.75

5. Inventory at December 31, 1974 @ base-year costs
$$\left(\frac{1,800,000}{1.4375}\right)$$
                                               1,252,200

Inventory at December 31, 1973, at base-year costs   1,200,000

6. 1974 increment at base-year costs   52,200

   Index of earliest-year costs for 1974 to 1973 average costs   110%

   LIFO increment at earliest-year costs:

     Earliest-year cost index (as above)   110%

     Prior-year cumulative average cost index   ×125

     Cumulative earliest cost index   137.50%

   1974 LIFO increment at earliest-year costs ($52,200 × 137.50%)   71,775

Inventory at December 31, 1974, at LIFO:

Inventory	Base-Year Cost	LIFO
1972	$1,000,000	$1,000,000
1973	200,000	230,000
1974	52,200	71,775
	$1,252,200	$1,301,775

It should be noted that if average cost, rather than earliest-year costs, were used to value LIFO increments, the December 31, 1974, LIFO inventory would be $1,325,037, determined as follows:

Inventory	Base-Year Cost	Cumulative Index for Average Cost	LIFO
1972	$1,000,000	100.00	$1,000,000
1973	200,000	125.00	250,000
1974	52,200	143.75	75,037
			$1,325,037

24

Installment Sales of Personal Property

Introduction

Dealers in personal property, including retailers, manufacturers, and wholesalers, who regularly sell on the installment plan, are permitted to report the income from installment sales for tax reporting purposes by the installment method under IRC Section 453(a). This method of reporting income recognizes that each cash collection contains two elements: recovery of cost and realization of gross profit. Accordingly, the gross profit is taken into income only when and if received. In effect, gross profits earned on installment sales are taxed over the periods when received, rather than at the time of sale under the conventional accrual method. Although the installment method of reporting income is permitted for tax purposes, it is not generally acceptable for financial accounting purposes ". . . unless the circumstances are such that the collection of the sale price is not reasonably assured." (See Accounting Principles Board Opinion No. 10.)

The installment method election is advantageous since it generates cash flow benefits through the deferral of income tax payments. In effect, the gross profit inherent in the accounts receivable qualifying for installment treatment is not recognized for tax reporting purposes pending cash collection. Moreover, as the retail operation expands and the volume of installment sales increases, there is a corresponding increase in the amount of installment accounts receivable outstanding and in the related amount of gross profit deferred. The following example illustrates the potential cash flow advantage of the installment method:

Total qualifying installment accounts receivable at year end	$1,000,000
Gross profit percentage	40%
Gross profit to be deferred	$ 400,000
Tax rate (assumed)	50%
Income tax deferred at year end	$ 200,000

This deferral is equivalent to an interest-free loan which can almost be viewed as permanent in nature, provided the amount of tax deferred at each subsequent year end does not decline. After the first year the amount of tax deferral will vary in accordance with changes in the annual gross profit percentage, the amount of qualifying installment receivables at year end, and the rate of tax.

Included below is a discussion of the procedures for determining qualified installment sales and the related deferred gross profit; the election of the installment method; and the allowance for doubtful installment accounts. The rules governing installment sales under revolving-type credit plans are included in some detail because of the widespread use of such plans by retailers. They are replacing ordinary 30-day charge accounts and, to some extent, the traditional type of individually tailored installment accounts covering "big ticket" items.

Qualification of Property for Installment Method

The basic purpose of the Code section governing installment sales is to permit anyone who sells personal property regularly on the installment basis to report the gross profit on the sales in the same proportion as the actual receipts bear to the total contract price. Sales by manufacturers to their customers may also qualify for installment treatment. The Treasury is empowered to establish detailed regulations which have the effect of law, and which are binding on all taxpayers who (voluntarily) elect to adopt the installment method. Taxpayers may elect to adopt the method without obtaining advance permission from the IRS. Retail sales reported on the installment plan are classified broadly as traditional installment sales or sales under revolving-type credit plans.

Certain types of sales do not qualify as installment sales: non-personal property sales which include sales of services and sales by leased departments in department stores. However, services which are incidental to and rendered contemporaneously with the sale of personal property do qualify. Thus, charges for items such as installation of storm windows and alteration of clothing would qualify if the charges for the service were made at the same time as the charges were rendered for the merchandise. However, charges for items such as watch or jewelry repairs, beauty parlor treatments, and appliance repairs would not qualify. [Reg. § 1.453–2(d)(6)(ii) and (iv).]

Federal excise taxes and those state and local sales taxes which are levied on the retailer as a vendor are includible for purposes of determining cost and gross profit for installment sales purposes. Presumably, state and local sales taxes levied on the consumer but collected by the retailer would not qualify. [Rev. Rul. 68–163; 1969–1 C.B. 201.]

Whether finance or service charges qualify as installment sales depends on the type of sale. Such charges on sales made under a traditional installment plan do qualify if the service charge or interest is added contemporaneously with the sale when recorded on the books of account of the retailer. [Reg. § 1.453–2(c)(2)(ii).] However, similar charges which are applied to revolving credit sales do not qualify. Under the rules governing revolving credit accounts, cash collections must first be applied against any outstanding finance or service charges. The practical effect of this requirement is a reduction in the amount of ineligible service charges at year end. Consequently, in the normal course of business, only a very minor portion of the year-end receivable balances will consist of finance or service charges, essentially representing the service charges for the last billing month. [Reg. § 1.453–2(d)(6)(i) and (v).]

The Regulations state that sales made by leased departments do not qualify. However, the retailer may be able to justify the eligibility of such sales by proving that, under the terms of the lease and through customary business practices, the sales by leased departments were legally made by the retailer.

It has been held that factory-built homes or shell houses may qualify if sold by the manufacturer, whereas finance companies may not be treated as dealers in personal property.

The retailer must eliminate the amount attributable to non-personal property sales from the year-end total revolving credit accounts receivable. To accomplish this, the retailer may compute the total non-personal property sales for the year as a percentage of total sales. This percentage may then be applied to the total revolving credit receivable balances at year end to determine the portion attributable to non-personal property sales. [Reg. § 1.453-2(d)(5).]

Requirement for Regularity of Sales

Vendors who sell personal property on the installment plan may qualify as dealers eligible for the installment method of reporting income only if the sales are made regularly. A dealer making only isolated sales on the installment plan will not qualify for the installment method. [Reg. § 1.453-2(c).] The proportion of installment sales is not controlling. The representation to the public that such sales could be made, their frequency, and the number of such sales are the decisive factors [*Davenport Machine and Foundry Co.*, 18 T.C. 39 (1952) (acq.)]. Since most retailers selling merchandise on the installment basis generally prefer to do so on a recurring basis, there should be no difficulty in meeting this requirement.

Computing the Unrealized Gross Profit—Traditional Installment Plan

Dealers selling on the traditional or other type of installment plan should compute the gross profit percentage on an overall annual basis related to the total installment sales for the year. If the dealer can demonstrate that income is clearly reflected, the gross profit percentage may be based on the total credit sales or the total sales (credit and cash). Collections must be allocated to the receivable balances and related gross profit percentages applicable to the year of sale. [Reg. § 1.453-2(c).]

Similarly, if dealers selling on the revolving credit plan can demonstrate that the gross profit percentage for all sales or all credit sales does not materially differ from sales under the revolving credit plan, the gross profit percentage may be based on the total sales or all credit sales. The year-end total revolving credit accounts receivable may be treated as sales pertaining to the current year if income will be clearly reflected. This would be the case if the gross profit percentage for the prior year was not materially different from the current year, or if an insubstantial amount of sales from the prior year were included in the current year-end balances. [Reg. § 1.453–2(d).]

Illustration. Following is a computation of the unrealized gross profit as of the beginning and end of a taxable year for traditional installment accounts. The illustration does not differentiate between collections and accounts written off as uncollectible, which are discussed below.

Year Ended January 31	Installment Sales °	Cost of Goods Sold	Gross Profit	Gross Profit Ratio
1974	$100,000	$64,350	$35,650	35.65%
1975	120,000	77,436	42,564	35.47
1976	150,000	97,200	52,800	35.20
1977	150,000	95,805	54,195	36.13

° As noted earlier, these amounts may include service or interest charges.

Sales of Year Ended January 31	Uncollected Installments, January 31, 1976	Gross Profit Ratio	Unrealized Gross Profit
1974	$ 10,000	35.65%	$ 3,565
1975	40,000	35.47	14,188
1976	90,000	35.20	31,680
	$140,000		
Unrealized gross profit, beginning of taxable year			$49,433

Sales of Year Ended January 31	Uncollected Installments, January 31, 1977	Gross Profit Ratio	Unrealized Gross Profit
1974	$ 2,000	35.65%	$ 713
1975	10,000	35.47	3,547
1976	40,000	35.20	14,080
1977	80,000	36.13	28,904
	$132,000		
Unrealized gross profit, end of taxable year			$47,244
Decrease in unrealized gross profit for year ended January 31, 1977, representing the net amount of realized gross profit to be included in taxable gross income for year			$ 2,189

Proof of Net Decrease in Unrealized Gross Profit

A proof of the change in unrealized gross profit during the fiscal year ended January 31, 1977, relating it directly to the relevant sales and collections made during that year, is shown below:

Decreases in unrealized gross profit:
35.65 per cent of $8,000 collected on sales of year ended January 31, 1974; or	$ 2,852
35.47 per cent of $30,000 collected on sales of year ended January 31, 1975, or	10,641
35.20 per cent of $50,000 collected on sales of year ended January 31, 1976, or	17,600
	31,093

Increase in unrealized gross profit:
36.13 per cent of $80,000 sales during year ended January 31, 1977, uncollected at that date	28,904
Net decrease in unrealized gross profit	$ 2,189

The foregoing method of computation effectively provides for the inclusion in taxable income of gross profit realized in the year ended January 31, 1977, on $70,000 collections from sales made in that year at 36.13 per cent, or $25,291, plus realized gross profits of $31,093 on collections from sales made in the years ended January 31, 1974, 1975, and 1976, or a total gross profit of $56,384.

Traditional Installment Plans

A traditional installment sale generally provides for the execution of a separate installment contract for each sale of personal property items and the retention by the dealer of some type of security interest in the property. The security could be in the form of a lien or chattel mortgage, or title might be retained until completion of payments. The Regulations do not require the dealer to retain a security interest in order to qualify for installment method treatment. [Reg. § 1.453-2(a).] The terms of each sale must provide for two or more payments. [Reg. § 1.453-2(b)(1).] Payments received must be allocated to the year of sale and the appropriate gross profit percentage is applied for each sales year. See page 461 for an example of the computation of unrealized gross profit. [Reg. § 1.453-2(c)(1).]

Revolving Credit Plans

It is unnecessary to have a separate contract for each sale under a revolving credit plan. The requisite minimum monthly payment under such a plan is either a fixed amount or a variable amount, depending on the balance of the account. If the payment is variable, the dealer may elect to compute the minimum based either on the last billing month of the year or the billing month of sale, for all such accounts. The customer's credit rating will, of course, affect the maximum which may be purchased on credit.

The terms of a revolving credit plan might include the following:

1. A credit limit is established for each customer, usually from six to nine times the required monthly payment.
2. The customer may make purchases up to the credit limit but must make a payment each month as long as there is a balance outstanding.
3. Any purchases which are allowed in excess of the credit limit must be paid for in the following month.
4. After a payment is received, the customer may make purchases which increase the balance outstanding up to the established credit limit.
5. A finance or service charge is computed as a percentage of the unpaid balance at the beginning of each month after deducting payments and credits.
6. No security interest is retained.

The terms must contemplate that each sale will be paid for in two or more payments, at least two payments must actually be made, and each sale must be greater than the required monthly payment. For this purpose, the *aggregate* amount of sales charged during the billing month is treated as if one sale was made. The rule as to two or more payments is satisfied if the first payment received after the month of sale is less than the account balance at the close of that month of sale. [Reg. § 1.453–2(d)(3)(i).]

A coupon book installment plan was considered to be ineligible for treatment as a traditional installment plan and did not meet the requisite proof of two or more payments, as required under revolving credit plans. [*W. T. Grant Co.*, 483 F.2d 115, *rev'g* 58 T.C. 290 (1973) (*cert. den.*).]

Regulations § 1.453–(2)(d)(2) and (3) provide rules for determining percentage of customers' accounts receivable at the year end which will be treated as arising from sales which qualified under the installment plan. A sample is taken of all revolving credit accounts having balances in the cycle billing-month ending within the last month of the taxpayer's year. The sample must be taken in accordance with generally accepted sampling techniques, or by following certain specific sampling procedures provided by the Treasury, as discussed below. The dollar amount of the accounts sampled which qualify for installment tax treatment is expressed as a percentage of the total amounts sampled. That percentage is applied to the year-end accounts receivable balances representing personal property sales.

The computation of the deferred amount of gross profit at the year end is explained in Reg. § 1.453-2(d)(7), and is summarized as follows:

1. The total revolving credit accounts receivable as of the last day of the taxable year is reduced by the estimated portion attributable to non-personal property sales.
2. The amount of receivables attributable to personal property sales is multiplied by the percentage of qualifying installment sales which was determined in the sampling procedure.
3. The gross profit percentage on sales made under the revolving plan (or for the entire store sales if not materially different in gross profit margin) will be applied to the amount determined in item 2 above to arrive at the gross profit to be deferred.

Illustration

1. Year-end balances of revolving credit accounts receivable	$2,000,000
Deduct: Approximately 5 per cent non-personal property sales (percentage of non-personal property sales to total sales made during the year)	100,000
Balance, personal property sales	$1,900,000
2. Percentage of sales qualifying on installment plan @ 70 per cent (per sample as explained below)	$1,330,000
3. Gross profit percentage (@ 40 per cent) to be deferred	$ 532,000

Computation of percentage of sales qualifying on installment plan:	
Random selection of account balances aggregating	$100,000
Deduct: Disregarded balances—accounts reflecting no payment received since billing-month of sale up to and including first billing-month ended after year end	10,000
Balance	$ 90,000
Analyzed as follows:	
Sales which qualify on installment plan	$ 63,000 (70%)
Sales which do not qualify	$ 27,000 (30%)

Sampling Methods

The following sampling methods are available:

1. A 100 per cent sample—usually deemed to be impractical;
2. A custom sample—any sampling procedure, in accordance with

generally accepted probability sampling techniques. The taxpayer must maintain records in sufficient detail to show the method of computing and applying the sample; or

3. The sampling procedure provided by Rev. Proc. 64–4, §5, 1964–1 C.B. (Part 1) 644, titled "An Acceptable Procedure for Sampling," Rev. Proc. 65–5, 1965–1 C.B. 720, modifying and amplifying Rev. Proc. 64–4.

Use of a professional statistician to develop an acceptable sample under method 2 may be warranted if the number of customers' accounts is substantial, since the use of the sampling procedure in method 3 above may result in an excessively large number of accounts to be analyzed. However, the IRS will not issue an advance ruling on whether a custom sampling procedure is acceptable. [Rev. Proc. 72–9, 1972–1 C.B. 718.]

For those who do not wish to engage the services of a statistician in developing a sampling selection procedure and maintaining it annually, method 3 must be used. Revenue Procedure 64–4 requires a listing of all accounts (the "population") under the dealer's revolving credit plan. (See later discussion of Rev. Proc. 65–5.)

Revenue Procedure 64–4 prescribes specific sampling procedures which must be followed. The population from which the sample is to be selected consists of all revolving credit accounts as of the last billing-month ending within the taxable year. Some retailers believe that using the population for the next to last billing-month is a reasonable alternative if no significant change in the population is anticipated. This procedure permits acceleration of the process of selecting accounts to be analyzed and a more rapid determination of the amount of income taxes to be deferred.

It is necessary to have a sequential listing of all accounts to be sampled. While it is desirable to list only revolving credit accounts, if the normal listing source also contains various types of other accounts, e.g., 30-day optional charge accounts and traditional installment accounts, such list may be used if all the revolving credit accounts are included therein.

Some retailers permit customers the option of paying each month-end balance in full during the following month (charge account basis), to avoid a service charge. Instead of paying the balance, the customer may exercise an option to treat the account as if it were a sale under a revolving credit plan. As a practical matter, these accounts are maintained usually in one file without any distinction being made between optional and revolving credit balances. If it is feasible, however, such 30-day optional accounts should be culled out at year end in order to reduce the size of the sample. Likewise, certain of the "null" accounts and all traditional installment accounts should be separated from revolving credit account balances in order to reduce the sample size.

Null accounts represent accounts with a zero or credit balance and accounts that must be "disregarded" because after the month of sale no payment was received up to and including the first billing-month of the following taxable year. The absence of any payment makes it impossible to determine whether the two-payment rule will ever be met. If the zero and credit balance accounts are culled out, there should be a significant reduction in the sample size. Of course, a percentage of the sample will always contain nulls to the extent that some balances must be disregarded.

A relatively recent development in methods of accounting for installment and other accounts receivable is the use of data processing equipment. In conjunction with such systems, programs for selecting the samples and analyzing these accounts for the amount of qualified installment sales have been developed which are effective in minimizing the effort required to obtain all necessary data.

Rules of Sampling Procedure Provided by Revenue Procedure 64-4

The following listing sequences are permitted under Revenue Procedure 64-4: alphabetic, ascending or descending sequence by account number, or a combination of the two. In addition, sequencing can be applied for the taxpayer as a whole, or for each division or store of the taxpayer which maintains the accounting records for revolving credit accounts. After sequencing, the list must be serially numbered. The method of sequencing cannot be changed without the consent of the District Director.

For many taxpayers, the most convenient source of the list will be the source of addresses used in billing or mailing the customers' statements for the last billing-month in the taxable year. It is most important that the listing used in selecting the sample, as well as schedules showing the application of the sample, be preserved as part of the records. Failure to do so might require a recomputation of the sample.

After the list is completed, the number of sample accounts to be analyzed is determined as follows:

1. Determine the total number of accounts in the list.
2. Calculate the minimum sample, as follows:

Total Accounts in the List	Minimum Number of Accounts Required in Sample
Under 40,000	240
40,000 to 800,000	0.6% of total
Over 800,000	7,200

(The above minimum sample size in Rev. Proc. 65–5 supersedes the one shown in Rev. Proc. 64–4.)
3. Each sample account should be classified as:
    a. A "null" account, i.e., an account with a zero or credit balance or an account which is "disregarded" since, after the month of sale, no payment was received up to and including the first billing-month of the following taxable year (it therefore being impossible to determine at that time whether the two-payment rule will ever be met), or
    b. An account that does not qualify as a revolving credit account (a traditional installment account, a regular charge account, or an optional installment account); or
    c. An "allocable" account, representing all other accounts. The balances in each "allocable" account must then be analyzed as to qualifying and nonqualifying amounts based on the aggregate monthly sales and payment tests.
4. Additional accounts in excess of the minimum sample are required since there are always "nulls" (disregarded accounts) in the frame. To determine the number of additional accounts required (the null correction factor), estimate the percentage of the number of allocable accounts in the frame and increase the minimum sample by an amount equal to the minimum sample divided by the square of the estimated percentage of allocable accounts. The allocable accounts contain both qualifying and nonqualifying sales. The estimate of allocable accounts can be based on historical information or on a review of a relatively small number of accounts selected on a random basis.

Example of Acceptable Method of Sampling Procedure in Revenue Procedure 64–4

Assume 125,000 accounts in frame; the minimum sample is 750 accounts (125,000 × .006). It is estimated that only 50 per cent are allocable accounts, and 50 per cent are null accounts. The sample size is computed as follows:

$$\frac{\text{Initial sample}}{(1 - \text{null ratio})^2} = \text{sample size}$$

$$\frac{.006 \times 125,000}{(1 - .5)^2} = \frac{750}{.25} = 3,000 \text{ accounts to be sampled}$$

Selecting the Accounts To Be Analyzed. Selection of the required 3,000 accounts is made by establishing five starting points in the list and using a constant skip interval.

The skip interval is a sampling technique that insures an even distribution of the sample throughout the population. It is calculated by multiplying the total number of accounts in the list by five and dividing the product by the number of accounts in the initial sample. As a result the taxpayer is required to select five separate subsamples of approximately 600 accounts each. In this example the skip interval is 200, determined as follows:

$$125,000 \times 5 = 625,000$$
$$625,000 \div 3,000 = 208$$
$$\text{Reduced to} \quad 200 \text{ *}$$

* The taxpayer may reduce the size of the skip interval if a slightly smaller skip interval is more convenient.

The starting points for each of the five subsamples are determined by adding the last digit of the employer's identification number to the last digit of the calendar year. If the sum is greater than nine, subtract ten from the sum. This number indicates the proper column to enter in Table 1, which lists the starting points for various skip intervals. Exhibits 1, 2, and 3, and Tables 1 and 2, shown on pages 469–74, must be followed under the Procedure.

If any starting point in the appropriate column is greater than the skip interval or is equal to the skip interval plus a previously selected starting point, it is disregarded and the next number is used. If necessary, the next column should be used. In our example the starting points are determined as follows:

Identification Number 53–087–1108	8
Calendar Year 1974	4
Total	12
Less	10
Column Number	2

Exhibit 1.—SEGREGATION OF REVOLVING CREDIT SALES INTO PORTION WHICH MAY BE TREATED AS INSTALLMENT SALES

Company .... Subsample number ....
Location .... Skip interval ....
Date .... Starting random number ....

| List serial number | Account identification || Account balance as of last billing date of the fiscal year | Disregarded balances | Charges (in dollars) ||
	Name	Address			Which are treated as installment sales	Which are not treated as installment sales
(1)	(2)	(3)	(4)	(5)	(6)	(7)

Footnote: Transfer the totals of column (6) and (7) to the worksheet of Exhibit 2, lines 1 and 2, respectively, and the columns corresponding to this subsample number.

Copyright © 1974, Commerce Clearing House, Inc.

Exhibit 2.—PERCENT ALLOCATION OF REVOLVING CREDIT ACCOUNTS

Name of taxpayer	Skip interval used	Number of accounts in frame	Date					
Address								
			Subsample number					Total of all subsamples
Item	1	2	3	4	5			
1. Total charges treated as installment sales [1]								
2. Total charges not treated as installment sales [2]								
3. Line 1 plus line 2								
4. Line 1 divided by line 3 (express as a %)								
5. Highest and lowest percentages on line 4 (enter only 2)								
6. Difference between highest and lowest percentages divided by 5								
7. Acceptability test level (from table 2)								
8. Line 6 divided by line 7								
9. Number of additional subsamples required (from table 3)								
10. Total account balances [3]								
11. Account balance for sample account with largest balance								
12. Number of accounts in sample								
13. Number of sample accounts that are nulls								
14. Percent of sample accounts that are nulls (line 13 ÷ 12)								

[1] Total of column 6 of worksheet of Exhibit 1.
[2] Total of column 7 of worksheet of Exhibit 1.
[3] Total of column 4 of worksheet of Exhibit 1.

Copyright © 1974, Commerce Clearing House, Inc.

Ch. 24   INSTALLMENT SALES OF PERSONAL PROPERTY   471

Exhibit 3.—AMOUNT OF GROSS PROFIT
TO BE DEFERRED

1. "Accounts Receivable—Revolving Credit" at end of fiscal year after reduction by nonpersonal property sales .... $............

2. Percent allocation (line 4, "total" column of Exhibit 2)............... %

3. Portion to be treated as installment sales (line 1 x line 2)............ $............

4. Gross profit percentage .... %

5. Gross profit to be deferred (line 3 x line 4)........................ $............

6. Statement as to removal of inactive accounts (see section 5.022 of this Revenue Procedure):

7. Statement as to method of sequencing the list or lists (see section 5.025(f) of this Revenue Procedure):

8. Sample data were based on: (check one)
   Sec. 4 Standards of Probability Sampling   ☐
   Sec. 5 An Acceptable Procedure for Sampling ☐

Table 1.—LIST OF STARTING POINTS

Skip intervals 6 to 9										Skip intervals 10 to 19									
0	1	2	3	4	5	6	7	8	9	0	1	2	3	4	5	6	7	8	9
1	7	2	8	9	6	4	8	1	6	2	13	1	5	18	9	14	11	14	2
4	8	7	6	4	1	5	9	6	5	4	15	8	3	14	11	7	18	10	7
7	6	4	1	5	4	3	6	5	2	11	4	4	11	17	12	19	6	13	1
6	1	3	4	1	7	6	3	7	9	7	1	5	13	2	6	3	3	15	11
9	4	5	3	7	2	2	4	3	4	8	16	2	8	15	17	4	8	16	3
3	3	9	2	6	5	7	5	8	1	18	10	9	2	4	16	9	13	2	19
5	5	1	5	8	9	8	1	2	7	5	8	7	18	19	3	1	7	19	6
2	2	8	9	2	8	9	2	4	8	6	5	17	7	7	7	2	15	7	8
—	—	—	—	—	—	—	—	—	—	1	12	10	4	9	4	5	12	1	9
—	—	—	—	—	—	—	—	—	—	19	19	3	9	3	8	17	5	6	18

Skip intervals 20 to 49										Skip intervals 50 to 99									
0	1	2	3	4	5	6	7	8	9	0	1	2	3	4	5	6	7	8	9
33	37	41	49	18	12	47	43	36	33	87	51	14	27	19	69	81	01	61	82
3	18	33	13	43	14	30	2	1	47	76	03	55	59	99	32	85	98	85	16
34	12	39	47	22	47	4	33	47	8	58	28	23	98	66	54	30	29	16	73
47	17	49	19	42	42	15	42	22	27	98	46	99	65	82	30	23	41	17	48
38	31	43	37	20	44	38	4	2	17	52	89	50	85	20	84	95	27	57	55
30	5	17	40	44	40	11	48	49	47	90	93	49	54	61	77	01	16	36	62
49	9	18	39	47	41	40	23	5	18	20	54	46	71	30	26	26	14	73	01
23	39	48	30	17	34	7	19	29	29	25	49	95	29	12	57	24	31	12	80
36	11	22	46	11	35	49	8	42	45	68	85	52	93	72	78	50	76	40	64
2	21	37	33	26	6	27	46	41	7	30	01	10	73	21	13	33	20	71	29

Copyright © 1974, Commerce Clearing House, Inc.

Table 1.—LIST OF STARTING POINTS—Continued

Skip intervals 100 to 199

0	1	2	3	4	5	6	7	8	9
2	147	100	148	149	147	171	23	195	112
159	168	124	115	137	181	188	58	3	186
37	64	113	87	154	39	111	30	88	191
34	152	50	144	175	76	160	184	21	148
77	121	34	179	155	185	140	86	69	171
199	64	30	101	170	48	175	189	174	151
98	147	161	171	12	132	19	89	79	158
36	83	127	78	40	70	96	148	56	64
80	148	133	5	50	13	181	36	46	185
86	199	82	51	171	164	64	32	16	59

Skip intervals 200 to 499

0	1	2	3	4	5	6	7	8	9
76	376	402	198	17	335	367	369	334	480
459	114	80	488	406	14	314	263	55	45
35	117	474	175	241	45	238	411	405	435
215	137	353	417	74	48	449	31	362	401
206	180	234	222	356	23	190	191	483	252
499	22	266	208	354	300	477	484	348	101
469	378	181	207	222	375	399	396	479	409
496	15	476	477	442	109	58	328	244	86
119	465	305	340	365	441	60	249	229	413
321	37	215	78	464	236	479	222	70	62

Skip intervals 500 to 999

0	1	2	3	4	5	6	7	8	9
853	571	577	512	613	143	088	400	550	977
841	311	169	504	096	794	031	994	788
272	746	672	182	431	297	268	842	780	127
993	950	193	167	350	482	863	061	217	126
727	364	021	418	054	341	023	655	594	438
690	551	116	688	570	711	242	895	649	347
396	988	678	845	540	134	845	619	825	737
817	831	355	891	468	770	033	316	754	732
879	157	847	777	627	961	307	089	223	637
077	861	406	445	703	467	535	787	469	134

Skip intervals 1,000 to 1,999

0	1	2	3	4	5	6	7	8	9
27	925	1,704	458	636	1,013	730	861	87	88
102	691	1,772	1,824	1,202	530	1,507	618	6	58
1,542	788	1,262	1,747	789	921	1,918	461	681	1,857
125	1,870	1,737	1,288	478	272	962	1,853	364	445
325	918	1,941	547	1,231	1,254	1,696	1,510	863	1,136
803	1,621	471	930	1,149	954	1,161	768	1,205	1,867
543	1,945	1,387	694	1,348	1,457	199	1,950	503	1,844
1,642	1,685	1,141	726	1,066	1,092	572	993	183	859
53	1,128	1,623	612	603	768	1,468	34	1,556	161
1,169	1,776	193	630	1,428	1,596	232	1,237	1,460	20

Copyright © 1974, Commerce Clearing House, Inc.

\multicolumn{10}{c	}{Skip intervals 2,000 to 4,999}
0	1	2	3	4	5	6	7	8	9
2,602	2,910	838'	1,710	351	4,553	2,175	1,063	2,827	2,701
574	3,806	4,858	187	4,293	4,031	3,461	4,735	3,014	2,120
2,052	4,414	4,940	4,706	2,524	2,728	4,128	497	4,694	9
2,325	1,841	4,418	932	974	737	625	4,561	3,588	2,127
603	4,907	3,890	131	3,910	655	2,311	1,331	3,360	4,819
1,250	4,034	1,721	2,454	1,605	2,641	2,954	3,993	1,688	3,181
3,713	507	2,566	2,341	3,483	3,713	3,440	1,534	1,367	2,396
4,364	3,211	2,549	3,311	1,535	3,107	3,490	4,266	3,794	1,609
4,918	2,311	4,934	1,321	723	4,006	3,915	3,635	4,324	1,685
1,523	3,737	4,686	2,863	1,437	4,660	590	4,639	4,018	2,677

\multicolumn{10}{c	}{Skip intervals 5,000 to 9,999}
0	1	2	3	4	5	6	7	8	9
2,825	8,210	7,406	4,415	1,531	6,718	9,945	418	9,798	4,108
4,453	533	224	411	4,597	9,382	8,171	4,770	6,201	6,825
830	3,423	671	6,604	6,341	5,443	1,649	7,049	1,883	1,835
4,580	525	7,329	5,917	2,660	7,251	2,232	4,979	6,913	587
9,578	853	7,107	1,983	651	174	8,893	9,911	5,212	9,230
5,387	2,499	2,748	7,176	7,471	1,579	8,622	5,916	4,476	7,507
2,465	3,497	8,319	5,302	3,691	8,059	8,805	7,696	2,665	8,285
9,689	834	1,912	9,273	42	4,762	61	6,942	1,163	6,854
958	2,023	9,424	405	4,955	7,334	4,040	7,243	9,469	4,104
9,956	9,840	9,548	3,956	3,974	4,370	7,080	864	949	5,693

Table 2.—ACCEPTABILITY TEST LEVEL BY NUMBER OF ACCOUNTS

Number of accounts	Acceptability test level As a percentage of allocable revolving credit sales)
Under 12,000	8.0%
12,000—15,999	7.0
16,000—21,999	6.0
22,000—31,999	5.0
32,000—49,999	4.0
50,000—64,999	3.5
65,000—84,999	3.0
85,000—119,999	2.5
120,000—199,999	2.0
200,000—299,999	1.6
300,000—399,999	1.4
400,000—549,999	1.2
550,000—699,999	1.1
700,000 and over	1.0

Copyright © 1974, Commerce Clearing House, Inc.

Table 3.—NUMBER OF ADDITIONAL SUBSAMPLES REQUIRED

Entry on Line 8 of Exhibit 2	Number of Additional Subsamples Required
1.00 or less	None
Over 1.00 up to 1.10	1
Over 1.10 up to 1.18	2
Over 1.18 up to 1.26	3
Over 1.26 up to 1.34	4
Over 1.34 up to 1.41	5
Over 1.41 up to 1.48	6
Over 1.48 up to 1.55	7
Over 1.55 up to 1.61	8
Over 1.61 up to 1.67	9
Over 1.67 up to 1.73	10
Over 1.73 up to 1.79	11
Over 1.79 up to 1.84	12
Over 1.84 up to 1.90	13
Over 1.90 up to 1.95	14
Over 1.95 up to 2.00*	15

* For values over 2.00, square the entry on line 8 of Exhibit 2, subtract 1 and multiply the difference by 5 to obtain the number of additional subsamples required. Raise any decimal remainder to the next higher number. E.g., if the entry on line 8 of Exhibit 2 is 2.01, the computation is $[(2.01)^2 - 1] \times 5 = 15.20$, which should be raised to 16 subsamples.

Copyright © 1974, Commerce Clearing House, Inc.

Reading down column 2 and continuing to column 3 of Table 1 for "skip intervals 200 to 499" (includes 200, as above) the appropriate starting points are 80, 181, 175, and 78.

Subsample Work Sheets. Once having determined the skip interval and the five starting points, it is necessary to prepare separate work sheets for each of the five or more subsamples on Exhibit 1 which must be preserved by the taxpayer for the purpose of any IRS examination. Exhibit 1 is used as a work sheet and is not required to be submitted with the return.

The first subsample serial numbers in the above example would be 80 as a starting point, 280 (80 + 200), 480 (280 + 200), etc. (See Exhibit 1.) Columns 4 to 7 are completed for each account, which is analyzed as discussed below.

Analysis of Customers' Accounts. In determining whether charges in each customer's account are treated as installment sales (Exhibit 1, column 6) or as non-installment sales (column 7), three criteria must be considered:

1. Disregarded balances. Account balances are "disregarded" where no payment has been received after the month of sale up to and

including the first billing-month of the next taxable year. Such account balances are entered in column 5. Accounts with credit balances are similarly disregarded.
2. Monthly sales test. If the aggregate amount of sales charges during a billing-month exceeds the required monthly payment, such sales are considered to be eligible for installment sales treatment.
3. Payment test. If the first payment after the billing-month of a sale does not liquidate the entire balance in the account, the sales for that billing-month do qualify. For this test, the balance is reduced by any return or allowance credited to the account after the close of the billing-month of sale and before the close of the billing-month of the first payment, unless the taxpayer can demonstrate that the return or allowance is attributable to a sale made subsequent to the billing-month of sale.

Finance or service charges are not considered to be part of the selling price and are ineligible for installment treatment. Each payment received from a customer must first be applied to the finance and service charges. However, finance and service charges recorded in the last billing-month of the year are invariably treated as unpaid.

Illustration. Assuming a January 31 fiscal year, a sample customer's account is shown as follows:

Month Ending	Aggregate Sales in Month	Returns and Allowances	Service Charges	Payments	Account Balances	Required Minimum Payment
October, 1973	$71.00			$20.00	$51.00	
November, 1973	21.00		$1.00		73.00	$25.00
December, 1973	25.00		1.00		99.00	25.00
January, 1974	30.00	$10.00	1.00	40.00	80.00	25.00

The analysis of the January 31, 1974, balance follows: °

October sales (balancing amount)	$ 3.00
November sales	21.00
December sales	25.00
January sales	30.00
January service charges	1.00
Balance	$80.00

° The aggregate of $60.00 payments is first applied to the November and December service charges. The unapplied balance of $58.00 plus the $10.00 credit ($68.00) is then applied to the earliest charges.

There are three possible results as to a payment which may be received during February, 1974:

1. Assume no payment. The account is treated as a "disregarded balance" since no payment was received in February, 1974, after the January, 1974, sale of $30.00.
2. Assume a payment of $80.00 in full during February, 1974. Of the $80.00 balance, $3.00 will qualify and $77.00 will not qualify for installment treatment. The sales in November and December of $21.00 and $25.00, respectively, did not exceed the required minimum monthly payment of $25.00 and therefore do not qualify. The January, 1974, service charge of $1.00 does not qualify automatically. The January, 1974, sales in the amount of $30.00 do not qualify, since the full "payment test" was not met. The first payment after the January, 1974, billing-month was not less than the balance of the account at the end of January.

   The October sale of $3.00 (the balance) qualifies since both the "aggregate monthly sales test" and the full payment test are met. The former is met since the aggregate sales for October in the amount of $51.00 exceed the required minimum monthly payment ($25.00). The latter is met since the first payment received in November ($20.00) was less than the balance of the account at the end of October; or
3. Any other payment if less than $80.00. $33.00 will qualify and $47.00 will not qualify.

   The explanation as to qualifying amounts remains the same as that in item 2 above as to the $3 balance of October sale. The January, 1974, sale of $30.00 also qualifies since the "full payment test" was met, being less than the account balance.

After the work sheets for the five subsamples are completed on Exhibit 1 (which is retained by the taxpayer), they must be summarized on Exhibit 2 which is submitted with the tax return. It should be noted from Exhibit 2, lines 6 to 9, that additional subsamples may be required. (See Tables 2 and 3.)

The calculation of the gross profit to be deferred is to be shown on Exhibit 3, which must also be submitted with the tax return.

Sampling Procedure Under Revenue Procedure 65–5

A taxpayer may adopt the more liberal sampling procedures under Rev. Proc. 65–5 if the requirements of Rev. Proc. 64–4 have been followed for the initial year. The basic difference in these Revenue Procedures is the reduction in (1) the minimum sample size, (2) the number of listed accounts required to be listed, and (3) the null correction factor. The Rev. Proc. 65–5 schedule of minimum sample size is shown on page 467 and is applicable for all taxable years including the first year under the installment method for which Rev. Proc. 64–4 is otherwise applicable.

The listing comprises only those accounts which make up randomly selected alphabetic segments, resulting in a smaller list.

The null correction formula is illustrated using the same facts shown under Rev. Proc. 64–4 on pages 467–68. The sample size is computed as follows:

$$\frac{\text{Initial sample} \times 1 + \text{null ratio}}{1 - \text{null ratio}} = \text{sample size}$$

Utilizing the above illustrative data, this would result in a required sample of 2,250 accounts as follows:

$$\frac{.006 \times 125,000}{1 - .5} = \frac{750 \times 1.5}{1 - .5} = \frac{1,125}{.5} = 2,250 \text{ accounts to be sampled (compared with 3,000 under Rev. Proc. 64–4).}$$

Election To Report on the Installment Method

Income tax laws generally have recognized two major methods of reporting income, namely, the accrual and the cash basis methods. Initially, the use of the installment method was permitted only by Treasury Regulations. The procedure to be followed and the validity of the method itself were the subject of much disagreement and conflicting court decisions. Finally, the procedure and the conditions of its adoption and use were included in the Internal Revenue Code and the Regulations.

It is not the purpose of the present discussion to set forth the historical background or discuss the various procedures which were allowable in certain periods and not in others. Disputes centered largely around the procedure to be followed at the time the method was to be changed. For example, when the installment method was adopted for tax purposes, the store would have reported the gross profit on all sales made up to that time on the accrual basis; under the installment sales basis, it would have reported only the gross profit on collections made. Prior to the 1939 Code the unresolved question was whether gross profit on collections from sales of prior periods, previously reported on the accrual basis, was subject to inclusion in taxable income in both taxable years.

A new retailer, or an existing retailer reporting sales on the installment method for the first time (after selling the installment account balances at the close of the preceding year; see below) attaches a statement to the tax return for the year of election indicating that the installment method is being adopted and specifying the type or types of sales included in such election. [Reg. § 1.453–8(a).] The dealer may adopt the installment method for traditional installment sales only, for revolving credit sales only, or for both types. Since the cash-flow advantages of the installment method are significant, it is unlikely that the taxpayer's election will be limited to only one form of installment selling. Advance permission from the IRS is not required to adopt the installment method.

The 1939 Code required the imposition of a double tax when a taxpayer elected to change from the accrual to the installment method. Notwithstanding that uncollected installment sales had been taxed in a previous year under the earlier accrual method, a second tax was imposed in each subsequent year under the newly elected installment method when the taxpayer received collections on such prior-year sales. The 1954 Code [Sec. 453(c)] affords some, but not full, relief by way of a credit against this double tax. The following is an excerpt from the House Ways and Means Committee Report No. 1337:

> Under subsection (c) an adjustment is provided to eliminate the double taxation of income when a taxpayer changes from an accrual method to the installment method. The adjustment is in the form of a reduction in tax for the year in which the item is includible the second time. The reduction is the amount of the tax attributable to the item in the prior year but not in excess of the tax attributable to the item in the year in which it is includible the second time. The tax attributable to an item is that percentage of the tax for the year which the gross profit from installment sales bears to the gross income. For example:

	Year 1	Year 2	Year 3 (year of change)
Gross profit from installment sales (receivable in five installments)	$100,000	$ 50,000	$ 20,000 ° 10,000 † 20,000 °°
Other income	80,000	200,000	150,000
Gross income	180,000	250,000	200,000
Deductions	60,000	50,000	50,000
Taxable income	$120,000	$200,000	$150,000
Assuming a tax rate of	30%	50%	40%
Tax would be	$ 36,000	$100,000	$ 60,000

° From year 1 sales.
† From year 2 sales.
°° From year 3 sales.

COMPUTATION OF ADJUSTMENT
Year 1 Item

In year 3:

Tax attributable to year 1 item	$= \dfrac{\$ 20,000}{\$200,000} \times \$ 60,000$	
Tax attributable to second inclusion		6,000

In year 1:

Tax attributable to prior inclusion	$= \dfrac{\$ 20,000}{\$180,000} \times \$ 36,000$	
Tax attributable to original inclusion is		4,000
Adjustment in respect of year 1 item is		4,000

Year 2 Item

In year 3:

Tax attributable to year 2 item	$= \dfrac{\$ 10,000}{\$200,000} \times \$ 60,000$	
Tax attributable to second inclusion is		3,000

In year 2:

Tax attributable to prior inclusion	$= \dfrac{\$ 10,000}{\$250,000} \times \$100,000$	
Tax attributable to original inclusion is		4,000
Adjustment in respect of year 2 item is		3,000

The tax would be reduced by $4,000 plus $3,000, or a total of $7,000. The tax would then be $53,000 in year 3.

The adjustment shall be made if the change of method occurs in a taxable year beginning after December 31, 1953, for all amounts required to be included a second time without regard to whether the prior inclusion of the amount occurred in a taxable year beginning before, on, or after December 31, 1953.

Thus the taxpayer is paying a double tax of $5,000 [40% × ($20,000 + $10,000) less $7,000].

The Regulations [§ 1.453–7(b)] include substantially the same illustration. Even with partial relief, there could be duplicate taxation to a considerable extent, which would reduce the potential benefit from the deferment of taxes. Furthermore, if the year 1 in the above example were a loss year, no credit would be allowable in the year 3.

Avoiding the Partially Double Tax

Inasmuch as a taxpayer electing the installment method of reporting income is required to pay a partially double tax, it is necessary to follow a method of avoidance which is acceptable to the IRS. A taxpayer may sell customers' installment obligations to a bank or other institution as of the last day of a particular taxable year and then elect to adopt the installment method of reporting income for the following year. Any loss arising from the sale of the accounts is treated as an ordinary loss. [Sec. 1221(4).] If the taxpayer is treated no longer as the "owner" of the installment obligations sold, the amounts collected from the customers which are attributable to installment obligations previously sold would not be included again in computing the taxpayer's taxable income. In Rev. Rul. 59–343 (1959–2 C.B. 136) the IRS, in acquiescing to *City Stores Co. v. Smith et al.*, 154 Fed. Supp. 348 (1957), held that this type of arrangement would be acceptable for eliminating the "double inclusion" of income if a "bona fide" sale has taken place.

IRS Ruling Request

It is usually possible to obtain an advance ruling that a prospective transaction would constitute a bona fide sale; it is not recommended that taxpayers dispense with a ruling. However, since the distinction between a bona fide sale and a loan may be somewhat narrow, the Internal Revenue Service will rule favorably only when all aspects of a proposed sales transaction meet the established IRS requirements. The Service has ruled favorably on prospective transactions which incorporate the following characteristics:

1. The selling price of the receivables is at a discount from face. The amount of discount need not be specified in the ruling request; however, the percentage must be fixed by the time of closing and cannot be dependent on subsequent events.
2. Since the taxpayer may not know the exact dollar balance of the accounts to be sold at the time the transaction is consummated, the accounts can be sold for an estimated amount. However, at such subsequent date (the contract usually indicates a reasonable time), payment should be made to adjust for differences between the estimated and actual dollar balances of the accounts. It is permissible for the parties to provide for interest on the adjustment; moreover, the rate charged does not have to be the same for an underpayment as for an overpayment.
3. Collections from the customers may be received by the taxpayer, as agent, but the Service requires that the finance charges be given to the bank; such finance charges cannot be retained by the taxpayer as compensation for action as a collection agent.
4. Settlement of collections should be provided on a monthly basis. The seller usually supplies the purchaser with a schedule of an-

ticipated collections. If actual collections are less than indicated on the schedule, damages, i.e., interest, can be paid. This schedule would then be used by the financial institution in order to determine the amount of discount from the face amount of the receivables.

5. A percentage of the sales price, not in excess of 10 per cent, can be retained by the purchaser as collateral for breach of warranties; however, the reserve must be reduced as collections are made. It is the Service's position that the reserve balance be the greater of 10 per cent of the outstanding uncollected balance or ¾ of one per cent of the initial amount sold. The latter provides a floor when most accounts have been collected.

6. The sale must pass title to the accounts, without recourse. Although the taxpayer may have the option to repurchase defaulted obligations, and any defaulted obligations not repurchased may be charged against the reserve, the taxpayer must not be required to purchase defaulted obligations. However, the taxpayer can be obligated to repurchase accounts on which warranties are breached. The records of the receivables should be identified (stamped) as being the property of the purchaser.

7. The Service usually requires a statement regarding the intended use of the sales proceeds. Under no circumstances can the seller be required to leave a compensating balance on account with the bank or to purchase certificates of deposit from the bank. In the event the taxpayer subsequently purchases certificates of deposit of the bank, a question of fact may arise as to whether the purchases were required.

Realizing that there are many variables in a contract of this nature which can be negotiated to provide a satisfactory yield to a purchasing bank, it is suggested that any retailer intending to enter into such a transaction conform as nearly as possible to the outlined arrangement. The desired yield can easily be arranged by providing an appropriate discount, thereby eliminating the necessity of including variations to which the Service may not agree.

In order to expedite the processing of the ruling request, a draft of the proposed sales agreement should be submitted to the IRS under the "two-part ruling request" procedure. The "summary" statement of facts will, in effect, become the substance of the ruling letter. A complete statement of facts is also submitted. (Rev. Proc. 72–3, Sec. 6.03; 1972–1 C.B. 698. The *City Stores* decision and Rev. Rul. 59–343, *supra,* are usually cited as the authorities.)

The ruling should state that a bona fide sale of the installment receivables balances has been made; that the loss on the sale (discount) is deductible as an ordinary loss; and that amounts collected subsequently by the taxpayer in respect of the balances sold will not be taxable under Sec. 453(c).

Usually, the ruling will require that the purchaser must not require the seller to purchase certificates of deposits or to maintain compensating balances. Also, the entire amount of reserve for bad debts relating to the receivables sold must be included in income when the accounts are sold. Furthermore, the ruling usually states that no opinion is being expressed regarding the establishment of a bad debt reserve under the taxpayer's contingent liability as a guarantor. [Sec. 166(g).] See discussion below under reserve for bad debts arising from liability as guarantor.

A copy of the ruling must be attached to the return covering the year of sale.

Changing from Installment Method

Where a store has been using the installment sales basis for years, it may be advantageous to continue or, at least, disadvantageous to change. Nevertheless, for some stores the question may arise as to whether it is desirable to discontinue the installment method and reinstitute the accrual method.

The Tax Reform Act of 1969 added Sec. 453(c)(4) and (5) to the Internal Revenue Code of 1954. The effect of this amendment is to permit dealers in personal property who previously elected to report income on the installment basis to revoke the election at any time within three years (including extensions) of the year of original election.

The revocation may be made by filing amended returns for the year of election and subsequent years on the accrual basis. In general, once the revocation is made, taxpayers are precluded from re-electing the installment method for a period of five years following the year of revocation. [Sec. 453(c)(5).] Furthermore, the Service may assess deficiencies (i.e., additional tax payments) for prior taxable years for a period of two years following the revocation if the deficiencies are attributable to such revocation. [Sec. 453(c)(4).]

If a retailer is not eligible to revoke the installment method election under Sec. 453(c)(4) and (5), but wishes to change from the installment basis to the accrual method, permission to do so must be requested from the Treasury not later than 180 days after the beginning of the taxable year for which permission to change is requested. At the time of change the tax will have to be paid on the total unrealized gross profits deferred at that date under the installment basis. If the 180-day period has expired, a similar effect can be obtained, without requesting permission, by making a sale, distribution, or other disposition of the accounts at the end of the fiscal year. [Sec. 453(d).] It is preferable taxwise that a change to the accrual basis be made in a year for which unused operating losses are anticipated in sufficient amount to absorb the unrealized gross income to be added to taxable income. Operating loss carry-forward and carry-back provisions are additional factors that would complicate such decisions.

If the taxpayer wishes to borrow money and is required to pledge installment receivables as collateral, it should be clear from the loan agreement that the accounts are not being sold or "discounted." The best procedure is to receive collections on the accounts rather than turn the accounts over to the financial institution for collection. [Rev. Rul. 65–185, 1965–2 C.B. 153; *L. H. Elmer,* 65 F.2d 568 (1933), *aff'g* 22 B.T.A. 224; *Town & Country Food Co., Inc.,* 51 T.C. 1049 (1969) (acq.).]

Bad Debts. Prior to 1966 the IRS had taken the position that the portion of the allowance for bad debts attributable to installment accounts which had been sold must be included in taxable income, in the year of sale. [Rev. Rul. 62–214, 1962–2 C.B. 72.] The correct treatment was in controversy, since the Tax Court had held in favor of the Service [*Mike Persia Chevrolet, Inc. v. Comm'r,* 41 T.C. 198 (1963)] while several circuit courts had ruled in favor of the taxpayer [*Foster Frosty Foods, Inc. v. Comm'r,* 332 F.2d 230 (10th Cir. 1964); *Burbank Liquidating Corp. v. Comm'r,* 335 F.2d 125 (9th Cir. 1964)].

In 1966, Sec. 166(g) was added to the Code. It provides that a retailer may include a reasonable amount in the allowance for bad debts "which may arise out of his liability as a guarantor, endorser, or indemnitor of debt obligations arising out of the sale by him of real property or tangible personal property (including related services). . . ."

Bad debts may be deducted in either one of two methods: (1) the deduction of specific debts when they become worthless in whole or in part; or (2) a reasonable addition to a reserve for bad debts. A taxpayer filing a first return may elect either method, subject to Treasury approval. The method adopted must be adhered to, unless permission to change is obtained.

Repossessions on Installment Accounts. The procedure with respect to bad debts may be somewhat affected when merchandise is repossessed. The simplest procedure is to reflect the repossessed goods in inventory at their fair market value at date of repossession. Any excess of unrecovered cost over the fair market value at repossession is treated as a loss. Unrecovered cost is original cost (retail sales price less gross profit percentage), less a portion of original cost received in installments, i.e., amounts received on account, less the gross profit portions thereof which were taxable.

In the unlikely event that the fair market value at repossession exceeds unrecovered cost, a gain will be reported rather than a loss, unless unrecovered cost or value, whichever is lower, is used in recognizing valuation of repossessed merchandise. [This rule was upheld in *Blum's, Inc. v. Comm'r*, 7 B.T.A. 737 (1927) (NA).] From a practical standpoint, this question is relatively unimportant, because fair market values at repossession will generally be less than the unrecovered cost.

Regulations § 1.453-1(d) state in part: "The fair market value of the property repossessed shall be reflected in appropriate permanent records of the vendor at the time of such repossession." As a practical procedure the fair market value at time of repossession may be obtained by estimating the selling price and reducing such amount by the estimated gross profit ratio. Effectively, this fair market value will be charged to merchandise and credited to the account receivable. If the credit to the latter is less than the outstanding balance, the uncollectible difference will be charged off directly to bad debt expense or to the reserve for bad debts, as the case may be. If the credit is greater than the outstanding balance, the difference may be credited against bad debt losses or to the reserve for bad debts.

The following is a typical example which illustrates the overall profit and loss impact of a sale on account and the subsequent repossession of merchandise.

Illustration. Assume an original sale on account, $60; a gross profit percentage, 40%; a fair value of repossessed merchandise, $10.

Under these circumstances, there is an overall loss of $26, determined as follows:

Account receivable	$60
Fair market value of repossessed merchandise	10
Balance written off as bad debt	50
Included in income, 40 per cent of original sale of $60	24
Loss	$26

Stated differently, there has been a diminution in value of the merchandise represented by the difference between the original cost of the merchandise of $36 (60 per cent of $60) and the current estimated fair market value of $10, or a "net loss" of $26.

Illustration of Various Classes of Credits

When unrealized gross profit on installment sales is computed on the basis of open balances, the credits to receivables for merchandise repossessed and for bad debts written off have, for all practical purposes, the same effect as cash collections. This presupposes that the amounts written off will be charged to bad debt expense and the repossessed merchandise will be recognized in the accounts at estimated fair market value. The accuracy of this methodology is evidenced by the following example which illustrates that the same result is obtained by analyzing cash collections only and alternatively by treating these other items of bad debts and value of repossessed merchandise separately.

The facts and figures used are the same as in a preceding illustration of the method of computing unrealized gross profit, with additional data as stated.

The amounts credited to the installment accounts in the year ended January 31, 1977, in the illustration on pages 461–62 were as follows:

Accounts Arising in Year Ended January 31	Amount of Credit in Year Ended January 31, 1977
1974	$ 8,000
1975	30,000
1976	50,000
1977	70,000

In this example the credits were considered in total, with no differentiation among cash collections, bad debts, or value of repossessed merchandise; or alternatively, it may be assumed that all credits represented cash collections. The result in the illustration was a taxable gross profit comprising:

36.13 per cent of $70,000 collections from sales made
in the year ended January 31, 1977 = $25,291
Realized gross profits of collections made on
prior-year sales, as follows:

Year Ended January 31	Gross Profit Percentage	Collections	Realized Gross Profits
1974	35.65%	$ 8,000	$ 2,852
1975	35.47	30,000	10,641
1976	35.20	50,000	17,600
Total taxable gross profit			$56,384

In the above example the credits to accounts receivable (i.e., "collections") were deemed to represent solely cash collections, with no reduction in receivable balances attributable to the write-off of bad debts. For illustrative purposes, let us assume that the credits to accounts receivable are to be classified between cash collected and accounts receivable written off, as follows:

Accounts Arising in Year Ended January 31	Total Credits to Accounts in Year Ended January 31, 1977	Cash	Accounts Written Off	Merchandise Repossessed at Inventory Value
1974	$ 8,000	$ 6,000	$1,500	$ 500
1975	30,000	26,000	3,000	1,000
1976	50,000	45,000	3,000	2,000
1977	70,000	65,000	2,000	3,000
	$158,000	$142,000	$9,500	$6,500

Analysis of Collections. The determination of taxable income for the year ended January 31, 1977, by an analysis of the collections during the year would be made as follows:

Year Ended January 31	Cash Collected	Gross Profit Percentage	Realized Income
1974	$ 6,000	35.65%	$ 2,139.00
1975	26,000	35.47	9,222.20
1976	45,000	35.20	15,840.00
1977	65,000	36.13	23,484.50
			$50,685.70

From this realized income of $50,685.70 there would be deductible, for tax purposes, the bad debt loss on the installment basis, determined as follows:

Year Ended January 31	Gross Value of Accounts Not Collectible (Total Credits of $158,000 Less Cash Collections of $142,000)	Gross Profit Percentages	Unrealized Profit in Credits Except Cash	Unrecovered Costs, or Cost of Credits Except Cash	Salvage Value of Merchandise Repossessed	Tax Deductions for Bad Debts
1974	$ 2,000	35.65%	$ 713.00	$ 1,287.00	$ 500	$ 787.00
1975	4,000	35.47	1,418.80	2,581.20	1,000	1,581.20
1976	5,000	35.20	1,760.00	3,240.00	2,000	1,240.00
1977	5,000	36.13	1,806.50	3,193.50	3,000	193.50
	$16,000		$5,698.30	$10,301.70	$6,500	$3,801.70

The gross profit of $50,685.70 realized on cash collections during the year is offset to the extent of $3,801.70 for the net cost of bad debt losses, leaving a taxable gross income of $46,884.

Analysis of Balances. As noted above, the shorter method of analyzing balances at the close of the year results in taxable gross profit of $56,384 if all credits to the accounts represent cash collections. If that method is used in connection with the data presented above regarding accounts written off during the year, the taxable income for the year is similarly determined to be $46,884, as follows:

Gross profit on sales in year ended January 31, 1977 (36.13 per cent of $150,000)	$54,195
Reduction in reserve for unrealized gross profit	2,189
	56,384
Less: Uncollectible accounts written off books	9,500
Net income	$46,884

25

Leasing of Real and Personal Property by Retailers

Introduction

In recent years, an increasing number of retailers have turned to leasing as a means of financing stores, warehouses, and furniture and fixtures. The ability to lease enables the retailer to acquire assets without having initially to raise funds equal to the purchase price. This attribute of leasing has made it a particularly attractive vehicle with which to finance expansion programs since it allows the retailer to proceed with expansion and benefit from the new assets without actually owning them.

Furthermore, major retailers have turned to leasing to act as lessor as well as lessee. Thus, many shopping centers are owned by major retailers who, in turn, lease space to other retailers. By acting as owner–developers of shopping centers, retailers have attempted to reduce their overall cost of renting prime space since they receive the benefit of any appreciation in the center.

This chapter will explore leasing with a view to supplying the retailer with the background necessary to assist in making the best economic decision when acquiring an asset.

Leasing Versus Ownership

When planning the acquisition of a capital asset, there are numerous financing methods available, ranging from outright purchase to short-term rentals. The differences in these extremes, and the gradations between them, are primarily related to the degrees of ownership. When an asset is purchased outright for cash, the buyer has full rights of ownership. As soon as the buyer obtains outside financing, the degree of control begins to diminish. For example, in an installment purchase, the buyer will generally have full ownership rights with the exception of the ability to sell. The right of sale will be limited by the lien of the lender. If a potential buyer obtains full financing by using a long-term lease, he retains operating risks of obsolescence and maintenance, but relinquishes residual rights except to the extent of purchase options at the end of the lease. Finally, in a short-term rental, the buyer relinquishes almost all risks of ownership. The lessor bears such risks, and the rental is priced accordingly.

When operating decisions, such as risk of maintenance or risk of rapid decline in value, are key factors, the decision should be to own/lease or rent. That is, management may presume that the economic risks of acquiring the asset, whether by outright sale or lease, are sufficiently great that they would prefer to rent the asset and pay an appropriate premium for being spared the risk. The decision to own/lease versus rent should be based on management's judgment regarding the operation of the asset. Accordingly, this decision is not discussed in the chapter. Rather, this chapter will focus on the differences between owning and leasing as opposed to the own/lease versus rent decision.

The decision as to whether to lease or buy is one that can be made only after a careful analysis of the advantages and disadvantages, and the resultant cash flows, from the two basic options. The "analysis" cannot be made by the simplistic approach of comparing on the one hand one current (total) payment and full ownership with extended payments (which in the aggregate exceed the one payment) and no ownership on the other hand. Aside from being economically doubtful, the foregoing type of decision can no longer be made in the current era of low profit margins and high costs of money. Using the same logic, the retailer would pay a salesman ten years' salary when hired, as opposed to paying him on a weekly basis. If this seems ludicrous, why does it automatically make sense, for example, to buy outright a fixture with a ten-year life, instead of making monthly payments as the fixture, in effect, generates income? The example is obviously simplistic, but the point is still valid of consideration: "turning capital investment" is becoming more and more a critical aspect of profitability for the retailer, as "turning inventory" always has been.

While the examples given stress the advantages of leasing, there are equally impressive disadvantages. This chapter will highlight the pros and cons of leasing, detail the accounting and tax considerations, present methods for making a quantitative "buy or lease" decision, and offer some subjective points for consideration.

Pros and Cons

For comparative purposes, the pros and cons from both the lessee's and the lessor's point of view are presented. To provide a framework for the subsequent technical discussions, the following summarizes the advantages and disadvantages of leasing.

Lessee—Advantages

1. One hundred per cent financing of the cost of the property, on attractive terms.
2. Possible avoidance of existing loan indenture restrictions on new debt financing. Consequently, a retailer may increase the debt base as lease obligations are generally not reflected on the balance sheet, although the lease obligation will probably require footnote disclosure to the financial statements. In this connection, however, it should be noted that a number of the more recent loan indentures place restrictions on lease commitments.
3. Increased leverage at overall lower cost. Indirect financing via the use of leases effectively makes possible a larger amount of overall financing at an overall aggregate lower capital cost. Institutional lenders conventionally utilize various financial statement objective ratios and relationships to measure a company's creditworthiness. Successive amounts of debt financing which are reflected on a company's balance sheet could thereby adversely affect a company's credit standing, a fact which quickly translates into higher interest rates. Accordingly, many companies seek to minimize overall costs of capital by maintaining relative balances of indirect financings and debt financings, with increasing equity amounts.

4. Rental deductions generally allowable for tax purposes for the term of the lease without problems or disputes about depreciable life of the property.
5. Possible improvement of net book income during the earlier years of the basic lease term. Rental payments in the earlier years of a lease are generally less than the combined interest expense and depreciation (even on the straight-line method) which a corporate property owner would otherwise have charged in the income statement.
6. Potential reduction in state and city franchise and income taxes since the property factor, which is generally one of the three factors in the allocation formula, is reduced.
7. Full deductibility for tax purposes of rent payment, notwithstanding that the rent is partially based on the cost of the land.

Lessee—Disadvantages

1. Loss of residual rights to the property at the end of the lease. If the lessee had full residual rights, the transaction would have been a financing instead of a true lease. The lessee may have purchase and/or renewal options, but the renewals result in payments to the lessor after the full cost of the property has been amortized.
2. Rentals greater than comparable debt service. Since the lessor borrows funds with which to buy the asset to be leased, the rent is based on the lessor's debt service plus a profit factor. This amount may exceed the debt service that the lessee would have had to pay had such lessee purchased the property.
3. Loss of operating and financing flexibility. If an asset was owned outright and a new, improved model became available, the owner could sell or exchange the old model for the new one. This flexibility may not be available under a lease. If interest rates decreased, lease payments would remain constant, whereas the owner of the asset could refinance the debt at a lower rate of interest.
4. Loss of tax benefits from accelerated depreciation and high interest expense deductions in early years which would have produced a temporary cash savings assuming that equivalent financing had been obtained.

Lessor—Advantages

1. Higher rate of return than on investment in straight debt. To compensate for risk and lack of marketability, the lessor can

charge the lessee a higher effective rate, particularly after considering the lessor's tax benefits, than would be available directly to the lessee.
2. Lessor's claim to a specific asset. Should the lessee have financial trouble, the lessor can look to a specific asset as opposed to being just a general creditor.
3. Retention of residual value of the property at the end of the lease. The cost of the asset is amortized over the basic lease term. At that time, the lessee will abandon, renew, or purchase. In the first instance, the lessor can then sell the asset. In the latter alternatives, the lessor will receive payments that represent substantially all profit.

Lessor—Disadvantages

1. Dependence on ability of lessee to pay rent on a timely basis.
2. Potential detriment from unexpected changes in the tax law which could reduce tax benefits and related cash flow.
3. Potential change in the depreciable life, thereby altering lessor's return. If the Internal Revenue Service significantly extends the depreciable life of the asset, the projected return upon which the lessor made the investment would diminish.
4. Negative cash flow in later years. As the lease progresses, an increasing percentage of the rent goes toward nondeductible principal amortization. The interest and depreciation tax deductions both decline as the lease progresses.
5. Potentially large tax on disposition resulting from depreciation recapture provisions of the Internal Revenue Code.

As the above comparisons indicate, there are many facets of leasing which must be considered before the decision is made. The pros and cons cited must be reviewed subjectively by the potential lessor and lessee to determine how the advantages and disadvantages apply to their respective financial and tax status. A critical advantage to one retailer may well have no bearing on the decision of another. For example, the benefit of not recording additional debt by leasing may be a great advantage to a heavily leveraged company, but may be insignificant to a firm with a small debt load.

Evaluation Techniques

The quantitative analysis of the buy–versus–lease decision is basically a cash flow comparison, and as such is essentially a capital budgeting type of question. The potential lessee must determine what the cash position would be under each alternative, and then compare the results using an approach which is believed to be the most appropriate for the particular company. Such comparison may be based on rate of return, present value of cash flows, or net cash position—to name a few currently used criteria. The policies and criteria that a company uses in its capital budgeting procedures should carry over to the lease analysis so that the company's return on investment from a lease will be viewed against the same frame of reference. It is not, however, the purpose of this chapter to discuss and evaluate capital budgeting.[1] Accordingly, the discussion here will center on the pertinent factors to be considered in a lease-or-buy comparison. The financial effects of an outright purchase will be examined first.

When a company purchases an asset, cash must be paid out to the extent of the purchase price. This cash will be financed either by obtaining a new loan specifically for the purchase or from the company's funds made available by current borrowings. In either case, the interest cost associated with the funds should be recognized. For purposes of the lease-versus-buy analysis, the costs the company must carry, related to the asset, are the interest on the debt and the depreciation of the asset. Operating expenses such as insurance and maintenance are excluded since the lease would typically be a net lease with such expenses borne by the lessee whether owned or leased. Thus, at the time of purchase, the company receives a sum of money from some debt source which it disburses to purchase the asset. The company will then pay a yearly debt service over the life of the loan and will have a non-cash depreciation charge over the life of the asset. The asset will have some salvage or residual value which will accrue to the company. The cash outlays of the buyer consist of the initial purchase cost and the yearly interest and principal payments. The cash inflows are the loan, the tax benefits of the yearly interest and depreciation expense, and the salvage value. Given the above facts and assuming that the company has sufficient taxable income which will enable it to obtain the full benefit of the interest and depreciation deductions, the yearly and cumulative cash flow can be calculated.

In a lease, the cash flows are more easily defined. The lessee pays a yearly rental which is fully deductible. The rent is based

---

[1] See *The Capital Budgeting Process* by Hunt, Gannon, and Martinelli, © 1968, Lybrand, Ross Bros. & Montgomery.

BUY VERSUS LEASE ANALYSIS
$100,000 ASSET

Buy

Period	Debt Service[a]	Principal Repayment	Interest Payment	Depreciation[b]	Interest Plus Depreciation	Tax Benefit at 50%	After-Tax Cash Cost	Cumulative After-Tax Cash Cost
1	$ 11,507	$ 3,614	$ 7,893	$ 12,500	$ 20,393	$10,197	$ 1,310	$ 1,310
2	11,507	3,912	7,595	11,667	19,262	9,631	1,876	3,186
3	11,507	4,234	7,273	10,833	18,106	9,053	2,454	5,640
4	11,507	4,583	6,924	10,000	16,924	8,462	3,045	8,685
5	11,507	4,961	6,546	9,167	15,713	7,856	3,651	12,336
6	11,507	5,370	6,137	8,333	14,470	7,235	4,272	16,608
7	11,507	5,813	5,694	7,500	13,194	6,598	4,910	21,518
8	11,507	6,292	5,215	6,667	11,882	5,941	5,566	27,084
9	11,507	6,810	4,697	5,833	10,530	5,265	6,242	33,326
10	11,507	7,372	4,135	5,000	9,135	4,567	6,940	40,266
11	11,507	7,979	3,528	4,167	7,695	3,848	7,659	47,925
12	11,507	8,637	2,870	3,333	6,203	3,101	8,406	56,331
13	11,507	9,349	2,158	2,500	4,658	2,329	9,178	65,509
14	11,507	10,120	1,387	1,667	3,054	1,527	9,980	75,489
15	11,507	10,954	552	833	1,385	693	10,814	86,303
	$172,605	$100,000	$72,605	$100,000	$172,605	$86,302	$86,303[d]	

Lease

Rental[c]	Tax Benefit at 50%	After-Tax Cash Cost	Cumulative After-Tax Cash Cost
$ 10,990	$ 5,495	$ 5,495	$ 5,495
10,990	5,495	5,495	10,990
10,990	5,495	5,495	16,485
10,990	5,495	5,495	21,980
10,990	5,495	5,495	27,475
10,990	5,495	5,495	32,970
10,990	5,495	5,495	38,465
10,990	5,495	5,495	43,960
10,990	5,495	5,495	49,455
10,990	5,495	5,495	54,950
10,990	5,495	5,495	60,445
10,990	5,495	5,495	65,940
10,990	5,495	5,495	71,435
10,990	5,495	5,495	76,930
10,990	5,495	5,495	82,425
$164,850	$82,425	$82,425[e]	

[a]$100,000 of debt borrowed at 8%. The debt service, payable quarterly in arrears, will be sufficient to fully amortize the loan over 15 years.
[b]Asset cost of $100,000 will be depreciated over 15 years using the sum-of-the-years-digits method. It was assumed that the asset had no salvage value.
[c]Rental on a 15-year lease will be payable quarterly in arrears. The rental was based on an interest factor of 7¾%. It was assumed that the lessee's credit would require 8% interest. Since the lessor retains the depreciation benefits of the asset, he can charge a rent based on 7¾% even though he has financed the acquisition at 8%.
[d]Present worth of $86,303 cost of buying, at 8%, is $41,198.
[e]Present worth of $82,425 cost of leasing, at 8%, is $47,034.

FIG. 45. Buy-versus-lease analysis of an asset.

on the debt service the lessor must pay plus a profit return to the lessor. The interest on the debt is generally a function of the creditworthiness of the lessee, rather than the lessor, since the lender is basically looking to the financial viability of the lessee for the debt repayment. Thus, the cash flow analysis of the lessee consists of level annual outflows over the lease period, less the related tax benefit. Salvage or residual value considerations are inapplicable since the lessee has no rights of ownership in the asset leased. Figure 45 illustrates the application of the above quantitative principles to a buy-versus-lease decision.

At this point, the annual cash flows from an outright sale and from a lease have been developed. The next step is to compare the flows, by an accepted method such as the discounted present value, to determine which results in the greater cash benefit or yield.

In making the cash flow analysis, the potential lessee must consider the effects of changes in the assumptions used. For example, what will the resultant cash flow be if the Internal Revenue Service requires a longer depreciation period than originally calculated? How will a ½ per cent change in interest rates affect the decision? Ideally, the result of the quantitative comparison should be a series of judgments which could then be assigned probabilities.

Thus, the results of the analysis could be similar to the following:

1. With a ten-year life and an 8 per cent borrowing, outright purchase is better by X dollars.
2. A two-year increase in useful life reduces the benefit of outright purchase to $(X - Y)$ dollars.
3. A ½ per cent increase in interest reduces the benefit of outright purchase to $(X - Z)$ dollars.
4. There is a 30 per cent chance that the life will be increased two years.
5. There is a 10 per cent chance that interest rates will increase ½ per cent.

Once hypotheses and computations similar to the above have been made, a decision can be arrived at which would give the most realistic net dollar benefit.

However, it should be recognized that the most critical aspect of the buy-versus-lease analysis is that the decision must not be made solely on the basis of the quantitative comparisons. The dollar or percentage benefit must be weighed against the other advantages and disadvantages discussed earlier, i.e., impact on the financial statements, desire for operational flexibility, and loan restrictions. Rate of return is not an absolute, and it must be tempered by a consideration of the many other accounting, tax, economic, and financial considerations to arrive at a comprehensive decision that is correct for the particular company at a specific point in time.

Accounting Treatment

The current status of accounting for leases is covered by Opinion No. 5, as amended (relating to lessees) and Opinions No. 7, as amended, and No. 27 (relating to lessors) of the Accounting Principles Board (APB) of the American Institute of Certified Public Accountants. Pertinent provisions of these opinions follow.

APB Opinion No. 5, issued in September, 1964, highlighted the problem area by stating: "The central question is whether assets and liabilities are created by leases which convey the rights to use property if no equity is accumulated in the property by the lessee." The Board looked at leases from two extremes. On the one hand, it was felt that a lease which exchanges the right to use property for rent does not create equity for the lessee. "The rights and obligations under leases which convey merely the right to use property, without an equity in the property accruing to the lessee, fall into the category of pertinent information which should be disclosed in schedules or notes rather than by recording assets and liabilities in the financial statements." On the other hand, some lease agreements are essentially equivalent to installment purchases of property. "The property and related obligation should be included as an asset and liability in the balance sheet if the terms of the lease result in the creation of a material equity in the property."

The key as to whether a lease must be capitalized on the books of the lessee is, therefore, the determination of an equity in the property by the lessee. The Opinion gives certain guidelines in paragraphs 10 and 11 to assist in making such determination:

1. "It is unlikely that such an equity can be created under a lease which either party may cancel unilaterally for reasons other than the occurrence of some remote contingency."
2. A noncancelable lease would tend to be considered a purchase if:
    a. The initial lease term is materially shorter than the property's

useful life and the lessee may renew for the balance of the useful life at a bargain rental;
b. The lessee has purchase or lease renewal options which are clearly at bargain prices;
c. The lessor acquired the property to meet the special needs of the lessee and the property will probably be usable only for that purpose and only for the lessee;
d. The lessee assumes all of the incidents of ownership such as taxes, insurance, and maintenance;
e. The lessee has guaranteed the obligations of the lessor with respect to the property leased;
f. The lessee has treated the property as a purchase for tax purposes.

If the facts indicate that the lease is in substance a purchase, it should be capitalized by appropriately discounting the aggregate future lease rental payments. If the lease is deemed to be a true lease, it should be disclosed in a footnote to the financial statements. Such footnote should be sufficient for the reader to assess the effect of lease commitments upon the financial position and results of operations, both present and prospective, of the lessee.

In practice, many accountants generally use the following rule of thumb in determining the need for capitalization: If all purchase options and the present value of future renewal options at the beginning of the applicable renewal periods exceed the undepreciated book balance of the assets at the respective option or renewal dates, a material equity has not been created and capitalization is not required. While the above rule of thumb is generally used, it must be kept in mind that it is just that—a rule of thumb. Even if the "rule" is met, the accountant may properly determine that the transaction is in substance a purchase and that accordingly it should be accounted for as such in the financial statements.

The prescribed accounting treatment for lessors was set forth in APB Opinion No. 7, as amended, which was issued in May, 1966. This Opinion defines two alternative treatments for lessors: the financing method and the operating method.

The financing method should be used by companies that act as lessors primarily as a result of being in the business of lending money, such as banks and insurance companies. Leases entered into by such institutions generally pass the risks and rewards of ownership on to the lessee and satisfy their own investment goals by recovering their investment along with an adequate return. The income of the lessor is, in effect, interest income, and is defined in APB Opinion No. 7 as the excess of aggregate rentals over the cost (less residual value at the termination of the lease) of the leased property. This excess is taken into income as interest on a comparable loan would be—in other words, at a rate similar to sum of the years' digits.

The operating method, on the other hand, should be used by lessors who retain the incidents of ownership, such as building owners or car rental companies. The income reported is the amount of rent receivable due under the lease.

The accounting treatment of the lessor is, therefore, dependent upon the lessor's business, the objectives in entering into the lease, and the risks of ownership retained.

Two other provisions of APB Opinions No. 7 and 27 should be pointed out because of their potential effect on financial statements:

1. Paragraph 11 of APB Opinion No. 7 allows the lessor to expense "initial costs" (costs of negotiating and closing the lease) as incurred and to recognize as revenue in the same period, in addition to normal revenue, a portion of the unearned revenue equal to the initial costs. (This is commonly known as "front-loading.")
2. Paragraphs 4, 5, and 6 of APB Opinion No. 27 allow manufacturers who lease their product as a method of marketing to record, in the year the lease is entered into, the same manufacturing revenues, costs, and profits as would have been reported had the product been sold outright (provided certain specified conditions are met). The obvious danger is the recognition of the profit for financial reporting purposes in the year of lease, whereas the cash proceeds may not be fully realized for an extended period of time.

A major problem of the three Opinions is the inconsistency in their interrelationship. This can be illustrated by the question: If a lease meets the criteria requiring reporting under the financing method of APB Opinion No. 7, does it then have to be capitalized on the books of the lessee? The Board answered this in APB Opinion No. 7 by effectively stating that the decision as to treatment by the lessee should be made independently of the lessor's treatment and vice versa. The Financial Accounting Standards Board (FASB) is currently studying the inconsistencies among APB Opinions No. 5, No. 7, and No. 27 as well as other problems in reporting and disclosing leases, and expects to issue a new opinion in the future. Preliminary indications are that the rules requiring capitalization of leases by lessees will be made more definitive and more stringent.

Disclosure of Lease Commitments

In Opinion No. 31 the APB promulgated the financial statement disclosure requirements of lessees regarding noncapitalized lease commitments. As set forth principally in paragraphs 8 and 9 of this pronouncement, the following disclosures should be made "as an integral part of the financial statements":

Total Rental Expense
8. Total rental expense (reduced by rentals from subleases, with disclosure of such amounts) entering into the determination of results of operations for each period for which an income statement is presented should be disclosed. Rental payments under short-term leases for a month or less which are not expected to be renewed need not be included. Contingent rentals, such as those based upon usage or sales, should be reported separately from the basic or minimum rentals.

Minimum Rental Commitments
9. The minimum rental commitments under all noncancelable leases should be disclosed, as of the date of the latest balance sheet presented, in the aggregate for:
   a. Each of the five succeeding fiscal years,
   b. Each of the next three five-year periods, and
   c. The remainder as a single amount.

The amounts so determined should be reduced by rentals to be received from existing noncancelable subleases (with disclosure of the amounts of such rentals). The total of the amounts included in (a), (b) and (c) should also be classified by major categories of properties, such as real estate, aircraft, truck fleets, and other equipment.

The Securities and Exchange Commission (SEC) was somewhat critical of APB Opinion No. 31, contending that the lease disclosure requirements included therein were inadequate "to meet the needs of investors." Accordingly, in Accounting Series Release No. 147, issued October 5, 1973, it adopted certain amendments to Regulation S-X (the regulation governing the form and content of financial statements) requiring additional lease disclosure. In essence, the SEC mandated the "disclosure of the present value of financing leases and of the impact on net income of capitalization of such leases." A financing lease was defined as:

. . . a lease which during the noncancelable lease period, either (i) covers 75 percent or more of the economic life of the property or (ii) has terms which assure the lessor a full recovery of the fair market value (which would normally be represented by his investment) of the property at the inception of the lease plus a reasonable return on the use of the assets invested subject only to limited risk in the realization of the residual interest in the property and the credit risks generally associated with secured loans.

In more specific terms, the SEC required the following disclosures with respect to all noncapitalized financing leases:

1. The present values of the minimum lease commitments in the aggregate and by major categories of properties, such as real estate, aircraft, truck fleets and other equipment. Present values shall be computed by discounting net lease payments (after subtracting, if practicable, estimated, or actual amounts, if any, applicable to taxes, insurance, maintenance and other operating expenses) at the interest rate implicit in the terms of each lease at the time of entering into the lease. Such disclosure shall be made as of the date of any balance sheet presented.

2. The impact upon net income for each period for which an income statement is presented if all noncapitalized financing leases were capitalized, related assets were amortized on a straight-line basis and interest cost was accrued on the basis of the outstanding lease liability. The amounts of amortization and interest cost included in the computation shall be separately identified. If the impact on net income is less than three percent of the average net income for the most recent three years, that fact may be stated in lieu of this disclosure.

Tax Considerations

In the field of leasing, there are two basic areas of tax considerations: the treatment of gain or loss on the sale and leaseback, and the actual treatment of the lease as a true lease or as a financing.

The asset sold in a sale and leaseback is generally a "Section 1231 asset"—that is, a depreciable asset or land used in the taxpayer's trade or business. The Internal Revenue Code provides that the net gain on the sale of 1231 assets that are not subject to depreciation recapture should be treated as a capital gain, whereas net losses may be deducted from income as an ordinary loss. This treatment allows the future lessee great flexibility in timing a sale and leaseback to best fit the tax posture. For example, in a high-bracket year, the retailer could sell and lease back an asset that has a market value substantially below book and obtain a large ordinary deduction. The danger here is that the Internal Revenue Service could declare the transaction a sham and disallow the loss deduction. The typical attack of the Service has been that a sale has not really taken place. Rather, the corporation has retained control over the asset while obtaining financing with the asset as collateral. The Service's position has been the strongest in cases where the terms of the sale and the lease were not at fair market value and the lease was for an extended period. Accordingly, the taxpayer's strongest defense has been where arm's-length negotiations are apparent, the terms are clearly at fair market value, the buyer/lessor is not a related party, and the basic lease term is under 30 years.[2] These defenses cannot be overemphasized. Case law has gone both ways, but the taxpayer has generally been successful where it has been possible to prove that the sale price and the rent were not less than fair market value.

Once the lease has been entered into, there are two ways it can be treated for tax purposes. If the Internal Revenue Service recognizes the lease as a true lease, the lessee will be entitled to deduct, in the appropriate period, annual rent expenses for purposes of federal income taxes. Normally, the appropriate period will be that in which liability for rent is incurred, in accordance with the terms of the lease, assuming the timing of such rent liability is not unreasonable. If, however, the Service looks upon the lease as a financing, the lessee is deemed to be the equitable owner of the property and is permitted to deduct the depreciation and interest expense. As discussed earlier in the chapter, the former treatment allows a level deduction over the period of the lease with no disputes about depreciable life. The latter results in higher deductions in earlier years and lower deductions later, although the depreciable life may be contested by the Service.

The test the Service applies to determine whether a lease is a financing is basically an analysis of the purchase options. If the lessee can purchase the property for an amount less than fair market value or for an amount approximately equal to what the debt balance would have been had the asset been bought outright, the transaction is viewed as a financing. If the lessee has a purchase option in an amount substantially in excess of probable fair market value or of the debt balance, the transaction receives lease status.

Comparing the accounting treatment to the tax treatment, there are many similarities. However, generally accepted accounting principles are not necessarily in accord with the rules and regulations governing the determination of taxable income, and modifica-

---

[2] The specific case relied on is *Jordan Marsh Co.*, 269 F.2d 453 (1959), rev'g T.C.M. 1957–237.

tions in financial reporting and tax reporting rules are made with the passage of time. Accordingly, it is entirely possible to view a lease agreement as a lease for financial reporting purposes, whereas it is deemed a financing for federal income taxes.

Other Considerations

A final aspect of the lease–buy decision relates to the lessor–lessee relationship. The user of the property can make a thorough analysis resulting in a decision to lease and then subsequently wind up in difficulty if the lessor encounters financial difficulties. It is essential that the lessee evaluate the lessor to determine the financial condition of the lessor, the reputation of the lessor in the financial community, and the relationship of the lessor to clients. Regardless of the legal protection that can and should be built into the lease, delays and difficulties will probably be avoided if the relationship between the lessor and the lessee is one of mutual trust and confidence. Toward this end, the lessee should look at the lessor's goals in entering into a lease and then see how these coincide or conflict with the lessee's own desires. The discussions in this chapter have presented both sides of the picture so that the potential lessee can see how the lessee's decisions affect the lessor. An understanding, by each side, of the other's goals will greatly assist in the negotiations leading to a mutually beneficial lease.

Conclusion

This chapter has discussed the varied facets of leasing that should be considered by management when faced with a buy-or-lease decision. Many of these factors are currently undergoing change. The FASB is reviewing the treatment of leases by lessors and lessees, tax courts are deliberating the recognition of gain and loss on sale and leaseback, and the financial community is becoming more and more sophisticated in evaluating the lease commitments and in determining return on investment. Thus, the individual in a decision-making capacity must be certain that all assumptions used in the analysis are currently valid. Finally, and this cannot be overemphasized, the decision to lease is a very complex one which requires a comprehensive analysis and weighing of the many objective and subjective factors before an economically correct decision can be made.

Index

Accounts receivable
  aging, 241-45
    individually tailored installment accounts, 243-44
    multipurpose use of, 243
    option accounts, 244-45
    revolving credit accounts, 244
  branch stores, at, 287-88
  cycle billing, 236-40
    multiple controls, 236-38
    single control, 237, 239
    two-cycle control, 239-40
  evaluation, techniques for, 241-42
  "post-audit," 233
  "preaudit," 233
  quality of, 240-41
Allowances from vendors, 150-51
Alteration and workroom costs (net), definition, 32
Alterations
  costs
    control over, 305-10
    per-garment, 307-8
    point of sale, losses at, 309-10
    store policy, 307
Anticipations, 178-79
Aprons; see Bill aprons

Bad debts, installment sales method, 483-84, 485-87
Bill aprons, 211-12, 213, 214-15
Branch stores
  expansion of, 280-81
  financial reporting, 291-97
    allocable expenses, 292, 293-95
    assignable expenses, 292-93
    branch operating statement, 292-95
    central organization expenses, 293-95
    contribution profit, 292-95
    controllable expenses, 292-95
    direct expenses, 292-93
    gross margin data, 295

    noncontrollable expenses, 292-95
    nonoperating revenue and expenses, 295
    sales data, 295-97
  manager, importance of, 282
  organization of, 282-83
  performance, evaluation of, 291-97
  procedures, financial and operating, 284-91
    accounts receivable, 287-88
    cash, 284-87
      transfers of, 286-87
    credit control, 287-88
    departmental inventory pools, 289-91
    inventory, 289-91
    payroll, 286
    separate location inventories, 291
  shopping centers, located in, 282
  suburban dependent branches, 281
Budgeting
  advertising, 90
  balance sheets, forecasted, 91
  cash receipts and disbursements, 91
  divisions of budget, 72-73
  expense centers, 86-89
  expense classifications, 86-91
  fixed expenses, 86
  goals, establishment of, 72
  merchandise budget, 75-76
  operating budget, 74-75
  payroll, 89-90
  periods of budget, 73-74
  variable expenses, 86
Bureau of Labor Statistics
  indexes used for LIFO valuation purposes, 383-85, 392
  price indexes
    adjustment of, 411
    cost indexes, derivation and use of, 438-41
    cost percentages applied to retail indexes, 412, 438-41

INDEX

Bureau of Labor Statistics (*Continued*)
  price indexes (*Continued*)
    department groups, 404–6, 410
    department stores, applied to, 404–10
    different departments, application to, 40
    different stores, application to, 410
    eligibility for use of, 442
    specialty stores, application to, 412, 438
    variety stores, application to, 411
    years 1942 through 1976, 407–9

Cash at branch stores, 284–87
Cash receipts and disbursements, budget, 91
Chain stores, 10–11
Chargebacks, 215, 217–18, 226
Claims against vendors, 269
C.O.D. sales, 245–46
Consigned stock, 267
Consignment purchases, 219–20
Contract department; *see* Discount sales
Contribution profit, 9
Corrections of retail
  definition, 27–28
  rebates by vendors, 27–28
Cost indexes, 438–41
Cost multiplier, definition, 25
Cost-no-retail items, 301–2
Cost percentage, definition, 25
Cost selling departments, 299, 303
Credit control at branches, 287–88
Cumulative markon
  definition, 24
  discounts, effect of, 32
  disposition of markon, 129–32
  inventories, valuation of, 37–38
  markdowns, effect of, 27
  markups, effect of, 25
  percentage, 24, 127
  sales discounts, effect of, 29
  shrinkages, effect of, 30
Customers' credits, 256–58
Cycle billing, 236–40

Deferred payment sales, 250–51
Department operating statement, 341–45
Department stores
  branch stores, 9
  definition and characteristics, 9–10
  organization, 13–21
Departments, classifications of, 35
Deposit sales, 246–47
Discount department; *see* Discount sales
Discount sales, 249–50
Discount stores, 11–12, 279

Discounts; *see also* Purchase discounts
  cash, accounting treatment, 33
Discounts earned
  accounting treatment, 33
  definition, 32–33
Dollar-value LIFO; *see* LIFO, dollar-value

Expense budget; *see also* Budgeting
  advertising, 90
  expense centers, 86–89
  expense classifications, 86–91
  fixed expenses, 86
  payroll, 89–90
  variable expenses, 86
Expense centers, 334–35, 337
  budgeting, 86–89
  responsibility accounting, 22
Expense service departments, 301
Expense statistics, 340–45
Expense summaries, 333–34, 335–37
Expenses
  allocation of, 8–10, 12
  percentages of sales, 352

Financial planning; *see* Profit planning
Financial statements
  department operating statement, 341–45
  income statement
    budget, comparisons with, 323, 336–37
    captions included, 322
    cost of merchandise handled, items included in, 327–30
    cost of merchandise sold, 330
    discounts earned, 330
    expense statistics, supporting, 340–45
    external reporting format, 337, 339–40
    form of, 322–24
    freight-in, 330
    gross margin, 331
    gross margin—owned, 330
    inventory
      beginning of period, 327
      end of period, 330
    leased department sales, presentation of, 325
    merchandise handled, net cost of, 330
    merchandise purchases, 327, 330
    merchandise sold, gross cost of, 330
    merchandise statistics, supporting, 340–45
    operating expenses, 331
    other costs of sales, 330–31

other income, net, 331–32
sales, 326
standard form, adaptation of, 332–33
LIFO
  adoption of, 380–81
  use of, 390–92
merchandise and expense analyses, supplemental, 342–45
non-retail operations, 346–47
operating expenses, 333–37
  expense centers, 334–35, 337
  expense summaries, 333–34, 335–37
  natural divisions of expenses, 335, 337, 338
Floor audit, 234–35
Form 970, 393–94
Formulas; *see* Mathematics of retail merchandise accounting

Gift certificates, 248
Gross margin
  budgeting, 73–85
  definition, 34
  derivation, 119–20
  formulas, 124–29
  percentages
    conversion from markon percentages before and after discounts, 34, 366–68
    markon and retail stock reductions, as related to, 356–58, 372–73
    workroom costs, 358–60, 365–66, 374–75
    prime cost add-ons and retail stock reductions, added discount and loading factors, as related to, 360–63, 376–77
Gross margin statement, 121–22

Imported merchandise, 218–19
Income statement; *see* Financial statements
Indirect manufacturing departments, 300–1, 304–5
Installment sales, 250–51
Installment sales method
  advantages of adoption, 457–58
  bad debts, 483–84, 485–87
  changing from, 482–83
  credits, impact of various, 485–87
  double tax on change from accrual method, 478–79
  avoidance of, 479–82
  election to report on, 477–78
  explanation of, 457
  finance charges, qualification as installment sales, 459

financial reporting, inapplicability for, 457
gross profit percentages, use of, 460–62
IRS ruling request, characteristics of, 480–82
leased department sales, qualification of, 459
non-personal property sales, exclusion of, 459–60
payments, two or more required, 462
property, inclusions in cost of, 459
qualification of property for, 458–60
regularity of sales, requirement for, 460
repossessions, 484–87
revocation of, 482–83
revolving credit plans
  qualifying terms, 462–64
  sampling methods and procedures, 463–77
  terms of, 462–63
sale of installment accounts
  prior to adoption of method, 479–82
  ruling requested from IRS, 479–82
security interest, no need to retain, 462
services, sales of, 458–59
unrealized gross profit, computation of traditional installment accounts, 460–62, 485–87
Installment sales of personal property; *see* Installment sales method
Internal audit group, inventory shortages, role in prevention of, 265–66
Inventories
  book records, 56
  branches, at, 289–91
  control of; *see* Inventory control
  cost method; *see* Inventory control, cost method
  departmental pools, 289–91
  departmental subdivision, 56–59
  markdown procedure and analysis, 59–60
  market value, 37
  merchandise classifications, subdivisions by, 56–59
  merchandise statistics, 63–64
  movements, controls over, 65–66
  retail method; *see* Retail method of inventory
  separate location inventories, 291
  slow-selling merchandise reports, 60–61
  taking physical; *see* Physical inventories
  unearned discount, deduction of, 158–60, 163, 166–67, 169–77
Inventory control
  cost method, 95–99

INDEX

Inventory control (*Continued*)
  methods of, 94
  physical inventories, by, 94–95
  retail method; *see* Retail method of inventory
Inventory shortages
  branch stores, increase in, 262, 272
  classification by origin, 263
  consigned stocks, problems of, 267
  contributory factors, expansion-related, 261–62, 272
  definition, 30, 261
  deterrents, 263
  markdowns, unrecorded, 270–71
  paperwork problems, 262, 263, 266
  personnel policies, inadequate, 262–63
  physical inventory as basis for, 267
  prevention
    deliveries, control over, 273
    devices, mechanical and electronic, 277
    internal audit group, role of, 265–66
    management concern, manifestation of, 264
    marking, control over, 269–70
    non-sales merchandise, control over movement of, 273
    paperwork errors, 266–67
    physical layout of store, 276, 277
    purchase orders, control over, 267–68
    receipt of merchandise, control over, 269, 271–72
    re-marking, control over, 271, 274
    returns to vendors, control over, 273
    sales personnel, guidelines for, 276
    security department, role of, 265
    selling floor, errors on, 272–73
    shrinkage control department, 264–65
    theft by employees, 265, 274–75
    theft by non-employees, 275–77
    training programs for employees, 264
    transfers of merchandise, control over, 271–72
  separate store records, advantages of, 266–67
  shoplifting, 262, 263, 275–77
Inventory Taking Manual of NRMA, 197
Invoice register, 214–15
Invoices in transit, 225–26

Last-in, first-out method of inventory; *see* LIFO; LIFO, dollar-value
Leased departments
  advantages to lessee, 315–16
  advantages to store, 314–15, 316
  arrangements formalized in lease agreement, 311, 317–21

definition, 311
departments usually leased, 316–17
lease agreement
  advertising, payment for, 319
  charge accounts, responsibility for, 320
  deliveries, payment for, 319
  employees, payment and hiring of, 319, 320
  insurance coverage, 320
  monthly reporting to lessee, 319–20
  other provisions, 320–21
  rental, 318
  term of agreement, 318
lessor–lessee relations, 313–14
organization and theory of, 312–13
profitability, contribution to store, 315
purpose of, 311, 314–15, 316
responsibilities of lessee, 312–13
responsibilities of lessor, 312
Leasing
  accounting treatment, 496–99
  advantages to lessee, 488, 490–91
  advantages to lessor, 491–92
  buy-versus-lease
    comparative cash flow analysis, 492–96
    quantitative analysis, 492–96
  capitalization of leases, necessity for, 496–97
  disadvantages to lessee, 491
  disadvantages to lessor, 492
  disclosure of lease commitments, 499–500
  equity, creation of, 496–97
  "financing leases," definition and disclosure of, 499–500
  financing method of accounting for lessors, 497–98
  lessor, importance of financial condition of, 502
  operating method of accounting for lessors, 497, 498
  other considerations, 502
  ownership versus
    analysis of, 489–90, 492–95
    risks and rights, 489–90
  purchase options, 497, 501
  sale and leaseback, 500–1
  tax considerations, 500–2
  tax criterion involving purchase options, 501
Lessees and lessors; *see* Leased departments; Leasing
LIFO
  advantages of, economic, 378–80
  bargain purchases, treatment of, 393
  Bureau of Labor Statistics, price indexes supplied by, 383–85, 392

business combinations, treatment in, 391
carryover of inventory methods in nontaxable transactions, 394–97, 400–3
cash flow, increase in, 379–80
computations on retail method
   adjustments in first year, book and tax, 414–15
   combined departments, handling of, 432–37
   cost, conversion to, 414–15
   cost multipliers, development of departmental, 415–19
   data sheets used for departmental cost multipliers and LIFO computations, 415–22
   departmental computations, specimen, 420–27
   factory profit, elimination of, 438
   markdowns and markups, adjustments for, 414
   pooled stock ledger, all locations, 438
   purchase discounts, handling of, 427–30
   retail price indexes, use of, 413
   special problems, 438–41
   split departments, handling of, 430–32
cost method, 383–84, 387, 389–90, 414–15
decision to adopt, factors influencing, 378–79, 386–93
disadvantages
   bonus and profit-sharing plans, impact on, 381
   comparisons with competitors, 380–81
   financial reporting, 380
   loan indentures, impact on, 381
   prospective sale of securities, 381
election
   exclusions from LIFO, 392, 394
   making, 392–94
   scope of, 392–93
   timing of, 392–93
   unilateral, of taxpayer, 386
financial statements, impacts on, 390–92
Form 970, use in election of, 393–94
Hutzler decision, 383–84
income taxes, reduced, 379–80
inventory levels, 387, 388
inventory valuation, LIFO vs. retail method, 383–84
markdowns, effect of, 383–84
merchandise in transit, inclusion or exclusion of, 393–94
net markon method, 383–84

nontaxable transfers to subsidiary, 398
opening inventory, restatement to cost of, 389–90
pools, 387–88, 392
"positive adjustment," 399–400
price indexes, use of, 382–85
price trends, forecast of future, 387–88
quantity changes, forecast of, 388
recomputation of prior year's taxable income, 389–90
reporting, required uniformity of book and tax, 380, 390–92
retail method, as contrasted to, 383–84
revisions of method, 398
revocation of method, 390
specialty stores, application to, 384–85
technological changes, forecast of, 388–89
termination of method, 399–400
unsalable merchandise, 389–90
unusable merchandise, 389–90
variety stores, application to, 385
LIFO, dollar-value
   base-year costs, definition of, 443
   current-year costs, options in valuing, 446, 448
   double-extension method of computation, 446, 452–55
      requirement for use of, 445
   efficiency factor, elimination of, 451–52
   election to use, 443, 450–51
   extent of election, selectivity in, 450–51
   index computed using statistical methods, 447
   index method of computation, 447
   indexes used as deflation factor, 382, 384–85
   "in-house" index, necessity to develop, 443
   link-chain method of computation, 447–49, 450, 455–56
   new items, treatment of, 449–50
   overhead index, computation of, 451–52
   pooling arrangement, 443
   pools, 387–88, 392
      computations by, 443
      election of, 443
      multiple, 444
      natural-business-unit, 444, 445
      raw material content, 445
   retail LIFO method, contrasted with, 443
   U. S. Treasury, approval of, 445, 450
Loaded discounts
   formula for add-on to cost, 174–75
   prime cost percentage add-ons, 360–63, 376–77

INDEX

Loan merchandise, 226-28

Mail-order houses, 12-13
Markdown cancellations, definition, 27
Markdowns
  causative factors, 59-60
  definition, 26
  LIFO method, impact on, 383-84
  procedure and analysis, 59-60
  reserves for, 38-39
  unrecorded, 270-71
Marking of merchandise, 229
Markon
  complement of markon percentage, 25
  cumulative, 24
  definition, 23-24
  disposition of, 129-32
  percentages
    conversion to gross margin percentages before and after discounts, 366-68
    gross margin and retail stock reductions, as related to, 356-58, 372-73
    workroom costs, 358-60, 365-66, 374-75
    marked retail and markups, as related to, 24
    prime cost add-ons, 358-60, 365-66, 374-75
Markup cancellations, definition, 26
Markups, definition, 25
Mathematics of retail merchandise accounting
  cost percentages converted to markon percentages, 352-56, 371
  discount percentages on sales converted to percentages on cost, 369
  markon percentages
    converted to cost percentages, 352-56, 371
    converted to gross margin percentages
      discounts, 366-68
      retail stock reductions, 356-58, 372-73
      workroom costs, 358-60, 365-66, 374-75
    prime cost percentage add-ons, 360-63, 376-77
    purchase markon percentages, 368-69
Memorandum merchandise, 226-28
Memorandum sales, 249
Merchandise budget; *see also* Budgeting; Merchandise plan
  alteration and workroom costs, planned, 81-82
  gross margin, planned, 82-83
  markdowns, planned, 78

merchandise classifications, 84
purchase discounts, planned, 83-84
purchase markon, planned, 80-81
purchases, planned, 79-81, 84-85
retail stock, planned, 79
revision, 84-85
sales, planned, 77-78
sales discounts, planned, 78
shrinkages, planned, 78
units, budgeting of, 85
Merchandise certificates, 248
Merchandise classifications, and merchandise control, 56-59
Merchandise control
  accounting tools, 42
  definition, 41
Merchandise management accounting
  averaging techniques, problems of, 351
  broad approach, 350
  cost accounting, application of, 349-51
  definition, 349
  departmental profitability, 350, 351
  detailed or item approach, 350
  fixed vs. variable expenses, 350-51
  intermediate or departmental approach, 350, 351
  item profitability, 350, 351
  percentage approach, 350, 351
  purpose of, 349
Merchandise plan, definition, 42
Merchandise service workrooms, 299-300, 303-4
Merchandise statistics, 63-64, 340-45
Merchandise turnover
  definition, 39
  illustrations, 154-57

Natural divisions of expenses, 335, 337, 338
Net markon
  definition, 28
  inventories, valuation of, 37-38
Non-retail operations
  accounting procedures
    cost selling departments, 303
    manufacturing workrooms, 304-5
    service workrooms, 303-4
  categories of, 299-301
  cost-no-retail, 301-2
  cost selling departments, 299
  expense service departments, 301
  financial statements, 346-47
  indirect manufacturing departments, 300-1
  merchandise service workrooms, 299-300
  purpose of, 298
  recordkeeping for, 302-3
  workroom charges, 301, 302, 303-4

INDEX

workroom costs, 299–300, 301, 302, 303–10
  control over, 305–10

Open-to-buy
  accounting and unit control systems, integration with, 47–56
  definition, 42–44
  purchase orders, control of, 211
Operations, centralization of function, 209–10

Percentages, limitations in, 348–49
Physical inventories
  arrangement of stock, 185, 187
  checking, 184–85, 187
  counting, 184–85
  cutoff procedures, establishment and verification of, 186, 187, 199–200, 200–1, 203
  definition, 181
  forms and supplies, 183–84, 187, 197–200
  frequency of, 200–2
  identification of merchandise, 185–86
  instructions, 186–91
  insurance coverage, basis for, 182
  Inventory Taking Manual of NRMA, 197
  layout of departments, 183–84
  listing, 184–85
  necessity for, 181–82
  overages, 206–8
  personnel, assignment of, 185
  personnel requirements, 183
  planning for, 182–83
  problems, 183–86
  purpose, 181, 184
  reconciliation of book and physical control figures, 203, 206–7
  responsibility for, 182
  segregation of merchandise, 185–86
  shortages, 206–8
  summarization, useful reports arising from, 208
  ticketing, review for proper, 185
  time of, 200–2
  unit controls, 206
Pre-retailing, 211, 213
Price indexes
  Bureau of Labor Statistics
    adjustment of indexes, 411
    cost indexes, derivation and use of, 438–41
    cost percentages applied to retail indexes, 412, 438–41
    department groups, 404–6, 410
    department stores, applied to, 404–10
    different departments, application to, 410
    different stores, application to, 410
    eligibility for use of, 442
    specialty stores, application to, 412, 438
    variety stores, application to, 411
    years 1942 through 1976, 407–9
  LIFO, use with, 382–85
Profit planning
  benefits anticipated, 71
  budgeting, 72–76
  management commitment, 70–71
Purchase discounts
  accrual basis, 160–61
  added discounts, 173–77
  anticipations, 178–79
  cash discounts, 33, 158
  deductible, or receivable, 162–63
  departmental discount rates, 164–66, 167
  earned, 32–33, 158–60, 163
    interim reporting of, 167–68
    reflected in the income statement, 168–73
  loaded discounts, 173–77
  lost, 161
  percentage on sales converted to percentage on cost, 369
  received, 161
  store-wide rate, 165–66, 167
  trade discounts, 158
  unearned discounts, 163
Purchase orders, controls over, 267–68
Purchase record, 215–16, 217
Purchases
  bill aprons, 211–12, 213, 214–15
  chargebacks, 215, 217–18, 226
  on consignment, 219–20
  definition, 31–32
  department transfers, 32
  discounts
    recorded gross of, 158–60, 164
    recorded net of, 158–60, 163–64
  foreign, 218–19
  imported merchandise, 218–19
  invoice register, 214–15
  invoices, control of, 210–14
  invoices in transit, 225–26
  loading of other purchase costs, 177–78
  loan, merchandise on, 226–28
  marking of merchandise, control of, 209–10, 229
  markon percentage, adequacy of, 368–69
  memorandum merchandise, 226–28
  merchandise transfers, 32
  "no retail" bills, 221
  payments, control over, 216–17

510 INDEX

Purchases (*Continued*)
  percentages of cost converted to markon percentages, 352–56, 371
  pre-retailing, 211, 213
  purchase orders, control of, 209, 210–14
  purchase record, 215–16, 217
  receipt of merchandise, control of, 209–10, 228–29
  reserve stock, 230
  returns to vendors, 217–18
  short shipments, 218, 228
  stocking of merchandise, control of, 209–10
  transfers, department merchandise, 221–25
  transportation costs, 218
  workroom bills, 220–21

Rebates, by vendors, 27–28
Receipt of merchandise, 228–29
Receiving and marking, centralization of, 209–10
Repair charges, 255–56
Repossessions, 251, 484–87
Reserve stock, 230
"Retail Accounting Manual—Revised" (1976)
  expense accounting and reporting, 333–37
  expense centers, 334–35, 337
  expense classifications, 86–88
  expense summaries, 333–34, 335–37
  finance charge income, treatment of, 331
  natural divisions of expenses, 335, 337, 338
  reporting results of operations, 322–23
  responsibility accounting, underlying concept of, 22
Retail businesses
  chain stores, 10–11
  department stores, 8–10
  discount stores, 11–12
  general stores, 7
  mail-order houses, 12–13
  miscellaneous, 13
  single-line stores, 7–8
  specialty stores, 8
  types, 7–13
Retail inventory method; *see* Retail method of inventory
Retail method of accounting, problems, 133–54
Retail method of inventory, 23, 99–100
  abnormal relationships, problem of, 140–42
  advantages, 100
  allowances from vendors, 150–51
  alteration and workroom costs, net, 118–19
  as averaging method, 100–1
  closing inventory, 118
  cumulation period, choice of, 145
  definitions, 36–37
  departmentalization, reduction of inaccuracies by, 138–39
  formulas, 124–29
  gross margin before discounts, 119–20
  gross margin statement, 121–22
  high-markon and low-markon goods, effect of averaging, 137
  imported vs. domestic goods, separate markons for, 139–40
  invoices in transit, 113–14
  loaded discounts, elimination of, 176–77
  markdowns, 115–16
  markdowns and markups, cancellation of, 134–37
  marked-down goods in stock, effect of applying cumulative markons to, 140
  markon, disposition of, 129–32
  markon percentages
    averages and trends of, 142–43
    monthly calculation of, 144–45
    seasonal calculation of, 144–45
  mercantile percentage, 114–15
  merchandise handled, 111–13
  merchandise turnover, 154–57
  operation of, 102–3
  purchase discount computations, 169–73, 176–77
  purchases entered gross of discounts, 164
  purchases entered net of discounts, 163–64
  sales, net, 115
  sales discounts, 117
  shrinkages, 117
  special sales events, 148–49
  stock ledger, 103–24
    controls over, 122–24
  transfers, departmental, 151–54
  variable prices, 149–50
Retail price indexes; *see* Price indexes
Retail stock reductions
  definition of, 30
  percentages
    markon and gross margin, as related to, 356–58, 372–73
    workroom costs, 358–60, 365–66, 374–75
Retailing
  distinctive features, 3–5
  problems, 3–5

INDEX

procedures, responsive to problems, 6
Revolving credit plans
  installment sales method, use of, 462–77
  terms of, 462–63

Sales
  accounts receivable
    aging, 241–45
    quality of, 240–41
  audit procedures, 233–36
    floor audit, 234–35
    sales check number control, 235–36
    tally audit, 233–34
  carrying charges, 251
  C.O.D., methods of handling, 245–46
  compilation of, by clerks, 245
  credit media, compilation of, 232–33
  cycle billing, 236–40
  deposit sales, methods of recording, 246–48
  discount sales, 249–50
  forward sales orders, 251–53
  gift certificates, description and recording of, 248
  gross, compilation of, 232–33
  installment, time, or deferred payment, 250–51
  layaway sales, 247–48
  memorandum sales, 249
  merchandise certificates, description and recording of, 248
  net, definition of, 30
  non-sales items, 258–59
  repair charges, 255–56
  repossessed merchandise, 251
  returns, compilation of, 232–33
Sales Audit Office, 231–32
  audit procedures, 233–36
  functions, 231–32
  gross sales, compilation of, 232–33
  special orders, 251–53
  storage charges, 254–55
  trading stamps, description and accounting for, 259–60
  unsalable merchandise, 258–59
  will-call, 247–48
  will-notify transactions, 253–54
Sales discounts, definition, 29
Sales returns
  compilation of, 232–33
  customers' credits, 256–58
Security department, and prevention of inventory shortages, 265

Shoplifting, 262, 263, 275–77
Shopping centers, branch stores in, 282
Shortages; see Inventory shortages
Shrinkages, definition, 30, 261; see also Inventory shortages
Single-line stores, 7–8
Slow-selling merchandise, reporting of, 60–62
Specialty stores, 8
Statements reporting operating results; see Financial statements
Stock ledger, 103–24
Stock-to-sales ratio
  definition, 39–40
  merchandise classifications, subdivisions by, 56–57
Storage charges, 254–55

Taking of physical inventories; see Physical inventories
Tally audit, 233–34
Theft; see Inventory shortages; Shoplifting
Trading stamps, 259–60
Transfers of merchandise
  definition, 32
  between departments, 221–25
  problems, accounting, 151–54
Transportation costs, 218
Turnover; see Merchandise turnover

Unit stock control
  accounting and open-to-buy systems, integration with, 47–56
  advantages, 46–47
  budgeting of units, 85
  nature of, 45–46

Wholesale price indexes, 438–41
Workrooms; see also Non-retail operations
  alteration costs per garment, 307–8
  alteration policy of store, 307
  bills for, 220–21
  charges, schedule of, 302
  costs, 299–300, 301
    control over, 305–10
    and markon percentages, 358–60, 365–66, 374–75
  deficiencies, operating, 305–6
  fitters, importance of, 309–10
  point of sale, losses at, 309–10
  productivity, 305–7, 308–9
  standards, use of, 307, 308